PEARSON CUSTOM BUSINESS RESOURCES

Compiled by

Corporate Finance
University of Baltimore

Pearson Learning Solutions

New York   Boston   San Francisco
London   Toronto   Sydney   Tokyo   Singapore   Madrid
Mexico City   Munich   Paris   Cape Town   Hong Kong   Montreal

Senior Vice President, Editorial and Marketing: Patrick F. Boles
Associate Editor: Ana Díaz-Caneja
Development Editor: Abbey Lee Briggs
Marketing Manager: Jack Cooney
Operations Manager: Eric M. Kenney
Production Manager: Jennifer Berry
Rights Manager: Jillian Santos
Art Director: Renée Sartell
Cover Designer: Renée Sartell

Cover Art: Courtesy of EyeWire/Getty Images and PhotoDisc/Getty Images. Photodisc, "Globe surrounded by business people on computer monitors," courtesy of Photodisc/Getty Images. Dave Cutler (Artist), "Man Dropping Coins Into Glass Jar,"courtesy of David Cutler/Images.com. Dave Cutler (Artist), "Three Coins in Glass Jar," courtesy of David Cutler/Images.com. Dean Turner, "Stock Vector: Global Finance" Courtesy of Dean Turner/iStockphoto. Hal Bergman, "Refinery Silhouette" Courtesy of Hal Bergman/iStockphoto. Dan Barnes, "Cargo Container Ship Aerial View" Courtesy of Dan Barnes/iStockphoto. Franc Podgorsek, "Stock Numbers" Courtesy of Franc Podgorsek/iStockphoto. "Customer in Line at Grocery Store" Courtesy of Digital Vision Photography/Veer Inc. Owaki-Kulla, "Pumping Gas" Courtesy of Flirt Photography/Veer Inc. Lynn Johnson, "Yunnan Province, People's Republic of China" Courtesy of Lynn Johnson/Getty Images, Inc. Thomas Bendy, "Student Typing" Courtesy of Thomas Bendy/iStockphoto.

This special edition published in cooperation with Pearson Learning Solutions.

Printed in the United States of America.

Please visit our web site at *www.pearsoncustom.com.*

Attention bookstores: For permission to return any unsold stock, contact us at *pearsonscustomreturns@pearson.com.*

Pearson Learning Solutions, 501 Boylston Street, Suite 900, Boston, MA 02116
A Pearson Education Company
www.pearsoned.com

ISBN 10: 0-558-95355-7
ISBN 13: 978-0-558-95355-3

Editorial Advisory Board

Contents

An Introduction to the Foundations of Financial Management

From Chapter 1 of *Foundations of Finance*, 7/e. Arthur J. Keown. John D. Martin. J. William Petty. Copyright © 2011 by Pearson Education.
Published by Prentice Hall. All rights reserved.

An Introduction to the Foundations of Financial Management

Learning Objectives

After reading this chapter, you should be able to:

 Identify **the goal of the firm.**

 Understand **the five basic principles of finance and business, the consequences of forgetting those basic principles of finance, and the importance of ethics and trust in business.**

 Describe **the role of finance in business.**

 Distinguish **between the different legal forms of business.**

 Explain **what has led to the era of the multinational corporation.**

Apple Computer (AAPL) ignited the personal computer revolution in the 1970s with the Apple II and reinvented the personal computer in the 1980s with the Macintosh. But by 1997, it looked like it might be nearing the end for Apple. Mac users were on the decline, and the company didn't seem to be headed in any real direction. It was at that point that Steve Jobs reappeared, taking back his old job as CEO of Apple, the company he cofounded in 1976. To say the least, things began to change. In fact, between then and September 2009, the price of Apple's common stock has climbed by over forty-one-fold!

How did Apple accomplish this? The company did it by going back to what it does best, which is to produce products that make the optimal trade-off between ease of use, complexity, and features. Apple took its special skills and applied them to more than just computers, introducing new products such as the iPod, iTunes, the sleek iMac, the MacBook Air, iPod Touch, and the iPhone along with its unlimited "apps." Although all these products have done well, the success of the iPod has been truly amazing. Between the introduction of the iPod in October 2001 and the beginning of 2005, Apple sold more than 6 million of the devices. Then, in 2004, it came out with the iPod Mini, about the length and width of a business card, which has also been a huge success, particularly among women. How successful has this new product been? By 2004, Apple was selling more iPods than its signature Macintosh desktop and notebook computers.

How do you follow up on the success of the iPod? You keep improving your products and you keep developing and introducing new products that consumers want. With this in mind, in March 2009, Apple unveiled its

2

latest version of the iPod Shuffle. At half the size of the previous generation iPod Shuffle, it has 4GB of storage, is able to hold up to 1,000 songs, and is less than the size of a house key. It even has a new feature called VoiceOver that, with the press of a button, tells you the song title or artist.

How did Apple make a decision to introduce the original iPod and now the tiny iPod Shuffle? The answer is by identifying a customer need, combined with sound financial management. Financial management deals with the maintenance and creation of economic value or wealth by focusing on decision making with an eye toward creating wealth. As such, this text deals with financial decisions such as when to introduce a new product, when to invest in new assets, when to replace existing assets, when to borrow from banks, when to sell stocks or bonds, when to extend credit to a customer, and how much cash and inventory to maintain. All of these aspects of financial management were factors in Apple's decision to introduce and continuously improve the iPod, iPod Shuffle, and iPhone, and the end result is having a major financial impact on Apple.

In this chapter, we lay the foundation for the entire book by explaining the key goal that guides financial decision making: maximizing shareholder wealth. From there we introduce the thread that ties everything together: the five basic principles of finance. Finally, we discuss the legal forms of business. We close the chapter with a brief look at what has led to the rise in multinational corporations.

The Goal of the Firm

1 Identify the goal of the firm.

The fundamental goal of a business is to create value for the company's owners (that is, its shareholders). This goal is frequently stated as "maximization of shareholder wealth." Thus, the goal of the financial manager is to create wealth for the shareholders, by making decisions that will maximize the price of the existing common stock. Not only does this goal directly benefit the shareholders of the company, but it also provides benefits to society as scarce resources are directed to their most productive use by businesses competing to create wealth.

We have chosen maximization of shareholder wealth—that is, maximizing the market value of the existing shareholders' common stock—because the effects of all financial decisions ultimately affect the firm's stock price. Investors react to poor investment or dividend decisions by causing the total value of the firm's stock to fall, and they react to good decisions by pushing up the price of the stock. In effect, under this goal, good decisions are those that create wealth for the shareholder.

Obviously, there are some serious practical problems in using changes in the firm's stock to evaluate financial decisions. Many things affect stock prices; to attempt to identify a reaction to a particular financial decision would simply be impossible, but fortunately that is unnecessary. To employ this goal, we need not consider every stock price change to be a market interpretation of the worth of our decisions. Other factors, such as changes in the economy, also affect stock prices. What we do focus on is the effect that our decision *should have* on the stock price if everything else were held constant. The market price of the firm's stock reflects the value of the firm as seen by its owners and takes into account the complexities and complications of the real-world risk. As we follow this goal throughout our discussions, we must keep in mind one more question: Who exactly are the shareholders? The answer: Shareholders are the legal owners of the firm.

Concept Check

1. What is the goal of the firm?
2. How would you apply this goal in practice?

 Understand the five basic principles of finance and business, the consequences of forgetting those basic principles of finance, and the importance of ethics and trust in business.

Five Principles that Form the Foundations of Finance

To the first-time student of finance, the subject matter may seem like a collection of unrelated decision rules. This could not be further from the truth. In fact, our decision rules, and the logic that underlies them, spring from five simple principles that do not require knowledge of finance to understand. These five principles guide the financial manager in the creation of value for the firm's owners (the stockholders).

As you will see, while it is not necessary to understand finance to understand these principles, it is necessary to understand these principles in order to understand finance. Although these principles may at first appear simple or even trivial, they provide the driving force behind all that follows, weaving together the concepts and techniques presented in this text, and thereby allowing us to focus on the logic underlying the practice of financial management. Now let's introduce the five principles.

Principle 1: Cash Flow Is What Matters

You probably recall from your accounting classes that a company's profits can differ dramatically from its cash flows. But for now understand that cash flows, not profits, represent money that can be spent. Consequently, it is cash flow, not profits that determines the value of a business. For this reason when we analyze the consequences of a managerial decision we focus on the resulting cash flows, not profits.

In the movie industry, there is a big difference between accounting profits and cash flow. Many a movie is crowned a success and brings in plenty of cash flow for the studio, but doesn't produce a profit. Even some of the most successful box office hits—*Forrest Gump*, *Coming to America*, and *Batman*—realized no accounting profits at all after accounting for various movie studio costs. That's because "Hollywood Accounting" allows for overhead costs not associated with the movie to be added on to the true cost of the movie. In fact, the movie *My Big Fat Greek Wedding*, which was the fifth highest grossing movie of 2002, actually lost $20 million according to the accountants. Was *My Big Fat Greek Wedding* a successful movie? It sure was—in fact it grossed over $370 million on a budget of only $5 million. Without question it produced cash, but it didn't make any profits. Unfortunately for most of the cast, their contracts entitled them to a cut of the profits, not the cash flows. They learned a bitter lesson about the difference in cash flows and profits.

There is another important point we need to make about cash flows. Recall from your economics classes that we should always look at marginal, or **incremental cash flows** when making a financial decision. The incremental cash flow to the company as a whole is *the difference between the cash flows the company will produce both with and without the investment it's thinking about making.* To understand this concept let's think about the incremental cash flows of a movie like *Pirates of the Caribbean*. Not only did Disney make money on the movie, the movie also increased the number of people attracted to Disney theme parks to go on the "Pirates of the Caribbean" ride. So, if you were to evaluate that movie, you'd want to include its impact on sales throughout the entire company.

incremental cash flow the difference between the cash flows a company will produce both with and without the investment it is thinking about making.

Principle 2: Money Has a Time Value

Perhaps the most fundamental principle of finance is that money has a "time" value. Very simply, a dollar received today is more valuable than a dollar received one year from now because we can invest the dollar we have today to earn interest so that at the end of one year we will have more than one dollar.

For example, suppose you have a choice of receiving $1,000 either today or one year from now. If you decide to receive it a year from now, you will have passed up the opportunity to earn a year's interest on the money. Economists would say you suffered an "opportunity loss" or an "opportunity cost." The cost is the interest you could have earned on the $1,000 if you invested it for one year. The concept of opportunity costs is fundamental to the study of finance and economics. Very simply, the **opportunity cost** of any choice you make *is the highest-valued alternative that you had to give up when you made the choice.* So if you loan money to your brother at no interest, money that otherwise would have been loaned to a friend for 8 percent interest (who is equally likely to repay you), then the opportunity cost of making the loan to your brother is 8 percent.

In the study of finance, we focus on the creation and measurement of value. To measure value, we use the concept of the time value of money to bring the future benefits and costs of a project, measured by its cash flows, back to the present. Then, if the benefits or cash inflows outweigh the costs, the project creates wealth and should be accepted; if the costs or cash outflows outweigh the benefits or cash inflows, the project destroys wealth and should be rejected. Without recognizing the existence of the time value of money, it is impossible to evaluate projects with future benefits and costs in a meaningful way.

opportunity cost the next best alternative available to the decision maker for a given level of risk.

Principle 3: Risk Requires a Reward

Even the novice investor knows there are an unlimited number of investment alternatives to consider. But without exception, investors will not invest if they do not expect to receive a return on their investment. They will want a return that satisfies two requirements:

◆ *A return for delaying consumption.* Why would anyone make an investment that would not at least pay them something for delaying consumption? They won't—even if there is no risk. In fact, investors will want to receive at least the same return that is available for risk-free investments, such as the rate of return being earned on U.S. government securities.

◆ *An additional return for taking on risk.* Investors generally don't like risk. Thus, risky investments are less attractive—*unless* they offer the prospect of higher returns. That said, the more unsure people are about how an investment will perform, the higher the return they will demand for making that investment. So, if you are trying to persuade investors to put money into a risky venture you are pursuing, you will have to offer them a higher expected rate of return.

Figure 1 depicts the basic notion that an investor's rate of return should equal a rate of return for delaying consumption plus an additional return for assuming risk. For example, if you have $5,000 to invest and are considering either buying stock in International

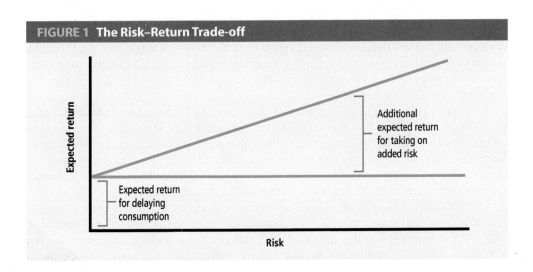

FIGURE 1 The Risk–Return Trade-off

Expected return (vertical axis)

Additional expected return for taking on added risk

Expected return for delaying consumption

Risk (horizontal axis)

Business Machines (IBM) or investing in a new bio-tech startup firm that has no past record of success, you would want the startup investment to offer the prospect of a higher expected rate of return than the investment in an established company like IBM.

Notice that we keep referring to the *expected* return rather than the *actual* return. As investors, we have expectations about what returns our investments will earn. However, we can't know for certain what they *will* be. For example, if investors could have seen into the future, no one would have bought stock in the women's retailer Ann Taylor Stores (XETRA: AAK.DE) on March 6, 2009. Why, because on that day, Ann Taylor announced a larger than expected fourth quarter loss. The result was that in minutes of the announcement, the company's stock price dropped a whopping 38 percent.

The risk–return relationship will be a key concept as we value stocks, bonds, and proposed new investment projects throughout this text. We will also spend some time determining how to measure risk. Interestingly, much of the work for which the 1990 Nobel Prize for economics was awarded centered on the graph in Figure 1 and how to measure risk. Both the graph and the risk-return relationship it depicts will reappear often in our study of finance.

Principle 4: Market Prices Are Generally Right

To understand how securities such as bonds and stocks are valued or priced in the financial markets, it is necessary to have an understanding of the concept of an efficient market. An **efficient market** is *one where the prices of the assets traded in that market fully reflect all available information at any instant in time.*

> **efficient market** a market in which the prices of securities at any instant in time fully reflect all publicly available information about the securities and their actual public values.

Security markets such as the stock and bond markets are particularly important to our study of finance since these markets are the place where firms can go to raise money to finance their investments. Whether a security market such as the New York Stock Exchange (NYSE) is efficient depends on the speed with which newly released information is impounded into prices. Specifically, an efficient stock market is characterized by a large number of profit-driven individuals who act very quickly by buying (or selling) shares of stock in response to the release of new information.

If you are wondering just how vigilant investors in the stock market are in watching for good and bad news, consider the following set of events. While Nike (NKE) CEO William Perez flew aboard the company's Gulfstream jet one day in November 2005, traders on the ground sold off a significant amount of Nike's stock. Why? Because the plane's landing gear was malfunctioning, and they were watching TV coverage of the event! Before Perez landed safely, Nike's stock dropped 1.4 percent. Once Perez's plane landed, Nike's stock price immediately bounced back. This example illustrates that in the financial market there are ever-vigilant investors who are looking to act even *in the anticipation* of the release of new information.

Another example of the speed with which stock prices react to new information deals with Disney. Beginning with *Toy Story* in 1995, Disney (DIS) and Pixar (PIXR) were on a roll, making animated hits one after another including *A Bug's Life*, *Toy Story 2*, *Monsters, Inc.*, *Finding Nemo*, and *The Incredibles*. So in 2006, the hopes for the animated movie *Cars* were very high. However, in the movie's opening weekend, it grossed only $60 million or about $10 million less than investors expected. How did the stock market respond? On the Monday following the opening weekend, Disney stock opened over two percent lower. Apparently, the news of the disappointing box office receipts was reflected in Disney's opening stock price, even before it traded!

The key learning point here is the following: Stock market prices are a useful barometer of the value of a firm. Specifically, managers can expect their company's share prices to respond quickly to investors' assessment of their decisions. If investors on the whole agree that the decision is a good one that creates value, then they will push up the price of the firm's stock to reflect that added value. On the other hand, if investors feel that a decision is bad for share prices, then the firm's share value will be driven down.

Unfortunately, this principle doesn't always work perfectly in the real world. You just need to look at the housing price bubble that helped bring on the economic downturn in 2008–2009 to realize that prices and value don't always move in lockstep. Like it or not, the psychological biases of individuals impact decision making, and as a result, our decision-making process is not always rational. Behavioral finance considers this type of behavior, and takes what we already know about financial decision making and adds in human behavior with all its apparent irrationality.

We'll try and point out the impact of human behavior on decisions throughout our study. But understand that the field of behavioral finance is a work in progress—we understand only a small portion of what may be going on. We can say, however, that behavioral biases have an impact on our financial decisions. As an example, people tend to be overconfident, and many times mistake skill for luck. As Robert Shiller, a well-known economics professor at Yale put it, "people think they know more than they do."[1] This overconfidence applies to their abilities, their knowledge and understanding, and in forecasting the future. Since they have confidence in their valuation estimates, they may take on more risk than they should. These behavioral biases impact everything in finance, from investment analysis, to analyzing new projects, to forecasting the future.

Principle 5: Conflicts of Interest Cause Agency Problems

Throughout this book we will describe how to make financial decisions that increase the value of a firm's shares. However, managers do not always follow through with these decisions. Often they make decisions that actually lead to a decrease in the value of the firm's shares. When this happens, it is frequently because the manager's own interest is best served by ignoring shareholder interests. In other words, there is a conflict of interest between what is best for the managers and the stockholders. For example, it may be the case that shutting down an unprofitable plant is in the best interests of the firm's stockholders but in so doing the managers will find themselves out of a job or having to transfer to a different job. This very clear conflict of interest might lead the management of the plant to continue running the plant at a loss.

Conflicts of interest lead to what are referred to by economists as an agency cost or **agency problem**. That is, managers are the agents of the firm's stockholders (the owners) and if the agents do not act in the best interests of their principal this leads to an agency cost. Although the goal of the firm is to maximize shareholder value, in reality the agency problem may interfere with the implementation of this goal. *The agency problem results from the separation of management and the ownership of the firm.* For example, a large firm may be run by professional managers or agents who have little or no ownership in the firm. Because of this separation of the decision makers and owners, managers may make decisions that are not in line with the goal of maximizing shareholder wealth. They may approach work less energetically and attempt to benefit themselves in terms of salary and perquisites at the expense of shareholders.

Managers might also avoid any projects that have risk associated with them—even if they are great projects with huge potential returns and a small chance of failure. Why is this so? Because if the project doesn't turn out, these agents of the shareholders may lose their jobs.

The costs associated with the agency problem are difficult to measure, but occasionally we see the problem's effect in the marketplace. If the market feels management is damaging shareholder wealth, there may be a positive reaction in stock price to the removal of that management. For example, on the announcement of the death of Roy Farmer, the CEO of Farmer Brothers (FARM), a seller of coffee-related products, Farmer Brothers' stock price rose about 28 percent. Generally, the tragic loss of a company's top executive raises concerns over a leadership void, causing the share price to drop, but in the case of Farmer Brothers, investors thought a change in management would have a positive impact on the company.

If the firm's management works for the owners, who are the shareholders, why doesn't the management get fired if it doesn't act in the shareholders' best interest? In theory, the shareholders pick the corporate board of directors and the board of directors in turn picks the management. Unfortunately, in reality the system frequently works the other way around. Management selects the board of director nominees and then distributes the ballots. In effect, shareholders are offered a slate of nominees selected by the management.

agency problem problems and conflicts resulting from the separation of the management and ownership of the firm.

---

[1]See Robert J. Shiller, *Irrational Exuberance*, Broadway Books, 2000, page 142.

The end result is that management effectively selects the directors, who then may have more allegiance to managers than to shareholders. This, in turn, sets up the potential for agency problems, with the board of directors not monitoring managers on behalf of the shareholders as they should.

The root cause of agency problems is conflicts of interest. Whenever they exist in business, there is a chance that individuals will do what is in their best interests rather than the best interests of the organization. For example, in 2000 Edgerrin James was a running back for the Indianapolis Colts and was told by his coach to get a first down and then fall down. That way the Colts wouldn't be accused of running up the score against a team they were already beating badly. However, since James' contract included incentive payments associated with rushing yards and touchdowns, he acted in his own self-interest and ran for a touchdown on the very next play.

We will spend considerable time discussing monitoring managers and trying to align their interests with shareholders. As an example, managers can be monitored by rating agencies and by auditing financial statements, and compensation packages may be used to align the interests of managers and shareholders. For example, the interests of managers and shareholders can be aligned by establishing management stock options, bonuses, and perquisites that are directly tied to how closely their decisions coincide with the interest of shareholders. In other words, what is good for shareholders must also be good for managers. If that is not the case, managers will make decisions in their best interest rather than maximizing shareholder wealth.

Avoiding Financial Crisis—Back to the Principles

Four significant economic events that have occurred during the last decade all point to the importance of keeping our eye closely affixed to the five principles of finance: the dot.com bubble; the accounting scandals headlined by Enron and WorldCom; the housing bubble; and, finally, the recent meltdown of the credit markets. Specifically, the problems that firms encounter in times of crisis are often brought on by, and made worse as a result of not paying close attention to the foundational principles of finance. To illustrate, consider the following:

- **Forgetting Principle 1: Cash Flow Is What Matters** (*Focusing on earnings instead of cash flow*). The financial fraud committed by WorldCom and others at the turn of the 21st century was a direct result of managerial efforts to manage the firm's reported earnings to the detriment of the firm's cash flows. The belief in the importance of current period earnings as the most important determinant of the market valuation of the firm's shares led some firms to sacrifice future cash flows in order to maintain the illusion of high and growing earnings.

- **Forgetting Principle 2: Money Has a Time Value** (*Focusing on the short run*). When trying to put in place a system that would align the interests of managers and shareholders, many firms tied managerial compensation to short-run performance. Consequently, the focus shifted in many firms from what was best in the long run to what was best in the short run.

- **Forgetting Principle 3: Risk Requires a Reward** (*Excessive risk taking due to underestimation of risk*). Relying on historical evidence, managers often underestimated the real risks that their decisions entailed. This underestimation of the underlying riskiness of their decisions led managers to borrow excessively. This excessive use of borrowed money (or financial leverage) led to financial disaster and bankruptcy for many firms as the economy slipped into recession. Moreover, the financial crisis was exacerbated by the fact that many times companies simply didn't understand how much risk they were taking on. For example, AIG (AIG), the giant insurance company that the government bailed out, was involved in investments whose value is based on the price of oil in 50 years. Let's face it, no one knows what the price of oil will be in a half a century—being involved in this type of investment is blind risk.

- **Forgetting Principle 4: Market Prices Are Generally Right** (*Ignoring the efficiency of financial markets*). Huge numbers of so-called hedge funds sprang up over the last decade and entered into investment strategies that pre-supposed that security prices could be predicted. Many of these same firms borrowed heavily in an effort to boost their returns and later discovered that security markets were a lot smarter than they thought and consequently realized huge losses on their highly-leveraged portfolios.

◆ **Forgetting Principle 5: Conflicts of Interest Cause Agency Problems** (*Executive compensation is out of control*). Executive compensation in the U.S. is dominated by performance-based compensation in the form of stock options and grants. The use of these forms of compensation over the last decade in the face of one of the longest bull markets in history has resulted in tremendous growth in executive compensation. The motivations behind these methods of compensation are primarily tied to a desire to make managers behave like stockholders (owners). Unfortunately, this practice has resulted in pay for non-performance in many cases and a feeling among the general public that executive compensation is excessive. We are reminded again that solving the principal-agent problem is not easy to do, but it has to be done!

In this edition of *Foundations of Finance* we believe that now, perhaps more than at any time in our memory, adhering to the fundamental principles of finance is critical. In addition, to further emphasize the "back to principles theme" we have created a new feature called "Cautionary Tales" that highlights specific examples where a failure to adhere to one or more of the five principles led to problems.

The Essential Elements of Ethics and Trust

While not one of the five principles of finance, ethics and trust are essential elements of the business world. In fact, without ethics and trust nothing works. This statement could be applied to almost everything in life. Virtually everything we do involves some dependence on others. Although businesses frequently try to describe the rights and obligations of their dealings with others using contracts, it is impossible to write a perfect contract. Consequently, business dealings between people and firms ultimately depend on the willingness of the parties to trust one another.

Ethics or rather a lack of ethics in finance is a recurring theme in the news. Financial scandals at Enron, WorldCom, and Arthur Andersen demonstrate the fact that ethical lapses are not forgiven in the business world. Not only is acting in an ethical manner morally correct, it is a necessary ingredient to long-term business and personal success.

Ethical behavior is easily defined. It's simply "doing the right thing." But what is the right thing? For example, Bristol-Myers Squibb (BMY) gives away heart medication to people who can't afford it. Clearly, the firm's management feels this is socially responsible and the right thing to do. But is it? Should companies give away money and products or should they leave such acts of benevolence to the firm's shareholders? Perhaps the shareholders should decide if they personally want to donate some of their wealth to worthy causes.

Like most ethical questions, there is no clear-cut answer to the dilemma posited above. We acknowledge that people have a right to disagree about what "doing the right thing" means, and that each of us has his or her personal set of values. These values form the basis for what we think is right and wrong. Moreover, every society adopts a set of rules or laws that prescribe what it believes constitutes "doing the right thing." In a sense, we can think of laws as a set of rules that reflect the values of a society as a whole.

You might ask yourself, "As long as I'm not breaking society's laws, why should I care about ethics?" The answer to this question lies in consequences. Everyone makes errors of judgment in business which is to be expected in an uncertain world. But ethical errors are different. Even if they don't result in anyone going to jail, they tend to end careers and thereby terminate future opportunities. Why? Because unethical behavior destroys trust, and businesses cannot function without a certain degree of trust.

Throughout this book, we will point out some of the ethical pitfalls that have tripped up managers. We encourage you to do the same so these mistakes don't happen to you. Taking "The Wall Street Journal Workplace-Ethics Quiz" in the Ethics in Financial Management box is a good place for you to begin.

ETHICS IN FINANCIAL MANAGEMENT

THE WALL STREET JOURNAL WORKPLACE-ETHICS QUIZ

Without question, when you enter the workforce you will be faced with a number of ethical dilemmas that you have never considered. The spread of technology into the workplace has raised a variety of new ethical questions, and many old ones still linger. The following is a quiz dealing with ethical questions that will both give you some questions to think about, and also allow you to compare your answers with those of other Americans surveyed.

Office Technology

1. Is it wrong to use company email for personal reasons?

   Yes   No

2. Is it wrong to play computer games on office equipment during the workday?

   Yes   No

3. Is it unethical to blame an error you made on a technological glitch?

   Yes   No

Gifts and Entertainment

4. Is a $50 gift to a boss unacceptable?

   Yes   No

5. Is a $50 gift FROM the boss unacceptable?

   Yes   No

6. Of gifts from suppliers: Is it OK to take a $200 pair of football tickets?

   Yes   No

7. Is it OK to take a $100 holiday food basket?

   Yes   No

8. Can you accept a $75 prize won at a raffle at a supplier's conference?

   Yes   No

Truth and Lies

9. Due to on-the-job pressure, have you ever abused or lied about sick days?

   Yes   No

10. Due to on-the-job pressure, have you ever taken credit for someone else's work or idea?

    Yes   No

Sources: Ethics Officer Association, Belmont, Mass.; Ethical Leadership Group, Wilmette, Ill.; surveys sampled a cross-section of workers at large companies and nationwide

Ethics Quiz Answers

1. 34% said personal email on company computers is wrong
2. 49% said playing computer games at work is wrong
3. 61% said it's unethical to blame your error on technology
4. 35% said a $50 gift to the boss is unacceptable
5. 12% said a $50 gift from the boss is unacceptable
6. 70% said it's unacceptable to take the $200 football tickets
7. 35% said it's unacceptable to take the $100 food basket
8. 40% said it's unacceptable to take the $75 raffle prize
9. 11% reported they lie about sick days
10. 4% reported they take credit for the work or ideas of others

Source: *The Wall Street Journal*, October 21, 1999, page B1 (Copyright © 1999, Dow Jones & Company, Inc.) All Rights Reserved.

Concept Check

1. According to Principle 3, how do investors decide where to invest their money?
2. What is an efficient market?
3. What is the agency problem and why does it occur?
4. Why are ethics and trust important in business?

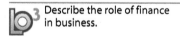
3 Describe the role of finance in business.

The Role of Finance in Business

Finance is the study of how people and businesses evaluate investments and raise capital to fund them. Our interpretation of an investment is quite broad. When Google designed its G1 Cell Phone, it was clearly making a long-term investment. The firm had to devote considerable expenses to designing, producing, and marketing the cell phone with the hope that the cell phone would eventually capture a sufficient amount of market share from the iPhone to make the investment worthwhile. Similarly, Google is making an investment decision whenever it hires a fresh new graduate, knowing that it will be paying a salary for at least 6 months before the employee will have much to contribute.

Thus, there are three basic types of issues that are addressed by the study of finance:

1. What long-term investments should the firm undertake? This area of finance is generally referred to as **capital budgeting**.
2. How should the firm raise money to fund these investments? The firm's funding choices are generally referred to as **capital structure decisions**.
3. How can the firm best manage its cash flows as they arise in its day-to-day operations? This area of finance is generally referred to as **working capital management**.

We'll be looking at each of these three areas of business finance—capital budgeting, capital structure, and working capital management—in the chapters ahead.

capital budgeting the decision-making process with respect to investment in fixed assets.

capital structure decision the decision-making process with funding choices and the mix of long-term sources of funds.

working capital management the management of the firm's current assets and short-term financing.

Why Study Finance?

Even if you're not planning a career in finance, a working knowledge of finance will take you far in both your personal and professional life.

Those interested in management will need to study topics like strategic planning, personnel, organizational behavior, and human relations, all of which involve spending money today in the hopes of generating more money in the future. For example, GM made a strategic decision to introduce an electric car and invested $740 million to produce the Chevy Volt, a decision GM expects to pay off in the future and save the company. Similarly, marketing majors need to understand and decide how aggressively to price products and the amount to spend on advertising. Since aggressive marketing today costs money, but allows firms to reap rewards in the future, it should be viewed as an investment that the firm needs to finance. Production and operations management majors need to understand how best to manage a firm's production and control its inventory and supply chain. These are all topics that involve risky choices that relate to the management of money over time, which is the central focus of finance. *While finance is primarily about the management of money, a key component of finance is the management and interpretation of information.* Indeed, if you pursue a career in management information systems or accounting, the finance managers are likely to be your most important clients. For the student with entrepreneurial aspirations, an understanding of finance is essential—after all, if you can't manage your finances, you won't be in business very long.

Finally, an understanding of finance is important to you as an individual. The fact that you are reading this book indicates that you understand the importance of investing in yourself. By obtaining a higher education degree, you are clearly making sacrifices in the hopes of making yourself more employable and improving your chances of having a rewarding and challenging career. Some of you are relying on your own earnings and the earnings of your parents to finance your education, whereas others are raising money or borrowing it from the **financial markets**, or *institutions and procedures that facilitate financial transactions.*

financial markets those institutions and procedures that facilitate transactions in all types of financial claims.

Although the primary focus of this book is on developing corporate finance tools that are used in business, much of the logic and tools we develop apply to the decisions you will have to make regarding your own personal finances. Financial decisions are everywhere, both for you and the firm you work for. In the future, both your business and personal life will be spent in the world of finance. Since you're going to be living in that world, it's time to learn the basics about it.

The Role of the Financial Manager

A firm can assume many different organizational structures. Figure 2 shows a typical presentation of how the finance area fits into a firm. The vice president for finance, also called the chief financial officer (CFO), serves under the firm's chief executive officer (CEO) and is responsible for overseeing financial planning, strategic planning, and controlling the firm's cash flow. Typically, a treasurer and controller serve under the CFO. In a smaller firm, the same person may fill both roles, with just one office handling all the duties. The treasurer generally handles the firm's financial activities, including cash and credit management, making capital expenditure decisions, raising funds, financial planning, and managing any foreign currency received by the firm. The controller is responsible for managing the firm's

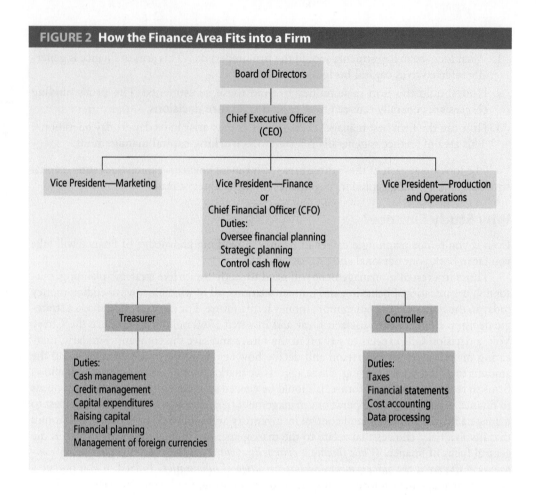

FIGURE 2 How the Finance Area Fits into a Firm

accounting duties, including producing financial statements, cost accounting, paying taxes, and gathering and monitoring the data necessary to oversee the firm's financial well-being. In this textbook, we focus on the duties generally associated with the treasurer and on how investment decisions are made.

Concept Check

1. What are the basic types of issues that are addressed by the study of finance?
2. What are the duties of a treasurer? Of a controller?

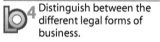
Distinguish between the different legal forms of business.

The Legal Forms of Business Organization

In the chapters ahead we focus on financial decisions for corporations because, although the corporation is not the only legal form of business available, it is the most logical choice for a firm that is large or growing. It is also the dominant business form in terms of sales in this country. In this section we explain why this is so.

Although numerous and diverse, the legal forms of business organization fall into three categories: the sole proprietorship, the partnership, and the corporation. To understand the basic differences between each form, we need to define each one and understand its advantages and disadvantages. As the firm grows, the advantages of the corporation begin to dominate. As a result, most large firms take on the corporate form.

Sole Proprietorships

sole proprietorship a business owned by a single individual.

A **sole proprietorship** is *a business owned by an individual*. The owner retains the title to the business's assets and is responsible, generally without limitation, for the liabilities incurred.

The proprietor is entitled to the profits from the business but must also absorb any losses. This form of business is initiated by the mere act of beginning the business operations. Typically, no legal requirement must be met in starting the operation, particularly if the proprietor is conducting the business in his or her own name. If a special name is used, an assumed-name certificate should be filed, requiring a small registration fee. Termination of the sole proprietorship occurs on the owner's death or by the owner's choice. Briefly stated, the sole proprietorship is for all practical purposes the absence of any formal *legal* business structure.

Partnerships

The primary difference between a partnership and a sole proprietorship is that the partnership has more than one owner. A **partnership** is *an association of two or more persons coming together as co-owners for the purpose of operating a business for profit*. Partnerships fall into two types: (1) general partnerships and (2) limited partnerships.

partnership an association of two or more individuals joining together as co-owners to operate a business for profit.

General Partnerships   In a **general partnership** *each partner is fully responsible for the liabilities incurred by the partnership*. Thus, any partner's faulty conduct, even having the appearance of relating to the firm's business, renders the remaining partners liable as well. The relationship among partners is dictated entirely by the partnership agreement, which may be an oral commitment or a formal document.

general partnership a partnership in which all partners are fully liable for the indebtedness incurred by the partnership.

Limited Partnerships   In addition to the general partnership, in which all partners are jointly liable without limitation, many states provide for **limited partnerships**. The state statutes permit *one or more of the partners to have limited liability, restricted to the amount of capital invested in the partnership*. Several conditions must be met to qualify as a limited partner. First, at least one general partner must have unlimited liability. Second, the names of the limited partners may not appear in the name of the firm. Third, the limited partners may not participate in the management of the business. Thus, a limited partnership provides limited liability for a partner who is purely an investor.

limited partnership a partnership in which one or more of the partners has limited liability, restricted to the amount of capital he or she invests in the partnership.

Corporations

The **corporation** has been a significant factor in the economic development of the United States. As early as 1819, U.S. Supreme Court Chief Justice John Marshall set forth the legal definition of a corporation as "an artificial being, invisible, intangible, and existing only in the contemplation of law."[2] This entity *legally functions separate and apart from its owners*. As such, the corporation can individually sue and be sued and purchase, sell, or own property, and its personnel are subject to criminal punishment for crimes. However, despite this legal separation, the corporation is composed of owners who dictate its direction and policies. The owners elect a board of directors, whose members in turn select individuals to serve as corporate officers, including the company's president, vice president, secretary, and treasurer. Ownership is reflected in common stock certificates, each designating the number of shares owned by its holder. The number of shares owned relative to the total number of shares outstanding determines the stockholder's proportionate ownership in the business. Because the shares are transferable, ownership in a corporation may be changed by a shareholder simply remitting the shares to a new shareholder. The shareholder's liability is confined to the amount of the investment in the company, thereby preventing creditors from confiscating stockholders' personal assets in settlement of unresolved claims. This is an extremely important advantage of a corporation. After all, would you be willing to invest in USAirways if you would be held liable if one of its planes crashed? Finally, the life of a corporation is not dependent on the status of the investors. The death or withdrawal of an investor does not affect the continuity of the corporation. Its managers continue to run the corporation when stock is sold or when it is passed on through inheritance.

corporation an entity that legally functions separate and apart from its owners.

---

[2] *The Trustees of Dartmouth College* v. *Woodard*, 4 Wheaton 636 (1819).

Organizational Form and Taxes: The Double Taxation on Dividends

Historically, one of the drawbacks of the corporate form was the double taxation of dividends. This occurs when a corporation earns a profit, pays taxes on those profits (the first taxation of earnings), and pays some of those profits back to the shareholders in the form of dividends, and then the shareholders pay personal income taxes on those dividends (the second taxation of those earnings). This double taxation of earnings does not take place with proprietorships and partnerships. Needless to say, that had been a major disadvantage of corporations. However, in an attempt to stimulate the economy, the tax rate on dividends was cut with the passage of the Tax Act of 2003.

Before the 2003 tax changes, you paid your regular, personal income tax rate on your dividend income, which could be as high as 35 percent. However, with the new law, qualified dividends from domestic corporations and qualified foreign corporations are now taxed at a maximum rate of 15 percent. Moreover, if your personal income puts you in the 10 percent or 15 percent income rate bracket, your dividends will be taxed at only 5 percent, and in 2008, this rate dropped to 0 percent. Unless Congress takes further action, this tax break on dividends will end after 2011 and individuals will once again be taxed at their regular personal tax rate.

S-Corporations and Limited Liability Companies (LLC)

One of the problems that entrepreneurs and small business owners face is that they need the benefits of the corporate form to expand, but the double taxation of earnings that comes with the corporate form makes it difficult to accumulate the necessary wealth for expansion. Fortunately, the government recognizes this problem and has provided two business forms that are, in effect, crosses between a partnership and a corporation with the tax benefits of partnerships (no double taxation of earnings) and the limited liability benefit of corporations (your liability is limited to what you invest).

S-corporation a corporation that, because of specific qualifications, is taxed as though it were a partnership.

The first is the **S-corporation**, which *provides limited liability while allowing the business's owners to be taxed as if they were a partnership*—that is, distributions back to the owners are not taxed twice as is the case with dividends distributed by regular corporations. Unfortunately, a number of restrictions accompany the S-corporation that detract from the desirability of this business form. Thus, an S-corporation cannot be used for a joint venture between two corporations. As a result, this business form has been losing ground in recent years in favor of the limited liability company.

limited liability company (LLC) a cross between a partnership and a corporation under which the owners retain limited liability but the company is run and is taxed like a partnership.

The **limited liability company (LLC)** is also *a cross between a partnership and a corporation*. Just as with the S-corporation, the LLC retains limited liability for its owners but runs and is taxed like a partnership. In general, it provides more flexibility than the S-corporation. For example, corporations can be owners in an LLC. However, because LLCs operate under state laws, both states and the IRS have rules for what qualifies as an LLC, and different states have different rules. But the bottom line in all this is that the LLC must not look too much like a corporation or it will be taxed as one.

Which Organizational Form Should Be Chosen?

Owners of new businesses have some important decisions to make in choosing an organizational form. Whereas each business form seems to have some advantages over the others, the advantages of the corporation begin to dominate as the firm grows and needs access to the capital markets to raise funds.

Because of the limited liability, the ease of transferring ownership through the sale of common shares, and the flexibility in dividing the shares, the corporation is the ideal business entity in terms of attracting new capital. In contrast, the unlimited liabilities of the sole proprietorship and the general partnership are deterrents to raising equity capital. Between the extremes, the limited partnership does provide limited liability for limited partners, which has a tendency to attract wealthy investors. However, the impracticality of having a large number of partners and the restricted marketability of an interest in a partnership prevent this form of organization from competing effectively with the corporation. Therefore, when developing our decision models we assume we are dealing with the corporate form and corporate tax codes.

Concept Check

1. What are the primary differences between a sole proprietorship, a partnership, and a corporation?
2. Explain why large and growing firms tend to choose the corporate form.
3. What is an LLC?

Finance and the Multinational Firm: The New Role

 5 Explain what has led to the era of the multinational corporation.

In the search for profits, U.S. corporations have been forced to look beyond our country's borders. This movement has been spurred on by the collapse of communism and the acceptance of the free market system in third world countries. All this has taken place at a time when information technology has experienced a revolution brought on by the personal computer and the Internet. Concurrently, the United States went through an unprecedented period of deregulation of industries. These changes resulted in the opening of new international markets, and U.S. firms experienced a period of price competition here at home that made it imperative that businesses look across borders for investment opportunities. The end result is that many U.S. companies, including General Electric, IBM, Walt Disney, and American Express have restructured their operations to expand internationally.

The bottom line is what you think of as a U.S. firm may be much more of a multinational firm than you would expect. For example, Coca-Cola earns over 80 percent of its profits from overseas sales and more money from its sales in Japan than it does from all its domestic sales. This is not uncommon. In fact, in 2008, 45 percent of the sales of S&P 500 listed companies came from outside the United States.

In addition to U.S. firms venturing abroad, foreign firms have also made their mark in the United States. You need only look to the auto industry to see what changes the entrance of Toyota, Honda, Nissan, BMW, and other foreign car manufacturers have had on the auto industry. In addition, foreigners have bought and now own such companies as Brooks Brothers, RCA, Pillsbury, A&P, 20th Century Fox, Columbia Pictures, and Firestone Tire & Rubber. Consequently, even if we wanted to, we couldn't keep all our attention focused on the United States, and even more important, we wouldn't want to ignore the opportunities that are available across international borders.

Concept Check

1. What has brought on the era of the multinational corporation?
2. Has looking beyond U.S. borders been a profitable experience for U.S. corporations?

Summary

This chapter outlines the framework for the maintenance and creation of shareholder wealth, which should be the goal of the firm and its managers. The goal of maximization of shareholder wealth is chosen because it deals well with uncertainty and time in a real-world environment. As a result, the maximization of shareholder wealth is found to be the proper goal for the firm.

The five basic principles of finance are:

 1 Identify the goal of the firm.

2 Understand the five basic principles of finance and business, the consequences of forgetting those basic principles of finance, and the importance of ethics and trust in business.

1. **Cash Flow Is What Matters**—incremental cash received and not accounting profits drives value.
2. **Money Has a Time Value**—a dollar received today is more valuable to the recipient than a dollar received in the future.

3. **Risk Requires a Reward**—the greater the risk of an investment, the higher will be the investor's required rate of return, and, other things remaining the same, the lower will be its value.

4. **Market Prices Are Generally Right**—For example, product market prices are often *slower* to react to important news than are prices in financial markets which tend to be very efficient and quick to respond to news.

5. **Conflicts of Interest Cause Agency Problems**—Large firms are typically run by professional managers who own a small fraction of the firms' equity. The individual actions of these managers are often motivated by self-interest, which may result in managers not acting in the best interests of the firm's owners. When this happens, the firm's owners will lose value.

While not one of the five principles of finance, ethics and trust are also essential elements of the business world, and without them, nothing works.

Describe the role of finance in business.

Finance is the study of how people and businesses evaluate investments and raise capital to fund them. There are three basic types of issues that are addressed by the study of finance: (1) What long-term investments should the firm undertake? This area of finance is generally referred to as capital budgeting. (2) How should the firm raise money to fund these investments? The firm's funding choices are generally referred to as capital structure decisions. (3) How can the firm best manage its cash flows as they arise in its day-to-day operations? This area of finance is generally referred to as working capital management.

Distinguish between the different legal forms of business.

The legal forms of business are examined. The sole proprietorship is a business operation owned and managed by an individual. Initiating this form of business is simple and generally does not involve any substantial organizational costs. The proprietor has complete control of the firm but must be willing to assume full responsibility for its outcomes.

The general partnership, which is simply a coming together of two or more individuals, is similar to the sole proprietorship. The limited partnership is another form of partnership sanctioned by states to permit all but one of the partners to have limited liability if this is agreeable to all partners.

The corporation increases the flow of capital from public investors to the business community. Although larger organizational costs and regulations are imposed on this legal entity, the corporation is more conducive to raising large amounts of capital. Limited liability, continuity of life, and ease of transfer in ownership, which increase the marketability of the investment, have contributed greatly in attracting large numbers of investors to the corporate environment. The formal control of the corporation is vested in the parties who own the greatest number of shares. However, day-to-day operations are managed by the corporate officers, who theoretically serve on behalf of the firm's stockholders.

Explain what has led to the era of the multinational corporation.

With the collapse of communism and the acceptance of the free market system in third world countries, U.S. firms have been spurred on to look beyond their own boundaries for new business. The end result has been that it is not uncommon for major U.S. companies to earn over half their income from sales abroad. Foreign firms are also increasingly investing in the United States.

Key Terms

Agency problem	Limited liability company (LLC)
Capital budgeting	Limited partnership
Capital structure decision	Opportunity cost
Corporation	Partnership
Efficient market	Sole proprietorship
Financial markets	S-corporation
General partnership	Working capital management
Incremental cash flow	

Review Questions

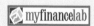

All Review Questions and Study Problems are available in MyFinanceLab.

1-1. What are some of the problems involved in implementing the goal of maximization of shareholder wealth?

1-2. Firms often involve themselves in projects that do not result directly in profits. For example, IBM and ExxonMobil frequently support public television broadcasts. Do these projects contradict the goal of maximization of shareholder wealth? Why or why not?

1-3. What is the relationship between financial decision making and risk and return? Would all financial managers view risk–return trade-offs similarly?

1-4. What is the agency problem and how might it impact the goal of maximization of shareholder wealth?

1-5. Define (a) sole proprietorship, (b) partnership, and (c) corporation.

1-6. Identify the primary characteristics of each form of legal organization.

1-7. Using the following criteria, specify the legal form of business that is favored: (a) organizational requirements and costs, (b) liability of the owners, (c) the continuity of the business, (d) the transferability of ownership, (e) management control and regulations, (f) the ability to raise capital, and (g) income taxes.

1-8. There are a lot of great business majors. Check out the Careers in Business Web site at www .careers-in-business.com. It covers not only finance but also marketing, accounting, and management. Find out about and provide a short write-up describing the opportunities investment banking and financial planning offer.

1-9. Like it or not, ethical problems seem to crop up all the time in finance. Some of the worst financial scandals are examined on the Financial Scandals Web site www.ex.ac.uk/~RDavies/arian/ scandals/classic.html. Take a look at the write-ups dealing with "The Credit Crunch," "The Dot-Com Bubble and Investment Banks" and "Bernard L. Madoff Investment Securities." Provide a short write-up on these events.

1-10. We know that if a corporation is to maximize shareholder wealth, the interests of the managers and the shareholders must be aligned. The simplest way to align these interests is to structure executive compensation packages appropriately to encourage managers to act in the best interests of shareholders. However, has executive compensation gotten out of control? Take a look at the Executive Pay Watch Web site at www.aflcio.org/corporatewatch/paywatch to see to whom top salaries have gone. What are the most recent total compensation packages for the head of Oracle (ORCL), Home Depot (HD), Disney (DIS), and ExxonMobil (XOM)?

Mini Case

The final stage in the interview process for an assistant financial analyst at Caledonia Products involves a test of your understanding of basic financial concepts. You are given the following memorandum and asked to respond to the questions. Whether you are offered a position at Caledonia will depend on the accuracy of your response.

To: Applicants for the position of Financial Analyst
From: Mr. V. Morrison, CEO, Caledonia Products
Re: A test of your understanding of basic financial concepts and of the corporate tax code

Please respond to the following questions:

  a. What is the appropriate goal for the firm and why?
  b. What does the risk–return trade-off mean?
  c. Why are we interested in cash flows rather than accounting profits in determining the value of an asset?
  d. What is an efficient market and what are the implications of efficient markets for us?
  e. What is the cause of the agency problem and how do we try to solve it?
  f. What do ethics and ethical behavior have to do with finance?
  g. Define (1) sole proprietorship, (2) partnership, and (3) corporation.

Understanding Financial Statements and Cash Flows

From Chapter 3 of *Foundations of Finance*, 7/e. Arthur J. Keown. John D. Martin. J. William Petty. Copyright © 2011 by Pearson Education.
Published by Prentice Hall. All rights reserved.

Understanding Financial Statements and Cash Flows

Learning Objectives

After reading this chapter, you should be able to:

1. Compute **a company's profits, as reflected by its income statement.**

2. Determine **a firm's financial position at a point in time based on its balance sheet.**

3. Measure **a company's cash flows.**

4. Compute **taxable income and income taxes owed.**

In Hewlett-Packard's (HP) 2008 annual report, Mark Hurd (CEO) describes the firm as follows:

> We are a leading global provider of products, technologies, software, solutions and services to individual consumers, small- and medium-sized businesses ("SMBs"), and large enterprises, including customers in the public and education sectors.

In his letter to the shareholders in the annual report, Hurd discusses the economic difficulties he believes the company will face in 2009, given the severe economic downturn.

> In the near term, we expect that economic conditions in 2009 will be extremely challenging. It will take continued discipline and tough decision making to stay the course and continue executing our strategy in the coming months.

In response to the anticipated challenges, he describes the firm's competitive advantages that he says will carry the firm through the difficult times:

> [O]ur company has significant competitive advantages:
>
> - A strong balance sheet
> - Diversified revenues with one-third of our revenue and well over half of our profits from recurring sources such as services and supplies
> - A lean, variable cost structure and commitment to continue to eliminate all costs that are not core to the company's success
> - Proven financial and operational discipline

> These advantages will be put to good use by our outstanding executive leadership team . . . Our plan is to get through this period without losing any muscle in the organization or changing our swing in the marketplace . . . We expect that HP's ability to execute in a challenging marketplace will differentiate us from our competitors and enable HP to emerge from the current environment as a stronger force in the industry.

In essence, Hurd is saying that when it comes to tough times, having strong financial statements is critical, and will provide a competitive advantage during these times. This chapter lays a foundation for your understanding financial statements, which in some ways is the "language" of business.

© Paul Sakuma/AP Wide World Photos

In this book we explained the workings of the financial markets. We found that these markets provide the means for bringing together investors (savers) with the users of capital (businesses that provide products and services to the consumer). There we looked at the world as the economist sees it, with an eye for understanding the marketplace where managers go to acquire capital. It is the investors in these financial markets who determine the value of a firm, and given our goal of maximizing shareholder value, no issue is more fundamental to our study. However, we want to alter our perspective for the time being.

In this chapter, we view the world of finance more as an accountant sees it. To begin, we examine the three basic financial statements that are used to understand how a firm is doing financially: the income statement, or what is sometimes called the profit and loss statement, the balance sheet, and the statement of cash flows. Our goal is not to make you an accountant, but instead to provide you with the tools to understand a firm's financial situation. With this knowledge, you will be able to understand the financial consequences of a company's decisions and actions—as well as your own.

The financial performance of a firm matters to a lot of groups—the company's management, its employees, and its investors, just to name a few. If you are an employee, the firm's performance is important to you because it may determine your annual bonus, your job security, and your opportunity to advance your professional career. This is true whether you are in the firm's marketing, finance, or human resources department. Moreover, an employee who can see how decisions affect a firm's finances has a competitive advantage. So regardless of your position in the firm, it is in your own best interest to know the basics of financial statements—even if accounting is not your greatest love.

Let's begin our review of financial statements by looking at the format and content of the income statement.

The Income Statement

An **income statement**, or **profit and loss statement**, indicates the amount of profits generated by a firm over a given time period, often 1 year. In its most basic form, the income statement may be represented as follows:

$$\text{Sales} - \text{expenses} = \text{profits} \qquad (1)$$

> ### REMEMBER YOUR PRINCIPLES
>
> **Principle** Two principles are especially important in this chapter. **Principle 1** tells us that **Cash Flow Is What Matters**. At times, cash is more important than profits. Thus, considerable time is devoted to measuring cash flows in this chapter. **Principle 5** warns us that there may be a conflict when managers and owners have different incentives. That is, **Conflicts of Interest Cause Agency Problems**. Because managers' incentives are at times different from those of owners, the firm's common stockholders, as well as other providers of capital (such as bankers), we need information that can be used to monitor the managers' actions. Because the owners of large companies do not have access to internal information about the firm's operations, they must rely on public information from any and all sources. One of the main sources of such information comes from the company's financial statements provided by the firm's accountants. Although this information is by no means perfect, it is an important source used by outsiders to assess a company's activities. In this chapter, we learn how to use data from the firm's public financial statements to monitor management's actions.

 Compute a company's profits, as reflected by its income statement.

income statement (profit and loss statement) a basic accounting statement that measures the results of a firm's operations over a specified period, commonly 1 year. Also known as the profit and loss statement. The bottom line of the income statement shows the firm's profit or loss for the period.

cost of goods sold the cost of producing or acquiring a product or service to be sold in the ordinary course of business.

gross profit sales or revenue minus the cost of goods sold.

operating expenses marketing and selling expenses, general and administrative expenses, and depreciation expense.

operating income (earnings before interest and taxes) sales less the cost of goods sold less operating expenses.

The format for an income statement is shown in Figure 1. The income statement begins with sales or revenue, from which we subtract the **cost of goods sold** (the cost of producing or acquiring the product or service to be sold) to yield **gross profits**. Next, **operating expenses** are deducted to determine **operating income** (also called **operating profits** or **earnings before interest and taxes** or **EBIT**). Notice that the operating expenses in the income statement consist of:

1. Marketing and selling expenses—the cost of promoting the firm's products or services to customers.
2. General and administrative expenses—the firm's overhead expenses, such as executive salaries and rent expense.
3. Depreciation expense—a noncash expense to allocate the cost of depreciable assets, such as plant and equipment, over the life of the asset.

In Figure 1, we see that operating income is the result of management's decisions relating only to the *operations* of the business, not its financing. In other words, the firm's

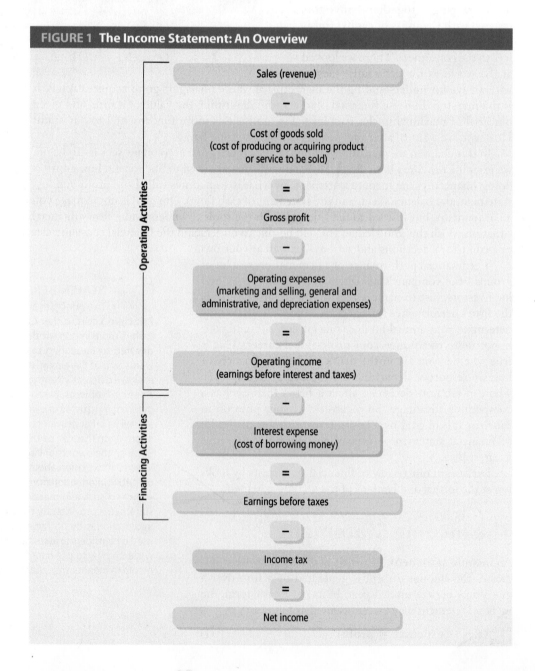

FIGURE 1 The Income Statement: An Overview

22

FINANCE AT WORK

THE LESSONS OF ADVERSITY

What has been learned from the most recent economic crisis? In the May 4, 2009 issue of *Fortune Magazine*, Rick Tetzeli concludes that "the survivors have been taught a few things about thinking long term and sticking to principles." He then suggests some lessons learned.

Gorging on easy profits can be fatal. Wall Street and Detroit tumbled for a lot of reasons, but high on the list is the fact that they thought the free buffet would be open indefinitely.

On Wall Street myriad bets were made on the belief that somehow accepting increasing risk would always pay off. Any reader of the account of the failure of Bear Stearns, *House of Cards*, by William Cohan will come away astonished at how little thought was given to the question, What if it doesn't last? The cabal of mega-losers on this list, led by AIG, answers that question pretty clearly.

As for Detroit, the more the bailout process exposes its decision-making process, the more we realize that, at least at GM, the assumption was that consumer preferences would be slow to change. Well, guess what?

Highly disciplined companies can thrive in all seasons. That doesn't mean they didn't suffer. From Apple to Berkshire, they did. But they didn't suffer nearly as much as others. . . . IBM has become the model for pushing itself up the technology learning curve, while Johnson & Johnson has relentlessly taken the long view. The average annual return on its stock since it went public in 1944 is 17.1%.

The next five years may redefine everything. Banking and automaking aren't the only industries that will be changed for good. Entertainment, publishing, and airlines face threats to their survival. And consider homebuilding—five companies fell right off the list this year: Hovnanian, KB Home, Lennar, NVR, and Toll Brothers.

In retailing, department stores like Macy's got clobbered, while discounters from Wal-Mart to Dollar Tree made new inroads. You won't find any $4.99 items for sale in Dollar Tree's stores—it only sells items for a buck, like tape, party supplies, and writing utensils. Says CEO Bob Sasser, "We are positioned well for any economy. We sell things people need every day." The American consumer's focus on value versus prestige may be changing in a lasting way.

American business—we hope—has been tempered by fire. If the next five years will be defining ones, they will also be years where we should see U.S. companies apply what they've learned from 2008. Robert Coury, CEO of Mylan a pharma maker new to the [Fortune 500] list, guided his company through two acquisitions in three years and increased his headcount from 3,500 to 15,000. "We've already gone through the most tumultuous change in the history of our company," he says. "We're tested warriors and tested leaders." Right now, the stock market agrees—Mylan's stock is up 143% since October.

Businesses will be more accountable. Anytime a business magazine writes something like this, it's worth noting the date, since these predictions are so often wishful thinking. But right now it's not such a reach. For starters, one result of the broad populist anger [against corporations] is that government is getting involved, with an eye toward restraining the worst corporate behavior. But even without federal involvement, businesses will have to answer to a higher authority.

According to Ram Charan, a consultant to CEOs of many Fortune 500 companies, the executives he works with "are very sensitive to the societal pressure, and you will see change." For starters, Charan foresees a shift in the composition of executive pay. Corporate boards will try to ease the grip of Wall Street by adopting pay structures that consider all stakeholders, including employees and customers. That would be a change we could all live with. And a sign that we actually learned something from the disaster.

Source: Rick Tetzeli, "The Lessons of Adversity," *Fortune Magazine*, May 4, 2009, pp. 62–63.

financing expenses (its interest expense resulting from the use of debt financing) have not been subtracted to this point. Thus, the operating income of a firm reports the results of the following activities:

1. The selling price of the products or services to be sold and the number of units sold (selling price × units sold = total sales)

2. The cost of producing or acquiring the goods or services that were sold (cost of goods sold)

3. Selling and marketing expenses (the expenses related to marketing, selling, and distributing the products or services)

4. The firm's overhead expenses (general and administrative expenses, and depreciation expenses)

We then determine the **earnings before taxes**, or **taxable income**, by deducting the **financing cost** (the interest expense on the firm's debt financing) from the operating income.[1]

earnings before taxes (taxable income) operating income minus interest expense.

financing cost cost incurred by a company that often includes interest expenses and preferred dividends.

[1]If a firm has issued preferred stock, it would pay preferred stock dividends, which would be shown in the income statement as an expense along with any interest paid on debt. For our purposes, we will assume that there is no preferred stock being used to finance the firm's assets.

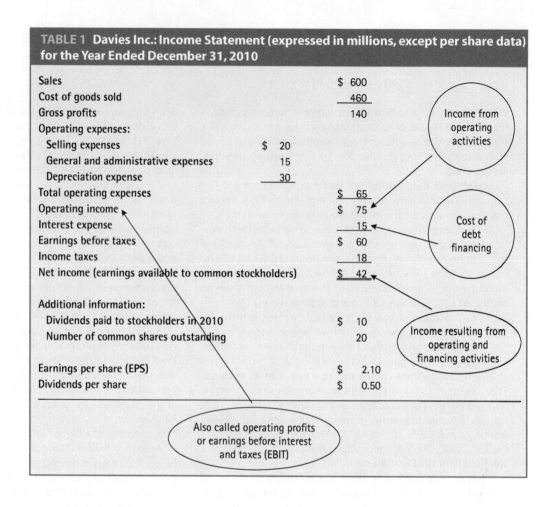

TABLE 1   Davies Inc.: Income Statement (expressed in millions, except per share data) for the Year Ended December 31, 2010

Sales		$ 600
Cost of goods sold		460
Gross profits		140
Operating expenses:		
Selling expenses	$ 20	
General and administrative expenses	15	
Depreciation expense	30	
Total operating expenses		$ 65
Operating income		$ 75
Interest expense		15
Earnings before taxes		$ 60
Income taxes		18
Net income (earnings available to common stockholders)		$ 42
Additional information:		
Dividends paid to stockholders in 2010		$ 10
Number of common shares outstanding		20
Earnings per share (EPS)		$ 2.10
Dividends per share		$ 0.50

(Annotations in figure: "Income from operating activities"; "Cost of debt financing"; "Income resulting from operating and financing activities"; "Also called operating profits or earnings before interest and taxes (EBIT)")

Next, the firm's income taxes are calculated, based on its earnings before taxes and the applicable tax rate for the amount of income reported. For instance, if a firm had earnings before taxes of $100,000, and its tax rate is 28 percent, then it would owe $28,000 in taxes (0.28 × $100,000 = $28,000).

The resulting number is the **net income**, or **earnings available to common stockholders**, which represents income that may be reinvested in the firm or distributed to its owners—provided, of course, the cash is available to do so. As you will come to understand, a positive net income on an income statement does not necessarily mean that a firm has generated positive cash flows.

Table 1 contains the 2010 income statement for Davies Inc., a manufacturer of accessories for small technology products. We see that the firm had *sales* of $600 million for the 12-month period ended December 31, 2010. The *cost of goods sold* was $460 million, resulting in *gross profits* of $140 million. The firm then had $65 million of operating expenses. After deducting the operating expenses, the firm's *operating income* (*earnings before interest and taxes*) was $75 million. To this point, we have calculated the profits resulting only from operating the business, without regard for any financing costs, such as the interest paid on money borrowed.

We next deduct the $15 million in interest expense (the amount paid for borrowing money) to arrive at the company's *earnings before taxes* (*taxable income*) of $60 million. We then subtract the income taxes of $18 million to determine the company's *net income*, or *earnings available to common stockholders*, of $42 million.

At this point, we have completed the income statement. However, the firm's owners (common stockholders) like to know how much income the firm made on a *per share* basis, or what is called **earnings per share**. We calculate earnings per share as net income divided

TABLE 2 Davies Inc.: Common-Sized Income Statement for the Year Ended December 31, 2010

	Dollars	Percentage of Sales	
Sales	$ 600	100.0%	
Cost of goods sold	460	76.7%	
Gross profits	$ 140	23.3%	← gross profit margin
Operating expenses	$ 65	10.8%	
Operating income	$ 75	12.5%	← operating profit margin
Interest	15	2.5%	
Earnings before taxes	$ 60	10.0%	
Income taxes	18	3.0%	
Net income	$ 42	7.0%	← net profit margin

by the number of common stock shares outstanding. Because Davies Inc. had 20 million shares outstanding in 2010 (see Table 1), its earnings per share was $2.10 ($2.10 = $42 million net income ÷ 20 million shares).

Investors also want to know the amount of dividends a firm pays for each share outstanding, or the **dividends per share**. In Table 1 we see that Davies Inc. paid $10 million in dividends during 2010. We can then determine that the firm paid $0.50 in dividends per share ($0.50 = $10 million total dividends ÷ 20 million shares outstanding).

What conclusions can we draw from Davies Inc.'s income statement? To answer this question, it is helpful to restate the numbers in the income statement as a percentage of sales. Such a revision is called a **common-sized income statement** and is presented in Table 2 for Davies Inc. The common-sized income statement allows us to express expenses and profits on a relative basis, so that we can more easily compare a firm's income performance across time and with competitors. The profits-to-sales relationships are defined as **profit margins**. For Davies Inc. we see that the firm earned

1. A 23.3 percent **gross profit margin** (23.3% = $140 million of gross profits ÷ $600 million of sales)
2. A 12.5 percent **operating profit margin** (12.5% = $75 million of operating income ÷ $600 million of sales)
3. A 7 percent **net profit margin** (7% = $42 million of net income ÷ $600 million of sales)

dividends per share the amount of dividends a firm pays for each share outstanding.

common-sized income statement an income statement in which a firm's expenses and profits are expressed as a percentage of its sales.

profit margins financial ratios (sometimes simply referred to as margins) that reflect the level of the firm's profits relative to its sales. Examples include the gross profit margin (gross profit divided by sales), operating profit margin (operating income divided by sales), and the net profit margin (net income).

gross profit margin gross profit divided by net sales. It is a ratio denoting the gross profit earned by the firm as a percentage of its net sales.

operating profit margin operating income divided by sales. This ratio serves as an overall measure of the company's operating effectiveness.

net profit margin net income divided by sales. A ratio that measures the net income of the firm as a percent of sales.

CAN YOU DO IT?

PREPARING AN INCOME STATEMENT

Given the information below for Menielle Inc., construct an income statement. What are the firm's gross profits, operating income, and net income? What is the firm's noncash expense? Calculate earnings per share and dividends per share assuming that there are 20,000 shares outstanding.

Interest expense	$35,000	Sales	$400,000
Cost of goods sold	$150,000	Common stock dividends	$15,000
Selling and marketing expenses	$40,000	Income taxes	$40,000
Administrative expenses	$30,000	Depreciation expense	$20,000

FIGURE 2 Hewlett-Packard's Income Statement

HEWLETT-PACKARD COMPANY AND SUBSIDIARIES

**Management's Discussion and Analysis of
Financial Condition and Results of Operations**

Hewlett-Packard's income statement was reported in its 2008 annual report as follows

Results of operations in dollars and as a percentage of net revenue were as follows for the following fiscal years ended October 31:

	2008		2007[2]		2006[2]	
			In millions			
Net revenue	$118,364	100.0%	$104,286	100.0%	$ 91,658	100.0%
Cost of sales[1]	89,921	76.0%	76,887	75.6%	69,427	75.7%
Gross profit	$ 28,443	24.0%	$ 25,399	24.4%	$ 22,231	24.3%
Research and development	3,543	3.0%	3,611	3.5%	3,591	3.9%
Selling, general and administrative	13,104	11.1%	12,226	11.7%	11,266	12.3%
Amortization of purchased intangible assets	967	0.9%	783	0.7%	604	0.7%
In-process research and development charges	45	—	190	0.2%	52	—
Restructuring charges	270	0.2%	387	0.4%	158	0.2%
Acquisition-related charges	41	—	—	—	—	—
Pension curtailments and pension settlements, net	—	—	(517)	(0.5)%	—	—
Earnings from operations	$ 10,473	8.8%	$ 8,719	8.4%	$ 6,560	7.2%
Interest and other, net	—	—	458	0.4%	631	0.6%
Earnings before taxes	$ 10,473	8.8%	$ 9,177	8.8%	$ 7,191	7.8%
Provision for taxes	2,144	1.8%	1,913	1.8%	993	1.0%
Net earnings	$ 8,329	7.0%	$ 7,264	7.0%	$ 6,198	6.8%

(1) Cost of products, cost of services and financing interest.
(2) Certain reclassifications have been made to prior year amounts in order to conform to the current year presentation.

Net Revenue

The components of weighted-average net revenue growth as compared to prior-year periods were as follows for the following fiscal years ended October 31:

	2008	2007
	Percentage points	
Personal Systems Group	5.6	7.9
HP Services	5.6	1.1
Imaging and Printing Group	0.9	1.8
Enterprise Storage and Servers	0.7	1.5
HP Software	0.5	1.2
HP Financial Services	0.4	0.3
Corporate Investments/Other	(0.2)	—
Total HP	13.5	13.8

In practice, managers pay close attention to the firm's profit margins. Profit margins are considered to be an important measurement of how well the firm is doing financially. Managers carefully watch for any changes in margins, up or down. They also compare the firm's margins with those of competitors. For the time being, simply remember that profit-to-sales relationships, or *profit margins*, are important in assessing a firm's performance. To observe the income statement from an actual company, Hewlett-Packard, see Figure 2

DID YOU GET IT?

PREPARING AN INCOME STATEMENT

We provided data for Menielle Inc. and asked you to prepare an income statement based on the information. Your results should be as follows:

Sales		$400,000
Cost of goods sold		150,000
Gross profit		$250,000
Operating expenses:		
Selling and marketing expenses	$40,000	
Administrative expenses	30,000	
Depreciation expense	20,000	
Total operating expenses		$ 90,000
Operating income		$160,000
Interest expense		35,000
Earnings before tax		$125,000
Income taxes		40,000
Net income		$ 85,000
Earnings per share ($85,000 net income ÷ 20,000 shares)		$ 4.25
Dividends per share ($15,000 dividends ÷ 20,000 shares)		$ 0.75

Concept Check

1. What can we learn by reviewing a firm's income statement?
2. What basic relationship can we see in an income statement?
3. How are gross profits, operating income, and net income different as they relate to the areas of business activity reported in the income statement?
4. What are earnings per share and dividends per share?
5. What is a profit margin? What are the different types of profit margins?

The Balance Sheet

A firm's income statement reports the results from operating the business *for a period of time*, such as 1 year. The firm's **balance sheet**, on the other hand, provides a snapshot of the firm's financial position *at a specific point in time*, presenting its asset holdings, liabilities, and owner-supplied capital (stockholders' equity). Figure 3 shows the difference in time perspectives

 Determine a firm's financial position at a point in time based on its balance sheet.

balance sheet a statement that shows a firm's assets, liabilities, and shareholder equity at a given point in time. It is a snapshot of the firm's financial position on a particular date.

FIGURE 3 The Income Statement and Balance Sheet as One Picture

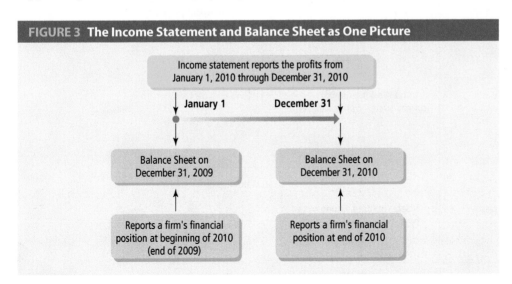

between an income statement and a balance sheet. By examining two balance sheets, one at the beginning of a year and one at the end of the year, along with the income statement for the year, we have a more complete picture of a firm's operations. For instance, we could see what a company looked like at the beginning of 2010 (by looking at its balance sheet on December 31, 2009), what happened during the year (by looking at its income statement for 2010), and the final outcome at the end of 2010 (by looking at its balance sheet on December 31, 2010).

In its simplest form, a balance sheet is represented by the following balance sheet "equation":

$$\text{Total assets} = \text{total liabilities (debt)} + \text{total shareholders' equity} \tag{2}$$

where *total assets* represent the resources owned by the firm, and *total liabilities* and *total shareholders' equity* indicate how those resources were financed.

The conventional practice is to report the value of the firm's various assets in the balance sheet by using the actual cost of acquiring them. Thus, the balance sheet does not represent the current market value of the company's assets, and consequently does not reflect the value of the company itself. Rather, *it reports historical transactions at their cost*. Therefore, the balance sheet reports a company's **accounting book value**, which is simply equal to a firm's total assets as listed in its balance sheet. It's important for you to understand that a company's accounting book value is not the same as the market value of the assets. Determining a fair or market value of a business or its assets is a different matter—an issue that we will give great attention to throughout future chapters.

Figure 4 shows us the basic components of a balance sheet. On the left side of Figure 4, the firm's assets are listed according to their type; on the right side, we see a listing of the different sources of financing a company could use to finance its assets.

Types of Assets

As shown in Figure 4, a company's assets fall into two categories: (1) current assets and (2) long-term (fixed) assets.

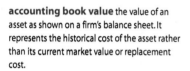

accounting book value the value of an asset as shown on a firm's balance sheet. It represents the historical cost of the asset rather than its current market value or replacement cost.

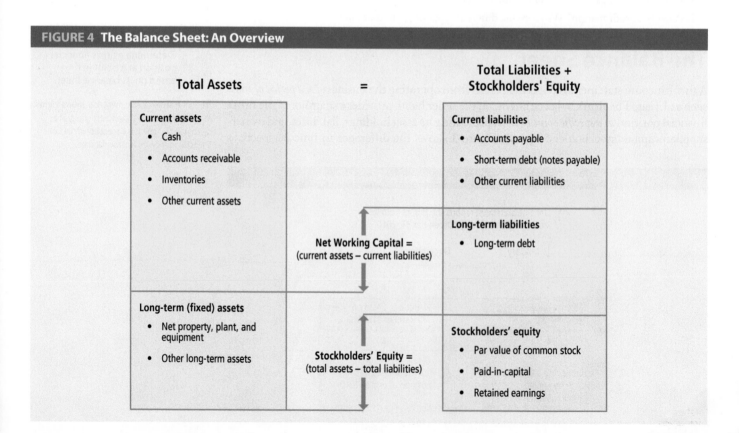

FIGURE 4 The Balance Sheet: An Overview

Current Assets   **Current assets**, or **gross working capital**, as it is sometimes called, are those assets that are relatively *liquid*, that is, those that are expected to be converted into cash within 12 months. Current assets include a firm's cash, accounts receivable, inventories, and other current assets.

- ◆ **Cash.**   Every firm must have **cash** to conduct its business operations. A reservoir of cash is needed because of the unequal flow of funds into (cash receipts) and out of (cash expenditures) the business.
- ◆ **Accounts receivable.**   A firm's **accounts receivable** are the amounts owed to the firm by its customers who buy on credit.
- ◆ **Inventories.**   A company's **inventories** consist of raw materials, works in process, and finished goods held by the firm for eventual sale.
- ◆ **Other current assets.**   Other current assets include such items as prepaid expenses. For example, a company's insurance premium might be due before the actual insurance coverage begins; or the firm's rent might have to be paid in advance. These expenditures are considered assets because they represent an investment that's been made by the company. Only when, for example, the insurance premium is used up following the coverage period is the premium considered an expense.

current assets (gross working capital) current assets consist primarily of cash, marketable securities, accounts receivable, inventories, and prepaid expenses.

cash cash on hand, demand deposits, and short-term marketable securities that can quickly be converted into cash.

accounts receivable money owed by customers who purchased goods or services from the firm on credit.

inventories raw materials, work in progress, and finished goods held by the firm for eventual sale.

Fixed Assets   **Fixed assets** are long term in nature, such as machinery and equipment, buildings, and land. These assets will be used over a number of years.

When a firm purchases a fixed asset, it does not immediately report the cost of the asset as an expense in its income statement. Instead, it is considered to be an asset and included in the balance sheet. Some of these assets, such as machinery and equipment, will depreciate in value over time due to obsolescence or daily wear and tear; others may not, such as land.

With depreciable assets, the original cost of an asset is allocated in the income statement over the asset's expected useful life. The amount allocated as the cost each year is shown as a **depreciation expense** in the income statement. The sum of all depreciation taken over the entire life of the asset is shown as **accumulated depreciation** in the balance sheet.

To illustrate, assume that a truck purchased for $20,000 is to be evenly depreciated over a 4-year life.[2] The depreciation expense to be reported in the income statement for each year would be $5,000 ($20,000 asset cost ÷ 4 years = $5,000). When a firm buys the truck, the $20,000 original cost of the asset is added to the balance sheet as a **gross fixed asset**. The cumulative depreciation taken over the asset's life is reported as *accumulated depreciation*. We subtract the accumulated depreciation each year from the gross fixed assets to determine **net fixed assets**. In this example, the income statements for each year and balance sheets over time would appear as follows:

fixed assets assets such as equipment, buildings, and land.

depreciation expense a noncash expense to allocate the cost of depreciable assets, such as plant and equipment, over the life of the asset.

accumulated depreciation the sum of all depreciation taken over the entire life of a depreciable asset.

gross fixed assets the original cost of a firm's fixed assets.

net fixed assets gross fixed assets minus the accumulated depreciation taken over the life of the assets.

Income Statement

	FOR THE YEAR ENDING			
	1	2	3	4
Depreciation expense	$5,000	$5,000	$5,000	$5,000

Balance Sheet

	END OF YEAR			
	1	2	3	4
Gross fixed assets	$20,000	$20,000	$20,000	$20,000
Accumulated depreciation	5,000	10,000	15,000	20,000
Net fixed assets	$15,000	$10,000	$ 5,000	$ 0

[2]In this instance, we are using a straight-line depreciation method. Other methods allow a firm to accelerate the depreciation expenses in the early years of the asset's life and report less in the later years.

FINANCE AT WORK

GOLDMAN SACHS ANNOUNCES FIRST QUARTER 2009 EARNINGS

Goldman Sachs Group, Inc. is a global investment-banking firm. Below are excerpts from the press release Goldman Sachs issued to report its first-quarter earnings for 2009. The excerpts are followed by parts of a *Wall Street Journal* article reporting on the release.

PRESS RELEASE
Relations: Lucas van Praag
Investor Relations: Dane E. Holmes

**Goldman Sachs Reports First Quarter
Earnings per Common Share of $3.39**

NEW YORK, April 13, 2009—The Goldman Sachs Group, Inc. (NYSE: GS) today reported net revenues of $9.43 billion and net earnings of $1.81 billion for its first quarter ended March 27, 2009. Diluted earnings per common share were $3.39 compared with $3.23 for the first quarter ended February 29, 2008 and a diluted loss per common share of $4.97 for the fourth quarter ended November 28, 2008. Annualized return on average common shareholders' equity was 14.3% for the first quarter of 2009.

"Given the difficult market conditions, we are pleased with this quarter's performance," said Lloyd C. Blankfein, Chairman and Chief Executive Officer. "Our results reflect the strength and diversity of our client franchise, the resilience of our business model and the dedication and focus of our people. We believe these attributes position the firm to continue to create value for our clients and actively fulfill our role in the capital markets."

A conference call to discuss the firm's results, outlook and related matters will be held Tuesday, April 14, 2009 at 7:00 A.M. (ET). The call will be open to the public. Members of the public who would like to listen to the conference call should dial 1-888-281-7154 (U.S. Domestic) or 1-706-679-5627 (international). The number should be dialed at least 10 minutes prior to the start of the conference call. The conference call will also be accessible as an audio webcast through the Investor Relations section of the firm's Web site, www.gs.com/shareholders. There is no charge to access the call.

And What Did the *Wall Street Journal* Have to Say?
Goldman Sachs Group Inc. announced robust earnings, along with its plan that would make it the first big financial firm to pay back the money it received from the government last fall. The Wall Street firm announced better-than-expected profit ahead of schedule after the close of trading Monday. The firm reported net income of $1.81 billion, or $3.39 a share, for the period ended March 27, compared with $1.51 billion, or $3.23, during the first quarter of last year. The firm had been scheduled to announce results Tuesday morning.

Driving the earnings was record performance in the fixed-income, currency, and commodities division, where the trading of products tied to interest rates and strength in commodities helped generate $6.56 billion in net revenue, a 34% rise from the comparable period last year. Those results offset a downturn in investment banking and money management.

Sources: http://www2.goldmansachs.com/our-firm/press/press-releases/current/2009-q1-results.html, accessed May 31, 2009; and Kate Kelly and Susanne Craig. "Goldman Flexes Its Profit Muscle—Share Sale Is Set as Better-Than-Expected Results Get Released Early," *Wall Street Journal*. (Eastern Edition). New York, N.Y.: April 14, 2009, p. C.1.

It is important to understand the distinction between *gross* fixed assets and *net* fixed assets and how depreciation expense in the income statement relates to accumulated depreciation in the balance sheet.

Other Assets Other assets are all of the firm's assets that are not current assets or fixed assets. They include, for example, long-term investments and intangible assets such as the company's patents, copyrights, and goodwill.

Types of Financing

We now turn to the right side of the balance sheet in Figure 4 labeled "Total Liabilities + Stockholders' Equity," which indicates how the firm finances its assets. **Debt** is money that has been borrowed and must be repaid at some predetermined date. **Equity**, on the other hand, represents the shareholders' (owners') investment in the company.

Debt (Liabilities) Debt capital is financing provided by a creditor. As shown in Figure 4, it is divided into (1) current or short-term debt and (2) long-term debt.

Current Debt The firm's **current debt**, or **short-term liabilities**, includes borrowed money that must be repaid within the next 12 months. The sources of a firm's current debt include the following:

◆ **Accounts payable.** The firm's **accounts payable** represents the credit suppliers have extended the firm when it purchased inventories. The purchasing firm may have 30, 60,

debt liabilities consisting of such sources as credit extended by suppliers or a loan from a bank.

equity stockholders' investment in the firm and the cumulative profits retained in the business up to the date of the balance sheet.

current debt (short-term liabilities) due to be paid within 12 months.

accounts payable money owed to suppliers for goods or services purchased in the ordinary course of business.

or even 90 days to pay for the inventory. This form of credit extension is also called **trade credit**.

◆ **Accrued expenses.** **Accrued expenses** are short-term liabilities that have been incurred in the firm's operations but not yet paid. For example, the company's employees might have done work for which they will not be paid until the following week or month, and these are recorded as accrued wages.

◆ **Short-term notes.** **Short-term notes** represent amounts borrowed from a bank or other lending source that are due and payable within 12 months.

Long-Term Debt The firm's **long-term debt** includes loans from banks or other sources that lend money for longer than 12 months. A firm might borrow money for 5 years to buy equipment, or it might borrow money for as long as 25 or 30 years to purchase real estate, such as land and buildings. Usually a loan to finance real estate is called a **mortgage**, where the lender has first claim on the property in the event the borrower is unable to repay the loan.

Equity Equity includes the shareholders' investment—both preferred stockholders and common stockholders—in the firm.

◆ **Preferred stockholders** generally receive a dividend that is fixed in amount. In the event of the firm being liquidated, these stockholders are paid after the firm's creditors but before the common stockholders.

◆ **Common stockholders** are the *residual owners* of a business. They receive whatever income is left over after paying all expenses. In the event the firm is liquidated, the common stockholders receive only what is left over—good or bad—after the creditors and preferred stockholders are paid. The amount of a firm's common equity as reported in the balance sheet is equal to the sum of two items:

1. **The amount a company receives from selling stock to investors.** This amount may simply be shown as **common stock** in the balance sheet or it may be divided into **par value** (the arbitrary value a firm puts on each share of stock prior to its being offered for sale) and **additional paid-in capital** above par (or just **paid-in capital** for short). Paid-in capital is the additional amount of capital the firm raises when buyers pay more than par value for the firm's stock. The amount of common stock issued will be offset by any stock that has been repurchased by the company, which is shown as **treasury stock.**

2. **The amount of the firm's retained earnings. Retained earnings** are the earnings (net income, to be exact) that have been retained in the business rather than being distributed to the shareholders. In other words, we take the *cumulative total of all the net income over the firm's life less the common stock dividends that have been paid over the years.* More simply, we can compute retained earnings at the end of a given year by taking the retained earnings at the end of the previous year, adding net income and subtracting dividends paid for the current year.[3] But remember, profits and cash are not the same; *so do not think of retained earnings as a big bucket of cash.* It is not!

Balance sheets for Davies Inc. are presented in Table 3 as of December 31, 2009, and December 31, 2010, along with the changes in each account between the two years. The balance sheet data shows that the firm ended 2010 with $438 million in assets, compared to $392 million at the end of 2009, for an increase of $46 million. As shown in the far right-hand column in Table 3, the increase resulted from (1) the additional investment in current assets (gross working capital) of $37 million (mostly from the increase in inventories), and (2) $39 million of new investments in fixed assets (based on the change in *gross* fixed assets, not *net* fixed assets). However, $30 million of the firm's fixed assets were depreciated during the year, as reflected by the increase in accumulated depreciation. Thus, the $46 million

---

trade credit credit made available by a firm's suppliers in conjunction with the acquisition of materials. Trade credit appears in the accounts payable section of the balance sheet.

accrued expenses expenses that have been incurred but not yet paid in cash.

short-term notes (debt) amounts borrowed from lenders, mostly financial institutions such as banks, where the loan is to be repaid within 12 months.

long-term debt loans from banks or other sources that lend money for longer than 12 months.

mortgage a loan to finance real estate where the lender has first claim on the property in the event the borrower is unable to repay the loan.

preferred stockholders stockholders who have claims on the firm's income and assets after creditors, but before common stockholders.

common stockholders investors who own the firm's common stock. Common stockholders are the residual owners of the firm.

common stock shares that represent ownership in a corporation.

par value the arbitrary value a firm puts on each share of stock prior to its being offered for sale.

additional paid-in capital the amount a company receives from selling stock to investors above par value.

treasury stock the firm's stock that has been issued and then repurchased by the firm.

retained earnings cumulative profits retained in a business up to the date of the balance sheet.

---

[3]Sometimes retained earnings will be affected by some unusual or extraordinary accounting transactions in addition to the reported net income and the dividends paid to stockholders. However, we are ignoring this possibility when explaining retained earnings.

31

TABLE 3 Davies Inc. Balance Sheets ($ millions) December 31, 2009 and 2010			
	2009	**2010**	**Change**
ASSETS			
Cash	$ 21	$ 20	$ (1)
Accounts receivable	31	36	5
Inventory	51	84	33
Other current assets	3	3	0
Total current assets	$106	$143	$37
Gross plant and equipment	$ 371	$ 410	$ 39
Less accumulated depreciation	(85)	(115)	(30)
Net plant and equipment	$286	$295	$ 9
Total assets	$392	$438	$46
DEBT AND EQUITY			
Accounts payable	$ 41	$ 42	$ 1
Accrued expenses	10	10	0
Short-term notes	14	12	(2)
Total current liabilities	$ 65	$ 64	$ (1)
Long-term debt	160	171	11
Total debt	$225	$235	$10
Common stockholders' equity			
Common stock—par value	$ 10	$ 11	$ 1
Paid-in capital	72	75	3
Retained earnings	85	117	32
Total common stockholders' equity	$167	$203	$36
Total liabilities and equity	$392	$438	$46

increase in total assets can be reconciled as follows: A $37 million increase in current assets, *plus* $39 million invested in new fixed assets, *less* $30 million in the depreciation of the firm's fixed assets.

In the debt and equity section of Table 3, notice that the $46 million increase in total debt and equity is exactly the same amount as the increase in total assets—as it must be. (Remember total assets = total debt + total equity.) The additional financing came primarily from a $36 million increase in common equity and secondarily from borrowing $11 million in long-term debt. The increase in common equity can be explained as follows (in $ millions):

December 31, 2009, common equity		$167
Sale of common stock		
Increase in par value	$ 1	
Increase in additional paid-in capital	3	
Total amount received from selling stock		$ 4
Increase in retained earnings		
Net income for 2010	$42	
Less 2010 common stock dividends	(10)	
Total increase in retained earnings		$ 32
Increase in common equity		$ 36
December 31, 2010, common equity		$203

There are two other issues revealed in the balance sheet that deserve special note: (1) the amount of a firm's working capital and (2) the mix of debt to equity used in financing the company. Let's consider each for Davies Inc.

Working Capital

Earlier we noted that the term *current assets* is also referred to as *gross working capital*. These two terms are used interchangeably. As we explained, gross working capital is equal to a company's current assets. By contrast, **net working capital** is equal to a company's current assets *less* its current liabilities. That is,

short term basis

Net working capital = current assets − current liabilities   (4)

net working capital the difference between a firm's current assets and its current liabilities. When the term *working capital* is used, it is frequently intended to mean net working capital.

Thus, net working capital compares the amount of current assets (assets that should convert into cash within the next 12 months) to the current liabilities (debt that must be paid within 12 months). The larger the net working capital a firm has, the more able the firm will be to pay its debt as it comes due. Thus, the amount of net working capital is important to a company's lenders who are always concerned about a company's ability to repay its loans. For Davies Inc. net working capital is computed as follows:

	2009	2010
Gross working capital (current assets)	$106,000,000	$143,000,000
Current liabilities	65,000,000	64,000,000
Net working capital	$41,000,000	$79,000,000

We see that the firm's net working capital increased $38 million, from $41 million to $79 million, mostly the result of increased amounts of inventories. The increase would prompt a lender or investor to know exactly why there was such a large increase in inventories, which could be good or bad. On one hand, it might mean that the firm is anticipating higher future sales and is stocking up on inventory. On the other hand, it might mean that firm's sales have declined and unsold inventory is piling up.

Most firms have a positive amount of net working capital because their current assets are greater than their current debts. There are a few exceptions. Take Disney and Starbucks, for example. These two firms actually have more current liabilities than current assets, which results in a negative net working capital position for each. How do you think this could happen? Very simply, these businesses involve mostly cash sales: The firms collect cash immediately from their customers and then quickly use it up again to keep their businesses operating. However, Disney's and Starbucks' suppliers have probably granted them 30 days or more to pay their bills. In other words, the two firms collect early and pay late.

Debt Ratio

A firm's **debt ratio** is *the percentage of a company's assets financed by debt*. Looking at Davies Inc., the debt ratios for 2009 and 2010 were 57.4 percent and 53.7 percent, respectively.

debt ratio a firm's total liabilities divided by its total assets. It is a ratio that measures the extent to which a firm has been financed with debt.

	2009	2010
Debt ratio = $\dfrac{\text{total debt}}{\text{total assets}}$	$\dfrac{\$225M}{\$392M} = 57.4\%$	$\dfrac{\$235M}{\$438M} = 53.7\%$

CAN YOU DO IT?

PREPARING A BALANCE SHEET

Given the information below for Menielle Inc., construct a balance sheet. What are the firm's current assets, net fixed assets, total assets, current or short-term debt, long-term debt, total equity, and total debt and equity?

Gross fixed assets 5	$75,000	Accounts receivable 2	$50,000
Cash 1	10,000	Long-term bank note 9	5,000
Other assets 4	15,000	Mortgage 10	20,000
Accounts payable 7	40,000	Common stock 11	100,000
Retained earnings 12	15,000	Inventories 3	70,000
Accumulated depreciation 6	20,000	Short-term notes 8	20,000

TABLE 4 Davies Inc. Common-Sized Balance Sheet ($ millions) December 31, 2009 and 2010					
		2009		2010	Change
ASSETS					
Cash		5.4%		4.6%	−0.8%
Accounts receivable		7.9%		8.2%	0.3%
Inventory		13.0%		19.2%	6.2%
Other current assets		0.8%		0.7%	−0.1%
Total current assets		27.0%		32.6%	5.6%
Gross plant and equipment	94.6%		93.6%		−1.0%
Less accumulated depreciation	−21.7%		−26.3%		−4.6%
Net plant and equipment		73.0%		67.4%	−5.6%
Total assets		100.0%		100.0%	0.0%
DEBT AND EQUITY					
Accounts payable and accrued expenses		13.0%		11.9%	−1.1%
Short-term notes		3.6%		2.7%	−0.8%
Total current liabilities		16.6%		14.6%	−2.0%
Long-term debt		40.8%		39.0%	−1.8%
Total debt		57.4%		53.7%	−3.7%
Common stockholders' equity					
Common stock—par value		2.6%		2.5%	0.0%
Paid-in capital		18.4%		17.1%	−1.2%
Retained earnings		21.7%		26.7%	5.0%
Total common stockholders' equity		42.6%		46.3%	3.7%
Total liabilities and equity		100.0%		100.0%	0.0%

The debt ratio is an important measure to lenders and investors because it indicates the amount of financial risk the company is bearing—the more debt a company uses to finance its assets, the greater is its financial risk.

Finally, we can gain additional perspective of a company's financial position by converting the balance sheet into a **common-sized balance sheet**. On a common-sized balance sheet, each item is shown as a percentage of total assets (and total debt and equity). Table 4 shows common-sized balance sheets for Davies Inc.

common-sized balance sheet a balance sheet in which a firm's assets and sources of debt and equity are expressed as a percentage of its total assets.

DID YOU GET IT?
PREPARING A BALANCE SHEET

We provided balance sheet data for Menielle Inc. and asked you to develop the balance sheet based on the information. Your results should be as follows:

Cash		$ 10,000	Accounts payable	$ 40,000
Accounts receivable		50,000	Short-term notes	20,000
Inventories		70,000	Total short-term debt	$ 60,000
Total current assets		$130,000		
Gross fixed assets	$ 75,000		Long-term bank note	$5,000
Accumulated depreciation	(20,000)		Mortgage	20,000
Net fixed assets		$ 55,000	Total long-term debt	$ 25,000
Other assets		15,000	Total debt	$ 85,000
Total assets		$200,000	Common stock	100,000
			Retained earnings	15,000
			Total equity	$115,000
			Total debt and equity	$200,000

Now we can observe that inventories increased from 13 percent of total assets to over 19 percent. Gross fixed assets declined 1 percent, whereas net fixed assets decreased 5.6 percent as a result of the additional depreciation taken on the assets. As already noted, the firm is using a bit less debt financing on a percentage basis due to the increase in equity, specifically, its retained earnings.

Earlier we showed the income statement for Hewlett-Packard. Now see Figure 5 for Hewlett-Packard's balance sheets.

Concept Check

1. Regarding the time frame reported, how is the balance sheet different from the income statement?
2. What does the basic balance sheet equation state, and what does it mean?
3. What is a firm's "accounting book value"?
4. What are a firm's two principal sources of financing? Of what do these sources consist?
5. What is gross working capital? Net working capital?
6. What is a debt ratio?

Measuring Cash Flows

 Measure a company's cash flows.

Although an income statement measures a company's profits, profits are not the same as cash flows; profits are calculated on an accrual basis rather than a cash basis. **Accrual basis accounting** records revenue when it is earned, whether or not the revenue has been received in cash, and records expenses when they are incurred, even if the money has not actually been paid out. For example, sales reported in the income statement include both cash sales and credit sales. Therefore, sales for a given year do not correspond exactly to the actual cash collected from sales. Similarly, a firm must purchase inventory, but some of the purchases are financed by trade credit rather than by an immediate cash payment, so the firm's expenses are not equal to its actual "out of pocket" cash flows. Also, under the accrual system, the purchase of equipment that will last for more than 1 year is not shown as an expense in the income statement. Instead, the amount is recorded as an asset and then expensed as depreciation over the useful life of the equipment. An annual depreciation expense (this is not a cash flow) is recorded as a way to match the use of the asset with sales generated from its service.

accrual basis accounting a method of accounting whereby revenue is recorded when it is earned, whether or not the revenue has been received in cash. Likewise, expenses are recorded when they are incurred, even if the money has not actually been paid out.

We could give you more examples to show why a firm's profits differ from its cash flows, but the point should be clear: *Profits and cash flows are not the same thing.* In fact, a business could be profitable but have negative cash flows, even to the point of going bankrupt. So, understanding a firm's cash flows is very important to its managers.

There are two common approaches used to measure a firm's cash flows. First, we can calculate a company's **free cash flows**. Once a firm has paid all of its operating expenses and taxes and made all of its investments, the remaining cash flows are *free* to be distributed to the creditors and shareholders—thus, the term *free cash flows*. Alternatively, we can use the conventional accountant's presentation called a *statement of cash flows*, which is always included in the financial section of a firm's annual report. This method for presenting cash flows focuses on identifying the sources and uses of cash that explain the change in a firm's cash balance reported in the balance sheet.

free cash flows the amount of cash available from operations after the firm pays for the investments it has made in operating working capital and fixed assets. This cash is available to distribute to the firm's creditors and owners.

During recent years, free cash flow has come to be viewed by many executives as an important measure of a firm's performance. Jack Welch, the former CEO of General Electric, explains the importance of free cash flows to management in these words:

> [T]here's cash flow, which is valuable because it just does not lie. All your other profit-and-loss numbers, like net income, have some art to them. They've been massaged through the accounting process, which is filled with assumptions. But free cash flow tells you the true condition of the business. It gives you a sense of your maneuverability—whether you can return cash to shareholders, pay down debt, borrow more to grow faster, or any combination of these options. Cash flow helps you understand and control your destiny.

We will use free cash flows in later chapters to evaluate capital investment opportunities. As we will see numerous times, the value of an investment is the present value of

FIGURE 5 Hewlett-Packard's Balance Sheet

HEWLETT-PACKARD COMPANY AND SUBSIDIARIES

Consolidated Balance Sheets

Hewlett-Packard reported the following balance sheet in its 2008 annual report.

	October 31	
	2008	2007
	In millions, except par value	

ASSETS

	2008	2007
Current assets:		
....	$ 10,153	$11,293
Short-term investments	93	152
Accounts receivable	16,928	13,420
Financing receivables	2,314	2,507
Inventory	7,879	8,033
Other current assets	14,361	11,997
Total current assets	$ 51,728	$47,402
Property, plant and equipment	10,838	7,798
Long-term financing receivables and other assets	10,468	7,647
Goodwill	32,335	21,773
Purchased intangible assets	7,962	4,079
Total assets	$113,331	$88,699

LIABILITIES AND STOCKHOLDERS EQUITY

	2008	2007
Current liabilities:		
Notes payable and short-term borrowings	$ 10,176	$ 3,186
Accounts payable	14,138	11,787
Employee compensation and benefits	4,159	3,465
Taxes on earnings	869	1,891
Deferred revenue	6,287	5,025
Accrued restructuring	1,099	123
Other accrued liabilities	16,211	13,783
Total current liabilities	$ 52,939	$39,260
Long-term debt	7,676	4,997
Other liabilities	13,774	5,916
Stockholders equity:		
Common stock, $0.01 par value (9,600 shares authorized; 2,415 and 2,580 shares issued and outstanding, respectively)	$ 24	$ 26
Additional paid-in capital	14,012	16,381
Retained earnings	24,971	21,560
Accumulated other comprehensive (loss) income	(65)	559
Total stockholders' equity	$ 38,942	$38,526
Total liabilities and stockholders' equity	$113,331	$88,699

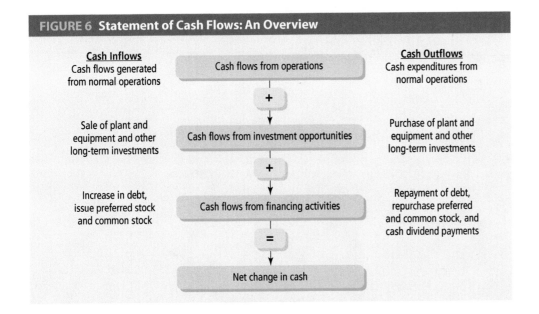

FIGURE 6 Statement of Cash Flows: An Overview

its free cash flows. But for now we will learn about the *statement of cash flows*. After all, it is a key financial statement, and we need to know what it is telling us, whether we are part of the management team, creditors, or shareholders.

As shown in Figure 6 above, there are three key activities that explain the cash inflows and outflows of a business, these being:

1. **Generating cash flows from day-to-day business operations.** It is informative to know how much cash is being generated in the normal course of operating a business on a daily basis, beginning with purchasing inventories on credit, selling on credit, paying for the inventories, and finally collecting on the sales made on credit.
2. **Investing in fixed assets and other long-term investments.** When a company purchases or sells fixed assets, like equipment and buildings, there can be significant cash inflows and outflows.
3. **Financing the business.** Cash inflows and outflows occur from borrowing or repaying debt, paying dividends, and from issuing stock (equity) or repurchasing stock from the shareholders.

If we know the cash flows from the activities above, we can easily explain a firm's cash flows in total. To understand how this is done, let's return to Davies' income statement (Table 1) and balance sheets (Table 3) to explain this process.

Cash Flows from Operations   Here we want to convert the company's income statement from an *accrual* basis to a *cash* basis. This conversion can be accomplished in two steps: (1) add back depreciation to net income since depreciation is not a cash expense, and (2) subtract any uncollected sales (increase in accounts receivables) and cash payments for inventories (increases in inventories less increases in accounts payables).

Why we add back depreciation should be clear. The changes in accounts receivables, inventories, and accounts payables may be less intuitive. Two comments might be helpful:

1. A firm's sales either are cash sales or credit sales. If accounts receivables increase, that means customers did not pay for everything they purchased. Thus, any increase in accounts receivables, as in the case for Davies Inc., needs to be subtracted from total sales to determine the cash that has been collected from customers.
2. The other activity occurring in the daily course of business is purchasing inventories. An increase in inventories shows that we bought inventories, but if accounts payables (credit extended by a supplier) increase, then we know that the firm did not pay for all

37

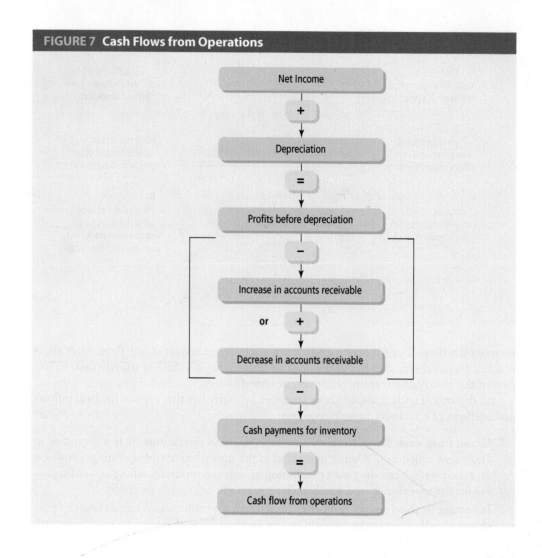

FIGURE 7 Cash Flows from Operations

the inventories purchased. Thus, the net payment for inventories is equal to the increase in inventories less what we have not paid for yet (increase in accounts payables).

Figure 7 shows a graphical presentation of the procedure for computing a firm's cash flows from operations.

Referring back to Davies Inc. income statement and balance sheets, we can compute the cash flows from operations (expressed in $ millions) as follows:

Net income	$42	
Plus depreciation	30	
Profits before depreciation		$72
Less the increase in accounts receivable (uncollected sales)		($ 5)
Less payments for inventories consisting of:		
Increase in inventories	(33)	
Less increase in accounts payables (inventories purchased on credit)	1	
Payments for inventories		($32)
Cash flows from operations		$ 35

Investing in Fixed Assets   When a company purchases fixed assets, such as equipment or buildings, these expenditures are shown as an increase in *gross* fixed assets (not the increase in *net* fixed assets) in the balance sheet. For instance, Davies Inc. spent $39 million on new plant and equipment in 2010, based on the change in *gross* fixed assets from $371 million to $410 million, as shown in their balance sheets (Table 3).

Financing a Business   Financing a business involves (1) paying dividends to the owners; (2) increasing or decreasing short-term and long-term debt, which means borrowing more money (an increase in debt) or paying off debt (a decrease in debt); and (3) selling shares of stock (source of cash) or repurchasing stock (use of cash).

Continuing with Davies Inc., we know from the income statement (Table 1) that they paid $10 million in dividends to the shareholders. Then from their balance sheets (Table 3), we see that short-term notes decreased $2 million (a use of cash) and long-term debt increased $11 million (a source of cash). Finally, Davies Inc. issued $4 million in common stock. This increase is reflected in the balance sheets in the combined increase in common stock par value of $1 million and additional paid in capital of $3 million. Thus, in net, Davies Inc. raised $3 million in financing cash flows:

Cash inflows from borrowing money	
Decrease in short-term notes	($ 2)
Increase in long-term debt	11
Issued new common stock (increase in par value and additional paid in capital)	4
Less dividends paid to owners	(10)
Financing cash flows	$ 3

To summarize, Davies Inc. generated $35 million in cash flows from operations; invested $39 million in plant and equipment; and received $3 million from financing activities, for a net decrease in cash of $1 million. This can be verified from the balance sheets (see Table 3), which show that Davies Inc.'s cash decreased $1 million during 2010 (from $21 million to $20 million). The complete statement of cash flows is provided in Table 5 below.

TABLE 5 Davies Inc. Statement of Cash Flows ($ millions) Year Ending December 31, 2010		
Operating activities:		
Net income	$42	
Plus depreciation	30	
Profits before depreciation		$72
Less increase in accounts receivable (uncollected sales)		($ 5)
Less payments for inventories consisting of:		
Increase in inventories	(33)	
Less increase in accounts payables (inventories purchased on credit)	1	
Payments for inventories		($32)
Cash flows from operations		$35
Investment activities:		
Less increase in gross fixed assets		($39)
Financing activities:		
Cash inflows from borrowing money		
Decrease in short-term notes	($ 2)	
Increase in long-term debt	11	
Issued new common stock (increase in par value and additional paid in capital)	4	
Less dividends paid to owners	(10)	
Financing cash flows		$ 3
Decrease in cash		($ 1)
Beginning cash		21
Ending cash		$20

CAN YOU DO IT?

HOW MUCH CAN YOU TRUST A BROTHER-IN-LAW?

Your brother-in-law has asked you to help him finance what he considers to be a "great investment opportunity." He plans to sell a new brand of European clothing that is becoming popular in the United States. He thinks that the university located nearby, from which you both graduated, would be an ideal location. He estimates that the financing can come mostly from a bank loan and credit from suppliers. However, the two of you will need to chip in a total of $5,000 to get the business going. He will invest $3,000, he says, and he wants you to invest the remaining $2,000.

It's not that you don't trust your brother-in-law, but you have decided to undertake your own investigation of the opportunity. After a few hours of work, you develop what you think are realistic estimates of the profits that can be earned from the venture. You also estimate how much money it will take to start the business.

There is a slight problem, however: Your new puppy chewed up your papers. After putting the dog in the backyard without any supper, you pick up the pieces and begin reconstructing your work. The remnants of your hard work—at least most of it—look as follows (numbers are in thousands):

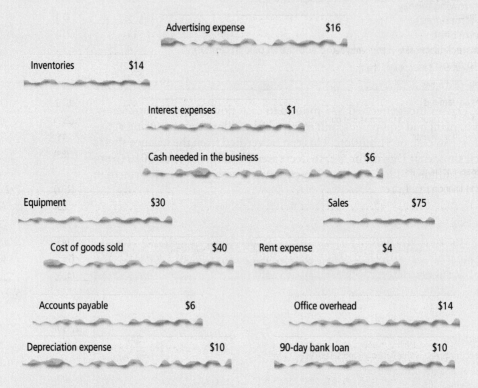

		Advertising expense		$16
Inventories	$14			
		Interest expenses		$1
		Cash needed in the business		$6
Equipment	$30		Sales	$75
Cost of goods sold	$40	Rent expense		$4
Accounts payable	$6	Office overhead		$14
Depreciation expense	$10	90-day bank loan		$10

Can you reconstruct the income statement and balance sheet using the bits of information provided above? What do you conclude about your brother-in-law's great opportunity?

The solution to your brother-in-law problem—hopefully after you have made a good-faith effort to solve it yourself.

In addition to the statement of cash flows for Davies Inc., see Figure 8 on the next page to see the statement of cash flows for Hewlett-Packard.

Based on our review of Davies Inc.'s financial statements, we can now draw some conclusions. To this point, we have learned that:

♦ For every dollar of sales, Davies earned 12.5 cents in operating income and 7 cents in net income.

♦ The firm finances its assets more with debt than with equity.

♦ The company's primary investments in 2010 were in additional inventories and fixed assets.

♦ Davies made significant investments ($39 million) in long-term assets that were financial from cash flows from operations and additional financing.

FIGURE 8 Hewlett-Packard's Consolidated Statements of Cash Flows

HEWLETT-PACKARD COMPANY AND SUBSIDIARIES
Consolidated Statements of Cash Flows

Hewlett-Packard reported the following statement of cash flows in its 2008 annual report.

	For the fiscal years ended October 31		
	2008	2007	2006
	In millions		
Cash flows from operating activities:			
Net earnings	$ 8,329	$ 7,264	$ 6,198
Adjustments to reconcile net earnings to net cash provided by operating activities:			
Depreciation and amortization	3,356	2,705	2,353
Stock-based compensation expense	606	629	536
Provision for doubtful accounts—accounts and financing receivables	275	47	4
Provision for inventory	214	362	267
Restructuring charges	270	387	158
Pension curtailments and pension settlements, net	—	(517)	—
In-process research and development charges	45	190	52
Acquisition-related charges	41	—	—
Deferred taxes on earnings	1,035	415	693
Excess tax benefit from stock-based compensation	(293)	(481)	(251)
Losses (gains) on investments	11	(14)	(25)
Other, net	(83)	(86)	18
Changes in assets and liabilities:			
Accounts and financing receivables	(261)	(2,808)	(882)
Inventory	89	(633)	(1,109)
Accounts payable	1,630	(346)	1,879
Taxes on earnings	(43)	502	(513)
Restructuring	(165)	(606)	(810)
Other assets and liabilities	(465)	2,605	2,785
Net cash provided by operating activities	$ 14,591	$ 9,615	$ 11,353
Cash flows from investing activities:			
Investment in property, plant and equipment	(2,990)	(3,040)	(2,536)
Proceeds from sale of property, plant and equipment	425	568	556
Purchases of available-for-sale securities and other investments	(178)	(283)	(46)
Maturities and sales of available-for-sale securities and other investments	280	425	94
Payments made in connection with business acquisitions, net	(11,248)	(6,793)	(855)
Net cash used in investing activities	$(13,711)	$ (9,123)	$ (2,787)
Cash flows from financing activities:			
Issuance (repayment) of commercial paper and notes payable, net	5,015	1,863	(55)
Issuance of debt	3,121	4,106	1,121
Payment of debt	(1,843)	(3,419)	(1,259)
Issuance of common stock under employee stock plans	1,810	3,103	2,538
Repurchase of common stock	(9,620)	(10,887)	(6,057)
Prepayment of common stock repurchase	—	—	(1,722)
Excess tax benefit from stock-based compensation	293	481	251
Dividends	(796)	(846)	(894)
Net cash used in financing activities	$ (2,020)	$ (5,599)	$ (6,077)
(Decrease) increase in cash and cash equivalents	(1,140)	(5,107)	2,489
Cash and cash equivalents at beginning of period	11,293	16,400	13,911
Cash and cash equivalents at end of period	$ 10,153	$11,293	$16,400

DID YOU GET IT?

HOW MUCH CAN YOU TRUST A BROTHER-IN-LAW?

Now that you understand how a firm's income statement and balance sheet are used, let's return to your brother-in-law's clothing-business proposition described. You have constructed the business's projected income statement and balance sheet from the fragments of paper your dog chewed up and found the following results (in $ thousands):

PROJECTED INCOME STATEMENT			PROJECTED BALANCE SHEET	
Sales		$ 75	Cash needed in the business	$ 6
Cost of goods sold		40	Inventories	14
Gross profit		$ 35	Equipment	30
			Total assets	$50
Operating expenses:				
Office overhead	$14		Accounts payable	$ 6
Advertising expense	16		90-day bank loan	10
Rent expense	4		Total debt	$16
Depreciation expense	10		Equity:	
Total operating expenses		$ 44	Brother-in-law	$ 3
Operating income		$ (9)	Your investment	2
Interest expense		1	Total equity	$ 5
Loss before taxes		$(10)	Total projected debt and equity	$21
Taxes		0	Additional financing needed	29
Net income		$(10)	Total debt and equity needed	$50

So, based on your estimates, the venture would expect to incur a loss of $10,000. Furthermore, the balance sheet suggests you will need $50,000 to purchase the business's assets. This would have to come from $16,000 in debt financing that you hope you can obtain, $3,000 from your brother-in-law, and $2,000 from you, which totals $21,000. However, this is still less than the $50,000 you actually need. Thus, the business will need an additional $29,000. Maybe, just maybe, this is not quite the opportunity your brother-in-law perceives it to be.

CAN YOU DO IT?

MEASURING CASH FLOWS

Given the following information for Menielle Inc., prepare a statement of cash flows.

Increase in accounts receivable	13	Dividends	5
Increase in inventories	25	Change in common stock	0
Net income	33	Increase in gross fixed assets	55
Beginning cash	15	Depreciation expense	7
Increase in accounts payable	20		
Increase in accrued expenses	5		
Increase in long-term notes payable	28		

(The solution can be found on next page.)

We will use the information included in this chapter to dig deeper and conduct a financial analysis of Davies Inc. Read on.

Concept Check

1. Why doesn't an income statement provide a measure of a firm's cash flows?

2. What are the three main parts of a statement of cash flows?

3. What does each part tell us about a company?

Income Taxes and Finance

 4 Compute taxable income and income taxes owed.

Income tax is one of the largest expenses that a business encounters, and as a result, it must be considered in making investment and financing decisions. But understanding income taxes is a profession unto itself. Tax accountants spend a lifetime attempting to remain current with the tax laws. So we will limit our discussion to the basic issue of computing a corporation's income taxes and let the tax accountants provide us counsel on the rest.

For our purposes, we simply need to know that **taxable income** for a corporation consists of two basic components: operating income and capital gains. Operating income, as we have already defined, is essentially gross profits less any operating expenses, such as marketing expenses, administrative expenses and so forth. **Capital gains** occur when a firm sells a capital asset, which is any asset that is not part of its ordinary operations. For example, when a company sells a piece of equipment or land, any gain (sales price less the cost of the asset) is thought to be a capital gain. Also, the *interest expense* paid on the firm's outstanding debt is a tax-deductible expense. However, dividends paid to the firm's stockholders are *not* deductible expenses, but rather distributions of income. Other taxable income includes the interest income and dividend income that the corporation receives.

taxable income gross income from all sources, except for allowable exclusions, less any tax-deductible expenses.

capital gains gains from selling any asset that is not part of the ordinary operations.

Computing Taxable Income

To demonstrate how to compute a corporation's taxable income, consider the J and S Corporation, a manufacturer of home accessories. The firm, originally established by Kelly Stites, had sales of $50 million for the year. The cost of producing the accessories totaled $23 million. Operating expenses were $10 million. The corporation has $12.5 million in debt outstanding, with an 8 percent interest rate, which resulted in $1 million interest expense ($12,500,000 × 0.08 = $1,000,000). Management paid $1 million in dividends to the firm's common stockholders. No other income, such as interest or dividend income, was received. The taxable income for the J and S Corporation would be $16 million, as shown in Table 6.

Once we know J and S Corporation's taxable income, we can determine the amount of taxes the firm owes.

TABLE 6 J and S Corporation Taxable Income

Sales		$50,000,000
Cost of goods sold		23,000,000
Gross profit		$27,000,000
Operating expenses		
Administrative expenses	$4,000,000	
Depreciation expenses	1,500,000	
Marketing expenses	4,500,000	
Total operating expenses		$10,000,000
Operating income		
(earnings before interest and taxes)		$17,000,000
Other income		0
Interest expense		1,000,000
Taxable income		$16,000,000

Dividends paid to common stockholders ($1,000,000) are not tax-deductible expenses.

Computing the Taxes Owed

The taxes to be paid by the corporation on its taxable income are based on the corporate tax rate structure. The specific rates for corporations, as of early 2007, are given in Table 7.

marginal tax rate the tax rate that would be applied to the next dollar of income.

The tax rates shown in Table 7 are defined as the **marginal tax rates**, or *rates applicable to the next dollar of income*. For instance, if a firm has earnings of $60,000 and is contemplating an investment that would yield $10,000 in additional profits, the tax rate to be used in calculating the taxes on this added income is 25 percent; that is, the marginal tax rate is 25 percent.

TABLE 7 Corporate Tax Rates

15%	$0–$50,000
25%	$50,001–$75,000
34%	$75,001–$10,000,000
35%	over $10,000,000
Additional surtax:	

- 5% on income between $100,000 and $335,000
- 3% on income between $15,000,000 and $18,333,333

The rates in Table 7 go up to a top marginal corporate tax rate of 35 percent for taxable income in excess of $10 million, and a surtax of 3 percent on taxable income between $15 million and $18,333,333. This means the corporation's marginal tax rate on income between $15 million and $18,333,333 is 38 percent (the 35 percent rate plus the 3 percent surtax). There is also a 5 percent surtax on taxable income between $100,000 and $335,000, which means the marginal rate on income between $100,000 and $335,000 is 39 percent (the 34 percent rate plus the 5 percent surtax). For example, the tax liability for J and S Corporation, which had $16 million in taxable earnings, would be $5,530,000, calculated as follows:

EARNINGS	×	MARGINAL TAX RATE	=	TAXES
$ 50,000	×	15%	=	$ 7,500
25,000	×	25%	=	6,250
9,925,000	×	34%	=	3,374,500
6,000,000	×	35%	=	2,100,000
				$5,488,250

Additional surtaxes:

- Add 5% surtax on income between
  $100,000 and $335,000
  (5% × [$335,000 – $100,000])   11,750
- Add 3% surtax on income between
  $15,000,000 and $18,333,333
  (3% × [$16,000,000 – $15,000,000])   30,000

Total tax liability $5,530,000

44

CAN YOU DO IT?

COMPUTING A CORPORATION'S INCOME TAXES

Assume that the Griggs Corporation had sales during the past year of $5 million; its cost of goods sold was $3 million; and it incurred operating expenses of $950,000. In addition, it received $185,000 in interest income. In turn, it paid $40,000 in interest and $75,000 in common stock dividends.

J and S Corporation's marginal tax rate is 38 percent (this is because $16 million falls into the 35% tax bracket *with* a 3% surtax); that is, any additional income will be taxed at a rate of 38 percent. However, after taxable income exceeds $18,333,333, the marginal tax rate declines to 35 percent, and the 3 percent surtax no longer applies.

For financial decision making, it's the *marginal tax rate* rather than the average tax rate that we are concerned with. Why? Because, generally speaking, the marginal rate is the rate that corporation pays on the next dollar that is earned. We always want to consider the tax consequences of any financial decision. The marginal tax rate is the rate that will be applicable for any changes in earnings that occur as a result of the decision being made. Thus, when making financial decisions involving taxes, always use the marginal tax rate in your calculations.[4]

DID YOU GET IT?

COMPUTING A CORPORATION'S INCOME TAXES

Sales		$5,000,000
Cost of goods sold		($3,000,000)
Gross profit		$2,000,000
Operating expenses		($ 950,000)
Operating income		$1,050,000
Other taxable income and expenses:		
Interest income	$185,000	
Interest expense	($ 40,000)	$ 145,000
Taxable income		$1,195,000
Tax computation		
15% × $ 50,000 =	$ 7,500	
25% × $ 25,000 =	$ 6,250	
34% × $1,120,000 =	380,800	
$1,195,000	$394,550	
Add 5% surtax for income		
Between $100,000 and		
$335,000	$ 11,750	
Tax liability	$406,300	

Analysis:
Note that the $75,000 Griggs paid in common stock dividends is not tax deductible. The marginal tax rate and the average tax rate both equal 34 percent; thus, we could have computed Griggs's tax liability as 34 percent of $1,195,000 or $406,300.

---

[4]On taxable income between $335,000 and $10 million, both the marginal and average tax rates equal 34 percent because of the imposition of the 5 percent surtax that applies to taxable income between $100,000 and $335,000. After the company's taxable income exceeds $18,333,333, both the marginal and average tax rates equal 35 percent because the 3 percent surtax on income between $15 million and $18,333,333 eliminates the benefits of having the first $10 million of income taxed at 34 percent rather than 35 percent.

Compute a company's profits, as reflected by its income statement.

Summary

A firm's profits may be viewed as follows:

Gross profit = sales − cost of goods sold

Earnings before interest and tax (operating profit) = sales − cost of goods sold − operating expenses

Net profit (net income) = sales − cost of goods sold − operating expenses − interest expense − taxes

The following five activities determine a company's net income:

1. The revenue derived from selling the company's product or service
2. The cost of producing or acquiring the goods or services to be sold
3. The operating expenses related to (1) marketing and distributing the product or service to the customer and (2) administering the business
4. The financing costs of doing business—namely, the interest paid to the firm's creditors
5. The payment of taxes

 Determine a firm's financial position at a point in time based on its balance sheet.

The balance sheet presents a company's assets, liabilities, and equity on a specific date. Its total assets represent all the investments that the firm has made in the business. The total assets must equal the firm's total debt and equity because every dollar of assets has been financed by the firm's lenders or stockholders. The firm's assets include its current assets, fixed assets, and other assets. Its debt includes both its short-term and long-term debt. The firm's equity includes (1) common stock, which may be shown as par value plus additional paid-in capital, and (2) retained earnings. All the numbers in a balance sheet are based on historical costs, rather than current market values.

Measure a company's cash flows.

A firm's profits are not an adequate measure of its cash flows. To measure a company's cash flows requires that we look both at the income statement and the changes in the balance sheet. There are three main parts of a statement of cash flows: cash flows from operations, investment cash flows, and financing cash flows. Examining these three parts of the statement of cash flows helps us understand where cash came from and how it was used.

 Compute taxable income and income taxes owed.

For the most part, taxable income for the corporation is equal to the firm's operating income plus capital gains less any interest expense. Tax consequences, particularly marginal tax rates, have a direct bearing on the decisions of the financial manager.

Key Terms

Accounting book value	Current debt
Accounts payable	Debt
Accounts receivable	Debt ratio
Accrual basis accounting	Depreciation expense
Accrued expenses	Dividends per share
Accumulated depreciation	Earnings before interest and taxes or EBIT
Additional paid-in capital	
Balance sheet	Earnings before taxes (taxable income)
Capital gains	Earnings per share
Cash	Equity
Common-sized balance sheet	Financing cost
Common-sized income statement	Fixed assets
Common stock	Free cash flows
Common stockholders	Gross fixed assets
Cost of goods sold	Gross profit
Current assets (gross working capital)	Gross profit margin

Income statement (profit and loss statement)	Operating income (earnings before interest and taxes)
Inventories	Operating profit margin
Long-term debt	Par value
Marginal tax rate	Preferred stockholders
Mortgage	Profit margins
Net fixed assets	Retained earnings
Net income (earnings available to common stockholders)	Short-term liabilities
	Short-term notes (debt)
Net profit margin	Taxable income
Net working capital	Trade credit
Operating expenses	Treasury stock

Review Questions

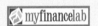

All Review Questions and Study Problems are available in MyFinanceLab.

3-1. A company's financial statements consist of the balance sheet, income statement, and statement of cash flows. Describe what each statement tells us.

3-2. How do gross profits, operating profits, and net income differ?

3-3. How do dividends and interest expense differ?

3-4. Why is it that the preferred stockholders' equity section of the balance sheet changes only when new shares are sold or repurchased, whereas the common stockholders' equity section changes from year to year regardless of whether new shares are bought or sold?

3-5. What is net working capital?

3-6. Why might one firm have positive cash flows and be headed for financial trouble, whereas another firm with negative cash flows could actually be in a good financial position?

3-7. Why is the examination of only the balance sheet and income statement not adequate in evaluating a firm?

3-8. Why are dividends paid to a firm's owners not a tax-deductible expense?

3-9. See the annual report for the Dell Corporation by going to www.dell.com. Scroll to the bottom of the page, then click "About Dell," then "Investors," and finally the link "Annual Reports." Scan the list to determine which year you would like to review. Alternatively, select one of the other links (such as "Financial History") to learn additional financial information about Dell Inc.

3-10. Go to www.homedepot.com for the home page of the Home Depot Corporation. Scroll to the bottom of the page and select the "Corporate Info" option, then "Investor Relations," and finally "Financial Reports." Look for key words in the income statement that appear in this chapter, such as sales, gross profits, and net income. What do you learn about the firm from its financial statements that you find interesting?

3-11. Go to the *Wall Street Journal* home page at www.wsj.com. Search for Barnes & Noble (ticker symbol BKS). Find the firm's earnings announcements. What did you learn about the company from the announcements? Also, search www.barnesandnoble.com to find the same information.

Self-Test Problems

The solution to this problem is provided at the end of the chapter.

ST-1. (*Interpreting financial statements and measuring cash flows*) Given the following information for the M & G Corporation:

    a. How much is the firm's net working capital and what is the debt ratio for 2010?

    b. Complete (1) a common-sized income statement and (2) a common-sized balance sheet. Interpret your results for 2010.

    c. Prepare a statement of cash flows for 2010. Interpret your results.

M & G Corporation Balance Sheet for December 31, 2009 and 2010

	2009	2010
Cash	$ 9,000	$ 500
Accounts receivable	12,500	16,000
Inventories	29,000	45,500
Total current assets	$ 50,500	$ 62,000
Land	20,000	26,000
Buildings and equipment	70,000	100,000
Less accumulated depreciation	(28,000)	(38,000)
Total fixed assets	$ 62,000	$ 88,000
Total assets	$112,500	$150,000
Accounts payable	$ 6,500	$ 17,000
Accrued expenses	4,000	5,000
Short-term bank notes	17,000	47,000
Total current liabilities	$ 27,500	$ 69,000
Long-term debt	28,750	22,950
Common stock	31,500	31,500
Retained earnings	24,750	26,550
Total debt and equity	$112,500	$150,000

M & G Corporation Income Statement for the Year Ending December 31, 2010

	2010
Sales (all credit)	$160,000
Cost of goods sold	96,000
Gross profit	$ 64,000
Operating expenses	
Fixed cash operating expenses	$ 21,000
Variable operating expenses	16,000
Depreciation	10,000
Total operating expenses	$ 47,000
Earnings before interest and taxes	$ 17,000
Interest expense	6,100
Earnings before taxes	$ 10,900
Income taxes	3,900
Net income	$ 7,000

ST-2. (*Corporate income tax*) The Dana Flatt Corporation had sales of $2 million this past year. Its cost of goods sold was $1.2 million and its operating expenses were $400,000. Interest expenses on outstanding debts were $164,000, and the company paid $40,000 in preferred stock dividends. The corporation received interest income of $12,000. Determine the corporation's taxable income and its tax liability.

Study Problems

3-1. (*Review of financial statements*) Prepare a balance sheet and income statement for Belmond Inc. from the following information.

Inventory	$ 6,500
Common stock	45,000
Cash	16,550
Operating expenses	1,350
Short-term notes payable	600
Interest expense	900
Depreciation expense	500
Net sales	12,800
Accounts receivable	9,600
Accounts payable	4,800
Long-term debt	55,000
Cost of goods sold	5,750
Buildings and equipment	$122,000
Accumulated depreciation	34,000
Taxes	1,440
General and administrative expense	850
Retained earnings	?

3-2. (*Computing cash flows*) Given the following information, prepare a statement of cash flows.

Increase in accounts receivable	$25
Increase in inventories	30
Operating income	75
Interest expense	25
Increase in accounts payable	25
Dividends	15
Increase in common stock	20
Increase in net fixed assets	23
Depreciation expense	12
Income taxes	17
Beginning cash	20

3-3. (*Review of financial statements*) Prepare a balance sheet and income statement for the Warner Company from the following scrambled list of items.

   a. What is the firm's net working capital and debt ratio?
   b. Complete a common-sized income statement and a common-sized balance sheet. Interpret your findings.

Depreciation expense	$ 66,000
Cash	225,000
Long-term debt	334,000
Sales	573,000
Accounts payable	102,000
General and administrative expense	79,000
Buildings and equipment	895,000
Notes payable	75,000
Accounts receivable	153,000
Interest expense	4,750
Accrued expenses	7,900
Common stock	289,000
Cost of goods sold	297,000
Inventory	99,300
Taxes	50,500
Accumulated depreciation	263,000
Prepaid expenses	14,500
Taxes payable	53,000
Retained earnings	262,900

3-4. (*Statement of cash flows*) Interpret the following information regarding Westlake Corporation's cash flows.

Net income	$ 680
Depreciation expense	125
Profits before depreciation	805
Increase in accounts receivables	(200)
Increase in inventories	(240)
Increase in accounts payables	120
Increase in accrued expenses	81
Cash flow from operations	$ 566
Investment activity	
Change in fixed assets	$(1,064)
Financing activity	
Increase in long-term debt	$ 640
Common stock dividends	(120)
Total financing activities	$ 520
Change in cash	$ 22
Beginning cash	500
Ending cash	$ 522

3-5. (*Computing cash flows*) Given the following information, prepare a statement of cash flows.

Dividends	$ 25
Increase in common stock	27
Increase in accounts receivable	65
Increase in inventories	5
Operating income	215
Increase in accounts payables	40
Interest expense	50
Depreciation expense	20
Increase in bank debt	48
Increase in accrued expenses	15
Increase in gross fixed assets	55
Income taxes	45

3-6. (*Cash flow analysis*) Interpret the following information regarding Maness Corporation's statement of cash flows.

Net income	$ 370
Depreciation expense	60
Profits before depreciation	430
Increase in accounts receivables	(300)
Increase in inventories	(400)
Increase in accounts payables	200
Increase in accrued expenses	40
Cash flow from operations	$ (30)
Investment activity	
Change in fixed assets	$(1,500)
Financing activity	
Increase in short-term notes	$ 100
Repayment of long-term debt	(250)
Repurchase common stock	(125)
Common stock dividends	(75)
Total financing activities	$ (350)
Change in cash	$(1,880)
Beginning cash	3,750
Ending cash	$ 1,870

3-7. (*Interpreting financial statements and measuring cash flows*) Given the information below for Pamplin Inc.:

a. How much is the firm's net working capital and what is the debt ratio?
b. Complete a common-sized income statement, a common-sized balance sheet, and a statement of cash flows for 2010. Interpret your results.

Pamplin Inc. Balance Sheet at 12/31/2009 and 12/31/2010

ASSETS

	2009	2010
Cash	$ 200	$ 150
Accounts receivable	450	425
Inventory	550	625
Current assets	$ 1,200	$ 1,200
Plant and equipment	$ 2,200	$ 2,600
Less accumulated depreciation	(1,000)	(1,200)
Net plant and equipment	$ 1,200	$ 1,400
Total assets	$ 2,400	$ 2,600

LIABILITIES AND OWNERS' EQUITY

	2009	2010
Accounts payable	$ 200	$ 150
Notes payable—current (9%)	0	150
Current liabilities	$ 200	$ 300
Bonds	$ 600	$ 600
Owners' equity		
Common stock	$ 900	$ 900
Retained earnings	700	800
Total owners' equity	$1,600	$1,700
Total liabilities and owners' equity	$2,400	$2,600

Pamplin Inc. Income Statement for Years Ending 12/31/2009 and 12/31/2010

	2009		2010	
Sales		$ 1,200		$ 1,450
Cost of goods sold		700		850
Gross profit		$ 500		$ 600
Selling, general, and administrative expenses	$ 30		$ 40	
Depreciation	220	250	200	240
Operating income		$ 250		$ 360
Interest expense		$ 50		64
Net income before taxes		$ 200		$ 296
Taxes (40%)		80		118
Net income		$ 120		$ 178

3-8. (*Interpreting financials statements and measuring cash flows*) Based on the information for T. P. Jarmon Company for the year ended December 31, 2010:

a. How much is the firm's net working capital and what is the debt ratio?
b. Complete a statement of cash flows for the period. Interpret your results.
c. Compute the changes in the balance sheets from 2009 to 2010. What do you learn about T. P. Jarmon from these computations? How do these numbers relate to the statement of cash flows?

T. P. Jarmon Company Balance Sheet for 12/31/2009 and 12/31/2010

ASSETS

	2009	2010
Cash	$ 15,000	$ 14,000
Marketable securities	6,000	6,200
Accounts receivable	42,000	33,000
Inventory	51,000	84,000
Prepaid rent	$ 1,200	$ 1,100
Total current assets	$ 115,200	$ 138,300
Net plant and equipment	286,000	270,000
Total assets	$ 401,200	$ 408,300

LIABILITIES AND EQUITY

	2009	2010
Accounts payable	$ 48,000	$ 57,000
Accruals	6,000	5,000
Notes payable	15,000	13,000
Total current liabilities	$ 69,000	$ 75,000
Long-term debt	$ 160,000	$ 150,000
Common stockholders' equity	$ 172,200	$ 183,300
Total liabilities and equity	$ 401,200	$ 408,300

T. P. Jarmon Company Income Statement for the Year Ended 12/31/2010

Sales		$ 600,000
Less cost of goods sold		460,000
Gross profit		$ 140,000
Operating and interest expenses		
General and administrative	$ 30,000	
Interest	10,000	
Depreciation	30,000	
Total operating and interest expenses		70,000
Earnings before taxes		$ 70,000
Taxes		27,100
Net income available to common stockholders		$ 42,900
Cash dividends		31,800
Change in retained earnings		$ 11,100

3-9. (*Measuring cash flows*) Prepare a statement of cash flows for Abrahams Manufacturing Company for the year ended December 31, 2010. Interpret your results.

Abrahams Manufacturing Company Balance Sheet for 12/31/2009 and 12/31/2010

	2009	2010
Cash	$ 89,000	$ 100,000
Accounts receivable	64,000	70,000
Inventory	112,000	100,000
Prepaid expenses	10,000	10,000
Total current assets	275,000	280,000
Gross plant and equipment	238,000	311,000
Accumulated depreciation	(40,000)	(66,000)
Total assets	$ 473,000	$ 525,000
Accounts payable	$ 85,000	$ 90,000
Accrued liabilities	68,000	63,000
Total current debt	153,000	153,000
Mortgage payable	70,000	0
Preferred stock	0	120,000
Common stock	205,000	205,000
Retained earnings	45,000	47,000
Total debt and equity	$ 473,000	$ 525,000

Abrahams Manufacturing Company Income Statement for the Year Ended 12/31/2010

	2010
Sales	$ 184,000
Cost of goods sold	60,000
Gross profit	$ 124,000
Selling, general, and administrative expenses	44,000
Depreciation expense	26,000
Operating income	$ 54,000
Interest expense	4,000
Earnings before taxes	$ 50,000
Taxes	16,000
Preferred stock dividends	10,000
Earnings available to common shareholders	$ 24,000

Additional Information

1. The only entry in the accumulated depreciation account is for 2010 depreciation.
2. The firm paid $22,000 in common stock dividends during 2010.

3-10. (*Corporate income tax*) The William B. Waugh Corporation is a regional Toyota dealer. The firm sells new and used trucks and is actively involved in the parts business. During the most recent year, the company generated sales of $3 million. The combined cost of goods sold and the operating expenses were $2.1 million. Also, $400,000 in interest expense was paid during the year. Calculate the corporation's tax liability.

3-11. (*Corporate income tax*) Sales for L. B. Menielle Inc. during the past year amounted to $5 million. The firm provides parts and supplies for oil field service companies. Gross profits for the year were $3 million. Operating expenses totaled $1 million. The interest income from the securities it owned was $20,000. The firm's interest expense was $100,000. Compute the corporation's tax liability.

3-12. (*Corporate income tax*) Sandersen Inc. sells minicomputers. During the past year, the company's sales were $3 million. The cost of its merchandise sold came to $2 million, and cash operating expenses were $400,000; depreciation expense was $100,000, and the firm paid $150,000 in interest on its bank loans. Also, the corporation paid $25,000 in the form of dividends to its own common stockholders. Calculate the corporation's tax liability.

Mini Case

In 2009, the auto industry was being devastated by the economic downturn. General Motors filed for bankruptcy and was renamed Motors Liquidation, an event that could not have been imagined in prior times. Toyota, historically a tough competitor for Detroit, was beginning to be affected as well, but not nearly to the same extent as GM. Below are the financial statements for the two firms. GM's fiscal year ends on December 31; thus, the statements are for the end-of-year for 2007 and 2008. Toyota, on the other hand, has a March 31 fiscal year; therefore the statements are for fiscal years 2008 and 2009. As a result, Toyota's financials are three months later than the financials for General Motors.

a. Prepare a common-sized income statement and common-sized balance sheet for each firm for both years.
b. How much profit (loss) was each company making per dollar of sales? To what would you attribute any differences?
c. What differences do you notice in the common-sized balance sheets that could account for the problems of GM relative to Toyota?
d. Conduct an Internet search on the two firms to gain additional insights as to causes of the financial differences between the firms in 2008 and continuing into 2009.
e. How are the two companies doing financially today?

Toyota Corp. Annual Income Statement
for Years Ending March 31, 2008 and 2009 (in $ millions except earnings per share)

	2008	2009
Sales	$262,394	$208,995
Cost of goods sold	199,912	172,663
Gross profits	$ 62,482	$ 36,332
Selling, general, and administrative expenses	24,938	25,804
Depreciation and amortization	14,883	15,221
Operating income	$ 22,661	$ (4,693)
Interest expense	460	477
Nonoperating income (expenses)	4,043	147
Earnings before tax	$ 26,244	$ (5,023)
Income taxes	9,098	(575)
Net income (loss)	$ 17,146	$ (4,448)
Common shares outstanding	1,589	1,570
Earnings per share	$ 10.79	$ (2.83)

Toyota Corp. Balance Sheet
for Years Ending March 31, 2008 and 2009 ($ millions)

ASSETS	MARCH 31, 2008	MARCH 31, 2009
Cash and short-term investments	$ 23,012	30,386
Receivables	68,519	57,181
Inventories	18,222	14,857
Other current assets	10,880	12,601
Total current assets	$120,633	$115,025
Gross fixed assets	$173,633	175,027
Accumulated depreciation and amortization	(95,661)	(99,677)
Net fixed assets	$ 77,972	$ 75,350
Other assets	125,363	105,482
TOTAL ASSETS	$323,968	$295,857

LIABILITIES		
Notes payable	$ 46,124	48,627
Accounts payable	22,086	13,229
Income taxes payable	3,050	522
Accrued expenses	16,039	15,684
Other current liabilities	31,882	29,739
Total current liabilities	$ 119,181	$ 107,801
Long-term debt	59,706	64,150
Deferred taxes	10,969	6,539
Other liabilities	15,642	14,942
TOTAL LIABILITIES	$205,498	$193,432

EQUITY		
Common stock	$ 3,963	4,042
Capital surplus	4,966	5,102
Retained earnings	121,443	106,117
Less: Treasury stock—total dollar amount	(11,902)	(12,836)
Total common equity	$ 118,470	$ 102,425
TOTAL LIABILITIES AND STOCKHOLDERS' EQUITY	$ 323,968	$ 295,857

General Motors Corp. Annual Income Statement
for Years Ending December 31, 2007 and December 31, 2008 (in $ millions except per share data)

	2007	2008
Sales	$179,984	$148,979
Cost of goods sold	160,856	149,311
Gross profits	$ 19,128	$ (332)
Selling, general, and administrative expenses	14,412	14,801
Depreciation and amortization	9,513	9,931
Operating income	$ (4,797)	$ (25,064)
Interest expense	3,307	3,055
Nonoperating income (expenses)	1,969	(975)
Taxable income	$ (6,135)	$ (29,094)
Income taxes	37,162	1,766
Income before extraordinary items	(43,297)	(30,860)
Extraordinary items	4,565	
Net income (loss)	$ (38,732)	$ (30,860)
Common shares outstandings	566	579
Earnings per share	$ (68.43)	$ (53.30)

General Motors Corp. Balance Sheets
for Years Ending December 31, 2007 and 2009 ($ millions)

ASSETS

	2007	2009
Cash and short-term investments	$ 26,956	$ 14,066
Receivables	9,659	7,711
Inventories—total	14,939	13,042
Other current assets	8,849	6,505
Total current assets	$ 60,403	$ 41,324
Gross fixed assets	97,319	86,919
Accumulated depreciation	(47,590)	(45,042)
Net fixed assets	$ 49,729	$ 41,877
Other assets—sundry	38,751	7,846
TOTAL ASSETS	$ 148,883	$ 91,047

LIABILITIES

	2007	2009
Notes payable	$ 6,047	$ 15,754
Accounts payable	29,439	22,236
Accrued expenses	34,024	35,921
Other current liabilities	5,813	1,822
Total current liabilities	$ 75,323	$ 75,733
Long-term debt	33,384	29,594
Post-retirement benefits	47,375	28,919
Pension	11,381	25,178
Other liabilities	18,514	17,777
Total liabilities	$ 185,977	$177,201

COMMON EQUITY

	2007	2009
Common stock	$ 943	$ 1,017
Capital surplus	15,319	15,755
Retained earnings	(53,356)	(102,926)
Total common equity	$ (37,094)	$ (86,154)
TOTAL DEBT AND EQUITY	$ 148,883	$ 91,047

Self-Test Solution

SS-1.

a. 2010 net working capital = current assets − current liabilities

$$= \$62,000 - \$69,000$$
$$= \$(7,000)$$

2010 debt ratio = total liabilities ÷ total assets

$$= \$91,950 \div 150,000$$
$$= 0.613 \text{ or } 61.3\%$$

(1)b. Common-sized income statement

	2010	% OF SALES
Sales (all credit)	$160,000	100.0%
Cost of goods sold	96,000	60.0%
Gross profit	$ 64,000	40.0%
Operating expenses		
Fixed cash operating expenses	$ 21,000	13.1%
Variable operating expenses	16,000	10.0%
Depreciation	10,000	6.3%
Total operating expenses	$ 47,000	29.4%
Earnings before interest and taxes	$ 17,000	10.6%
Interest expense	6,100	3.8%
Earnings before taxes	$ 10,900	6.8%
Income taxes	3,900	2.4%
Net income	$ 7,000	4.4%

From the common-sized income statement, we see that M & G Corporation's gross profit margin was 40 percent of sales. Furthermore, the firm earned an operating profit margin of 10.6 percent and a net profit margin of 4.4 percent.

(2) Common-sized balance sheet

Cash	$ 500	0.3%
Accounts receivable	16,000	10.7%
Inventories	45,500	30.3%
Total current assets	$ 62,000	41.3%
Land	$ 26,000	17.3%
Plant and equipment	100,000	66.7%
Accumulated depreciation	(38,000)	− 25.3%
Total fixed assets	$ 88,000	58.7%
Total assets	$150,000	100.0%
Accounts payable	$ 17,000	11.3%
Accrued expenses	$ 5,000	3.3%
Short-term bank notes	47,000	31.3%
Total current liabilities	$ 69,000	46.0%
Long-term debt	22,950	15.3%
Total debt	$ 91,950	61.3%
Common stock	$ 31,500	21.0%
Retained earnings	26,550	17.7%
Total common equity	$ 58,050	38.7%
Total liabilities and equity	$150,000	100.0%

M & G Corporation has about 41 percent in current assets and 59 percent in long-term assets. A large part of its debt is short term, mostly in the form of short-term bank notes.

c. Complete a statement of cash flows for the period. Interpret your results.

Net income	$ 7,000
Depreciation expense	10,000
Profits before depreciation	17,000
Increase in accounts receivables	(3,500)
Increase in inventories	(16,500)
Increase in accounts payables	10,500
Increase in accrued expenses	1,000
Cash flow from operations	$ 8,500
Investment activity	
Change in fixed assets	$(36,000)
Financing activity	
Increase in short-term bank notes	30,000
Decrease in long-term debt	$ (5,800)
Common stock dividends	(5,200)
Total financing activities	$ 19,000
Change in cash	$ (8,500)
Beginning cash	9,000
Ending cash	$ 500

Thus, M & G Corporation's managers invested more in fixed assets and land than was generated in cash flows from operations. The company then borrowed enough in short-term financing to cover its shortfall to make up the difference and to pay down its long-term debt, pay interest expense, and pay dividends.

SS-2.

Sales	$2,000,000
Cost of goods sold	(1,200,000)
Gross profits	$ 800,000
Operating expenses	(400,000)
Operating income	$ 400,000
Interest expense	(164,000)
Interest income	12,000
Taxable income	$ 248,000

Tax computation		
15% ×	$ 50,000	$ 7,500
25% ×	$ 25,000	$ 6,250
34% ×	$173,000	$ 58,820
	$248,000	$ 72,570
Add 5% surcharge for income		
between $100,000 and $248,000		$ 7,400
Tax liability		$ 79,970

Evaluating a Firm's Financial Performance

From Chapter 4 of *Foundations of Finance*, 7/e. Arthur J. Keown. John D. Martin. J. William Petty. Copyright © 2011 by Pearson Education.
Published by Prentice Hall. All rights reserved.

Evaluating a Firm's Financial Performance

Learning Objectives

After reading this chapter, you should be able to:

1. Explain **the purpose and importance of financial analysis.**

2. Calculate **and use a comprehensive set of measurements to evaluate a company's performance.**

3. Describe **the limitations of financial ratio analysis.**

The previous chapter was most likely a review for many students using this text, having taken a basic financial accounting course earlier in their studies. But hopefully the chapter served as a good refresher if some time has elapsed since studying accounting. After all, it is easy to forget.

In this chapter, we want to answer the question, "So what?" What significance do the financial statements tell the firm's managers, as well as its other stakeholders, such as suppliers, creditors, and stockholders, about the firm's financial performance? We now want to use the data in the financial statements to gain greater insights into a company's operations, just as Paul Polman did when he became the new chief executive of Unilever in January 2009.

Unilever—whose products include Ben & Jerry's ice cream, Dove soap, Lipton teas, and Hellmann's mayonnaise—increased prices in 2008, just as the recession was taking root. As a result, some consumers stopped buying its products, driving down sales volume in the first quarter of 2009.

As Unilever's new CEO, Polman vowed to drive volume with lower prices and aggressive marketing spending. The impact was immediate. Second-quarter sales rose 4.1 percent, a strong result given the global recession. (By comparison, at rival Procter & Gamble Co., sales over the same period fell 1 percent.) But at the same time, Unilever's profit margins fell to 12.6 percent in the second quarter from 13.2 percent in the year-earlier period, due to the lower prices and increases in the firm's advertising budget. Thus, dollar profits essentially remained unchanged.

In response, Polman intends to reverse the declining profit margins by reducing costs. "We're looking at opportunities to drive costs out of the system to reinvest the savings back in growth," Polman said at a media briefing in London. For example, since taking over, Polman has tried to increase the speed of decision making in the company, known for its sprawling bureaucracy and cautious culture. After his arrival, the company introduced "Thirty-Day Action Plans," for instance. The plans are designed to make executives take quick action to fix problems with individual products.

Polman is Unilever's first CEO who wasn't brought up from the company's internal ranks. The executive spent most of his career at Procter & Gamble Co. Analysts said it could take years to change the Unilever culture. "I believe [Mr. Polman] is the right man to do so but I am not so optimistic it will go through quickly," said Claudia Lenz, an analyst at Bank Vontobel in Switzerland.

It will be interesting to follow Unilever's performance in future years under Polman's leadership. His dilemma between increasing sales and lowering profit margins is one that all managers face.

In this chapter, we will see that either increasing sales alone or increasing profit margins alone will *not* give a manager the complete picture. Management should consider them together as they impact a firm's return on investment. Thus, understanding the relationships between decisions and the financial consequences are critical for managers, and is the topic of this chapter.

Source: Adapted from Aaron O. Patrick, "Unilever CEO's Push to Cut Prices Drives Increase in Sales," *Wall Street Journal*, August 5, 2009, p. B1.

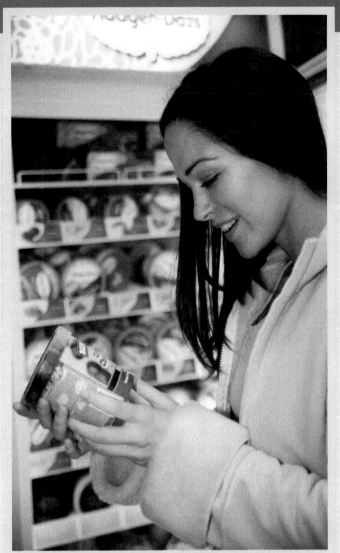

Ace Stock Limited

In this chapter, we restate financial statements in relative terms to understand how a firm is performing. Specifically, we look at key financial relationships in the form of ratios to understand three basic attributes of the firm's performance:

- The ability of the firm to meet its current liabilities as they come due, or what financial analysts refer to as *liquidity*
- Whether the firm's managers deliver acceptable, and hopefully, even superior profits on the capital entrusted to the firm
- Whether the firm's managers create or destroy shareholder value

In this chapter, we look at financial measurements, or metrics, used to manage a business. Is using metrics to help us manage a business important? John Thompson, CEO, Symantec Corporation, a high-growth Internet security firm, thinks so:

> I don't believe you can manage what you don't measure. A firm needs metrics that serve as an indication for the team about what you're paying attention to. If employees know you're measuring market growth and customer satisfaction, they'll pay attention to those considerations and will behave based on indicators that you, as the leader, provide to the organization. Metrics help the team focus on what's important for an organization.
>
> The best metrics are simple to understand, are simple to communicate, and make it relatively easy for everyone to get access to the data that represents the results. That makes your metrics an effective management tool. If you make your metrics difficult to gather, manage, or communicate, they won't be effective. Simplicity is key.
>
> My experience has proven to me the importance of picking a few metrics that are the most critical for running the business. Stick with them—and communicate them to both internal and external audiences.[1]

With this advice from an experienced CEO, we begin our study of the key financial metrics that can and must be used by companies, both large and small.

[1]David Liss, "Ask the CEO: Management by the Numbers," *Business Week Online*, New York: McGraw-Hill, at www.businessweek.com/technology/content/jul2003/tc20030721_6130.htm, accessed May 15, 2009.

Explain the purpose and importance of financial analysis.

The Purpose of Financial Analysis

The fundamental and core objective of financial management is to create shareholder value, as opposed to focusing on accounting numbers, such as earnings. In a perfect world, we would rely on market values relating to a firm's assets rather than its accounting data. However, we rarely have market values to guide decision making. Thus, accounting information can be very useful for this purpose.

However, financial analysts use accounting information differently than accountants do. Accountants focus on using the information to prepare financial statements according to generally accepted accounting principles (GAAP). By contrast, financial analysts use the information to measure a company's performance and make projections about and improve its future financial performance. The analysis is primarily based on the use of ratios that help us see critical relationships that might not otherwise be readily identifiable. Ratios are used to standardize financial information so that we can make comparisons. Otherwise, it is really difficult to compare the financial statements of two firms of different sizes or even the same firm at different times.

Financial ratios give us two ways of making meaningful comparisons of a firm's financial data: (1) We can examine the ratios across time (say, for the past 5 years) to compare a firm's current and past performance; and (2) we can compare the firm's ratios with those of other firms. In comparing a firm with other companies, we could select a peer group of companies, or we could use industry norms published by firms such as Dun & Bradstreet, Risk Management Association, Standard & Poor's, Value Line, and Prentice Hall. Dun & Bradstreet, for instance, annually publishes a set of 14 key ratios for each of 125 lines of business. The Risk Management Association (the association of bank loan and credit officers) publishes a set of 16 key ratios for more than 350 lines of business. The firms are grouped according to the North American Industrial Classification System (NAICS) codes. They are also segmented by firm size to provide the basis for more meaningful comparisons.

Figure 1 shows the financial statement information as reported by Risk Management Association (RMA) for new car dealers. The report shows the information by two asset-size and sales-size categories. In the complete report (not provided here), other size categories are presented. The balance sheet data in the report are provided as a percentage of total assets, or what we call a *common-sized balance sheet*. Likewise, the income statement data are reported as a percentage of sales, referred to as a *common-sized income statement*.[2] In presenting the financial ratios in the bottom portion of the report, RMA gives three results for each ratio—the firms at the 75th, 50th, and 25th percentiles, respectively.

Financial analysis is not just a tool for financial managers but also can be used effectively by investors, lenders, suppliers, employees, and customers. Within the firm, managers use financial ratios to:

financial ratios accounting data restated in relative terms in order to help people identify some of the financial strengths and weaknesses of a company.

REMEMBER YOUR PRINCIPLES

As we talked about financial statements, a primary rationale for evaluating a company's financial performance relates to **Principle 5: Conflicts of Interest Cause Agency Problems**. Thus, the firm's common stockholders need information that can be used to monitor managers' actions. Interpreting the firm's financial statements through the use of financial ratios is a key tool used in this monitoring. Of course, the firm's managers also need metrics to monitor the company's performance so corrective actions can be taken when necessary.

Principle 4: Market Prices Are Generally Right is also relevant when it comes to evaluating a firm's financial performance. By exceptionally profitable markets, we mean markets in which investments earn rates of return that exceed the opportunity cost of the money invested. Thus, rates of return are critical measures of whether or not managers are creating shareholder value. In addition, certain financial ratios can help us better know if managers are pursuing exceptionally good investments or bad ones.

Finally, **Principle 3: Risk Requires a Reward** is also at work in this chapter. As we will see, how managers choose to finance the business affects the company's risk and, as a result, the rate of return stockholders receive on their investments.

♦ Identify deficiencies in the firm's performance and take corrective action.

♦ Evaluate employee performance and determine incentive compensation.

♦ Compare the financial performance of the firm's different divisions.

[2]In this book, we presented a common-sized income statement and common-sized balance sheet for Davies Inc.

FIGURE 1 Financial Statement Data by Industry: Norms for New Car Dealers

RETAIL—NEW CAR DEALERS NAICS 4411 (SIC 5511)

CURRENT DATA SORTED BY ASSETS 50-100MM %	100-250MM %		CURRENT DATA SORTED BY SALES 10-25MM %	25MM and OVER %
		ASSETS		
7.3	8.7	Cash and Equivalents	8.1	10.3
10.0	10.9	Trade Receivables (net)	7.3	8.7
48.3	45.5	Inventory	67.9	60.0
4.4	2.5	All Other Current	2.7	2.9
70.0	67.6	Total Current	85.9	81.9
16.3	20.9	Fixed Assets (net)	8.3	10.9
2.6	1.5	Intangibles (net)	1.4	1.6
11.1	10.0	All Other Non-current	4.3	5.6
100.0	100.0	Total	100.0	100.0
		LIABILITIES		
42.2	42.5	Notes Payable Short Term	56.5	51.8
3.5	2.4	Cur. Mat.-L/T/D	2.0	2.4
3.5	4.2	Trade Payables	4.3	4.4
.1	.2	Income Taxes Payable	.1	.2
9.7	12.8	All Other Current	9.5	11.2
59.0	62.2	Total Current	72.3	70.0
14.6	16.0	Long Term Debt	6.5	7.5
.6	.3	Deferred Taxes	.1	.2
3.4	2.3	All Other Non-current	2.7	2.2
22.5	19.2	Net Worth	18.5	20.1
100.0	100.0	Total Liabilities and Net Worth	100.0	100.0
		INCOME DATA		
100.0	100.0	Net Sales	100.0	100.0
15.6	15.6	Gross Profit	12.3	12.1
13.2	14.0	Operating Expenses	11.9	11.2
2.4	1.6	Operating Profit	.3	.9
-.3	.3	All Other Expenses (net)	-.6	-.5
2.6	1.3	Profit Before Taxes	.9	1.4
		RATIOS		
1.3	1.2	Current	1.3	1.3
1.2	1.1		1.2	1.1
1.1	.9		1.1	1.0
.4	.4	Quick	.3	.4
.3	.3		.2 (768) / (1302)	.2
.2	.2		.1	.2
5 67.2	6 61.0	Sales/Receivables	3 127.5	4 102.8
10 36.1	11 33.1		5 70.6	6 60.7
17 21.6	17 21.9		9 38.6	10 37.5

CURRENT DATA SORTED BY ASSETS 50-100MM	%	100-250MM	%	RATIOS	10-25MM	%	25MM and OVER	%
52	7.1	53	6.9	Cost of Sales/Inventory	60	6.1	46	8.0
67	5.4	62	5.9		76	4.8	59	6.2
80	4.5	74	5.0		93	3.9	73	5.0
3	142.6	3	111.0	Cost of Sales/Payables	1	257.4	2	209.2
4	84.3	4	81.3		3	140.6	3	123.4
8	43.8	8	43.5		5	71.2	5	77.8
	16.7		30.5	Sales/Working Capital		17.5		21.9
	29.7		95.3			30.6		39.4
	53.0		-98.0			88.5		134.2
	8.4		12.7	EBIT/Interest		6.8		11.3
(32)	4.0	(20)	4.1		(597)	2.4	(938)	4.5
	1.5		2.5			1.0		1.9
	8.4			Net Profit+Depr., Dep., Amort./Cur. Mat. L/T/D		4.6		6.7
(10)	1.5				(64)	1.8	(174)	2.2
	1.0					.6		.9
	.2		.4	Fixed Assets/Net Worth		.2		.2
	.8		1.3			.4		.5
	1.3		4.9			1.2		1.2
	2.4		3.2	Debt/Net Worth		3.0		2.6
	3.7		5.3			5.8		4.8
	6.6		17.0			14.0		9.8
	39.3		77.4	% Profit Before Taxes/Tangible Net Worth		36.4		50.4
(36)	23.2	(25)	22.2		(692)	17.4	(1223)	28.0
	10.5		13.3			3.0		12.2
	8.6		7.7	% Profit Before Taxes/Total Assets		6.1		9.2
	4.4		5.0			2.3		4.8
	1.5		2.9			.1		1.6
	84.2		74.0	Sales/Net Fixed Assets		163.6		126.3
	22.9		17.7			77.4		67.2
	9.6		8.2			37.0		27.0
	4.0		3.9	Sales/Total Assets		4.5		5.2
	3.3		3.1			3.8		4.2
	1.9		2.5			3.0		3.4
	.3		.2	% Depr., Dep., Amort./Sales		.1		.1
(37)	.4	(21)	.5		(679)	.3	(1214)	.3
	1.0		.8			.4		.4
	.1			% Officers', Directors', Owners' Comp/Sales		.4		.2
(17)	.3				(501)	.6	(760)	.4
	1.1					1.1		1.0
	7968935M		13431196M	Net Sales ($)		13318098M		95427461M
	2604956M		3948948M	Total Assets ($)		3876849M		24306019M

M = $ thousand   MM = $ million

◆ Prepare, at both the firm and division levels, financial projections, such as those associated with the launch of a new product.

◆ Understand the financial performance of the firm's competitors.

◆ Evaluate the financial condition of a major supplier.

Outside the company, financial ratios can be used by:

♦ Lenders to decide whether or not to make a loan to the company
♦ Credit-rating agencies to determine the firm's creditworthiness
♦ Investors to decide whether or not to invest in a company
♦ Major suppliers to decide whether or not to grant credit terms to a company

The conclusion: Financial analysis tools can help a wide group of individuals for a variety of purposes. However, in this chapter we will focus on how the firm itself uses financial ratios to evaluate its performance. But remember that personnel in marketing, human resources, information systems, and other groups within a firm can use financial ratios for a variety of other reasons.

Concept Check

1. What is the basic purpose of doing a financial analysis?
2. How does a firm use financial ratios? Who else might use financial ratios and why?
3. Where can we find financial ratios for different companies or for peer groups?

Calculate and use a comprehensive set of measurements to evaluate a company's performance.

Measuring Key Financial Relationships

Instructors usually take one of two approaches to teach students about financial ratios. The first approach reviews the different types or categories of ratios, whereas the second approach uses ratios to answer important questions about a firm's operations. We prefer the latter approach and have chosen the following five questions to help you map out the process of using financial ratios:

1. How liquid is the firm?
2. Are the firm's managers generating adequate operating profits on the company's assets?
3. How is the firm financing its assets?
4. Are the firm's managers providing a good return on the capital provided by the shareholders?
5. Are the firm's managers creating shareholder value?

Let's look at each of these five questions in turn. In doing so, we will use Davies Inc. to illustrate the use of financial ratios. The company's financial statements are shown in Table 1 and Table 2.

TABLE 1 Davies Inc. Income Statement for Year Ending December 31, 2010 ($ millions)		
Sales		$ 600
Cost of goods sold		460
Gross profits		$ 140
Operating expenses:		
Selling expenses	$ 20	
General and administrative expenses	15	
Depreciation expense	30	
Total operating expenses		$ 65
Operating income (EBIT)		$ 75
Interest		15
Earnings before taxes		$ 60
Income taxes		18
Net income		$ 42
Number of common shares outstanding (millions)		20
Earnings per share (EPS)		$ 2.10
Dividends per share (DPS)		$ 0.50

TABLE 2 Davies Inc. Balance Sheets ($ millions) December 31, 2010		
Assets		
Cash		$ 20
Accounts receivable		36
Inventories		84
Other current assets		3
Total current assets		$ 143
Gross fixed assets	$ 410	
Accumulated depreciation	(115)	
Net fixed assets		$ 295
Total assets		$ 438
Debt and Equity		
Accounts payable		$ 42
Accrued expenses		10
Short-term notes		12
Total current liabilities		$ 64
Long-term debt		$ 171
Total liabilities		$ 235
Equity		
Common stockholders' equity		
Common stock—par value		$ 11
Paid-in capital		75
Retained earnings		117
Total common equity		$ 203
Total liabilities and equity		$ 438

To give us a basis for comparison, we also provide the average financial ratios for a peer group of businesses similar to Davies Inc. In the ratio computations, we have color coded the numbers so that you can readily determine whether a particular number is coming from the income statement (red numbers) or the balance sheet (blue numbers).

Question 1: How Liquid Is the Firm—Can It Pay Its Bills?

A liquid asset is one that can be converted quickly and routinely into cash at the current market price. So the **liquidity** of a business is a function of its ability to have cash available when needed to meet its financial obligations. Very simply, can we expect the company to be able to pay creditors on a timely basis?

This question can be answered by taking a look at two complementary perspectives: (1) by comparing the firm's assets that are relatively liquid (those that can be converted quickly and easily into cash) with the firm's debt owed in the near term, and (2) by examining the timeliness with which the firm's primary liquid assets—accounts receivable and inventories—are being converted into cash. Let's consider these two approaches.

liquidity a firm's ability to pay its bills on time. Liquidity is related to the ease and quickness with which a firm can convert its noncash assets into cash, as well as the size of the firm's investment in noncash assets relative to its short-term liabilities.

Measuring Liquidity: Perspective 1   The first angle for measuring liquidity is to look at the company's balance sheet and compare the firm's "liquid" assets (current assets) to its current (short-term) liabilities. Thus, the most commonly used measure of a firm's short-term solvency is the **current ratio**:

$$\text{Current ratio} = \frac{\text{current assets}}{\text{current liabilities}} \qquad (1)$$

current ratio a firm's current assets divided by its current liabilities. This ratio indicates the firm's degree of liquidity by comparing its current assets to its current liabilities.

For Davies Inc.:

$$\text{Current ratio} = \frac{\$143M}{\$64M} = 2.23$$

Peer group current ratio   1.80

CAUTIONARY TALE

FORGETTING PRINCIPLE 3: RISK REQUIRES A REWARD

Clearly, borrowing money carries risk—after all, you eventually have to pay off any debt you take on. Yet every day, forgetting this simple principle gets Americans in trouble. Between the mid-1980s and the early 2000s, the American household debt-to-income ratio doubled. In fact, this debt ratio spiked from between 45 and 60 percent to 135 percent! Interest on this household debt also increased substantially. At the same time, because interest on home mortgages is tax deductible, households had an incentive to borrow excessive amounts for home loans. This heavy debt burden—the risk of borrowing—meant that any unexpected expense, loss of a job, or increase in mortgage payments resulted in defaults.

Based on the current ratio, Davies Inc. is more liquid than the average firm in the peer group. The company has $2.23 in current assets for every $1 in short-term debt, compared to a peer-group average current ratio of $1.80.

When we use the current ratio, we assume that the firm's accounts receivable will be collected and turned into cash on a timely basis and that its inventories can be sold without any extended delay. However, a company's inventory is generally less liquid than its accounts receivable because inventory must first be sold before any cash can be collected. So, if we want to have a more stringent test of a firm's liquidity, we include only the firm's cash and accounts receivable in the numerator of our liquidity measure (and not its inventory). This revised ratio is called the **acid-test** (or **quick**) **ratio**. It is calculated as follows:

acid-test (quick) ratio a firm's cash and accounts receivable divided by its current liabilities. This ratio is a more stringent measure of liquidity than the current ratio in that it excludes inventories and other current assets (those that are least liquid) from current assets.

$$\text{Acid-test ratio} = \frac{\text{cash} + \text{accounts receivable}}{\text{current liabilities}} \tag{2}$$

For Davies Inc.:

$$\text{Acid-test ratio} = \frac{\$20M + \$36M}{\$64M} = 0.88$$

Peer group acid-test ratio	0.94

Based on the acid-test ratio, Davies Inc. appears to be slightly *less* liquid. It has $0.88 in cash and accounts receivable per $1 in current debt, compared to $0.94 for the average company in the peer group.

Measuring Liquidity: Perspective 2   The second angle for measuring liquidity examines the quality of a firm's accounts receivable and inventories in terms of the firm's ability to convert these assets into cash on a timely basis. A firm might have a higher current ratio or acid-test ratio than its competitors. However, it might also have more uncollectible receivables and/or be carrying a lot of obsolete inventory. So knowing the quality of these assets is necessary if we are to have a more complete understanding of a firm's liquidity.

Converting Accounts Receivable to Cash   The conversion of accounts receivable into cash can be measured by computing how long it takes to collect the firm's receivables. We can answer this question by computing a firm's days of sales outstanding, or its **average collection period**, as follows:[3]

average collection period a firm's accounts receivable divided by the company's average daily credit sales (annual credit sales ÷ 365). This ratio expresses how rapidly the firm is collecting its credit accounts.

$$\text{Average collection period} = \frac{\text{accounts receivable}}{\text{annual credit sales}/365} = \frac{\text{accounts receivable}}{\text{daily credit sales}} \tag{3}$$

---

[3]When computing a given ratio that uses information from both the income statement and the balance sheet, we should remember that the income statement is for a given time period (e.g., 2010), whereas balance sheet data are at a point in time (e.g., December 31, 2010). If there has been a significant change in an asset from the beginning of the period to the end of the period, it would be better to use the average balance for the year. For example, if the accounts receivable for a company have increased from $1,000 at the beginning of the year to $2,000 at the end of the year, it would be more appropriate to use the average accounts receivable of $1,500 in our computations. Nevertheless, in an effort to simplify, we will use year-end amounts from the balance sheet in our computations.

Assuming that Davies Inc. sells entirely on credit, the firm's average collection period would be found as follows:

$$\text{Average collection period} = \frac{\text{accounts receivable}}{\text{daily credit sales}}$$

For Davies Inc.:

$$\text{Average collection period} = \frac{\$36M}{\$600M/365} = \frac{\$36M}{\$1.64M/\text{day}} = 21.95 \text{ days}$$

Peer group average collection period	25.00 days

On average Davies Inc. collects its accounts receivable in 22 days compared to 25 days for the peer group, which suggests that the firm's receivables are more liquid than those of competing firms.

We could have reached the same conclusion by measuring how many times accounts receivable are "rolled over" during a year, using the **accounts receivable turnover ratio**. If Davies Inc. collects its accounts receivable every 21.90 days, then it is collecting 16.67 times per year (16.67 times = 365 days ÷ 21.90 days). The accounts receivable turnover can also be calculated as follows:

accounts receivable turnover ratio a firm's credit sales divided by its accounts receivable. This ratio expresses how often accounts receivable are "rolled over" during a year.

$$\text{Accounts receivable turnover} = \frac{\text{annual credit sales}}{\text{accounts receivable}} \qquad (4)$$

For Davies Inc.:

$$\text{Accounts receivable turnover} = \frac{\$600M}{\$36M} = 16.67X$$

Peer group accounts receivable turnover	14.60X

Whether we use the average collection period or the accounts receivable turnover ratio, the conclusion is the same. Davies Inc. collects its accounts receivable more quickly than competing firms. In other words, Davies Inc.'s accounts receivable are of better quality than the peer group average.

Converting Inventories to Cash   We now want to know the quality of Davies Inc.'s inventory, as indicated by how long the inventory is held before being sold; stated differently, we want to know how many times the company is turning over its inventory during the year. **Inventory turnover** is calculated as follows:[4]

inventory turnover a firm's cost of goods sold divided by its inventory. This ratio measures the number of times a firm's inventories are sold and replaced during the year, that is, the relative liquidity of the inventories.

$$\text{Inventory turnover} = \frac{\text{cost of goods sold}}{\text{inventory}} \qquad (5)$$

For Davies Inc.:

$$\text{Inventory turnover} = \frac{\$460M}{\$84M} = 5.48X$$

Peer group inventory turnover	7.00X

We see that Davies Inc. is moving (turning over) its inventory more slowly than the average peer group firm—5.48 times per year at Davies Inc., compared with 7.0 times for the peer group, which suggests that the firm's inventory is less liquid than that of the peer group on average.

---

[4]Note that sales has been replaced by cost of goods sold in the numerator. Because inventory (the denominator) is measured at cost, we want to use the cost-based measure of sales in the numerator. Otherwise our answer will vary from one firm to the next solely because of differences in how each firm marks up its sales over cost. However, some of the industry norms provided by financial services are computed using sales in the numerator. In those cases, we will want to use sales in our computation of inventory turnover.

CAN YOU DO IT?

EVALUATING DISNEY'S LIQUIDITY

The following information (expressed in $ millions) is taken from the Walt Disney Company's 2008 financial statements:

Current assets	$ 11,666
Accounts receivable	5,373
Cash	3,001
Inventories	1,124
Sales	37,843
Cost of goods sold	30,439
Total current liabilities	11,591

Evaluate Disney's liquidity based on the following norms in the broadcasting and entertainment industry:

Current ratio	1.17
Acid-test ratio	0.92
Accounts receivable turnover	10.08
Inventory turnover	18.32

We could also express the inventory turnover in terms of the number of days of sales in inventory. Davies Inc. turns its inventory over 5.48 times per year, so on average, it is carrying its inventory for 67 days (365 days ÷ 5.48 times per year), whereas the average peer firm carries its inventory only 52 days (365 days ÷ 7.0 times per year) on average.

To conclude, the current ratio indicates that Davies Inc. is more liquid than the competing firms on average, but this result assumes that the firm's inventory are of similar quality as the competitors, which is not the case given Davies' slower inventory turnover. The acid-test ratio, on the other hand, suggests that the firm is less liquid than its competitors, but we know that Davies' accounts receivable are more liquid than the average peer group firm. So we have a mixed outcome and cannot say definitely whether Davies Inc. is more or less liquid. Judgment suggests that Davies Inc. is probably similar in its liquidity to other firms on average.

Concept Check

1. What information about the firm is provided by liquidity measures?
2. Describe the two perspectives available for measuring liquidity.
3. Why might a very high current ratio actually indicate there's a problem with a firm's inventory or accounts receivable management? What might be another reason for a high current ratio?
4. Why might a successful (liquid) firm have an acid-test ratio that is less than 1?

Question 2: Are the Firm's Managers Generating Adequate Operating Profits on the Company's Assets?

We now switch to a different dimension of performance—the firm's profitability. The question is, "Do the firm's managers produce adequate profits from the company's assets?" From the perspective of the firm's shareholders, there is no more important question to be asked. One of the most important ways managers create shareholder value is to earn strong profits on the assets in which they have invested.

To answer this all-important question, think about the process of financing a company. In its simplest form, a firm's shareholders invest in a business. The company might also borrow additional money from other sources (banks and so forth). The cumulative effects of this process are reflected in a firm's balance sheet. For example, Figure 2 indicates that Davies Inc.'s shareholders have invested $203 million in the company, and the company has borrowed another $235 million to finance $438 million of assets. These assets were then used to produce $75 million in operating profits.

DID YOU GET IT?
EVALUATING DISNEY'S LIQUIDITY

	DISNEY	INDUSTRY
Current ratio	1.01	1.17
Acid-test ratio	0.72	0.92
Accounts receivable turnover	7.04X	10.1X
Inventory turnover	27.08X	18.3X

Based on these results, Disney is not as liquid as the average firm in the industry! The company has less liquid assets relative to its current liabilities than do its competitors on average. Nor does the firm convert its receivables to cash as quickly as its competitors. However, Disney's inventories turn over more quickly than those of its competitors.

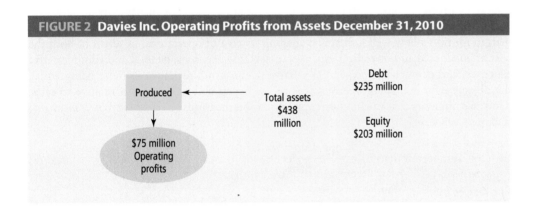

FIGURE 2 Davies Inc. Operating Profits from Assets December 31, 2010

Notice that we are using *operating profits* (the same as *operating income* or *earnings before interest and taxes*) rather than *net income*. Operating profits is the income generated from the firm's assets without regard to how the assets are financed. The effect of financing will be explicitly considered in the two questions that follow, but for now we want to isolate only the operating aspects of the company's profits.

To examine the level of operating profits relative to the firm's total assets, we use the **operating return on assets (OROA):**

$$\text{Operating return on assets} = \frac{\text{operating profits}}{\text{total assets}} \qquad (6)$$

operating return on assets (OROA) the ratio of a firm's operating income divided by its total assets. This ratio indicates the rate of return being earned on the firm's assets.

For Davies Inc.:

$$\text{Operating return on assets} = \frac{\$75M}{\$438M} = 0.171 = 17.1\%$$

Peer group operating return on assets   17.8%

Davies Inc. is earning a slightly lower return on its assets relative to the average firm in the peer group. Managers are generating 17.1 cents of operating profits for every \$1 of assets, compared to 17.8 cents on average for the peer group.

Because Davies Inc. is generating a return on the firm's assets that is less than the competition, the company's managers will want to know why the firm is not earning a competitive return on the assets. The answer lies in two areas: (1) *operations management*, which includes the day-to-day buying and selling of a firm's goods or services as reflected in the income statement, and (2) *asset management*, which relates to the balance sheet. We can relate operations management and asset management through a firm's *operating return on assets* using the product of two ratios; that is,

	OPERATIONS	ASSET MANAGEMENT

$$\text{Operating return on assets} = \text{operating profit margin} \times \text{total asset turnover} \qquad (7a)$$

which is calculated as follows:

$$\text{Operating return on assets} = \frac{\text{operating profits}}{\text{sales}} \times \frac{\text{sales}}{\text{total assets}} \qquad (7b)$$

Managing Operations The first component of the operating return on assets (OROA), the **operating profit margin**, is an indicator of how well the company manages its operations—that is, how well revenues are being generated and costs controlled. The operating profit margin measures how well a firm is managing its cost of operations, in terms of both the cost of goods sold and operating expenses (marketing expenses, general and administrative expenses, and depreciation expenses) relative to the firm's revenues. All else being equal, the objective for managing operations is to keep costs and expenses low relative to sales. Thus, we often say that the operating profit margin measures *how well the firm is managing its income statement.*

operating profit margin a firm's operating income (earnings before interest and taxes) divided by sales. This ratio serves as an overall measure of operating effectiveness.

$$\text{Operating profit margin} = \frac{\text{operating profits}}{\text{sales}} \qquad (8)$$

For Davies Inc.:

$$\text{Operating profit margin} = \frac{\$75M}{\$600M} = 0.125 = 12.5\%$$

Peer group operating profit margin	15.5%

The foregoing result clearly suggests that Davies Inc.'s managers are not as good at managing its cost of goods sold and operating expenses as comparable firms. The company has higher costs per sales dollar, which result in a lower operating profit margin. Put another way, Davies Inc. is not as good as competitors at managing its income statement.

total asset turnover a firm's sales divided by its total assets. This ratio is an overall measure of asset efficiency based on the relation between a firm's sales and the total assets.

asset efficiency how well a firm is managing its assets.

Managing Assets The second component in equation (7) is the **total asset turnover**. This ratio indicates how well the firm is managing its assets, or **asset efficiency**. It measures how efficiently a firm is using its assets to generate sales. To clarify, assume that Company A generates $3 in sales for every $1 invested in assets, whereas Company B generates the same $3 in sales but has invested $2 in assets. We can therefore conclude that Company A is using its assets more efficiently to generate sales, which leads to a higher return on the firm's investment in assets.

$$\text{Total asset turnover} = \frac{\text{sales}}{\text{total assets}} \qquad (9)$$

For Davies Inc.:

$$\text{Total asset turnover} = \frac{\$600M}{\$438M} = 1.37X$$

Peer group total asset turnover	1.15X

Davies Inc. is using its assets more efficiently than its competitors because it generates about $1.37 in sales per dollar of assets, whereas the competition produces only $1.15 in sales per every dollar of assets.

However, we should not stop here with our analysis of Davies Inc.'s asset utilization. We have learned that, in general, Davies Inc.'s managers are making effective use of the firm's assets, but this may not be the case for each and every type of asset. So we also want to know how well the firm is managing its accounts receivable, inventories, and fixed assets, respectively.

To answer the preceding question, we examine the turnover ratios for each asset category. Of course, we already calculated the turnover ratios for the company's accounts receivable and inventories, and concluded that Davies Inc.'s managers are managing the firm's accounts receivable more efficiently than its competitors, but not its inventories. But, we still need to compute the **fixed asset turnover** as follows:

$$\text{Fixed asset turnover} = \frac{\text{sales}}{\text{net fixed assets}} \qquad (10)$$

fixed asset turnover a firm's sales divided by its net fixed assets. This ratio indicates how efficiently the firm is using its fixed assets.

For Davies Inc.:

$$\text{Fixed asset turnover} = \frac{\$600M}{\$295M} = 2.03X$$

Peer group fixed asset turnover 1.75X

Thus, Davies Inc. has a smaller investment in fixed assets relative to the firm's sales than the average peer group firm.

We can now look at all the asset efficiency ratios together to summarize Davies Inc.'s asset management:

	DAVIES INC.	PEER GROUP
Total asset turnover	1.37X	1.15X
Accounts receivable turnover	16.67X	14.60X
Inventory turnover	5.48X	7.00X
Fixed asset turnover	2.03X	1.75X

Davies Inc.'s situation with respect to asset management is now clear. Overall, Davies Inc.'s managers are utilizing the firm's assets efficiently, as based on the firm's total asset turnover. This overall asset efficiency results from better management of the firm's accounts

FINANCE AT WORK

MANAGING BY THE NUMBERS

Dorian S. Boyland is taking care of business as he bustles about his 29,000-square-foot Honda dealership, located in Greenfield, Wisconsin. He is preparing for a grand opening, even though the store has been open since 2001.

Boyland, 48, is excited about the festivities, but he intends to get a return on this investment. Make no mistake about it; he is meticulous about how he spends money, keeping the company's advertising and sales salaries less than 10 percent of gross profits, respectively. No more than 10 percent of gross profits are paid in commissions to managers, and no more than 15 percent of gross profits are paid in commissions to sales managers.

The auto dealer operates with one goal in mind: net a 3 percent to 3.5 percent profit on sales from all seven of his auto dealerships. "I never ask how many cars we sold," says Boyland. "I ask my sales managers how much profit did we make. I operate on the premise that if I sell a car for $20,000, I know that 3 percent (or $600) of that amount is going to go to my bottom line. Now, how

I get that 3 percent is how we operate the store—from the bottom up."

Boyland's cost controls are a never-ending process. A financial analysis is generated monthly and reviewed by all store managers. This information sharing allows every general manager and sales manager to critique one another, exchange ideas, and establish goals and guidelines.

Volume is very important to dealers because manufacturers expect them to achieve a certain level of market penetration. But as Boyland sees it, "You can be No.1 in terms of volume, but if you are constantly losing money, you'll be taken out of business."

Boyland grows excited when discussing business strategies. "You have to have a passion for this business," he says. "There's a lot of money to be made and a lot of money to be lost. But whether you are selling cars or shoes, you go into business to make money. That's the bottom line."

Source: Carolyn M. Brown, "Maximum Overdrive," *Black Enterprise*, Vol. 33, No. 11 (June 2003), pp. 156–162. Copyright 2003 by Graves Ventures LLC.

CAN YOU DO IT?

EVALUATING DISNEY'S OPERATING RETURN ON ASSETS

Given the following financial information for the Walt Disney Company (expressed in $ millions), evaluate the firm's operating return on its assets (OROA).

Accounts receivable	$ 5,373
Inventories	1,124
Sales	37,843
Operating profits	4,427
Cost of goods sold	30,439
Net fixed assets	21,723
Total assets	62,497

The industry norms are as follows:

Operating return on assets	5.09%
Operating profit margin	11.30%
Total asset turnover	0.45X
Accounts receivable turnover	10.08X
Inventory turnover	18.32X
Fixed assets turnover	1.05X

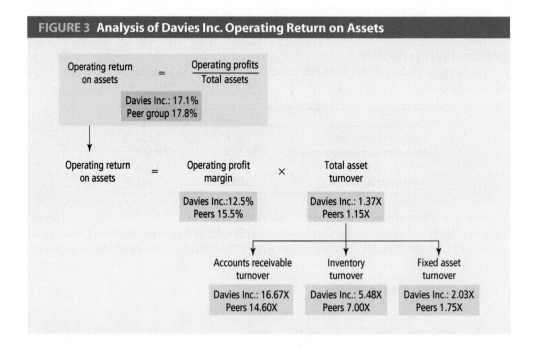

FIGURE 3 Analysis of Davies Inc. Operating Return on Assets

receivable and fixed assets (which have higher turnovers than the peer group), but the firm is not managing its inventories as well (which has a lower turnover than the peer group).

Figure 3 provides a summary of our evaluation of Davies Inc.'s operating and asset management performance. We began by computing the operating return on assets to determine if managers are producing good returns on the assets. We then broke the operating return on assets into its two pieces, operations management (operating profit margin) and asset management (asset turnover ratios), to explain why Davies Inc.'s operating return on assets is lower than the peer group.

Concept Check

1. Which number in a company's income statement should be used to measure its profitability relative to its total assets? Why?
2. What two broad areas of the firm's management does the operating return on assets assess?
3. What factors influence the operating profit margin?
4. A low total asset turnover indicates that a firm's total assets are not being managed efficiently. What additional information would you want to know when this is the case?

ETHICS IN FINANCIAL MANAGEMENT

FRAUD'S RED FLAGS

Directors and CEOs are more concerned than ever about understanding the corporate culture of their companies, and, if necessary, doing something to improve it. The consequences of lapses earlier in the decade that led to the great accounting scandals are still being felt today, both for those who are serving time in "Club Fed" and those serving on public boards.

Following are some examples of indicators that something might be amiss.

- **The old rules don't apply.** Most companies encourage creativity and value innovation. Yet when it comes to compliance with laws and regulations, and conducting business ethically, the old rules may be the best rules.
- **It seems too good to be true.** How many times do we say this or think it to ourselves? How often does it turn out that it was too good to be true?

One example is MassMutual's CEO's deferred-compensation account. According to press reports, its phenomenal success was not the result of investment acumen, but rather 20-20 hindsight in allocating portions of the account to hypothetical investments in companies whose shares had already appreciated in value.

- **We will do it just this once.** Robbing Peter to pay Paul is still robbery, and it's a slippery slope. The reports from the trials of WorldCom and HealthSouth executives contain numerous examples of this red flag.
- **Everybody else does it.** This is one of the most dangerous red flags because it is so common and it reflects an utter lack of thought about right and wrong. This is a rationale that is often used to justify accounting practices that may be technically defensible but do not result in "fair presentation" of financial results or conditions.

- **The lawyers, or accountants, said it is okay.** Here is another red flag that was apparently flown at Enron and WorldCom. You can just imagine how many times at each of these companies some senior or middle manager was told that something was okay because the attorneys, auditors, or boss said so. Yet, in many cases, the person asked to falsify the financial records or pass judgment on the special-purpose corporations knew better.
- **Conflicts of interest.** Dozens of companies have suffered serious scandals and shareholder revolt because management has had financial interests in enterprises that do business with, or compete against, their company. Just consider the "special-purpose entities" at Enron that created conflicts of interest for the company's CFO Andrew Fastow.
- **Too many euphemisms.** Labels are important. Would we eat as much sushi if it were called "raw fish," carpaccio if it were called "raw beef," or sweetbreads if they were called "organ meat"? The same idea is at work in the business world.

One of the recent reminders of the dangers of euphemisms is the Hewlett-Packard scandal over the investigation by the chairman of the board of outside directors' alleged leaks of confidential information. It seems unlikely that the company officers who were involved would have proceeded with "pretexting" if it were called "obtaining private, personal information under false pretenses."

Source: Excerpts from Michael Ross, "Fraud's Red Flags," *Directorship*, July 25, 2008, http://www.businessweek.com/managing/content/jul2008/ca20080725_953586.htm, accessed June 4, 2009.

Question 3: How Is the Firm Financing Its Assets?

We now turn to the matter of how a firm is financed. (We will return to the issue of profitability shortly.) Is it financed through debt or equity? To answer this question, we use two ratios. First, we ask *what percentage of the firm's assets is financed by debt*, including both short-term and long-term debt, realizing that the remaining percentage must be financed by equity. We compute the **debt ratio** as follows:[5]

$$\text{Debt ratio} = \frac{\text{total debt}}{\text{total assets}} \tag{11}$$

debt ratio a firm's total liabilities divided by its total assets. This ratio measures the extent to which a firm has been financed with debt.

For Davies Inc.:

$$\text{Debt ratio} = \frac{\$235M}{\$438M} = 0.54 = 54\%$$

Peer group debt ratio   35%

[5]Instead of using the debt ratio, we could use the debt–equity ratio. The debt–equity ratio is simply a transformation of the debt ratio:

$$\text{Debt–equity ratio} = \frac{\text{total debt}}{\text{total equity}} = \frac{\text{debt ratio}}{1 - \text{debt ratio}} \text{ and the debt ratio} = \frac{\text{debt/equity}}{1 + \text{debt/equity}}$$

times interest earned a firm's earnings before interest and taxes (EBIT) divided by interest expense. This ratio measures a firm's ability to meet its interest payments from its annual operating earnings.

Davies Inc. finances 54 percent of its assets with debt (taken from Davies Inc.'s balance sheet in Table 2), compared with the peer group average of 35 percent. Stated differently, Davies Inc. finances with 46 percent equity, whereas the average for the peer group is 65 percent equity. Thus, Davies Inc. uses significantly more debt than the peer group average. As we will see at several points in our study, more debt financing results in more financial risk.

Our second perspective regarding the firm's financing decisions comes by looking at the income statement. When the firm borrows money, it must at least pay the interest on what it has borrowed. Thus, it is informative to compare (1) the amount of operating income that is available to pay the interest with (2) the amount of interest that has to be paid. Stated as a ratio, we compute the number of times we are earning our interest. The **times interest earned** ratio is commonly used when examining a firm's debt position and is computed in the following manner:

$$\text{Times interest earned} = \frac{\text{operating profits}}{\text{interest expense}} \tag{12}$$

For Davies Inc.:

$$\text{Times interest earned} = \frac{\$75M}{\$15M} = 5.0X$$

Peer group times interest earned   7.0X

Davies Inc.'s interest expense is $15 million, which when compared to its operating income of $75 million, indicates that its interest expense is consuming 1/5 (20.0%) of its operating profits compared to 1/7 (14.29%) for the average peer group firm.

Why would Davies Inc. have a lower times interest earned ratio than the peer group? For one thing, Davies Inc. uses significantly more debt than the average company in the peer group, which leads to more interest expense. Second, its operating return on assets is slightly less than competitors, which means the firm has less operating income to cover the interest.

Before concluding our discussion regarding times interest earned, we should understand that interest is not paid with income but with cash. Moreover, in addition to the interest that must be paid, the firm might be required to repay some of the debt principal. Thus, the times interest earned ratio is only a crude measure of the firm's capacity to service its debt. Nevertheless, it does give us a general indication of a company's financial risk and its capacity to borrow.

CAN YOU DO IT?

EVALUATING DISNEY'S FINANCING DECISIONS

Given the information to the right (expressed in $ millions) for the Disney Corporation, calculate the firm's debt ratio and the times interest earned. How do Disney's ratios compare to those of the industry in which it operates? What are the implications of your findings?

Total debt	$30,174
Total common equity	
Common stock	3,991
Retained earnings	28,332
Total liabilities and equity	62,497
Operating profits	4,427
Interest expense	524
Industry norms:	
Debt ratio	34.21%
Times interest earned	4.50X

Concept Check

1. What information is provided by the debt ratio?
2. Why is it important to calculate the times interest earned ratio, even for firms that have low debt ratios?
3. Why does operating income not give a complete picture of a firm's ability to service its debt?

Question 4: Are the Firm's Managers Providing a Good Return on the Capital Provided by the Company's Shareholders?

We now want to look at the *accounting return on the common stockholders' investment*, or the **return on equity** (frequently shortened to ROE). We want to know if the earnings available to the firm's owners (shareholders) are attractive when compared with the returns earned for the owners of companies in the peer group. We measure the return on equity (ROE) as follows:

return on equity a firm's net income divided by its common book equity. This ratio is the accounting rate of return earned on the common stockholders' investment.

$$\text{Return on equity} = \frac{\text{net income}}{\text{common equity}} \qquad (13)$$

For Davies Inc.:

$$\text{Return on equity} = \frac{\$42M}{\$203M} = 0.207 = 20.7\%$$

Peer group return on equity	18.0%

In the preceding computation, the common equity includes all common equity in the balance sheet, including both common stock and retained earnings. (Understand that profits retained within the business are as much of an investment for the common stockholders as when the shareholders bought the company's stock.)

The return on equity for Davies Inc. and the peer group are 20.7 percent and 18.0 percent, respectively. Hence, the owners of Davies Inc. are receiving a higher return on their equity investment than the shareholders in the peer group firms on average. How are they doing it? To answer, we need to draw on what we have already learned, namely, that:

1. Davies Inc. is receiving a lower operating return on its assets. We learned earlier that the operating return on assets was 17.1 percent for Davies Inc., compared to 17.8 percent for the competition. A lower (higher) return on the firm's assets will always result in a lower (higher) return on equity.

DID YOU GET IT?
EVALUATING DISNEY'S FINANCING DECISIONS

A comparison of Disney's debt ratio and times interest earned with the industry is as follows:

	DISNEY	INDUSTRY
Debt ratio	48.28%	34.21%
Times interest earned	8.45X	4.50X

Disney uses significantly more debt financing than the average firm in the industry. The higher debt ratio implies that the firm has greater financial risk. Even so, Disney appears to have no difficulty servicing its debt, covering its interest 8.45 times compared only to 4.50 times for the average firm in the industry. Disney's higher times interest earned is attributable to a significantly higher operating return on assets, which more than offsets the higher debt ratio.

2. Davies Inc. uses significantly more debt (less equity) financing than the average firm in the industry—54 percent debt for Davies Inc. and 35 percent debt for the peer group. As we will see shortly, the more debt a firm uses, the higher its return on equity will be, provided that the firm is earning a return on assets greater than the interest rate on its debt. Conversely, the less debt a firm uses, the lower its return on equity will be (again, provided that the firm is earning a return on assets greater than the interest rate on its debt). Thus, Davies Inc. has increased its return for its shareholders by using more debt. That's the good news. The bad news for Davies Inc.'s shareholders is that the more debt a firm uses, the greater is the company's financial risk, which translates into more risk for the shareholders.

To help us understand the foregoing reason for Davies Inc.'s higher return on equity and its implications, consider the following example.

EXAMPLE 1

Firms A and B are identical in size. Both have $1,000 in total assets, and both have an operating return on assets of 14 percent. However, they are different in one respect: Firm A uses all equity and no debt financing; Firm B finances 60 percent of its investments with debt and 40 percent with equity. (For the sake of simplicity, we will assume that both firms pay interest at an interest cost of 6 percent, and there are no income taxes.) The financial statements for the two companies would be as follows:

	FIRM A	FIRM B
BALANCE SHEET		
Total assets	$1,000	$1,000
Debt (6% interest rate)	$ 0	$ 600
Equity	1,000	400
Total debt and equity	$1,000	$1,000
INCOME STATEMENT		
Operating income (OROA = 14%)	$ 140	$ 140
Interest expense (6%)	(0)	(36)
Net income	$ 140	$ 104

Computing the return on equity for both companies, we see that Firm B has a more attractive return of 26 percent compared with Firm A's 14 percent. The calculations are as follows:

			FIRM A		FIRM B	
Return on common equity	=	net income / common equity	=	$\dfrac{\$140}{\$1,000}$ = 14%	$\dfrac{\$104}{\$400}$ = 26%	

Why the difference? The answer is straightforward. Firm B is earning 14 percent on all of its $1,000 in assets, but only having to pay 6 percent to the lenders on the $600 debt principal. The difference between the 14 percent return on the firm's assets (operating return on assets) and the 6 percent interest rate goes to the owners, thus boosting Firm B's return on equity above that of Firm A.

This is an illustration of favorable financial leverage. What's favorable, you might ask? Well, you earn 14 percent on your investments while paying only 6 percent to the bankers, thus capturing an 8 percent spread on each dollar of debt financing. The result is an increase in the return on equity to Firm B when compared to Firm A. What a great deal for Firm B's shareholders! So if debt enhances owners' returns, why doesn't Firm A borrow money or Firm B borrow even more money?

The good outcome for Firm B shareholders is based on the assumption that the firm does in fact earn 14 percent operating return on the assets. But what if the economy falls into a deep recession, business declines sharply, and Firms A and B only earn a 2 percent operating return on their assets? Let's recompute the return on equity given the new conditions:

	FIRM A	FIRM B
Operating income (OROA = 2%)	$ 20	$ 20
Less interest expense	(0)	(36)
Net income	$ 20	($ 16)
Return on equity:		
$\dfrac{\text{net income}}{\text{common equity}}$	$\dfrac{\$\ 20}{\$1,000}$	$\dfrac{(\$\ 16)}{\$\ 400}$
Equals:	2%	−4%

Now the use of financial leverage has a negative influence on the return on equity, with Firm B earning less than Firm A for its owners. This results from Firm B earning less than the interest rate of 6 percent; consequently, the equity investors have to make up the difference. Thus, financial leverage is a two-edged sword; when times are good, financial leverage can make them very, very good, but when times are bad, financial leverage makes them very, very bad. Financial leverage can enhance the returns of the equity investors, but it also increases the possibility of losses, thereby increasing the uncertainty, or risk, for the owners.

Figure 4 on the next page provides a summary of our discussion of the return on equity relative to Davies Inc. and helps us visualize the two fundamental factors affecting a firm's return on equity:

1. There is a direct relationship between a firm's operating return on assets (OROA) and the resulting return on equity (ROE). As we have explained, the higher the

operating return on assets (OROA), the higher will be the return on equity (ROE). Even more precisely, the greater the difference between the firm's operating return on assets (OROA) and the interest rate (i) being paid on the firm's debt, the higher the return on equity will be. So increasing the operating return on assets relative to the interest rate (OROA-i) increases the return on equity (ROE). But if OROA-i decreases, then ROE will decrease as well.

2. Increasing the amount of debt financing relative to the amount of equity (increasing the debt ratio) increases the return on equity if the operating return on assets is higher than the interest rate being paid. If the operating return on assets falls below the interest rate, more debt financing will decrease the return on equity.

In short, the return on equity is driven by (1) the spread between the operating return on assets and the interest rate (OROA-i) and (2) changes in the debt ratio.

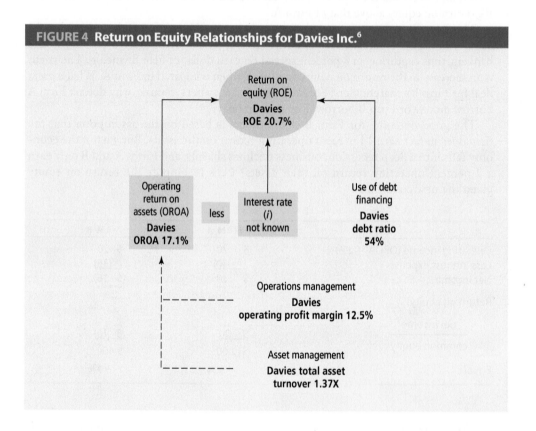

FIGURE 4 Return on Equity Relationships for Davies Inc.[6]

CAN YOU DO IT?

EVALUATING DISNEY'S RETURN ON EQUITY

The net income and also the common equity invested by Disney's shareholders (expressed in $ millions) are provided here, along with the average return on equity for the industry. Evaluate the rate of return being earned on the common stockholders' equity investment. In addition to comparing the Disney Corporation's return on equity to the industry, consider the implications Disney's operating return on assets and its debt financing practices have on the firm's return on equity.

Net income	$4,427
Common equity	
Common stock	3,991
Retained earnings	28,332
Industry average return on equity	4.31%

[6]This figure is a modified format of the "DuPont Analysis."

Concept Check

1. How is a company's return on equity related to the firm's operating return on assets?
2. How is a company's return on equity related to the firm's debt ratio?
3. What is the upside of debt financing? What is the downside?

DID YOU GET IT?
EVALUATING DISNEY'S RETURN ON EQUITY

Disney's return on equity is 13.7 percent (13.7% = $4,427 million net income/$32,323 million common equity), compared to 4.31 percent for the industry average. Disney's return on equity is due to the firm having a higher operating return on assets and using a lot more debt financing than the average firm in the industry.

Question 5: Are the Firm's Managers Creating Shareholder Value?

To this point, we have relied exclusively on accounting data to assess the performance of a firm's managers. We now want to look at management's performance in terms of creating or destroying shareholder value. To answer this question, we use two approaches: (1) We examine market-value ratios, and (2) we estimate the value being created for shareholders, as measured by a popular technique called Economic Value Added (EVA™).

Market-Value Ratios There are two commonly used ratios that compare the firm's stock price to the firm's earnings and the accounting book value of the equity. These two ratios indicate what investors think of management's past performance and future prospects.

Price/Earnings Ratio The **price/earnings** (P/E) **ratio** indicates how much investors are willing to pay for $1 of reported earnings. Returning to Davies Inc., the firm had net income in 2010 of $42 million and 20 million shares of common stock outstanding. (See Table 1.) Accordingly, its earnings per share were $2.10 ($2.10 = $42 million net income ÷ 20 million shares). At the time, the firm's stock was selling for $32 per share. Thus, the price/earnings ratio was 15.24 times, calculated as follows:

price/earnings ratio the price the market places on $1 of a firm's earnings. For example, if a firm has an earnings per share of $2, and a stock price of $30 per share, its price/earnings ratio is 15 ($30 ÷ $2).

$$\text{Price/earnings ratio} = \frac{\text{price per share}}{\text{earnings per share}} \qquad (14)$$

For Davies Inc.:

$$\text{Price/earning ratio} = \frac{\$32.00}{\$2.10} = 15.24\text{X}$$

Peer group average price/earnings ratio 19.0X

Davies Inc.'s price/earnings ratio tells us that the investors were willing to pay $15.24 for every dollar of earnings per share that Davies Inc. produced, compared to an average price/earnings ratio of 19 times for the firms making up the peer group. Thus, investors were not willing to pay as much for Davies Inc.'s earnings as were shareholders of the average peer group firm. Why might that be? The price/earnings ratio will be higher for companies that investors think have strong earnings growth prospects with less risk. Thus, investors must perceive Davies Inc. to have less growth potential and/or greater risk compared to the average company in the peer group.

Price/Book Ratio A second frequently used indicator of investors' assessment of the firm is its **price/book ratio**. This ratio compares the market value of a share of stock to the book

price/book ratio the market value of a share of the firm's stock divided by the book value per share of the firm's reported equity in the balance sheet.

CAN YOU DO IT?

COMPUTING DISNEY'S PRICE/EARNINGS RATIO AND PRICE/ BOOK RATIO

Disney's stock was selling for $23, while its net income was $4.427 billion ($4,427 million) and its common equity in the balance sheet (book equity) was $32.323 billion ($32,323 million). There were 1.823 billion shares outstanding. What was the firm's earnings per share and its book value per share? Calculate the price/earnings ratio and the price/book ratio. The average firm in the industry sold for 11 times earnings and 1.6 times book value. What do the shareholders think about the firm's performance and future growth prospects?

value per share of the firm's reported equity in its balance sheet. We already know that the market price of Davies Inc.'s common stock was $32. To determine the equity book value per share, we divide the firm's equity book value by the number of shares of stock outstanding. From Davies Inc.'s balance sheet (Table 2), we see that the equity book value was $203 million (including both common stock and retained earnings). Given that Davies Inc. had 20 million shares outstanding, the equity book value per share is $10.15 ($10.15 = $203 million book equity value ÷ 20 million shares). With this information, we determine the price/book ratio to be:

$$\text{Price/book ratio} = \frac{\text{market price per share}}{\text{equity book value per share}} \qquad (15)$$

For Davies Inc.:

$$\text{Price/book ratio} = \frac{\$32.00}{\$10.15} = 3.15X$$

Peer group 500 price/book ratio 3.7X

Given that the book value per share is an accounting number that reflects historical costs, we can roughly think of it as the amount shareholders have invested in the business over its lifetime. So, a ratio greater than 1 indicates that investors believe the firm is more valuable than the amount shareholders have invested in it. Conversely, a ratio less than 1 suggests that investors do not believe the stock is worth the amount shareholders have invested in it. Clearly, investors believe the stock of Davies Inc. is now worth more than shareholders paid, because they are now paying $3.15 for each dollar of book value. In comparison, the average firm in the peer group was selling for $3.70 for every $1 in book equity. Again, the investors are signaling that they believe that Davies Inc. has less growth prospects relative to its riskiness.

Economic Value Added (EVA™) The price/book ratio, as just described, indicates whether the shareholders value the firm's equity above or below the amount of capital they originally invested. If the firm's market value is above the accounting book value (price/book > 1), then management has created value for shareholders, but if the firm's market value is below book value (price/book < 1), then management has destroyed shareholder value.

How is shareholder value created or destroyed? Quite simply, shareholder value is created when a firm earns a rate of return on the capital invested that is greater than the investors' required rate of return. If we invest in a firm and have a 12 percent required rate of return, and the firm earns 15 percent on our capital, then the firm's managers have created value for investors. If instead, the firm earns only 10 percent, then value has been destroyed. This concept is regularly applied by firms when they decide whether or not to make large capital investments in plant and equipment; however, it has not been generally applied to the analysis of a firm's day-to-day operating results. Instead, managers have traditionally focused on accounting results, such as earnings growth, profit margins, and the return on equity.

80

DID YOU GET IT?
COMPUTING DISNEY'S PRICE/EARNINGS RATIO AND PRICE/BOOK RATIO

We compute Disney's price/earnings ratio and price/book ratio as follows:

$$\text{Earnings per share} = \frac{\text{net income}}{\text{number of shares}}$$

$$= \frac{4.427 \text{ billion}}{1.823 \text{ billion shares}} = \$2.43$$

$$\text{Equity book value per share} = \frac{\text{common equity}}{\text{number of shares}}$$

$$= \frac{\$32.323 \text{ billion}}{1.823 \text{ billion shares}} = \$17.73$$

$$\text{Price/earnings ratio} = \frac{\text{market price per share}}{\text{earning per share}} = \frac{\$23}{\$2.43} = 9.47$$

$$\text{Price/book ratio} = \frac{\text{market price per share}}{\text{equity book value per share}}$$

$$= \frac{\$23}{\$17.73} = 1.30$$

Disney's stock is selling for 9.47 times its earnings and 1.30 times its book value. At the same time, the average firm in the industry was selling for 11 times its earnings and 1.6 times its book value. Thus, investors see Disney as having lower growth prospects and/or greater risk.

More recently, however, people have begun assessing whether or not a firm's managers are creating shareholder value and then linking this assessment to managers' compensation, mostly through bonuses. Although several techniques have been developed for making this assessment, the one that has received the most attention is Economic Value Added (EVA™).

Economic Value Added is a financial performance measure developed by the investment consulting firm, Stern Stewart & Co. EVA attempts to measure a firm's economic profit, rather than accounting profit, in a given year. Economic profits assign a cost to the equity capital (the opportunity cost of the funds provided by the shareholders) in addition to the interest cost on the firm's debt—even though accountants recognize only the interest expense as a financing cost when calculating a firm's net income.

For example, assume a firm has total assets of $1,000; 40 percent ($400) is financed with debt, and 60 percent ($600) is financed with equity. If the interest rate on the debt is 5 percent, the firm's interest expense is $20 ($20 = $400 × 0.05) and would be reported in the firm's income statement. However, there would be no cost shown for the equity financing. To compute economic profits, we compute not only the $20 in interest expense but also the opportunity cost of the $600 equity capital invested in the firm. That is, if the shareholders could earn 15 percent on another investment of similar risk (their opportunity cost is, therefore, 15 percent), then we should count this cost just as surely as we do the interest expense. This would involve subtracting not only the $20 in interest but also $90 ($90 = $600 equity × 0.15) as the cost of equity. Thus, the firm has earned an economic profit only if its operating profit exceeds $110 ($20 + $90). Stated as a percentage, the firm must earn at least an 11 percent operating return on its assets (11% = $110 ÷ $1,000) in order to meet the investors' required rate of return.

We can calculate Economic Value Added (EVA)—the value created for the shareholders for a given year—as follows:

$$\text{EVA} = \left(\begin{array}{c}\text{operating return} \\ \text{on assets}\end{array} - \begin{array}{c}\text{cost of} \\ \text{all capital}\end{array}\right) \times \text{total assets} \tag{16}$$

where the cost of capital is the cost of all the firm's capital, both debt and equity. That is, the value created by management is determined by the amount the firm earns on its invested capital relative to the cost of these funds—both debt and equity—and the amount of capital invested in the firm, which are the total assets.[7]

[7]In this book, we will explain how the firm's cost of capital is calculated.

TABLE 3 Davies Inc. Financial Ratio Analysis

FINANCIAL RATIOS		DAVIES INC.	PEER GROUP
1. FIRM LIQUIDITY			
Current ratio	$\dfrac{\text{Current assets}}{\text{Current liabilities}}$	$\dfrac{\$143M}{\$64M} = 2.23$	1.80
Acid-test ratio	$\dfrac{\text{Cash} + \text{Accounts Receivable}}{\text{Current liabilities}}$	$\dfrac{\$20M + \$36M}{\$64M} = .88$	.94
Average collection period	$\dfrac{\text{Accounts receivable}}{\text{Daily credit sales}}$	$\dfrac{\$36M}{\$600M \div 365} = 21.90$	25
Accounts receivable turnover	$\dfrac{\text{Credit sales}}{\text{Accounts receivable}}$	$\dfrac{\$600M}{\$36M} = 16.67$	14.6
Inventory turnover	$\dfrac{\text{Cost of goods sold}}{\text{Inventory}}$	$\dfrac{\$460M}{\$84M} = 5.48$	7.00
2. OPERATING PROFITABILITY			
Operating return on assets	$\dfrac{\text{Operating profit}}{\text{Total assets}}$	$\dfrac{\$75M}{\$438M} = 17.1\%$	17.8
Operating profit margin	$\dfrac{\text{Operating profit}}{\text{Sales}}$	$\dfrac{\$75M}{\$600M} = 12.5\%$	15.5
Total asset turnover	$\dfrac{\text{Sales}}{\text{Total assets}}$	$\dfrac{\$600M}{\$438M} = 1.37$	1.15
Accounts receivable turnover	$\dfrac{\text{Credit sales}}{\text{Accounts receivable}}$	$\dfrac{\$600M}{\$36M} = 16.67$	14.6
Inventory turnover	$\dfrac{\text{Cost of goods sold}}{\text{Inventory}}$	$\dfrac{\$460M}{\$84M} = 5.48$	7.00
Fixed assets turnover	$\dfrac{\text{Sales}}{\text{Fixed assets}}$	$\dfrac{\$600M}{\$295M} = 2.03$	1.75
3. FINANCING DECISIONS			
Debt ratio	$\dfrac{\text{Total debt}}{\text{Total assets}}$	$\dfrac{\$235M}{\$438M} = 53.7\%$	35%
Times interest earned	$\dfrac{\text{Operating income}}{\text{Interest expense}}$	$\dfrac{\$75M}{\$15M} = 5.0X$	7.0X
4. RETURN ON EQUITY			
Return on equity	$\dfrac{\text{Net income}}{\text{Common equity}}$	$\dfrac{\$42M}{\$203M} = 20.7\%$	18%
5. MARKET-VALUE RATIOS			
Price/earnings ratio	$\dfrac{\text{Market price per share}}{\text{Earnings per share}}$	$\dfrac{\$32.00}{\$2.10} = 15.24X$	19.0X
Price/book ratio	$\dfrac{\text{Market price per share}}{\text{Equity book value per share}}$	$\dfrac{\$32.00}{\$10.15} = 3.15X$	3.7X

Continuing with our previous example, assume that our company is earning a 16 percent operating return on its assets (total invested capital). Then the firm's economic value added is $50, calculated as follows:

$$\text{EVA} = \left(\begin{array}{c} \text{operating return} \\ \text{on assets} \end{array} - \begin{array}{c} \text{cost of} \\ \text{all capital} \end{array} \right) \times \text{total assets}$$

$$\text{EVA} = (0.16 - 0.11) \times \$1000 = \$50$$

The foregoing explains the EVA concept in its simplest form. However, computing EVA requires converting a firm's financial statements from an accountant's perspective (GAAP) to an economic book value. This process is much more involved than we will go into here, but the basic premise involved in its computation is the same.

To conclude, with the exception of Economic Value Added, a summary of all the ratios we used to analyze the financial performance of Davies Inc. is provided in Table 3.

Concept Check

1. What determines if a firm is creating or destroying shareholder value?
2. What measures can we use to determine whether a firm is creating shareholder value?
3. What is indicated by a price/book ratio that is greater than 1? Less than 1?
4. How does the information provided by a firm's price/book ratio differ from that provided by its price/earnings ratio?
5. How do the profits shown in an income statement differ from economic profits?
6. What is Economic Value Added? What does it tell you?

The Limitations of Financial Ratio Analysis

 Describe the limitations of financial ratio analysis.

We conclude this chapter by offering several caveats about using financial ratios. We have described how financial ratios can be used to understand a company's financial position. That said, anyone who works with these ratios needs to be aware of the limitations related to their use. The following list includes some of the more important pitfalls you will encounter as you compute and interpret financial ratios:

1. It is sometimes difficult to determine the industry to which a firm belongs when the firm engages in multiple lines of business. In this case, you must select your own set of peer firms and construct your own norms.
2. Published peer group or industry averages are only approximations. They provide the user with general guidelines, rather than scientifically determined averages of the ratios for all, or even a representative sample, of the firms within an industry.
3. An industry average is not necessarily a desirable target ratio or norm. There is nothing magical about an industry norm. At best, an industry average provides an indication as to the financial position of the average firm within the industry. It does not mean it is the ideal or best value for the ratio. For various reasons, a well-managed company might be above the average, whereas another equally good firm might choose to be below the average.

DID YOU GET IT?

CALCULATING DISNEY'S ECONOMIC VALUE ADDED

Disney's Economic Value Added (EVA) is calculated as follows:

$$EVA = \left(\begin{array}{c} \text{operating return} \\ \text{on assets} \end{array} - \begin{array}{c} \text{cost of} \\ \text{all capital} \end{array} \right) \times \text{total assets}$$

$$= (7.08\% - 10\%) \times \$62.497 \text{ billion} = (\$1.824 \text{ billion})$$

Wow! In the year we are calculating Disney's EVA, 2008, the firm destroyed $1.824 billion in shareholder value by earning a rate of return on the firm's assets that was less than the investors' required rate of return.

4. Accounting practices differ widely among firms. For example, different firms choose different methods to depreciate their fixed assets. Differences such as these can make the computed ratios of different firms difficult to compare.

5. Financial ratios can be too high or too low. For example, a current ratio that exceeds the industry norm might signal the presence of excess liquidity, resulting in lower profits relative to the firm's investment in assets. On the other hand, a current ratio that falls below the norm might indicate (1) the possibility that the firm has inadequate liquidity and may at some future date be unable to pay its bills on time, or (2) the firm is managing its accounts receivable and inventories more efficiently than other similar firms.

6. Many firms experience seasonal changes in their operations. As a result, their balance sheet entries and their corresponding ratios will vary with the time of year the statements are prepared. To avoid this problem, an average account balance should be used (one calculated on the basis of several months or quarters during the year) rather than the year-end account balance. For example, an average of the firm's month-end inventory balance might be used to compute its inventory turnover ratio versus a year-end inventory balance.

In spite of their limitations, financial ratios provide us with a very useful tool for assessing a firm's financial condition. We should, however, be aware of their potential weaknesses. In many cases, the "real" value derived from the ratios is that they tell us what additional questions we need to ask about the firm.

Concept Check

1. When comparing a firm to its peers, why is it difficult to determine the industry to which the firm belongs?

2. Why do differences in the accounting practices of firms limit the usefulness of financial ratios?

3. Why should you be careful when comparing a firm with industry norms?

Explain the purpose and importance of financial analysis.

Calculate and use a comprehensive set of measurements to evaluate a company's performance.

Summary

A variety of groups find financial ratios useful. For instance, both managers and shareholders use them to measure and track a company's performance over time. Financial analysts outside of the firm who have an interest in its economic well-being also use financial ratios. An example of this group would be a loan officer of a commercial bank who wishes to determine the creditworthiness of a loan applicant and its ability to pay the interest and principal associated with the loan request.

Financial ratios are the principal tool of financial analysis. Sometimes referred to simply as benchmarks, ratios standardize the financial information of firms so comparisons can be made between firms of varying sizes.

Financial ratios can be used to answer at least five questions: (1) How liquid is the company? (2) Are the company's managers effectively generating profits on the firm's assets? (3) How is the firm financed? (4) Are the firm's managers providing a good return on the capital provided by the shareholders? (5) Are the firm's managers creating or destroying shareholder value?

Two methods can be used to analyze a firm's financial ratios. (1) We can examine the firm's ratios across time (say, for the past 5 years) to compare its current and past performance; and (2) we can compare the firm's ratios with those of other firms. In our example, a peer group was chosen for analyzing the financial position of Davies Inc.

Financial ratios provide a popular way to evaluate a firm's financial performance. However, when evaluating a company's use of its assets (capital) to create firm value, a financial ratio analysis based entirely on the firm's financial statements may not be enough. If we want to understand how the shareholders assess the performance of a company's managers, we can use the market price of the firm's stock relative to its accounting earnings and equity book value.

Economic Value Added (EVA™) provides another approach to evaluate a firm's performance in terms of shareholder value creation. EVA is equal to the return on a company's invested capital less the investors' opportunity cost of the funds times the total amount of the capital invested.

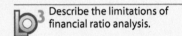

Describe the limitations of financial ratio analysis.

The following are some of the limitations that you will encounter as you compute and interpret financial ratios:

1. It is sometimes difficult to determine an appropriate industry within which to place the firm.
2. Published industry averages are only approximations rather than scientifically determined averages.
3. Accounting practices differ widely among firms and can lead to differences in computed ratios.
4. Some financial ratios can be too high or too low, which makes the results more difficult to interpret.
5. An industry average may not be a desirable target ratio or norm.
6. Many firms experience seasonal business conditions. As a result, the ratios calculated for them will vary with the time of year the statements are prepared.

In spite of their limitations, financial ratios provide us with a very useful tool for assessing a firm's financial condition.

Key Terms

Accounts receivable turnover ratio

Acid-test (quick) ratio

Asset efficiency

Average collection period

Current ratio

Debt ratio

Financial ratios

Fixed asset turnover

Inventory turnover

Liquidity

Operating profit margin

Operating return on assets (OROA)

Price/book ratio

Price/earnings ratio

Return on equity

Times interest earned

Total asset turnover

Review Questions

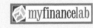

All Review Questions and Study Problems are available in MyFinanceLab.

4-1. Describe the "five-question approach" to using financial ratios.

4-2. Discuss briefly the two perspectives that can be taken when performing a ratio analysis.

4-3. Where can we obtain industry norms?

4-4. What are the limitations of industry average ratios? Discuss briefly.

4-5. What is liquidity, and what is the rationale for its measurement?

4-6. Distinguish between a firm's operating return on assets and operating profit margin.

4-7. Why is a firm's operating return on assets a function of its operating profit margin and total asset turnover?

4-8. What is the difference between a firm's gross profit margin, operating profit margin, and net profit margin?

4-9. What information do the price/earnings ratio and the price/book ratio give us about the firm and its investors?

4-10. Explain what determines a company's return on equity.

4-11. What is Economic Value Added? Why is it used?

4-12. Go to the Web site for IBM at www.ibm.com/investor. Click "Investor tools" and then "Investment guides" for a guide to reading financial statements. How does the guide differ from the presentation in Chapter 3 and this chapter?

Self-Test Problems

ST-1. (*Ratio analysis and short-term liquidity*) Ray's Tool and Supply Company in Austin, Texas, has been expanding its level of operation for the past 2 years. The firm's sales have grown rapidly as a result of the expansion of the Austin economy. However, Ray's is a privately held company, and the only source of available funds is a line of credit with the firm's bank. The company needs to expand its inventories to meet the needs of its growing customer base but also wishes to maintain a current ratio of at least 3. If Ray's current assets are $6 million, and its current ratio is now 4, how much can it expand its inventories (finance the expansion with its line of credit) before its target current ratio is violated?

ST-2. (*Ratio analysis*) The statements for M & G Industries are presented below:

M & G Industries Balance Sheet for December 31, 2009 and 2010

	2009		2010	
Cash		$ 9,000		$ 500
Accounts receivable		12,500		16,000
Inventories		29,000		45,500
Total current assets		$ 50,500		$ 62,000
Land	20,000		26,000	
Buildings and equipment	70,000		100,000	
Less accumulated depreciation	(28,000)		(38,000)	
Total fixed assets		$ 62,000		$ 88,000
Total assets		$ 112,500		$150,000
Accounts payable		$ 10,500		$ 22,000
Short-term bank notes		17,000		47,000
Total current liabilities		$ 27,500		$ 69,000
Long-term debt		28,750		22,950
Common stock		31,500		31,500
Retained earnings		24,750		26,550
Total debt and equity		$ 112,500		$150,000

M & G Industries Income Statement for the Years Ended December 31, 2009 and 2010

	2009		2010	
Sales (all credit)		$125,000		$160,000
Cost of goods sold		75,000		96,000
Gross profit		$ 50,000		$ 64,000
Operating expenses				
Fixed cash operating expenses	$ 21,000		$ 21,000	
Variable operating expenses	$ 12,500		16,000	
Depreciation	4,500		10,000	
Total operating expenses		$ 38,000		$ 47,000
Earnings before interest and taxes		$ 12,000		$ 17,000
Interest expense		$ 3,000		$ 6,100
Earnings before taxes		$ 9,000		10,900
Taxes		$ 4,500		$ 5,450
Net income		$ 4,500		$ 5,450

a. Based on the preceding statements, complete the following table:

M & G Industries Ratio Analysis

	INDUSTRY AVERAGES	ACTUAL 2009	ACTUAL 2010
Current ratio	1.80		
Acid-test ratio	0.70		
Average collection period	37.00		
Inventory turnover	2.50		
Debt ratio	58.0%		
Times interest earned	3.80		
Operating profit margin	10.0%		
Total asset turnover	1.14		
Fixed asset turnover	1.40		
Operating return on assets	11.4%		
Return on common equity	9.5%		

b. Evaluate the firm's financial position at the end of 2010 in terms of liquidity, operating return on assets, financing, and return on equity.

c. If in 2010 the firm has 5,000 shares of common stock outstanding selling for $15, what is the (1) firm's earnings per share, (2) price/earnings ratio, and (3) price/book ratio?

Study Problems

4-1. (*Ratio analysis*) Brashear Inc. currently has $2,145,000 in current assets and $858,000 in current liabilities. The company's managers want to increase the firm's inventory, which will be financed by a short-term note with the bank. What level of inventories can the firm carry without its current ratio falling below 2.0?

4-2. (*Ratio analysis*) The Allen Corporation had sales in 2008 of $65 million, total assets of $42 million, and total liabilities of $20 million. The interest rate on the company's debt is 6 percent and its tax rate is 30 percent. The operating profit margin was 12 percent. What was the 2008 operating income and net income? What was operating return on assets and return on equity? Assume that interest must be paid on all of the debt.

4-3. (*Ratio analysis*) Last year, Davies Inc. had sales of $400,000, with a cost of goods sold of $112,000. The firm's operating expenses were $130,000, and its increase in retained earnings was $58,000. There are currently 22,000 common stock shares outstanding and the firm pays a $1.60 dividend per share.

a. Assuming the firm's earnings are taxed at 34 percent, construct the firm's income statement.

b. Compute the firm's operating profit margin.

c. What was the times interest earned?

4-4. (*Ratio analysis*) Greene Inc.'s balance sheet shows a stockholders' equity value of $750,500. The firm's earnings per share was $3, resulting in a price/earnings ratio of 12.25. There are 50,000 shares of common stock outstanding. What is the price/book ratio? What does this indicate about how shareholders view Greene Inc.?

4-5. (*Ratio analysis*) The Mitchem Marble Company has a target current ratio of 2.0 but has experienced some difficulties financing its expanding sales in the past few months. At present the firm has a current ratio of 2.5 and current assets of $2.5 million. If Mitchem expands its receivables and inventories using its short-term line of credit, how much additional short-term funding can it borrow before its current ratio standard is reached?

4-6. (*Ratio analysis*) The balance sheet and income statement for the J. P. Robard Mfg. Company are as follows:

Balance Sheet ($000)

Cash	$ 500
Accounts receivable	2,000
Inventories	1,000
Current assets	3,500
Net fixed assets	4,500
Total assets	$ 8,000
Accounts payable	$ 1,100
Accrued expenses	600
Short-term notes payable	300
Current liabilities	$ 2,000
Long-term debt	2,000
Owners' equity	4,000
Total liabilities and owners' equity	$ 8,000

Income Statement ($000)

Net sales (all credit)	$ 8,000
Cost of goods sold	(3,300)
Gross profit	4,700
Operating expenses	
(includes $500 depreciation)	(3,000)
Operating income	$ 1,700
Interest expense	(367)
Earnings before taxes	$ 1,333
Income taxes (40%)	(533)
Net income	$ 800

Calculate the following ratios:

Current ratio	Operating return on assets
Times interest earned	Debt ratio
Inventory turnover	Average collection period
Total asset turnover	Fixed asset turnover
Operating profit margin	Return on equity

4-7. (*Analyzing operating return on assets*) The R. M. Smithers Corporation earned an operating profit margin of 10 percent based on sales of $10 million and total assets of $5 million last year.

a. What was Smithers' total asset turnover ratio?

b. During the coming year the company president has set a goal of attaining a total asset turnover of 3.5. How much must firm sales rise, other things being the same, for the goal to be achieved? (State your answer in both dollars and percentage increase in sales.)

c. What was Smithers' operating return on assets last year? Assuming the firm's operating profit margin remains the same, what will the operating return on assets be next year if the total asset turnover goal is achieved?

4-8. (*Using financial ratios*) The Brenmar Sales Company had a gross profit margin (gross profits ÷ sales) of 30 percent and sales of $9 million last year. Seventy-five percent of the firm's sales are on credit and the remainder are cash sales. Brenmar's current assets equal $1.5 million, its current liabilities equal $300,000, and it has $100,000 in cash plus marketable securities.

a. If Brenmar's accounts receivable are $562,500, what is its average collection period?

b. If Brenmar reduces its average collection period to 20 days, what will be its new level of accounts receivable?

c. Brenmar's inventory turnover ratio is 9 times. What is the level of Brenmar's inventories?

4-9. (*Ratio analysis*) Using Pamplin Inc.'s financial statements shown here:

a. Compute the following ratios for both 2009 and 2010.

	INDUSTRY NORM	2009	2010
Current ratio	5.00		
Acid-test (quick) ratio	3.00		
Inventory turnover	2.20		
Average collection period	90.00		
Debt ratio	0.33		
Times interest earned	7.00		
Total asset turnover	0.75		
Fixed asset turnover	1.00		
Operating profit margin	20%		
Return on common equity	9%		

b. How liquid is the firm?

c. Are its managers generating an adequate operating profit on the firm's assets?

d. How is the firm financing its assets?

e. Are its managers generating a good return on equity?

Pamplin Inc. Balance Sheet at 12/31/2009 and 12/31/2010

ASSETS

	2009		2010	
Cash		$ 200		$ 150
Accounts receivable		450		425
Inventory		550		625
Current assets		$ 1,200		$ 1,200
Plant and equipment	$ 2,200		$ 2,600	
Less accumulated depreciation	(1,000)		(1,200)	
Net plant and equipment		$ 1,200		$ 1,400
Total assets		$ 2,400		$ 2,600

Liabilities and Owners' Equity

	2009		2010	
Accounts payable		$ 200		$ 150
Notes payable—current (9%)		0		150
Current liabilities		$ 200		$ 300
Bonds (8.33% interest)		600		600
Total debt		$ 800		$ 900
Owners' equity				
Common stock	$ 300		$ 300	
Paid-in capital	600		600	
Retained earnings	700		800	
Total owners' equity		$ 1,600		$ 1,700
Total liabilities and owners' equity		$ 2,400		$ 2,600

Pamplin Inc. Income Statement for Years Ending 12/31/2009 and 12/31/2010

		2009		2010
Sales (all credit)		$1,200		$1,450
Cost of goods sold		700		850
Gross profit		$ 500		$ 600
Operating expenses	30		40	
Depreciation	220	250	200	240
Operating income		$ 250		$ 360
Interest expense		50		64
Net income before taxes		$ 200		$ 296
Taxes (40%)		80		118
Net income		$ 120		$ 178

4-10. (*Financial ratios—investment analysis*) The annual sales for Salco Inc. were $4.5 million last year. The firm's end-of-year balance sheet was as follows:

Current assets	$ 500,000	Liabilities	$1,000,000	
Net fixed assets	1,500,000	Owners' equity	1,000,000	
	$2,000,000		$2,000,000	

The firm's income statement for the year was as follows:

Sales	$4,500,000
Less cost of goods sold	(3,500,000)
Gross profit	$1,000,000
Less operating expenses	(500,000)
Operating income	$ 500,000
Less interest expense	(100,000)
Earnings before taxes	$ 400,000
Less taxes (50%)	(200,000)
Net income	$ 200,000

    a. Calculate Salco's total asset turnover, operating profit margin, and operating return on assets.

    b. Salco plans to renovate one of its plants, which will require an added investment in plant and equipment of $1 million. The firm will maintain its present debt ratio of .5 when financing the new investment and expects sales to remain constant. The operating profit margin will rise to 13 percent. What will be the new operating return on assets for Salco after the plant's renovation?

    c. Given that the plant renovation in part b occurs and Salco's interest expense rises by $50,000 per year, what will be the return earned on the common stockholders' investment? Compare this rate of return with that earned before the renovation.

4-11. (*Financial analysis*) The T. P. Jarmon Company manufactures and sells a line of exclusive sportswear. The firm's sales were $600,000 for the year just ended, and its total assets exceeded $400,000. The company was started by Mr. Jarmon just 10 years ago and has been profitable every year since its inception. The chief financial officer for the firm, Brent Vehlim, has decided to seek a line of credit from the firm's bank totaling $80,000. In the past, the company has relied on its suppliers to finance a large part of its needs for inventory. However, in recent months tight money conditions have led the firm's suppliers to offer sizable cash discounts to speed up payments for purchases. Mr. Vehlim wants to use the line of credit to replace a large portion of the firm's payables during the summer, which is the firm's peak seasonal sales period.

The firm's two most recent balance sheets were presented to the bank in support of its loan request. In addition, the firm's income statement for the year just ended was provided. These statements are found in the following tables:

T. P. Jarmon Company, Balance Sheet for 12/31/2009 and 12/31/2010

	2009	2010
Cash	$ 15,000	$ 14,000
Marketable securities	6,000	6,200
Accounts receivable	42,000	33,000
Inventory	51,000	84,000
Prepaid rent	1,200	1,100
Total current assets	$ 115,200	$ 138,300
Net plant and equipment	286,000	270,000
Total assets	$ 401,200	$ 408,300
Accounts payable	$ 48,000	$ 57,000
Notes payable	15,000	13,000
Accruals	6,000	5,000
Total current liabilities	$ 69,000	$ 75,000
Long-term debt	160,000	150,000
Common stockholders' equity	172,200	183,300
Total liabilities and equity	$ 401,200	$ 408,300

T. P. Jarmon Company, Income Statement for the Year Ended 12/31/2010

Sales (all credit)		$ 600,000
Less cost of goods sold		460,000
Gross profit		$ 140,000
Less operating and interest expenses		
General and administrative	$ 30,000	
Interest	10,000	
Depreciation	30,000	
Total		70,000
Earnings before taxes		$ 70,000
Less taxes		27,100
Net income available to common stockholders		$ 42,900
Less cash dividends		31,800
Change in retained earnings		$ 11,100

Jan Fama, associate credit analyst for the Merchants National Bank of Midland, Michigan, was assigned the task of analyzing Jarmon's loan request.

   a. Calculate the financial ratios for 2010 corresponding to the industry norms provided as follows:

RATIO	NORM
Current ratio	1.8
Acid-test ratio	0.9
Debt ratio	0.5
Times interest earned	10.0
Average collection period	20.0
Inventory turnover (based on cost of goods sold)	7.0
Return on common equity	12.0%
Operating return on assets	16.8%
Operating profit margin	14.0%
Total asset turnover	1.20
Fixed asset turnover	1.80

   b. Which of the ratios reported in the industry norms do you feel should be most crucial in determining whether the bank should extend the line of credit?
   c. Prepare Jarmon's statement of cash flows for the year ended December 31, 2010. Interpret your findings.
   d. Use the information provided by the financial ratios and the cash flow statement to decide if you would support making the loan.

4-12. (*Economic Value Added*) Stegemoller Inc.'s managers want to evaluate the firm's prior-year performance in terms of its contribution to shareholder value. This past year, the firm earned an operating income return on investment of 12 percent, compared to an industry norm of 11 percent. It has been estimated that the firm's investors have an opportunity cost on their funds of 14 percent. The firm's total assets for the year were $100 million. Compute the amount of economic value created or destroyed by the firm. How does your finding support or fail to support what you would conclude using ratio analysis to evaluate the firm's performance?

4-13. (*Ratio analysis*)

   a. Go to www.investor.reuters.com. (You will need to sign up for a free membership before being able to access all the information on the site.) Type in the symbol for Starbucks (SBUX) in the "Quote" box and then click "Go." Click the "Financial Statements" link on the left side of the Web page and examine Starbucks' financial statements.
   b. After becoming familiar with the financial statements for Starbucks, click on the "Ratios" link in the left margin to see a large number of ratios that have been calculated for the company. There are many more ratios than what we presented, and some have been calculated differently than we did—a problem that occurs frequently when using different sources of ratios. Which ratios are familiar to you? How have the ratios changed for Starbucks Corporation over the past 5 years (look at the 5-year averages)?

91

4-14. Being able to identify an industry to use for benchmarking your firm's results with similar companies is frequently not easy. Choose a type of business and go to www.naics.com. This Web site allows you to do a free search for the NAICS (North American Industry Classification System, pronounced Nakes) number for different types of businesses. Choose keywords such as "athletic shoes" or "auto dealers" and others to see to which industry they have been assigned.

4-15. (*Market-value ratios*) Bremmer Industries has a price per earnings ratio of 16.29X.

    a. If Bremmer's earnings per share is $1.35, what is the price per share of Bremmer's stock?

    b. Using the price per share you found in part (a), determine the price per book ratio if Bremmer's equity book value per share is $9.58.

4-16. (*Financing decisions*) Ellie's Electronics Incorporated has total assets of $63 million and total debt of $42 million. The company also has operating income of $21 million with interest expenses of $6 million.

    a. What is Ellie's debt ratio?

    b. What is Ellie's times interest earned?

    c. Based on the information above, would you recommend to Ellie's management that the firm is in a strong enough position to assume more debt and increase interest expense to $9 million?

4-17. (*Economic value added*) Callaway Concrete uses Economic Value Added as a financial performance measure. Callaway has $240 million in assets, and the firm has financed its assets with 37% equity and 63% debt with an interest rate of 6%. The firm's opportunity cost on its funds is 12%, while the operating return on the firm's assets is 14%.

    a. What is the Economic Value Added created or destroyed by Callaway Concrete?

    b. What does Economic Value Added measure?

Mini Case

Go to http://finance.yahoo.com/and locate current financial information for GM and Toyota, both in terms of the company's current financial statements and stock market prices. With this information:

    a. Compute the financial ratios for both firms for the most recent year, and evaluate the relative performance of the two firms in the following areas:

        1. Liquidity

        2. Operating profitability

        3. Financing practices

        4. Return on the shareholders' investment

    b. What is each firm's price/earnings ratio and market/book ratio? What do these ratios tell you?

    c. Assume that the cost of capital (investors' required rate of return) is 8 percent for both companies. Calculate the EVA for each company. Interpret your findings.

Self-Test Solutions

SS-1. Note that the current ratio for Ray's Tool and Supply Company before its inventory expansion is as follows:

current ratio = $6,000,000/current liabilities = 4

Thus, the firm's level of current liabilities is $1.5 million. If the expansion in inventories is financed entirely with borrowed funds, then the change in inventories is equal to the change in the firm's current liabilities. Thus, the firm's current ratio after the expansion can be defined as follows:

$$\text{current ratio} = \frac{\$6,000,000 + \text{change in inventory}}{\$1,500,000 + \text{change in inventory}} = 3$$

Note that we set the new current ratio equal to the firm's target of 3. Solving for the change in inventory in the equation, we determine that the firm can expand its inventories by $750,000, finance the expansion with current liabilities, and still maintain its target current ratio.

SS-2.

a. M & G Industries Ratio Analysis

	INDUSTRY AVERAGES	ACTUAL 2009	ACTUAL 2010
Current ratio	1.80	1.84	0.90
Acid-test ratio	0.70	0.78	0.24
Average collection period (based on a 365-day year and end-of-year figures)	37.00	36.50	36.50
Inventory turnover	2.50	2.59	2.11
Debt ratio	58%	50%	61.3%
Times interest earned	3.80	4.00	2.79
Operating profit margin	10%	9.6%	10.6%
Total asset turnover	1.14	1.11	1.07
Fixed asset turnover	1.40	2.02	1.82
Operating return on assets	11.4%	10.67%	11.3%
Return on common equity	9.5%	8.0%	9.4%

b. M & G's liquidity is poor, as suggested by its low current ratio and acid-test ratio in 2010; also, the firm's inventories are turning over slowly compared to the industry norm. In 2010, M & G's managers are doing a satisfactory job of generating profits on the firm's operating assets, as indicated by the operating return on assets. Note that the operating return on assets in 2010 is about the same as the industry average, owing to a slightly above-average operating profit margin combined with a slightly below-average total asset turnover ratio. The problem with the total asset turnover ratio comes from slow inventory turnover. M & G has increased its use of debt to the point of using slightly more debt than the average company in the industry. As a result, the firm's coverage of interest has decreased to a point well below the industry norm.

c.

1. $\text{Earnings per share} = \dfrac{\text{net income}}{\text{number of shares outstanding}} = \dfrac{\$5,450}{5,000} = \$1.09$

2. $\text{Price/earnings ratio} = \dfrac{\text{market price share}}{\text{earnings per share}} = \dfrac{\$15.00}{\$1.09} = 13.76$

3. $\text{Price/book ratio} = \dfrac{\text{market price share}}{\text{book value per share}} = \dfrac{\$15.00}{\$11.61} = 1.29$

where

$$\text{book value per share} = \dfrac{\text{total book equity value}}{\text{number of shares outstanding}}$$

$$= \dfrac{\$31,500 + \$26,550}{5,000 \text{ shares}}$$

$$= \dfrac{\$58,050}{5,000 \text{ shares}} = \$11.61$$

The Time Value of Money

From Chapter 5 of *Foundations of Finance*, 7/e. Arthur J. Keown. John D. Martin. J. William Petty. Copyright © 2011 by Pearson Education. Published by Prentice Hall. All rights reserved.

The Time Value
of Money

Learning Objectives

After reading this chapter, you should be able to:

LO 1 Explain **the mechanics of compounding, that is, how money grows over time when it is invested.**

LO 2 Discuss **the relationship between compounding and bringing the value of money back to the present.**

LO 3 Understand **annuities.**

LO 4 Determine **the future or present value of a sum when there are nonannual compounding periods.**

LO 5 Determine **the present value of an uneven stream of payments and understand perpetuities.**

LO 6 Explain **how the international setting complicates the time value of money.**

In business, there is probably no other single concept with more power or applications than that of the time value of money. In his landmark book, *A History of Interest Rates*, Sidney Homer noted that if $1,000 was invested for 400 years at 8 percent interest, it would grow to $23 quadrillion—that would work out to approximately $5 million per person on earth. He was not giving a plan to make the world rich but effectively pointing out the power of the time value of money.

The time value of money is certainly not a new concept. Benjamin Franklin had a good understanding of how it worked when he left £1,000 each to Boston and Philadelphia. With the gift, he left instructions that the cities were to lend the money, charging the going interest rate, to worthy apprentices. Then, after the money had been invested in this way for 100 years, they were to use a portion of the investment to build something of benefit to the city and hold some back for the future. Two hundred years later, Franklin's Boston gift resulted in the construction of the Franklin Union, has helped countless medical students with loans, and still has over $3 million left in the account. Philadelphia, likewise, has reaped a significant reward from his gift with its portion of the gift growing to over $2 million. Bear in mind that all this has come from a gift of £2,000 with some serious help from the time value of money.

The power of the time value of money can also be illustrated through a story Andrew Tobias tells in his book *Money Angles*. There he tells of a peasant who wins a chess tournament put on by the king. The king asks the peasant what he would like as the prize. The peasant answers that he would like for his village one piece of grain to be placed on the first square of his chessboard, two pieces of grain on the second square, four pieces on the third, eight on the fourth, and so forth. The king, thinking he was getting off easy, pledged on his word of honor that it would be done. Unfortunately for the king, by the time all 64 squares on the chessboard were filled, there were 18.5 million trillion grains of wheat on the board—the kernels were compounding at a rate of 100 percent over the 64 squares of the chessboard. Needless to say, no one in the village ever went hungry; in fact, that is so much wheat that if each kernel were one-quarter inch long (quite frankly, I have no idea how long a kernel of wheat is, but Andrew Tobias's guess is one-quarter inch), if laid end to end, they could stretch to the sun and back 391,320 times.

Mira.com/Terry Smith

Understanding the techniques of compounding and moving money through time is critical to almost every business decision. It will help you to understand such varied things as how stocks and bonds are valued, how to determine the value of a new project, how much you should save for your children's education, and how much your mortgage payments will be.

In this book, we focus on determining the value of the firm and the desirability of the investments it considers making. A key concept that underlies this material is the time value of money; that is, a dollar today is worth more than a dollar received a year from now. Intuitively this idea is easy to understand. We are all familiar with the concept of interest. This concept illustrates what economists call an opportunity cost of passing up the earning potential of a dollar today. This opportunity cost is the time value of money.

To evaluate and compare investment proposals, we need to examine how dollar values might accrue from accepting these proposals. To do this, all the dollar values must first be comparable. In other words, we must move all dollar flows back to the present or out to a common future date. An understanding of the time value of money is essential, therefore, to an understanding of financial management, whether basic or advanced.

Compound Interest and Future Value

 Explain the mechanics of compounding, that is, how money grows over time when it is invested.

We begin our study of the time value of money with some basic tools for visualizing the time pattern of cash flows. While timelines seem simple at first glance, they can be a tremendous help for more complicated problems.

Using Timelines to Visualize Cash Flows

As a first step in visualizing cash flows, we can construct a timeline, a linear representation of the timing of cash flows. A timeline identifies the timing and amount of a stream of cash flows—both cash received and cash spent—along with the interest rate it earns. Timelines are a critical first step used by financial analysts to solve financial problems. We will refer to them often throughout this text.

To illustrate how to construct a timeline, consider the following example, where we receive annual cash flows over the course of four years. The following timeline shows our cash inflows and outflows from time period 0 (the present) until the end of year 4:

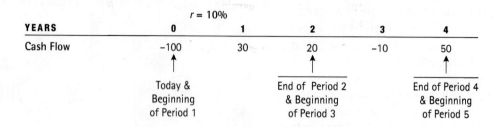

For our purposes, time periods are identified on the top of the timeline, and in this example, the time periods are measured in years, which are indicated on the far left of the timeline. Thus, time period 0 is both today and the beginning of the first year. The dollar amount of the cash flow received or spent at each time period is shown below the timeline. Positive values represent *cash inflows*. Negative values represent *cash outflows*. For example, in the timeline shown, a $100 cash outflow occurs today, or at time 0, followed by cash inflows of $30 and $20 at the end of years 1 and 2, a negative cash flow (a cash outflow) of $10 at the end of year 3, and finally a cash inflow of $50 at the end of year 4.

The units of measurement on the timeline are time periods and are typically expressed in years, but could be expressed as months, days, or any unit of time. However, for now, let's assume we're looking at cash flows that occur annually. Thus, the distance between 0 and 1 represents the period between today and the end of the first year. Consequently, time period 0 indicates today, while time period 1 represents the end of the first year, which is also the beginning of the second year. (You can think of it as being both the last second of the first year and the first second of the second year.) The interest rate, which is 10% in this example, is listed above the timeline.

In this chapter and throughout the text, we will often refer to the idea of moving money through time. Because this concept is probably not familiar to everyone, we should take a moment to explain it. Most business investments involve investing money today. Then, in subsequent years, the investment produces cash that comes back to the business. To evaluate an investment, you need to compare the amount of money the investment requires today with the amount of money the investment will return to you in the future, and adjust these numbers for the fact that a dollar today is worth more than a dollar in the future. Timelines simplify solving time value of money problems, and they are not just for beginners; experienced financial analysts use them as well. In fact, the more complex the problem you're trying to solve, the more valuable a timeline will be in terms of helping you visualize exactly what needs to be done.

Most of us encounter the concept of compound interest at an early age. Anyone who has ever had a savings account or purchased a government savings bond has received compound interest. **Compound interest** occurs when *interest paid on the investment during the first period is added to the principal; then, during the second period, interest is earned on this new sum.*

For example, suppose we place $100 in a savings account that pays 6 percent interest, compounded annually. How will our savings grow? At the end of the first year we have earned 6 percent, or $6 on our initial deposit of $100, giving us a total of $106 in our savings account, thus,

value at the end of year 1 = present value $\times$ (1 + interest rate)
$$= \$100(1 + 0.06)$$
$$= \$100(1.06)$$
$$= \$106$$

Carrying these calculations one period further, we find that we now earn the 6 percent interest on a principal of $106, which means we earn $6.36 in interest during the second

compound interest the situation in which interest paid on an investment during the first period is added to the principal. During the second period, interest is earned on the original principal plus the interest earned during the first period.

year. Why do we earn more interest during the second year than we did during the first? Simply because we now earn interest on the sum of the original principal and the interest we earned in the first year. In effect we are now earning interest on interest; this is the concept of compound interest. Examining the mathematical formula illustrating the earning of interest in the second year, we find

value at the end of year 2 = value at the end of year 1 $\times (1 + r)$

where r = the annual interest (or discount) rate

which, for our example, gives

$$\text{value at the end of year 2} = \$106 \times (1.06)$$
$$= \$112.36$$

Looking back, we can see that the **future value** at the end of year 1, or $106, is actually equal to the present value times $(1 + r)$, or $100(1 + 0.06)$. Moving forward to year 2 we find,

$$\text{value at the end of year 2} = \text{present value} \times (1 + r) \times (1 + r)$$
$$= \text{present value} \times (1 + r)^2$$

Carrying this forward into the third year, we find that we enter the year with $112.36 and we earn 6 percent, or $6.74 in interest, giving us a total of $119.10 in our savings account. This can be expressed as

$$\text{value at the end of year 3} = \text{present value} \times (1 + r) \times (1 + r) \times (1 + r)$$
$$= \text{present value} \times (1 + r)^3$$

By now a pattern is becoming apparent. We can generalize this formula to illustrate the future value of our investment if it is compounded annually at a rate of r for n years to be

future value = present value $\times (1 + r)^n$

Letting FV_n stand for the future value at the end of n periods and PV stand for the present value, we can rewrite this equation as,

$$FV_n = PV(1 + r)^n \qquad (1)$$

We also refer to $(1 + r)^n$ as the **future value factor**. Thus, to find the future value of a dollar amount, all you need to do is multiply that dollar amount times the appropriate future value factor,

future value = present value $\times$ (future value factor)

where future value factor = $(1 + r)^n$.

Figure 1 illustrates how this investment of $100 would continue to grow for the first 20 years at a compound interest rate of 6 percent. Notice how the amount of interest earned annually increases each year. Again, the reason is that each year interest is received on the sum of the original investment plus any interest earned in the past. The situation in which interest is earned on interest that was earned in the past is referred to as compound interest. *If you only earned interest on your initial investment*, it would be referred to as **simple interest**.

When we examine the relationship between the number of years an initial investment is compounded for and its future value, as shown graphically in Figure 2, we see that we can increase the future value of an investment by either increasing the number of years for which we let it compound or by compounding it at a higher interest rate. We can also see this from equation (1) because an increase in either r or n while the present value is held constant results in an increase in the future value.

future value the amount to which your investment will grow.

future value factor the value of $(1 + r)^n$ used as a multiple to calculate an amount's future value.

simple interest if you only earned interest on your initial investment it would be referred to as simple interest.

FIGURE 1 $100 Compounded at 6 Percent Over 20 Years

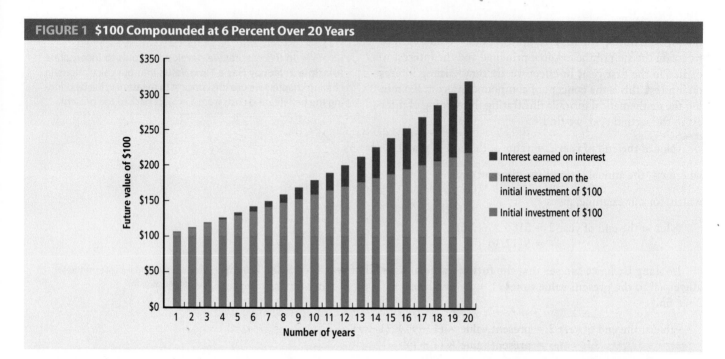

FIGURE 2 The Future Value of $100 Initially Deposited and Compounded at 0, 5, 10, and 15 Percent

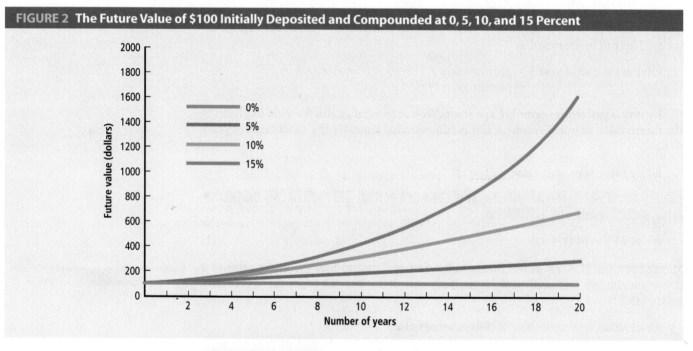

EXAMPLE 1

If we place $1,000 in a savings account paying 5 percent interest compounded annually, how much will our account accrue to in 10 years? Substituting present value = $1,000, r = 5 percent, and n = 10 years into equation (1), we get

$$\text{future value} = \text{present value} \times (1 + r)^n \qquad (1)$$
$$FV_n = PV(1 + r)^n$$
$$= \$1,000(1 + 0.05)^{10}$$
$$= \$1,000(1.62889)$$
$$= \$1,628.89$$

Thus, at the end of 10 years we will have $1,628.89 in our savings account.

Techniques for Moving Money Through Time

There are three different approaches that you can use to solve a time value of money problem. The first is to simply do the math. Financial calculators are a second alternative, and there are a number of them that do a good job of solving time value of money problems. Based on many years of experience, the Texas Instruments BA II Plus or the Hewlett-Packard 10BII calculators would be excellent choices. Finally, spreadsheets can move money through time, and in the real world, they are without question the tool of choice. Now let's take a look at all three alternatives.

Mathematical Calculations   If we want to calculate the future value of an amount of money, the mathematical calculations are relatively straightforward. However, as we will see, time value of money calculations are easier using a financial calculator or spreadsheet. Those are the chosen methods in the real world.

EXAMPLE 2

If we invest $500 in a bank where it will earn 8 percent interest compounded annually, how much will it be worth at the end of 7 years? Plugging in $n = 7$, $r = 8$ percent, and present value = $500 into equation (1), we find

$$\text{future value} = \text{present value} \times (1 + r)^n \tag{1}$$
$$= \$500(1 + 0.08)^7$$
$$= \$500(1.71382)$$
$$= \$856.91$$

Thus, we will have $856.91 at the end of 7 years.

   In the future we will find several uses for equation (1); not only can we find the future value of an investment, but we can also solve for the present value, r, or n.

Using a Financial Calculator   Before we review the use of the financial calculator, let's review the five "time value of money" keys on a financial calculator. Although the specific keystrokes used to perform time value of money calculations differ slightly when using financial calculators made by different companies, the symbols used are basically the same. Below are the keystrokes as they appear on a Texas Instruments BA II Plus calculator.

MENU KEY	DESCRIPTION
Menu Keys we will use in this chapter include:	
N	Stores (or calculates) the total number of payments or compounding periods.
I/Y	Stores (or calculates) the interest (or discount or growth) rate per period.
PV	Stores (or calculates) the present value of a cash flow (or series of cash flows).
FV	Stores (or calculates) the future value, that is, the dollar amount of a final cash flow (or the compound value of a single flow or series of cash flows).
PMT	Stores (or calculates) the dollar amount of each annuity (or equal) payment deposited or received.

The keys shown here correspond to the TI BA II Plus calculator. Other financial calculators have essentially the same keys. They are simply labeled a little differently. We should stop and point out that the labels on the keys of financial calculators are slightly different than what we have been using in our mathematical formulas. For example, we have used a lower case n to refer to the number of compounding periods, whereas an uppercase N appears on the Texas Instruments BA II Plus calculator. Likewise, the I/Y key refers to the rate of interest per period, whereas we have used r. Some financial calculators also have a CPT key, which stands for "compute." It is simply the key you press when you want the calculator to begin solving your problem. Finally, the PMT key refers to a fixed payment received or paid each period.

101

At this point you might be wondering exactly why we are using different symbols in this book than are used on calculators. The answer is that, unfortunately, the symbols used by the different companies that design and make financial calculators are not consistent. The symbols in Microsoft Excel are somewhat different as well.

An important thing to remember when using a financial calculator is that cash outflows (investments you make rather than receive) generally have to be entered as negative numbers. In effect, a financial calculator sees money as "leaving your hands" and therefore taking on a *negative* sign when you invest it. The calculator then sees the money "returning to your hands" and therefore taking on a *positive* sign after you've earned interest on it. Also, every calculator operates a bit differently with respect to entering variables. Needless to say, it is a good idea to familiarize yourself with exactly how your calculator functions.[1]

Once you've entered all the variables you know, including entering a zero for any variable with a value of zero, you can let the calculator do the math for you. If you own a Texas Instruments BA II Plus calculator, press the compute key (CPT), followed by the key corresponding to the unknown variable you're trying to determine. With a Hewlett-Packard calculator, once the known variables are entered, you need only press the key corresponding to the final variable to calculate its value.

A good starting place when working a problem is to write down all the variables you know. Then assign a value of zero to any variables that are not included in the problem. Once again, make sure that the sign you give to the different variables reflects the direction of the cash flow.

Calculator Tips—Getting It Right   Calculators are pretty easy to use. But there are some common mistakes that are often made. So, before you take a crack at solving a problem using a financial calculator ensure that you take the following steps:

1. **Set your calculator to one payment per year.** Some financial calculators use monthly payments as the default. Change it to annual payments. Then consider n to be the number of periods and r the interest rate per period.

2. **Set your calculator to display at least four decimal places or to floating decimal place (nine decimal places).** Most calculators are preset to display only two decimal places. Because interest rates are so small, change your decimal setting to at least four.

3. **Set your calculator to the "end" mode.** Your calculator will assume cash flows occur at the end of each time period.

When you're ready to work a problem, remember:

1. **Every problem must have at least one positive and one negative number.** The pre-programming within the calculator assumes that you are analyzing problems in which money goes out (outflows) and comes in (inflows) so you have to be sure to enter the sign appropriately. If you are using a BA II Plus calculator and get an "Error 5" message, that means you are solving for either r or n and you input both the present and future values as positive numbers—correct that and re-solve the problem.

2. **You must enter a zero for any variable that isn't used in a problem, or you have to clear the calculator before beginning a new problem.** If you don't clear your calculator or enter a value for one of the variables, your calculator won't assume that that variable is zero. Instead, your calculator will assume it carries the same number as it did during the previous problem. So be sure to clear out the memory (CLR, TVM) or enter zeros for variables not included in the problem.

3. **Enter the interest rate as a percent, not a decimal.** That means 10% must be entered as 10 rather than 0.10.

Two popular financial calculators are the Texas Instruments BA II Plus (TI BA II Plus) and the Hewlett-Packard 10BII (HP 10BII). If you're using one of these calculators and encounter

---

[1] Appendix in the back of the book provides a tutorial that covers both the Texas Instruments BA II Plus and the Hewlett-Packard 10BII calculators

any problems, take a look at Appendix A at the end of the book. It provides a tutorial for both of these calculators.

Spreadsheets   Practically speaking, most time value of money calculations are now done on computers with the help of spreadsheet software. Although there are competing spreadsheet programs, the most popular is Microsoft Corporation's Excel®. Just like financial calculators, Excel has "built-in" functions that make it really easy to do future value calculations.

Excel Tips—Getting It Right

1. **Take advantage of the formula help that Excel offers.** All Excel functions are set up the same way: First, with the "=" sign; second, with the function's name (for example, FV or PV); and third, with the inputs into that function enclosed in parentheses. The following, for example, is how the future value function looks:

   =FV(rate,nper,pmt,pv)

   When you begin typing in your Excel function in a spreadsheet cell (that is, a box where you enter a single piece of data), all the input variables will appear at the top of the spreadsheet in their proper order so you will know what variable must be entered next. For example, =FV(**rate**,nper,pmt,pv,type) will come into view, with **rate** appearing in bold because rate is the next variable to enter. This means you don't really need to memorize the functions because they will appear when you begin entering them.

2. **If you're lost, click on "Help."** On the top row of your Excel spreadsheet you'll notice the word *Help* listed—another way to get to the help link is to hit the F1 button. When you're lost, the help link is your friend. Click on it and enter "PV" or "FV" in the search bar, and the program will explain how to calculate each. All of the other financial calculations you might want to find can be found the same way.

3. **Be careful about rounding the *r* variable.** For example, suppose you're dealing with the interest rate 6.99% compounded monthly. This means you will need to enter the interest rate per month, which is =6.99%/12, and since you are performing division in the cell, you need to put an "=" sign before the division is performed. Don't round the result of 0.0699/12 to 0.58 and enter 0.58 as *r*. Instead, enter =6.99%/12 or as a decimal =0.0699/12 for *r*.

   Also, you'll notice that while the inputs using an Excel spreadsheet are almost identical to those on a financial calculator, the interest rate in Excel is entered *either* as a decimal (0.06) *or* a whole number followed by a % sign (6%) rather than a 6 (as you would enter if you were using a financial calculator).

4. **Don't let the Excel notation fool you.** Excel doesn't use *r* or I/Y to note the interest rate. Instead, it uses the term *rate*. Don't let this bother you. All of these notations refer to the same thing—the interest rate. Similarly, Excel doesn't use *n* to denote the number of periods. Instead, it uses *nper*. Once again, don't let this bother you. Both *n* and *nper* refer to the number of periods.

5. **Don't be thrown off by the "type" input variable.** You'll notice that Excel asks for a new variable that we haven't talked about yet, "type." Again, if you type "=FV(" in a cell, "=FV(**rate**,nper,pmt,pv,type)" will immediately appear just below that cell. Don't let this new variable, "type," throw you off. The variable "type" refers to whether the payments, pmt, occur at the end of each period (which is considered type=0) or the beginning of each period (which is considered type=1). But you don't have to worry about it at all because the default on "type" is 0. *Thus, if you don't enter a value for "type," it will assume that the payments occur at the end of each period.* We're going to assume they occur at the end of each period, and if they don't, we'll deal with them another way which will be introduced later in this chapter. You'll also notice that since we assume that all payments occur at the end of each period unless otherwise stated, we ignore the "type" variable.

103

Some of the more important Excel functions that we will be using throughout the book include the following (again, we are ignoring the "type" variable because we are assuming cash flows occur at the end of the period):

CALCULATION (WHAT IS BEING SOLVED FOR)	FORMULA
Present value	=PV(rate, nper, pmt, fv)
Future value	=FV(rate, nper, pmt, pv)
Payment	=PMT(rate, nper, pv, fv)
Number of periods	=NPER(rate, pmt, pv, fv)
Interest rate	=RATE(nper, pmt, pv, fv)

Reminders: First, just like using a financial calculator, the outflows have to be entered as negative numbers. In general, each problem will have two cash flows—one positive and one negative. Second, a small, but important, difference between a spreadsheet and a financial calculator. When using a financial calculator, you enter the interest rate as a percent. For example, 6.5% is entered as 6.5. However, with the spreadsheet, the interest rate is entered as a decimal, thus 6.5 percent would be entered as 0.065 or, alternatively, as 6.5 followed by a % sign.

EXAMPLE 3

If you put $1,000 in an investment paying 20 percent interest compounded annually, how much will your account grow to in 10 years?

Let's start with a timeline to help you visualize the problem:

	$r = 20\%$										
YEARS	0	1	2	3	4	5	6	7	8	9	10
Cash Flows	−1,000										Future Value = ?

USING THE MATHEMATICAL FORMULAS

Substituting present value = $1,000, r = 20 percent, and n = 10 years into equation (1), we get

$$\text{future value} = \text{present value} \times (1 + r)^n \qquad (1)$$
$$= \$1,000(1 + 0.20)^{10}$$
$$= \$1,000(6.19174)$$
$$= \$6,191.74$$

Thus, at the end of ten years, you will have $6,191.74 in your investment. In this problem we've invested $1,000 at 20 percent and found that it will grow to $6,191.74 after ten years. These are actually equivalent values expressed in terms of dollars from different time periods where we've assumed a 20 percent compound rate.

USING A FINANCIAL CALCULATOR

A financial calculator makes this even simpler.

Enter	10.	20.0	−1,000.	0	
	N	I/Y	PV	PMT	FV
Solve for					6,191.74

Notice that you input the present value with a negative sign. In effect, a financial calculator sees money as "leaving your hands" and therefore taking on a negative sign when you invest it. In this case you are investing $1,000 right now, so it takes on a negative sign—as a result, the answer takes on a positive sign.

USING AN EXCEL SPREADSHEET

You'll notice the inputs using an Excel spreadsheet are almost identical to those on a financial calculator. The only difference is that the interest rate in Excel is entered *either* as a decimal (0.20) *or* a whole number followed by a % sign (20%) rather than a 20 (as you would enter if you were using a financial calculator). Again, the present value should be entered with a negative value so that the answer takes on a positive sign.

	A	B
1	interest rate (rate) =	20.00%
2	number of periods (nper) =	10
3	payment (pmt) =	$0
4	present value (pv) =	($1,000)
5		
6	future value (fv) =	$6,191.74
7		
8	Excel formula =FV(rate,nper,pmt,pv)	
9	Entered in cell b6: =FV(b1,b2,b3,b4)	

Two Additional Types of Time Value of Money Problems

Sometimes the time value of money does not involve determining either the present value or future value of a sum, but instead deals with either the number of periods in the future, n, or the rate of interest, r. For example, to answer the following question you will need to calculate the value for n.

◆ How many years will it be before the money I have saved will be enough to buy a second home?

Similarly, questions such as the following must be answered by solving for the interest rate, r.

◆ What rate do I need to earn on my investment to have enough money for my newborn child's college education ($n = 18$ years)?
◆ What interest rate has my investment earned?

Fortunately, with the help of a financial calculator or an Excel spreadsheet, you can easily solve for r or n in any of the above situations. It can also be done using the mathematical formulas, but it's much easier with a calculator or spreadsheet, so we'll stick to them.

Solving for the Number of Periods Suppose you want to know how many years it will take for an investment of $9,330 to grow to $20,000 if it's invested at 10 percent annually. Let's take a look at solving this using a financial calculator and an Excel spreadsheet.

Using a Financial Calculator With a financial calculator, all you do is substitute in the values for I/Y, PV, and FV, and solve for N:

Enter		10.0	−9,330.	0	20,000.
	N	I/Y	PV	PMT	FV
Solve for	8.0				

You'll notice that *PV* is input with a negative sign. In effect the financial calculator is programmed to assume that the $9,330 is a cash outflow, whereas the $20,000 is money that you receive. If you don't give one of these values a negative sign, you can't solve the problem.

Using an Excel Spreadsheet With Excel, solving for *n* is straightforward. You simply use the =NPER function and input values for rate, pmt, pv, and fv.

	A	B
1	interest rate (rate) =	0.10
2	payment (pmt) =	0
3	present value (pv) =	($9,330)
4	future value (fv) =	$20,000
5		
6	number of periods (nper) =	8
7		
8	Excel formula =nper(rate,pmt,pv,fv)	
9	Entered in cell b6: =nper(b1,b2,b3,b4)	

Solving for the Rate of Interest You have just inherited $34,946 and want to use it to fund your retirement in 30 years. If you have estimated that you will need $800,000 to fund your retirement, what rate of interest would you have to earn on your $34,946 investment? Let's take a look at solving this using a financial calculator and an Excel spreadsheet to calculate the interest rate.

Using a Financial Calculator With a financial calculator, all you do is substitute in the values for N, PV, and FV, and solve for I/Y:

Enter	30.		–34,946.	0.	800,000.
	N	I/Y	PV	PMT	FV
Solve for		11.0			

Using an Excel Spreadsheet With Excel, the problem is also very easy. You simply use the =RATE function and input values for nper, pmt, pv, and fv.

	A	B
1	number of periods (nper) =	30
2	payment (pmt) =	0
3	present value (pv) =	($34,946)
4	future value (fv) =	$800,000
5		
6	interest rate (rate) =	11.00%
7		
8	Excel formula =rate(nper,pmt,pv,fv)	
9	Entered in cell b6: =rate(b1,b2,b3,b4)	

Applying Compounding to Things Other Than Money

While this chapter focuses on moving money through time at a given interest rate, the concept of compounding applies to almost anything that grows. For example, let's assume you're interested in knowing how big the market for wireless printers will be in five years and assume the demand for them is expected to grow at a rate of 25 percent per year over the next five years. We can calculate the future value of the market for printers using the same formula we used to calculate future value for a sum of money. If the market is currently 25,000 printers per year, then 25,000 would be the present value, *n* would be 5, *r* would be 25%, and substituting into equation (1) you would be solving *FV*,

$$\text{future value} = \text{present value} \times (1 + r)^n \tag{1}$$
$$= 25{,}000(1 + 0.25)^5 = 76{,}293$$

In effect, you can view the interest rate, r, as a compound growth rate, and solve for the number of periods it would take for something to grow to a certain level—what something will grow to in the future. Or you could solve for r, that is, solve for the rate that something would have to grow at in order to reach a target level.

Concept Check

1. Principle 2 states that "money has a time value." Explain this statement.
2. How does compound interest differ from simple interest?
3. Explain the formula $FV_n = PV(1 + r)^n$.

Present Value

 Discuss the relationship between compounding and bringing the value of money back to the present.

Up to this point we have been moving money forward in time; that is, we know how much we have to begin with and are trying to determine how much that sum will grow in a certain number of years when compounded at a specific rate. We are now going to look at the reverse question: What is the value in today's dollars of a sum of money to be received in the future? The answer to this question will help us determine the desirability of investment projects. In this case we are moving future money back to the present. We will determine the **present value** of a lump sum, which in simple terms is the *current value of a future payment*. In fact, we will be doing nothing other than inverse compounding. The differences in these techniques come about merely from the investor's point of view. In compounding, we talked about the compound interest rate and the initial investment; in determining the present value, we will talk about the discount rate and present value of future cash flows. Determining the discount rate can be defined as the rate of return available on an investment of equal risk to what is being discounted. Other than that, the technique and the terminology remain the same, and the mathematics are simply reversed. In equation (1) we were attempting to determine the future value of an initial investment. We now want to determine the initial investment or present value. By dividing both sides of equation (1) by $(1 + r)^n$, we get

present value the value in today's dollars of a future payment discounted back to present at the required rate of return.

$$\text{present value} = \text{future value at the end of year } n \times \left[\frac{1}{(1 + r)^n}\right]$$

or

$$PV = FV_n\left[\frac{1}{(1 + r)^n}\right] \qquad (2)$$

The term in the brackets in equation (2) is referred to as the **present value factor**. Thus, to find the present value of a future dollar amount, all you need to do is multiply that future dollar amount times the appropriate present value factor,

present value factor the value of $\frac{1}{(1 + r)^n}$ used as a multiplier to calculate an amount's present value.

$$\text{present value} = \text{future value (present value factor)}$$

$$\text{where present value factor} = \left[\frac{1}{(1 + r)^n}\right]$$

Because the mathematical procedure for determining the present value is exactly the inverse of determining the future value, we also find that the relationships among n, r, and present value are just the opposite of those we observed in future value. The present value of a future sum of money is inversely related to both the number of years until the payment will be received and the discount rate. This relationship is shown in Figure 3. Although the present value equation [equation (2)] is used extensively to evaluate new investment proposals, it should be stressed that the equation is actually the same as the future value, or compounding equation [equation (1)], only solves for present value instead of future value.

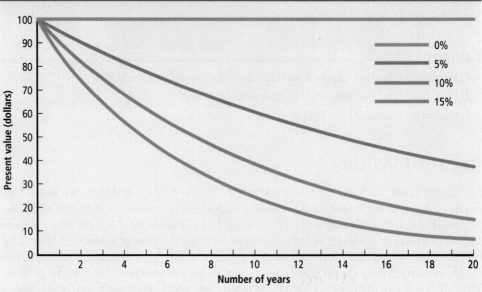

FIGURE 3 The Present Value of $100 to Be Received at a Future Date and Discounted Back to the Present at 0, 5, 10, and 15 Percent

EXAMPLE 4

What is the present value of $500 to be received 10 years from today if our discount rate is 6 percent? Substituting $FV_{10} = \$500$, $n = 10$, and $r = 6$ percent into equation (2), we find

$$\text{present value} = \$500\left[\frac{1}{(1 + 0.06)^{10}}\right]$$

$$= \$500\left(\frac{1}{1.791}\right)$$

$$= \$500(0.5584)$$

$$= \$279.20$$

Thus, the present value of the $500 to be received in 10 years is $279.20.

CALCULATOR SOLUTION

Data Input	Function Key
10	N
6	I/Y
−500	FV
0	PMT

Function Key	Answer
CPT	
PV	279.20

EXAMPLE 5

You're on vacation in a rather remote part of Florida and see an advertisement stating that if you take a sales tour of some condominiums "you will be given $100 just for taking the tour." However, the $100 that you get is in the form of a savings bond that will not pay you the $100 for 10 years. What is the present value of $100 to be received 10 years from today if your discount rate is 6 percent? Substituting $FV_{10} = \$100$, $n = 10$, and $r = 6\%$ into equation (2) you find,

$$\text{present value} = \$100\left[\frac{1}{(1 + 0.06)^{10}}\right]$$

$$= \$100(0.5584)$$

$$= \$55.84$$

Thus, the value in today's dollars of that $100 savings bond is only $55.84.

CALCULATOR SOLUTION

Data Input	Function Key
10	N
6	I/Y
−100	FV
0	PMT

Function Key	Answer
CPT	
PV	55.84

108

CAUTIONARY TALE

FORGETTING PRINCIPLE 4: MARKET PRICES ARE GENERALLY RIGHT

In this book, we have looked at the role the mortgage crisis played in the financial collapse of 2009 from the viewpoint of conflicts of interest and failed corporate governance. But there are many lenses through which we can look to analyze the crisis. One such lens is the principle of efficient markets.

In 2007, several U.S. real estate markets entered a housing bubble. To look more closely at the underlying factors that led to the recent housing bubble (and burst), let's take a step back for a moment.

Beginning in the mid-1990s, the federal government made moves to relax conventional lending standards. In one such move, the government required the Federal National Mortgage Association, commonly known as Fannie Mae, and the Federal Home Loan Mortgage Corporation, known as Freddie Mac, to increase their holdings of loans to low- and moderate-income borrowers. Then in 1999, the U.S. Department of Housing and Urban Development (HUD) regulations required Fannie Mae and Freddie Mac to accept more loans with little or no down payment. As a result, the government had opened the door to very risky loans that would not have been made without this government action.

After the 2001 terrorist attack on the World Trade Center, the government made another move which acted against what we know about competitive markets. The Fed lowered short-term interest rates to insure that the economy did not seize up. These low, short-term interest rates made adjustable rate loans with low down payments highly attractive to homebuyers. As a result

of the low interest rate, when individuals took out variable rate mortgages, they often qualified for bigger mortgages than they could have afforded during a normal interest rate period. But in 2005 and 2006, to control inflation, the Fed returned these short-term interest rates to higher levels and the adjustable rates reset, causing the monthly payments on these loans to increase. Housing prices began to fall and defaults soared.

These actions prevented supply and demand from acting naturally. As a result, housing prices were unnaturally inflated and the listed value of the mortgages, when packaged as securities, was a poor indicator of their actual worth. When homeowners defaulted on their loans in spades, investors were left holding the bad mortgages. These defaulted mortgages also led to a lot more houses on the market that the banks couldn't sell, which led to the market drying up, as it then became very difficult for anyone to get a *new* loan.

We now know that these events put into motion the housing bubble that contributed to the 2009 financial crisis. Competitive markets operate with natural forces of supply and demand, and while they tend to eliminate huge returns, competitive markets can also help to prevent the occurrence of short-lived false values—such as the temporarily low monthly interest payments for new homebuyers—that lead to an eventual crash. If we take one lesson away from this, it should be this: Don't mess with efficient markets. If the markets move interest rates to higher levels, it's for a reason.

Again, we have only one present-value–future-value equation; that is, equations (1) and (2) are different formats of the same equation. We have introduced them as separate equations to simplify our calculations; in one case we are determining the value in future dollars, and in the other case the value in today's dollars. In either case the reason is the same: to compare values on alternative investments and to recognize that the value of a dollar received today is not the same as that of a dollar received at some future date. In other words, we must measure the dollar values in dollars of the same time period. For example, if we looked at these projects—one that promised $1,000 in 1 year, one that promised $1,500 in 5 years, and one that promised $2,500 in 10 years—the concept of present value allows us to bring their flows back to the present and make those projects comparable. Moreover, because all present values are comparable (they are all measured in dollars of the same time period), we can add and subtract the present value of inflows and outflows to determine the present value of an investment. Let's now look at an example of an investment that has two cash flows in different time periods and determine the present value of this investment.

CAN YOU DO IT?

SOLVING FOR THE PRESENT VALUE WITH TWO FLOWS IN DIFFERENT YEARS

What is the present value of an investment that yields $500 to be received in 5 years and $1,000 to be received in 10 years if the discount rate is 4 percent?

STEP 1
CALCULATOR SOLUTION

Data Input	Function Key
7	N
6	I/Y
−1,000	FV
0	PMT

Function Key	Answer
CPT	
PV	665.06

STEP 2
CALCULATOR SOLUTION

Data Input	Function Key
10	N
6	I/Y
−1,000	FV
0	PMT

Function Key	Answer
CPT	
PV	558.39

STEP 3
Add the two present values that you just calculated together:

$ 665.06
558.39
$1,223.45

3 Understand annuities.

annuity a series of equal dollar payments made for a specified number of years.

ordinary annuity an annuity where the cash flows occur at the end of each period.

compound annuity depositing an equal sum of money at the end of each year for a certain number of years and allowing it to grow.

EXAMPLE 6

What is the present value of an investment that yields $1,000 to be received in 7 years and $1,000 to be received in 10 years if the discount rate is 6 percent? Substituting the values of $n = 7$, $r = 6$ percent, and $FV_7 = \$1,000$; and $n = 10$, $r = 6$ percent, and $FV_{10} = \$1,000$ into equation (2) and adding these values together, we find

$$\text{present value} = \$1,000\left[\frac{1}{(1 + 0.06)^7}\right] + \$1,000\left[\frac{1}{(1 + 0.06)^{10}}\right]$$

$$= \$1,000(0.66506)^\prime + \$1,000(0.55839)$$

$$= \$665.06 + \$558.39 = \$1,223.45$$

Again, present values are comparable because they are measured in the same time period's dollars.

With a financial calculator, this becomes a three-step solution, as shown in the margin. First, you'll solve for the present value of the $1,000 received at the end of 7 years, then you'll solve for the present value of the $1,000 received at the end of 10 years, and finally, you'll add the two present values together. Remember, once you've found the present value of those future cash flows you can add them together because they're measured in the same period's dollars.

Concept Check

1. What is the relationship between the present-value equation (2) and the future-value, or compounding, equation (1)?

2. Why is the present value of a future sum always less than that sum's future value?

Annuities

An **annuity** is a *series of equal dollar payments for a specified number of years*. When we talk about annuities, we are referring to **ordinary annuities** unless otherwise noted. With an ordinary annuity *the payments occur at the end of each period*. Because annuities occur frequently in finance—for example, as bond interest payments—we treat them specially. Although compounding and determining the present value of an annuity can be dealt with using the methods we have just described, these processes can be time consuming, especially for larger annuities. Thus, we have modified the single cash flow formulas to deal directly with annuities.

Compound Annuities

A **compound annuity** involves *depositing or investing an equal sum of money at the end of each year for a certain number of years and allowing it to grow*. Perhaps we are saving money for education, a new car, or a vacation home. In any case, we want to know how much our savings will have grown at some point in the future.

Actually, we can find the answer by using equation (1), our compounding equation, and compounding each of the individual deposits to its future value. For example, if to provide for a college education we are going to deposit $500 at the end of each year for the next 5 years in a bank where it will earn 6 percent interest, how much will we have at the end of 5 years? Compounding each of these values using equation (1), we find that we will have $2,818.50 at the end of 5 years.

$$FV_5 = \$500(1 + 0.6)^4 + \$500(1 + 0.6)^3 + \$500(1 + 0.6)^2 + \$500(1 + 0.6) + \$500$$

$$= \$500(1.262) + \$500(1.191) + \$500(1.124) + \$500(1.060) + \$500$$

$$= \$631.00 + \$595.50 + \$562.00 + \$530.00 + \$500.00$$

$$= \$2,818.50$$

110

DID YOU GET IT?

SOLVING FOR THE PRESENT VALUE WITH TWO FLOWS IN DIFFERENT YEARS

There are several different ways you can solve this problem—using the mathematical formulas, a financial calculator, or a spreadsheet—each one giving you the same answer.

1. **Using the Mathematical Formula.** Substituting the values of $n = 5, r = 4$ percent, and $FV_5 = \$500$; and $n = 10, r = 4$ percent, and $FV_{10} = \$1,000$ into equation (2) and adding these values together, we find

$$present\ value = \$500\left[\frac{1}{(1 + 0.04)^5}\right] + \$1,000\left[\frac{1}{(1 + 0.04)^{10}}\right]$$
$$= \$500(0.822) + \$1,000(0.676)$$
$$= \$411 + \$676 = \$1,087$$

2. **Using a Financial Calculator.** Again, it is a three-step process. First calculate the present value of each cash flow individually, and then add the present values together.

STEP 1 CALCULATOR SOLUTION	
Data Input	Function Key
5	N
4	I/Y
−500	FV
0	PMT
Function Key	Answer
CPT	
PV	410.96

STEP 2 CALCULATOR SOLUTION	
Data Input	Function Key
10	N
4	I/Y
−1,000	FV
0	PMT
Function Key	Answer
CPT	
PV	675.56

STEP 3
Add the two present values that you just calculated together:

$ 410.96
675.56
$1,086.52

3. **Using an Excel Spreadsheet.** Using Excel, the cash flows are brought back to the present using the =PV function. If the future values were entered as positive values, our answer will come out as a negative number.

By examining the mathematics involved and the graph of the movement of money through time in Table 1, we can see that all we are really doing is adding up the future values of different cash flows that initially occurred in different time periods. Fortunately, there is also an equation that helps us calculate the future value of an annuity:

$$future\ value\ of\ an\ annuity = PMT\left[\frac{future\ value\ factor - 1}{r}\right]$$
$$= PMT\left[\frac{(1 + r)^n - 1}{r}\right] \quad (3)$$

To simplify our discussion, we will refer to the value in brackets in equation (3) as the **annuity future value factor**. It is defined as $\left[\frac{(1 + r)^n - 1}{r}\right]$.

Using this new notation, we can rewrite equation (3) as follows:

annuity future value factor the value of $\left[\frac{(1 + r)^n - 1}{r}\right]$ used as a multiplier to calculate the future value of an annuity.

$$FV_n = PMT\left[\frac{(1 + r)^n - 1}{r}\right] = PMT(annuity\ future\ value\ factor)$$

Rather than asking how much we will accumulate if we deposit an equal sum in a savings account each year, a more common question to ask is how much we must deposit each

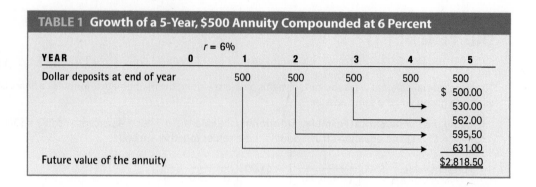

TABLE 1 Growth of a 5-Year, $500 Annuity Compounded at 6 Percent

YEAR	0	1	2	3	4	5
Dollar deposits at end of year		500	500	500	500	500
						$ 500.00
						530.00
						562.00
						595.50
						631.00
Future value of the annuity						$2,818.50

r = 6%

year to accumulate a certain amount of savings. This problem frequently occurs with respect to saving for large expenditures.

For example, if we know that we need $10,000 for college in 8 years, how much must we deposit in the bank at the end of each year at 6 percent interest to have the college money ready? In this case we know the values of n, r, and FV_n in equation (3); what we do not know is the value of PMT. Substituting these example values in equation (3), we find

$$\$10,000 = PMT\left[\frac{(1 + 0.06)^8 - 1}{0.06}\right]$$

$$\$10,000 = PMT(9.8975)$$

$$\frac{\$10,000}{9.8975} = PMT$$

$$\$1,010.36 = PMT$$

Thus, we must deposit $1,010.36 in the bank at the end of each year for 8 years at 6 percent interest to accumulate $10,000 at the end of 8 years.

EXAMPLE 7

How much must we deposit in an 8 percent savings account at the end of each year to accumulate $5,000 at the end of 10 years? Substituting the values $FV_{10} = \$5,000$, $n = 10$, and $r = 8$ percent into equation (3), we find

$$\$5,000 = PMT\left[\frac{(1 + 0.08)^{10} - 1}{0.08}\right]$$

$$\$5,000 = PMT(14.4866)$$

$$\frac{5,000}{14.4866} = PMT$$

$$\$345.15 = PMT$$

Thus, we must deposit $345.15 per year for 10 years at 8 percent to accumulate $5,000.

The Present Value of an Annuity

Pension payments, insurance obligations, and the interest owed on bonds all involve annuities. To compare these three types of investments we need to know the present value of each. For example, if we wish to know what $500 received at the end of each of the next 5 years is worth today given a discount rate of 6 percent, we can simply substitute the

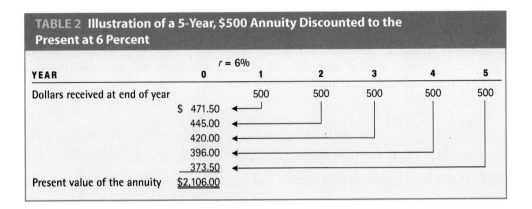

TABLE 2 Illustration of a 5-Year, $500 Annuity Discounted to the Present at 6 Percent

appropriate values into equation (2), such that

$$PV = \$500\left[\frac{1}{(1 + 0.06)^1}\right] + \$500\left[\frac{1}{(1 + 0.06)^2}\right] + \$500\left[\frac{1}{(1 + 0.06)^3}\right]$$

$$+ \$500\left[\frac{1}{(1 + 0.06)^4}\right] + \$500\left[\frac{1}{(1 + 0.06)^5}\right]$$

$$= \$500(0.943) + \$500(0.890) + \$500(0.840) + \$500(0.792) + \$500(0.747)$$

$$= \$2,106$$

Thus, the present value of this annuity is $2,106.00. By examining the mathematics involved and the graph of the movement of money through time in Table 2, we can see that all we are really doing is adding up the present values of different cash flows that initially occurred in different time periods. Fortunately, there is also an equation that helps us calculate the present value of an annuity:

$$\text{present value of an annuity} = PMT\left[\frac{1 - \text{present value factor}}{r}\right]$$

$$= PMT\left[\frac{1 - (1 + r)^{-n}}{r}\right] \tag{4}$$

To simplify our discussion, we will refer to the value in the brackets in equation (4) as the **annuity present value factor**. It is defined as $\left[\dfrac{1 - (1 + r)^{-n}}{r}\right]$.

annuity present value factor the value of $\left[\dfrac{1 - (1 + r)^{-n}}{r}\right]$ used as a multiplier to calculate the present value of an annuity

EXAMPLE 8

What is the present value of a 10-year $1,000 annuity discounted back to the present at 5 percent? Substituting n = 10 years, r = 5 percent, and PMT = $1,000 into equation (4), we find

$$PV = \$1,000\left[\frac{1 - (1 + 0.05)^{-10}}{0.05}\right]$$

$$PV = \$1,000(7.722)$$

$$= \$7,722$$

Thus, the present value of this annuity is $7,722.

CALCULATOR SOLUTION

Data Input	Function Key
10	N
5	I/Y
−1,000	PMT
0	PV

Function Key	Answer
CPT	
PV	7,722

When we solve for PMT, the financial interpretation of this action would be: How much can be withdrawn, perhaps as a pension or to make loan payments, from an account that earns

r percent compounded annually for each of the next n years if we wish to have nothing left at the end of n years? For example, if we have \$5,000 in an account earning 8 percent interest, how large of an annuity can we draw out each year if we want nothing left at the end of 5 years? In this case the present value, PV, of the annuity is \$5,000, $n = 5$ years, $r = 8$ percent, and PMT is unknown. Substituting this into equation (4), we find

$$\$5{,}000 = PMT\left[\frac{1 - (1 + 0.08)^{-5}}{0.08}\right] = PMT(3.993)$$

$$\$1{,}252 = PMT$$

Thus, this account will fall to zero at the end of 5 years if we withdraw \$1,252 at the end of each year.

Annuities Due

annuity due an annuity in which the payments occur at the beginning of each period.

Annuities due are really just *ordinary annuities in which all the annuity payments have been shifted forward by 1 year*. Compounding them and determining their future and present value is actually quite simple. With an annuity due, each annuity payment occurs at the beginning of each period rather than at the end of the period. Let's first look at how this affects our compounding calculations.

Because an annuity due merely shifts the payments from the end of the year to the beginning of the year, we now compound the cash flows for one additional year. Therefore, the compound sum of an annuity due is simply

future value of an annuity due = future value of an annuity $\times\ (1 + r)$

$$FV_n(\text{annuity due}) = PMT\left[\frac{(1 + r)^n - 1}{r}\right](1 + r) \qquad (5)$$

In an earlier example on saving for college, we calculated the value of a 5-year ordinary annuity of \$500 invested in the bank at 6 percent to be \$2,818.50. If we now assume this to be a 5-year annuity due, its future value increases from \$2,818.50 to \$2,987.66.

$$FV_5 = \$500\left[\frac{(1 + 0.06)^5 - 1}{0.06}\right](1 + 0.06)$$

$$= \$500(5.637093)(1.06)$$

$$= \$2{,}987.66$$

Likewise, with the present value of an annuity due, we simply receive each cash flow 1 year earlier—that is, we receive it at the beginning of each year rather than at the end of each year. Thus, because each cash flow is received 1 year earlier, it is discounted back for one less period. To determine the present value of an annuity due, we merely need to find the present value of an ordinary annuity and multiply that by $(1 + r)$, which in effect cancels out 1 year's discounting.

present value of an annuity due = present value of an annuity $\times\ (1 + r)$

$$PV(\text{annuity due}) = PMT\left[\frac{1 - (1 + r)^{-n}}{r}\right](1 + r) \qquad (6)$$

Reexamining the earlier college saving example in which we calculated the present value of a 5-year ordinary annuity of \$500 given a discount rate of 6 percent, we now find that if it is an annuity due rather than an ordinary annuity, the present value increases from \$2,106 to \$2,232.55.

$$PV = \$500\left[\frac{1 - (1 + 0.06)^{-5}}{0.06}\right](1 + 0.06)$$

$$= \$500(4.21236)(1.06)$$

$$= \$2{,}232.55$$

With a financial calculator, first treat it as if it were an ordinary annuity and find the future or present value. Then multiply the present value times $(1 + r)$, in this case times 1.06; this is shown in the margin.

The result of all this is that both the future and present values of an annuity due are larger than those of an ordinary annuity because in each case all payments are received earlier. Thus, when *compounding*, an annuity due compounds for one additional year, whereas when *discounting*, an annuity due discounts for one less year. Although annuities due are used with some frequency in accounting, their usage is quite limited in finance. Therefore, in the remainder of this text, whenever the term *annuity* is used, you should assume that we are referring to an ordinary annuity.

EXAMPLE 9

The Virginia State Lottery runs like most other state lotteries: You must select 6 out of 44 numbers correctly in order to win the jackpot. If you come close, there are some significantly lesser prizes, which we ignore for now. For each million dollars in the lottery jackpot, you receive $50,000 per year for 20 years, and your chance of winning is 1 in 7.1 million. A recent advertisement for the Virginia State Lottery went as follows: "Okay, you got two kinds of people. You've got the kind who play Lotto all the time, and the kind who play Lotto some of the time. You know, like only on a Saturday when they stop in at the store on the corner for some peanut butter cups and diet soda and the jackpot happens to be really big. I mean, my friend Ned? He's like 'Hey, it's only $2 million this week.' Well, hellloooo, anybody home? I mean, I don't know about you, but I wouldn't mind having a measly 2 mill coming *my* way. . . ."

What is the present value of these payments? The answer to this question depends on what assumption you make about the time value of money. In this case, let's assume that your required rate of return on an investment with this level of risk is 10 percent. Keeping in mind that the Lotto is an annuity due—that is, on a $2 million lottery you would get $100,000 immediately and $100,000 at the end of each of the next 19 years. Thus, the present value of this 20-year annuity due discounted back to present at 10 percent becomes:

$$PV(\text{annuity due}) = PMT\left[\frac{1 - (1 + r)^{-n}}{r}\right](1 + r) \quad (6)$$

$$= \$100,000\left[\frac{1 - (1 + 0.10)^{-20}}{0.10}\right](1 + 0.10)$$

$$= \$100,000(8.51356)(1.10)$$

$$= \$851,356(1.10)$$

$$= \$936,492$$

Solving this is a two-step process. In step 1, you treat the jackpot as if it were an ordinary annuity and find the present value. Then multiply the present value times $(1 + r)$, in this case times 1.10; this is shown in the margin.

Thus, the present value of the $2 million Lotto jackpot is less than $1 million if 10 percent is the discount rate. Moreover, because the chance of winning is only 1 in 7.1 million, the expected value of each dollar "invested" in the lottery is only (1/7.1 million) × ($936,492) = 13.19¢. That is, for every dollar you spend on the lottery you should expect to get, on average, about 13 cents back—not a particularly good deal. Although this ignores the minor payments for coming close, it also ignores taxes. In this case, it looks like "my friend Ned" is doing the right thing by staying clear of the lottery. Obviously, the main value of the lottery is entertainment. Unfortunately, without an understanding of the time value of money, it can sound like a good investment.

Present value of an annuity due:

STEP 1
CALCULATOR SOLUTION

Data Input	Function Key
20	N
10	I/Y
−100,000	PMT
0	FV

Function Key	Answer
CPT	
PV	851,356

STEP 2

$851,356
×1.10
$936,492

Amortized Loans

The procedure of solving for *PMT*, the annuity payment value when *r*, *n*, and *PV* are known, is also used to determine what payments are associated with paying off a loan in equal installments over time. *Loans that are paid off this way, in equal periodic payments*, are called **amortized loans**. Actually, the word *amortization* comes from the Latin word meaning "about to die." When you pay off a loan using regular, fixed payments, that loan is amortized. Although the payments are fixed, different amounts of each payment are applied toward the principal and the interest. With each payment you owe a bit less toward the principal. As a result, the amount that has to go toward the interest payment declines with each payment, whereas the portion of each payment that goes toward the principal increases. Figure 4 illustrates the process of amortization.

For example, suppose a firm wants to purchase a piece of machinery. To do this, it borrows $6,000 to be repaid in four equal payments at the end of each of the next 4 years, and the interest rate that is paid to the lender is 15 percent on the outstanding portion of the loan. To determine what the annual payments associated with the repayment of this debt will be, we simply use equation (4) and solve for the value of *PMT*, the annual annuity. In this case, we know *PV*, *r*, and *n*. *PV*, the present value of the annuity, is $6,000; *r*, the annual interest rate, is 15 percent; and *n*, the number of years for which the annuity will last, is 4 years. *PMT*, the annuity payment received (by the lender and paid by the firm) at the end of each year, is unknown. Substituting these values into equation (4), we find

$$\$6,000 = PMT\left[\frac{1 - (1 + 0.15)^{-4}}{0.15}\right]$$

$$\$6,000 = PMT(2.85498)$$

$$\$2,101.59 = PMT$$

amortized loan a loan that is paid off in equal periodic payments.

CALCULATOR SOLUTION

Data Input	Function Key
4	N
15	I/Y
−6,000	PV
0	FV

Function Key	Answer
CPT	
PMT	2,101.59

Concept Check

1. How does an annuity due differ from an ordinary annuity?

2. Why are both the future and present values greater for an annuity?

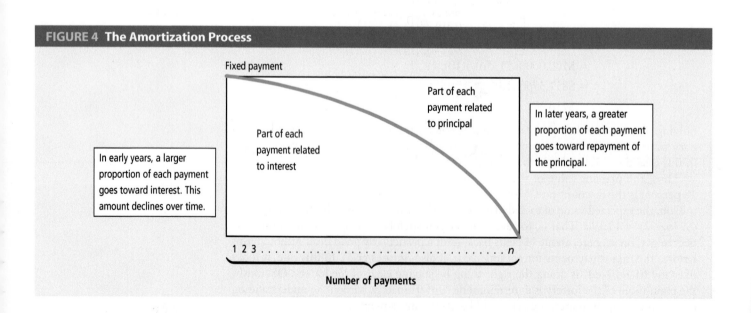

FIGURE 4 **The Amortization Process**

TABLE 3 Loan Amortization Schedule Involving a $6,000 Loan at 15 Percent to Be Repaid in 4 Years

Year	Annuity	Interest Portion of the Annuity[a]	Repayment of the principal Portion of the Annuity[b]	Outstanding Loan Balance After the Annuity Payment
0	0	0	0	$6,000.00
1	$2,101.59	$900.00	$1,201.59	4,798.41
2	2,101.59	719.76	1,381.83	3,416.58
3	2,101.59	512.49	1,589.10	1,827.48
4	2,101.59	274.12	1,827.48	

[a]The interest portion of the annuity is calculated by multiplying the outstanding loan balance at the beginning of the year by the interest rate of 15 percent. Thus, for year 1 it was $6,000 × 0.15 = $900.00, for year 2 it was $4,798.41 × 0.15 = $719.76, and so on.

[b]Repayment of the principal portion of the annuity was calculated by subtracting the interest portion of the annuity (column 2) from the annuity (column 1).

To repay the principal and interest on the outstanding loan in 4 years, the annual payments would be $2,101.59. The breakdown of interest and principal payments is given in the *loan amortization schedule* in Table 3, with very minor rounding error. As you can see, the interest portion of the payment declines each year as the loan outstanding balance declines.

Now let's use a spreadsheet to look at a loan amortization problem and calculate the monthly mortgage payment, and then determine how much of a specific payment goes toward interest and principal.

To buy a new house you take out a 25-year mortgage for $100,000. What will your monthly payments be if the interest rate on your mortgage is 8 percent? To solve this problem, you must first convert the annual rate of 8 percent into a monthly rate by dividing it by 12. Second, you have to convert the number of periods into months by multiplying 25 years times 12 months per year for a total of 300 months.

	A	B
1	interest rate (rate) =	0.6667%
2	number of periods (nper) =	300
3	present value (pv) =	$100,000
4	future value (fv) =	$0
5		
6	payment (pmt) =	($771.82)
7		
8	Excel formula =pmt(rate,nper,pv,fv)	
9	Entered in cell b6: =pmt((8/12)%,b2,b3,b4	

You can also use Excel to calculate the interest and principal portion of any loan amortization payment. You can do this using the following Excel functions:

CALCULATION	FUNCTION
Interest portion of payment	=IPMT(rate, per, nper, pv, fv)
Principal portion of payment	=PPMT(rate, per, nper, pv, fv)
where per refers to the number of an individual periodic payment	

For this example, you can determine how much of the 48th monthly payment goes toward interest and principal as follows,

	A	B
1	interest rate (rate) =	0.6667%
2	payment number (per) =	48
3	number of periods (nper) =	300
4	present value (pv) =	$100,000
5	future value (fv) =	$0
6		
7	Interest portion of the 48th payment =	($628.12)
8	Principal portion of the 48th loan payment =	($143.69)
9		
10	Entered values in cell b7: =IPMT((8/12)%,b2,b3,b4,b5)	
11	Entered values in cell b8: =PPMT((8/12)%,b2,b3,b4,b5)	

Concept Check

1. What is an amortized loan?
2. What functions in Excel help determine the amount of interest and principal in a mortgage payment?

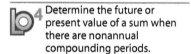 **4** Determine the future or present value of a sum when there are nonannual compounding periods.

Making Interest Rates Comparable

In order to make intelligent decisions about where to invest or borrow money, it is important that we make the stated interest rates comparable. Unfortunately, some rates are quoted as compounded annually, whereas others are quoted as compounded quarterly or compounded daily. But it is not fair to compare interest rates with different compounding periods to each other. Thus, the only way interest rates can logically be compared is to convert them to a common compounding period.

In order to understand the process of making different interest rates comparable, it is first necessary to define the nominal, or quoted, interest rate. The nominal, or quoted, rate is the rate of interest stated on the contract. For example, if you shop around for loans and are quoted 8 percent compounded annually and 7.85 percent compounded quarterly, then 8 percent and 7.85 percent would both be nominal rates. Unfortunately, because on one rate the interest is compounded annually, but on the other interest is compounded quarterly, the two rates are not comparable. In fact, it is never appropriate to compare nominal rates *unless* they include the same number of compounding periods per year. To make them comparable, we must calculate their equivalent rate at some common compounding period. We do this by calculating the **effective annual rate (EAR)**. This is *the annual compound rate that produces the same return as the nominal or quoted rate.*

Let's assume that you are considering borrowing money from a bank at 12 percent compounded monthly. If you borrow $1 at 1 percent per month for 12 months you'd owe,

$$\$1.00(1.01)^{12} = \$1.126825$$

In effect, you are borrowing at 12.6825 percent rather than just by 12 percent. Thus, the EAR for 12 percent compounded monthly is 12.6825. It tells us the annual rate that would produce the same loan payments as the nominal rate. In other words, you'll end up with the same monthly payments if you borrow at 12.6825 percent compounded annually, or 12 percent compounded monthly. Thus, 12.6825 is the effective annual rate (EAR) for 12 percent compounded monthly.

Generalizing on this process, we can calculate the EAR using the following equation:

$$EAR = \left(1 + \frac{\text{quoted rate}}{m} \right)^m - 1 \tag{7}$$

where *EAR* is the effective annual rate and *m* is the number of compounding periods within a year. Given the wide variety of compounding periods used by businesses and banks,

effective annual rate (EAR) the annual compound rate that produces the same return as the nominal, or quoted, rate when something is compounded on a nonannual basis. In effect, the EAR provides the true rate of return.

118

it is important to know how to make these rates comparable so that logical decisions can be made.

> ### EXAMPLE 10
>
> You've just received your first credit card and the problem is the rate. It looks pretty high to you. The quoted rate is 21.7 percent, and when you look closer, you notice that the interest is compounded daily. What's the EAR, or effective annual rate, on your credit card?
>
> To calculate the EAR we can use equation (7)
>
> $$EAR = \left[1 + \frac{\text{quoted rate}}{m} \right]^m - 1 \tag{7}$$
>
> where the quoted rate is 21.7 percent, or 0.217, and m is 365. Substituting, we get
>
> $$EAR = \left[1 + \frac{0.217}{365} \right]^{365} - 1$$
>
> $$EAR = 1.242264 - 1 = 0.242264 \text{ or } 24.2264 \text{ percent}$$
>
> Thus, in reality, the effective annual rate is actually 24.2264 percent.

Finding Present and Future Values with Nonannual Periods

The same logic that applies to calculating the EAR also applies to calculating present and future values when the periods are semiannual, quarterly, or any other nonannual period. Previously when we moved money through time we assumed that the cash flows occurred annually and the compounding or discounting period was always annual. However, it need not be, as evidenced by the fact that bonds generally pay interest semiannually and most mortgages require monthly payments.

For example, if we invest our money for 5 years at 8 percent interest compounded semiannually, we are really investing our money for 10 6-month periods during which we receive 4 percent interest each period. If it is 8 percent compounded quarterly for 5 years, we receive 2 percent interest per period for 20 3-month periods. This process can easily be generalized, giving us the following formula for finding the future value of an investment for which interest is compounded in nonannual periods:

$$FV_n = PV \left[1 + \frac{r}{m} \right]^{m \cdot n} \tag{8}$$

where FV_n = the future value of the investment at the end of n years

n = the number of years during which the compounding occurs

r = annual interest (or discount) rate

PV = the present value or original amount invested at the beginning of the first year

m = the number of times compounding occurs during the year

In fact, all the formulas for moving money through time can be easily modified to accommodate nonannual periods. In each case, we begin with the formulas we introduced in this chapter, and make two adjustments—the first where n, the number of years appears, and the second where r, the annual interest rate appears. Thus, the adjustment involves two steps:

- ◆ n becomes the number of periods or n (the number of years) times m (the number of times compounding occurs per year). Thus, if it is monthly compounding for 10 years, n becomes $10 \times 12 = 120$ months in 10 years, and if it is daily compounding over 10 years, it becomes $10 \times 365 = 3,650$ days in 10 years.
- ◆ r becomes the interest rate per period or r (the annual interest rate) divided by m (the number of times compounding occurs per year). Thus, if it is a 6 percent annual rate with monthly compounding, r becomes $6\% \div 12 = 0.5$ percent per month, and if it is a 6 percent annual rate compounded daily, then r becomes ($6\% \div 365$) per day.

119

CAN YOU DO IT?

HOW MUCH CAN YOU AFFORD TO SPEND ON A HOUSE? AN AMORTIZED LOAN WITH MONTHLY PAYMENTS

You've been house shopping and aren't sure how big a house you can afford. You figure you can handle monthly mortgage payments of $1,250, and you can get a 30-year loan at 6.5 percent. How big of a mortgage can you afford? In this problem, you are solving for *PV*, which is the amount of money you can borrow today.

TABLE 4 The Value of $100 Compounded at Various Intervals

	FOR 1 YEAR AT *r* PERCENT			
r =	**2%**	**5%**	**10%**	**15%**
Compounded annually	$102.00	$105.00	$110.00	$115.00
Compounded semiannually	102.01	105.06	110.25	115.56
Compounded quarterly	102.02	105.09	110.38	115.87
Compounded monthly	102.02	105.12	110.47	116.08
Compounded weekly (52)	102.02	105.12	110.51	116.16
Compounded daily (365)	102.02	105.13	110.52	116.18
	FOR 10 YEARS AT *r* PERCENT			
r =	**2%**	**5%**	**10%**	**15%**
Compounded annually	$121.90	$162.89	$259.37	$404.56
Compounded semiannually	122.02	163.86	265.33	424.79
Compounded quarterly	122.08	164.36	268.51	436.04
Compounded monthly	122.10	164.70	270.70	444.02
Compounded weekly (52)	122.14	164.83	271.57	447.20
Compounded daily (365)	122.14	164.87	271.79	448.03

We can see the value of intrayear compounding by examining Table 4. Because "interest is earned on interest" more frequently as the length of the compounding period declines, there is an inverse relationship between the length of the compounding period and the effective annual interest rate: The shorter the compounding period is, the higher the effective interest rate will be. Conversely, the longer the compounding period is, the lower the effective interest rate will be.

CALCULATOR SOLUTION

Data Input	Function Key
20	N
12/4	I/Y
100	PV
0	PMT

Function Key	Answer
CPT	
FV	−180.61

EXAMPLE 11

If we place $100 in a savings account that yields 12 percent compounded quarterly, what will our investment grow to at the end of 5 years? Substituting $n = 5$, $m = 4$, $r = 12$ percent, and $PV = \$100$ into equation (8), we find

$$FV_5 = \$100\left(1 + \frac{0.12}{4}\right)^{4 \cdot 5}$$

$$= \$100(1 + 0.03)^{20}$$

$$= \$100(1.8061)$$

$$= \$180.61$$

Thus, we will have $180.61 at the end of 5 years. In this problem, N becomes the number of quarters in 5 years while I/Y becomes the interest rate per period. In effect 3 percent per quarter for 20 quarters.

DID YOU GET IT?

HOW MUCH CAN YOU AFFORD TO SPEND ON A HOUSE?
AN AMORTIZED LOAN WITH MONTHLY PAYMENTS

There are several different ways you can solve this problem—using the mathematical formulas, a financial calculator, or a spreadsheet—each one giving you the same answer.

1. **Using the Mathematical Formulas.** Again, you need to multiply n times m, and divide r by m, where m is the number of compounding periods per year. Thus,

$$PV = \$1{,}250 \left[\frac{1 - \dfrac{1}{\left(1 + \dfrac{.065}{12}\right)^{30 \cdot 12}}}{\dfrac{.065}{12}} \right]$$

$$PV = \$1{,}250 \left[\frac{1 - \dfrac{1}{(1 + .00541667)^{360}}}{.00541667} \right]$$

$$PV = \$1{,}250 \left[\frac{1 - \dfrac{1}{6.99179797}}{.00541667} \right]$$

$$PV = \$1{,}250(158.210816)$$

$$PV = \$197{,}763.52$$

2. **Using a Financial Calculator.** First, you must convert everything to months. To do this you would first convert n into months by multiplying n times m (30 times 12) and enter this into $\boxed{N}$. Next you would enter the interest rate as a monthly rate by dividing r by m and entering this number into $\boxed{I/Y}$. Finally, make sure that the value entered as $\boxed{PMT}$ is a monthly figure, that is, it is the monthly payment value.

CALCULATOR SOLUTION

Data Input	Function Key
360	$\boxed{N}$
6.5/12	$\boxed{I/Y}$
−1,250	$\boxed{PMT}$
0	$\boxed{FV}$

Function Key	Answer
$\boxed{CPT}$	
$\boxed{PV}$	197,763.52

3. **Using an Excel Spreadsheet.**

	A	B
1	interest rate (rate) =	0.5417%
2	number of periods (nper) =	360
3	payment (pmt) =	1250
4	future value (fv) =	0
5		
6	present value (pv) =	($197,763.52)
7	Entered values in cell b6: =PV((6.5/12)%,b2,b3,b4)	
8		

EXAMPLE 12

In 2009 the average U.S. household owed about $10,000 in credit card debt, and the average interest rate on credit card debt was 13.0 percent. On many credit cards the minimum monthly payment is 4 percent of the debt balance. If the average household paid off 4 percent of the initial amount it owed each month, that is, made payments of $400 each month, how many months would it take to repay this credit card debt? Use a financial calculator to solve this problem.

You'll notice in the solution that appears in the margin that the value for *PMT* goes in as a negative. The answer is over 29 months.

CALCULATOR SOLUTION

Data Input	Function Key
13.0/12	$\boxed{I/Y}$
10,000	$\boxed{PV}$
−400	$\boxed{PMT}$
0	$\boxed{FV}$

Function Key	Answer
$\boxed{CPT}$	
$\boxed{N}$	29.3

Concept Check

1. Why does the future value of a given amount increase when interest is compounded nonannually as opposed to annually?

2. How do you adjust the present- and future-value formulas when interest is compounded monthly?

5 Determine the present value of an uneven stream of payments and understand perpetuities.

The Present Value of an Uneven Stream

Although some projects will involve a single cash flow, and some will involve annuities, many projects will involve uneven cash flows over several years. In this book, we will be comparing not only the present value of cash flows generated by different projects but also the cash inflows and outflows generated by a particular project to determine that project's present value. However, this will not be difficult because the present value of any cash flow is measured in today's dollars and thus can be compared, through addition for inflows and subtraction for outflows, to the present value of any other cash flow also measured in today's dollars. For example, if we wished to find the present value of the following cash flows

YEAR	CASH FLOW	YEAR	CASH FLOW
1	$ 0	6	500
2	200	7	500
3	−400	8	500
4	500	9	500
5	500	10	500

given a 6 percent discount rate, we would merely discount the flows back to the present and total them by adding in the positive flows and subtracting the negative ones. However, this problem is complicated by the annuity of $500 that runs from years 4 through 10. To accommodate this, we can first discount the annuity back to the beginning of period 4 (or end of period 3) and get its present value at that point in time. We then bring this single cash flow (which is the present value of the 7-year annuity) back to the present. In effect we discount twice, first back to the end of period 3, then back to the present. This is shown graphically in Table 5 and numerically in Table 6. Thus, the present value of this uneven stream of cash flows is $2,185.69.

Remember, once the cash flows from an investment have been brought back to the present, they can be combined by adding and subtracting to determine the project's total present value.

STEP 1

Bring the $200 at the end of year 2 back to present:

CALCULATOR SOLUTION

Data Input	Function Key
2	N
6	I/Y
200	FV
0	PMT

Function Key	Answer
CPT	
PV	−178.00

STEP 2

Bring the negative $400 at the end of year 3 back to present:

CALCULATOR SOLUTION

Data Input	Function Key
3	N
6	I/Y
0	PMT
−400	FV

Function Key	Answer
CPT	
PV	335.85

STEP 3

Bring the 7-year, $500 annuity beginning at the end of year 4 back to the beginning of year 4, which is the same as the end of year 3:

CALCULATOR SOLUTION

Data Input	Function Key
7	N
6	I/Y
500	PMT
0	FV

Function Key	Answer
CPT	
PV	−2,791.19

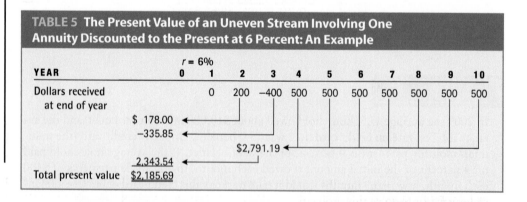

TABLE 5 The Present Value of an Uneven Stream Involving One Annuity Discounted to the Present at 6 Percent: An Example

TABLE 6 Determining the Present Value of an Uneven Stream Involving One Annuity Discounted to the Present at 6 Percent: An Example

1. Present value of $200 received at the end of 2 years at 6% =	$178.00
2. Present value of a $400 outflow at the end of 3 years at 6% =	−335.85
3. (a) Value at end of year 3 of a $500 annuity, years 4–10 at 6% = $2,791.19	
(b) Present value of $2,791.19 received at the end of year 3 at 6% =	2,343.54
4. Total present value =	$2,185.69

Concept Check

1. How would you calculate the present value of an investment that produced cash flows of $100 received at the end of year 1 and $700 at the end of year 2?

Perpetuities

A **perpetuity** is *an annuity that continues forever*; that is, every year following its establishment this investment pays the same dollar amount. An example of a perpetuity is preferred stock that pays a constant dollar dividend infinitely. Determining the present value of a perpetuity is delightfully simple; we merely need to divide the constant flow by the discount rate. For example, the present value of a $100 perpetuity discounted back to the present at 5 percent is $100/0.05 = $2,000. Thus, the equation representing the present value of a perpetuity is

$$PV = \frac{PP}{r} \tag{9}$$

where: PV = the present value of the perpetuity
PP = the constant dollar amount provided by the perpetuity
r = the annual interest (or discount) rate

EXAMPLE 13

What is the present value of a $500 perpetuity discounted back to the present at 8 percent? Substituting PP = $500 and r = 0.08 into equation (9), we find

$$PV = \frac{\$500}{0.08} = \$6,250$$

Thus, the present value of this perpetuity is $6,250.

Concept Check

1. What is a perpetuity?
2. When r, the annual interest (or discount) rate, increases, what happens to the present value of a perpetuity? Why?

Quoted Versus Effective Rate

The Multinational Firm: The Time Value of Money

From **Principle 3: Risk Requires a Reward**, we found that investors demand a return for delaying consumption, as well as an additional return for taking on added risk. The discount rate that we use to move money through time should reflect this return for delaying consumption; and as we have seen with the Fisher Effect, this discount rate should reflect anticipated inflation. In the United States, anticipated inflation has historically been quite low, although it does tend to fluctuate over time. Elsewhere in the world, however, the inflation rate is difficult to predict because it can be dramatically high and fluctuate tremendously.

Let's look at Argentina, keeping in mind that similar examples abound in Central and South America and Eastern Europe. At the beginning of 1992, Argentina introduced its fifth currency in 22 years, the new peso. The austral, the currency that was replaced, was introduced in June 1985 and was initially equal in value to $1.25 U.S. currency. Five and a half

---

STEP 4

Bring the value we just calculated, which is the value of the 7-year annuity of $500 at the end of year 3, back to present.

CALCULATOR SOLUTION

Data Input	Function Key
3	N
6	I/Y
2,791.19	FV
0	PMT

Function Key	Answer
CPT	
PV	−2,343.54

STEP 5

Add the present value of the cash inflows and subtract the present value of the cash outflow (the $400 from the end of year 3) calculated in steps 1, 2, and 4.

$ 178.00
−335.85
+2,343.54
$ 2,185.69

perpetuity an annuity with an infinite life.

6 Explain how the international setting complicates the time value of money.

3
Principle

years later, it took 100,000 australs to equal $1. Inflation had reached the point at which the stack of money needed to buy a candy bar was bigger and weighed more than the candy bar itself, and many workers received their week's wages in grocery bags. Needless to say, if we were to move australs through time, we would have to use an extremely high interest or discount rate.

Unfortunately, in countries suffering from hyperinflation, inflation rates tend to fluctuate dramatically, and this makes estimating the expected inflation rate even more difficult. For example, in 1989 the inflation rate in Argentina was 4,924 percent; in 1990 it dropped to 1,344 percent; in 1991 it was only 84 percent; in 1992, only 18 percent; in 2000 it was close to zero, and by 2009 it was back up again, with some forecasts for 2010 putting it in the 20 percent range. Finally, here are two cases at the extreme: In July 1946 in Hungary, the rate of inflation was so high that prices doubled every 15 hours; while in November 2008, the *daily* inflation rate hit 98% in Zimbabwe with prices doubling virtually every day.

The bottom line on all this is that for companies doing business internationally, dramatic fluctuations in inflation rates can make choosing the appropriate discount rate to move money through time an extremely difficult process.

Concept Check

1. How does the international setting complicate the choice of the appropriate interest rate to use when discounting cash flows back to the present?

TABLE 7 Summary of Time Value of Money Equations

Calculation	Equation
Future value of a single payment	$FV_n = PV(1 + r)^n$
Present value of a single payment	$PV = FV_n \left[\dfrac{1}{(1 + r)^n} \right]$
Future value of an annuity	$FV \text{ of an annuity} = PMT \left[\dfrac{(1 + r)^n - 1}{r} \right]$
Present value of an annuity	$PV \text{ of an annuity} = PMT \left[\dfrac{1 - (1 + r)^{-n}}{r} \right]$
Future value of an annuity due	$FV_n(\text{annuity due}) = \text{future value of an annuity} \times (1 + r)$
Present value of an annuity due	$PV(\text{annuity due}) = \text{present value of an annuity} \times (1 + r)$
Effective annual return (EAR) =	$\left[1 + \dfrac{\text{quoted rate}}{m} \right]^m - 1$
Future value of a single payment with nonannual compounding	$FV_n = PV \left(1 + \dfrac{r}{m} \right)^{mn}$
Present value of a perpetuity	$PV = \dfrac{PP}{r}$

Notations: FV_n = the future value of the investment at the end of n years
   n = the number of years until payment will be received or during which compounding occurs
   r = the annual interest or discount rate
   PV = the present value of the future sum of money
   m = the number of times compounding occurs during the year
   PMT = the annuity payment deposited or received at the end of each year
   PP = the constant dollar amount provided by the perpetuity

Summary

Compound interest occurs when interest paid on an investment during the first period is added to the principal; then, during the second period, interest is earned on this new sum. The formula for this appears in Table 7.

Although there are several ways to move money through time, they all give you the same result. In the business world, the primary method is through the use of a financial spreadsheet, with Excel being the most popular. If you can use a financial calculator, you can easily apply your skills to a spreadsheet.

Actually, we have only one formula with which to calculate both present value and future value—we simply solve for different variables—FV and PV. This single compounding formula is $FV_n = PV(1 + r)^n$ and is presented in Table 7.

An annuity is a series of equal payments made for a specified number of years. In effect, it is calculated as the sum of the present or future value of the individual cash flows over the life of the annuity. The formulas for several types of annuities are given in Table 7.

If the cash flows from an annuity occur at the end of each period, the annuity is referred to as an ordinary annuity. If the cash flows occur at the beginning of each period, the annuity is referred to as an annuity due. We will assume that cash flows occur at the end of each period unless otherwise stated.

The procedure for solving for PMT, the annuity payment value when r, n, and PV are known, is also used to determine what payments are associated with paying off a loan in equal installments over time. Loans that are paid off this way, in equal periodic payments, are called amortized loans. Although the payments are fixed, different amounts of each payment are applied toward the principal and the interest. With each payment you make, you owe a bit less on the principal. As a result, the amount that goes toward the interest payment declines with each payment made, whereas the portion of each payment that goes toward the principal increases.

With nonannual compounding, interest is earned on interest more frequently because the length of the compounding period is shorter. As a result, there is an inverse relationship between the length of the compounding period and the effective annual interest rate. The formula for solving for the future value of a single payment with nonannual compounding is given in Table 7.

Although some projects will involve a single cash flow, and some will involve annuities, many projects will involve uneven cash flows over several years. However, finding the present or future value of these flows is not difficult because the present value of any cash flow measured in today's dollars can be compared, by adding the inflows and subtracting the outflows, to the present value of any other cash flow also measured in today's dollars.

A perpetuity is an annuity that continues forever; that is, every year following its establishment the investment pays the same dollar amount. An example of a perpetuity is preferred stock, which pays a constant dollar dividend infinitely. Determining the present value of a perpetuity is delightfully simple. We merely need to divide the constant flow by the discount rate.

For companies doing business internationally, dramatic fluctuations in inflation rates from country to country can make choosing the appropriate discount rate to move money through time an extremely difficult process.

 Explain the mechanics of compounding, that is, how money grows over time when it is invested.

 Discuss the relationship between compounding and bringing the value of money back to the present.

 Understand annuities.

 Determine the future or present value of a sum when there are nonannual compounding periods.

 Determine the present value of an uneven stream of payments and understand perpetuities.

Explain how the international setting complicates the time value of money.

Key Terms

Amortized loan

Annuity

Annuity due

Annuity future value factor

Annuity present value factor

Compound annuity

Compound interest

Effective annual rate (EAR)

Future value

Future value factor

Ordinary annuity

Perpetuity

Present value

Present value factor

Simple interest

Review Questions

All Review Questions and Study Problems are available in MyFinanceLab.

5-1. What is the time value of money? Why is it so important?

5-2. The process of discounting and compounding are related. Explain this relationship.

5-3. How would an increase in the interest rate (r) or a decrease in the holding period (n) affect the future value (FV_n) of a sum of money? Explain why.

5-4. Suppose you were considering depositing your savings in one of three banks, all of which pay 5 percent interest; bank A compounds annually, bank B compounds semiannually, and bank C compounds daily. Which bank would you choose? Why?

5-5. What is an annuity? Give some examples of annuities. Distinguish between an annuity and a perpetuity.

5-6. Compare some of the different financial calculators that are available on the Internet. Look at *Kiplinger Online calculators* (www.kiplinger.com/tools/index.html) which include saving and investing, mutual funds, bonds, stocks, home, auto, credit cards, and budgeting online calculators. Also go to www.dinkytown.net, www.bankrate.com/calculators.aspx, and www.interest.com and click on the "Calculators" link. Which financial calculators do you find to be the most useful? Why?

Self-Test Problems

Solutions to these problems are provided at the end of the chapter.

ST-1. You place $25,000 in a savings account paying an annual compound interest of 8 percent for 3 years and then move it into a savings account that pays 10 percent interest compounded annually. By how much will your money have grown at the end of 6 years?

ST-2. You purchase a boat for $35,000 and pay $5,000 down. You also agree to pay the rest over the next 10 years in 10 equal end-of-the-year payments plus 13 percent compound interest on the unpaid balance. What will be the amount of each payment?

Study Problems

5-1. (*Compound interest*) To what amount will the following investments accumulate?
  a. $5,000 invested for 10 years at 10 percent compounded annually
  b. $8,000 invested for 7 years at 8 percent compounded annually
  c. $775 invested for 12 years at 12 percent compounded annually
  d. $21,000 invested for 5 years at 5 percent compounded annually

5-2. (*Compound value solving for n*) How many years will the following take?
  a. $500 to grow to $1,039.50 if invested at 5 percent compounded annually
  b. $35 to grow to $53.87 if invested at 9 percent compounded annually
  c. $100 to grow to $298.60 if invested at 20 percent compounded annually
  d. $53 to grow to $78.76 if invested at 2 percent compounded annually

5-3. (*Compound value solving for r*) At what annual rate would the following have to be invested?
  a. $500 to grow to $1,948.00 in 12 years
  b. $300 to grow to $422.10 in 7 years
  c. $50 to grow to $280.20 in 20 years
  d. $200 to grow to $497.60 in 5 years

5-4. (*Present value*) What is the present value of the following future amounts?
  a. $800 to be received 10 years from now discounted back to the present at 10 percent
  b. $300 to be received 5 years from now discounted back to the present at 5 percent
  c. $1,000 to be received 8 years from now discounted back to the present at 3 percent
  d. $1,000 to be received 8 years from now discounted back to the present at 20 percent

5-5. (*Compound annuity*) What is the accumulated sum of each of the following streams of payments?
  a. $500 a year for 10 years compounded annually at 5 percent
  b. $100 a year for 5 years compounded annually at 10 percent
  c. $35 a year for 7 years compounded annually at 7 percent
  d. $25 a year for 3 years compounded annually at 2 percent

5-6. (*Present value of an annuity*) What is the present value of the following annuities?

    a. $2,500 a year for 10 years discounted back to the present at 7 percent

    b. $70 a year for 3 years discounted back to the present at 3 percent

    c. $280 a year for 7 years discounted back to the present at 6 percent

    d. $500 a year for 10 years discounted back to the present at 10 percent

5-7. (*Compound value*) Stanford Simmons, who recently sold his Porsche, placed $10,000 in a savings account paying annual compound interest of 6 percent.

    a. Calculate the amount of money that will have accrued if he leaves the money in the bank for 1, 5, and 15 years.

    b. If he moves his money into an account that pays 8 percent or one that pays 10 percent, rework part (a) using these new interest rates.

    c. What conclusions can you draw about the relationship between interest rates, time, and future sums from the calculations you have completed in this problem?

5-8. (*Future value*) Sarah Wiggum would like to make a single investment and have $2 million at the time of her retirement in 35 years. She has found a mutual fund that will earn 4 percent annually. How much will Sarah have to invest today? What if Sarah were a finance major and learned how to earn a 14 percent annual return, how much would she have to invest today?

5-9. (*Compound interest with nonannual periods*)

    a. Calculate the future sum of $5,000, given that it will be held in the bank 5 years at an annual interest rate of 6 percent.

    b. Recalculate part (a) using compounding periods that are (1) semiannual and (2) bimonthly.

    c. Recalculate parts (a) and (b) for a 12 percent annual interest rate.

    d. Recalculate part (a) using a time horizon of 12 years (annual interest rate is still 6 percent).

    e. With respect to the effect of changes in the stated interest rate and holding periods on future sums in parts (c) and (d), what conclusions do you draw when you compare these figures with the answers found in parts (a) and (b)?

5-10. (*Solving for r with annuities*) Nicki Johnson, a sophomore mechanical engineering student, receives a call from an insurance agent, who believes that Nicki is an older woman ready to retire from teaching. He talks to her about several annuities that she could buy that would guarantee her an annual fixed income. The annuities are as follows:

ANNUITY	INITIAL PAYMENT INTO ANNUITY (AT $t = 0$)	AMOUNT OF MONEY RECEIVED PER YEAR	DURATION OF ANNUITY (YEARS)
A	$50,000	$8,500	12
B	$60,000	$7,000	25
C	$70,000	$8,000	20

If Nicki could earn 11 percent on her money by placing it in a savings account, should she place it instead in any of the annuities? Which ones, if any? Why?

5-11. (*Future value*) Sales of a new finance book were 15,000 copies this year and were expected to increase by 20 percent per year. What are expected sales during each of the next 3 years? Graph this sales trend and explain.

5-12. (*Future value*) Albert Pujols hit 47 home runs in 2009. If his home-run output grew at a rate of 12 percent per year, what would it have been over the following 5 years?

5-13. (*Loan amortization*) Mr. Bill S. Preston, Esq., purchased a new house for $80,000. He paid $20,000 down and agreed to pay the rest over the next 25 years in 25 equal end-of-year payments plus 9 percent compound interest on the unpaid balance. What will these equal payments be?

5-14. (*Solving for PMT of an annuity*) To pay for your child's education, you wish to have accumulated $15,000 at the end of 15 years. To do this you plan on depositing an equal amount into the bank at the end of each year. If the bank is willing to pay 6 percent compounded annually, how much must you deposit each year to reach your goal?

5-15. (*Solving for r in compound interest*) If you were offered $1,079.50 10 years from now in return for an investment of $500 currently, what annual rate of interest would you earn if you took the offer?

5-16. (*Future value of an annuity*) In 10 years you are planning on retiring and buying a house in Oviedo, Florida. The house you are looking at currently costs $100,000 and is expected to increase in value each year at a rate of 5 percent. Assuming you can earn 10 percent annually on your investments, how much must you invest at the end of each of the next 10 years to be able to buy your dream home when you retire?

5-17. (*Compound value*) The Aggarwal Corporation needs to save $10 million to retire a $10 million mortgage that matures in 10 years. To retire this mortgage, the company plans to put a fixed amount into an account at the end of each year for 10 years, with the first payment occurring at the end of 1 year. The Aggarwal Corporation expects to earn 9 percent annually on the money in this account. What equal annual contribution must it make to this account to accumulate the $10 million in 10 years?

5-18. (*Compound interest with nonannual periods*) After examining the various personal loan rates available to you, you find that you can borrow funds from a finance company at 12 percent compounded monthly or from a bank at 13 percent compounded annually. Which alternative is more attractive?

5-19. (*Present value of an uneven stream of payments*) You are given three investment alternatives to analyze. The cash flows from these three investments are as follows:

END OF YEAR	INVESTMENT		
	A	B	C
1	$10,000		$10,000
2	10,000		
3	10,000		
4	10,000		
5	10,000	$10,000	
6		10,000	50,000
7		10,000	
8		10,000	
9		10,000	
10		10,000	10,000

Assuming a 20 percent discount rate, find the present value of each investment.

5-20. (*Present value*) The Kumar Corporation is planning on issuing bonds that pay no interest but can be converted into $1,000 at maturity, 7 years from their purchase. To price these bonds competitively with other bonds of equal risk, it is determined that they should yield 10 percent, compounded annually. At what price should the Kumar Corporation sell these bonds?

5-21. (*Perpetuities*) What is the present value of the following?

    a. A $300 perpetuity discounted back to the present at 8 percent
    b. A $1,000 perpetuity discounted back to the present at 12 percent
    c. A $100 perpetuity discounted back to the present at 9 percent
    d. A $95 perpetuity discounted back to the present at 5 percent

5-22. (*Solving for n with nonannual periods*) About how many years would it take for your investment to grow fourfold if it were invested at 16 percent compounded semiannually?

5-23. (*Complex present value*) How much do you have to deposit today so that beginning 11 years from now you can withdraw $10,000 a year for the next 5 years (periods 11 through 15) plus an *additional* amount of $20,000 in that last year (period 15)? Assume an interest rate of 6 percent.

5-24. (*Loan amortization*) On December 31, Beth Klemkosky bought a yacht for $50,000, paying $10,000 down and agreeing to pay the balance in 10 equal end-of-year installments and 10 percent interest on the declining balance. How big would the annual payments be?

5-25. (*Solving for r of an annuity*) You lend a friend $30,000, which your friend will repay in five equal annual end-of-year payments of $10,000, with the first payment to be received 1 year from now. What rate of return does your loan receive?

5-26. (*Solving for r in compound interest*) You lend a friend $10,000, for which your friend will repay you $27,027 at the end of 5 years. What interest rate are you charging your "friend"?

5-27. (*Loan amortization*) A firm borrows $25,000 from the bank at 12 percent compounded annually to purchase some new machinery. This loan is to be repaid in equal installments at the end of each year over the next 5 years. How much will each annual payment be?

5-28. (*Present-value comparison*) You are offered $1,000 today, $10,000 in 12 years, or $25,000 in 25 years. Assuming that you can earn 11 percent on your money, which should you choose?

5-29. (*Compound annuity*) You plan on buying some property in Florida 5 years from today. To do this you estimate that you will need $20,000 at that time for the purchase. You would like to accumulate these funds by making equal annual deposits in your savings account, which pays 12 percent annually. If you make your first deposit at the end of this year, and you would like your account to reach $20,000 when the final deposit is made, what will be the amount of your deposits?

5-30. (*Complex present value*) You would like to have $50,000 in 15 years. To accumulate this amount you plan to deposit each year an equal sum in the bank, which will earn 7 percent interest compounded annually. Your first payment will be made at the end of the year.

  a. How much must you deposit annually to accumulate this amount?
  b. If you decide to make a large lump-sum deposit today instead of the annual deposits, how large should this lump-sum deposit be? (Assume you can earn 7 percent on this deposit.)
  c. At the end of 5 years you will receive $10,000 and deposit this in the bank toward your goal of $50,000 at the end of 15 years. In addition to this deposit, how much must you deposit in equal annual deposits to reach your goal? (Again assume you can earn 7 percent on this deposit.)

5-31. (*Comprehensive present value*) You are trying to plan for retirement in 10 years, and currently you have $100,000 in a savings account and $300,000 in stocks. In addition you plan on adding to your savings by depositing $10,000 per year in your savings account at the end of each of the next 5 years and then $20,000 per year at the end of each year for the final 5 years until retirement.

  a. Assuming your savings account returns 7 percent compounded annually, and your investment in stocks will return 12 percent compounded annually, how much will you have at the end of 10 years? (Ignore taxes.)
  b. If you expect to live for 20 years after you retire, and at retirement you deposit all of your savings in a bank account paying 10 percent, how much can you withdraw each year after retirement (20 equal withdrawals beginning 1 year after you retire) to end up with a zero balance upon your death?

5-32. (*Loan amortization*) On December 31, Son-Nan Chen borrowed $100,000, agreeing to repay this sum in 20 equal end-of-year installments and 15 percent interest on the declining balance. How large must the annual payments be?

5-33. (*Loan amortization*) To buy a new house you must borrow $150,000. To do this you take out a $150,000, 30-year, 10 percent mortgage. Your mortgage payments, which are made at the end of each year (one payment each year), include both principal and 10 percent interest on the declining balance. How large will your annual payments be?

5-34. (*Present value*) The state lottery's million-dollar payout provides for $1 million to be paid over 19 years in 20 payments of $50,000. The first $50,000 payment is made immediately, and the 19 remaining $50,000 payments occur at the end of each of the next 19 years. If 10 percent is the appropriate discount rate, what is the present value of this stream of cash flows? If 20 percent is the appropriate discount rate, what is the present value of the cash flows?

5-35. (*Solving for r in compound interest—financial calculator needed*) In September 1963, the first issue of the comic book *X-MEN* was issued. The original price for that issue was $0.12. By September 2009, 46 years later, the value of this comic book had risen to $22,000. What annual rate of interest would you have earned if you had bought the comic in 1963 and sold it in 2009?

5-36. (*Comprehensive present value*) You have just inherited a large sum of money, and you are trying to determine how much you should save for retirement and how much you can spend now. For retirement, you will deposit today (January 1, 2011) a lump sum in a bank account paying 10 percent compounded annually. You don't plan on touching this deposit until you retire in 5 years (on January 1, 2016), and you plan on living for 20 additional years and then dropping dead on December 31, 2035. During your retirement you would like to receive income of $50,000 per year to be received the first day of each year, with the first payment on January 1, 2016, and the last payment on January 1, 2035. Complicating this objective is your desire to have one final 3-year fling during which time you'd like to track down all the living original cast members of *Leave It to Beaver* and *The Brady Bunch* and get their autographs. To finance this effort you want to receive $250,000 on January 1, 2031, and *nothing* on January 1, 2032, and January 1, 2033, as you will be on the road. In addition, after you pass on (January 1, 2036), you would like to have a total of $100,000 to leave to your children.

  a. How much must you deposit in the bank at 10 percent on January 1, 2011, to achieve your goal? (Use a timeline to answer this question.)
  b. What kinds of problems are associated with this analysis and its assumptions?

5-37. (*Spreadsheet problem*) If you invest $900 in a bank in which it will earn 8 percent compounded annually, how much will it be worth at the end of 7 years? Use a spreadsheet to do your calculations.

5-38. (*Spreadsheet problem*) In 20 years you'd like to have $250,000 to buy a vacation home, but you have only $30,000. At what rate must your $30,000 be compounded annually for it to grow to $250,000 in 20 years? Use a spreadsheet to calculate your answer.

5-39. (*Spreadsheet problem*) To buy a new house you take out a 25-year mortgage for $300,000. What will your monthly payments be if the interest rate on your mortgage is 8 percent? Use a spreadsheet to calculate your answer. Now, calculate the portion of the 48th monthly payment that goes toward interest and principal.

5-40. (*Future and present value using a calculator*) Over the past few years Microsoft founder Bill Gates's net worth has fluctuated between $20 billion and $130 billion. In 2010 Gates was worth about $28 billion after he reduced his stake in Microsoft from 21 percent to around 14 percent by moving billions into his charitable foundation. Let's see what Bill Gates can do with his money in the following problems.

   a. I'll take Manhattan? Manhattan's native tribe sold Manhattan Island to Peter Minuit for $24 in 1626. Now, 384 years later in 2010, Bill Gates wants to buy the island from the "current natives." How much would Bill have to pay for Manhattan if the "current natives" want a 6 percent annual return on the original $24 purchase price? Could he afford it?
   b. (*Nonannual compounding using a calculator*) How much would Bill have to pay for Manhattan if the "current natives" want a 6% return compounded monthly on the original $24 purchase price?
   c. Microsoft Seattle? Bill Gates decides to pass on Manhattan and instead plans to buy the city of Seattle, Washington, for $60 billion in 10 years. How much would Mr. Gates have to invest today at 10 percent compounded annually in order to purchase Seattle in 10 years?
   d. Now assume Bill Gates wants to invest only about half his net worth today, $14 billion, in order to buy Seattle for $60 billion in 10 years. What annual rate of return would he have to earn in order to complete his purchase in 10 years?
   e. Margaritaville? Instead of buying and running large cities, Bill Gates is considering quitting the rigors of the business world and retiring to work on his golf game. To fund his retirement, Bill Gates would invest his $28 billion fortune in safe investments with an expected annual rate of return of 7 percent. Also, Mr. Gates wants to make 40 equal annual withdrawals from this retirement fund beginning a year from today. How much can Mr. Gates's annual withdrawal be in this case?

5-41. (*Compounding using a calculator*) Bart Simpson, age 10, wants to be able to buy a really cool new car when he turns 16. His really cool car costs $15,000 today, and its cost is expected to increase 3 percent annually. Bart wants to make one deposit today (he can sell his mint-condition original *Nuclear Boy* comic book) into an account paying 7.5 percent annually in order to buy his car in 6 years. How much will Bart's car cost, and how much does Bart have to save today in order to buy this car at age 16?

5-42. (*Compounding using a calculator*) Lisa Simpson wants to have $1 million in 45 years by making equal annual end-of-the-year deposits into a tax-deferred account paying 8.75 percent annually. What must Lisa's annual deposit be?

5-43. (*Compounding using a calculator and annuities due*) Springfield mogul Montgomery Burns, age 80, wants to retire at age 100 in order to steal candy from babies full time. Once Mr. Burns retires, he wants to withdraw $1 billion at the beginning of each year for 10 years from a special offshore account that will pay 20 percent annually. In order to fund his retirement, Mr. Burns will make 20 equal end-of-the-year deposits in this same special account that will pay 20 percent annually. How much money will Mr. Burns need at age 100, and how large of an annual deposit must he make to fund this retirement account?

5-44. (*Compounding using a calculator and annuities due*) Imagine Homer Simpson actually invested $100,000 5 years ago at a 7.5 percent annual interest rate. If he invests an additional $1,500 a year at the beginning of each year for 20 years at the same 7.5 percent annual rate, how much money will Homer have 20 years from now?

5-45. (*Nonannual compounding using a calculator*) Prof. Finance is thinking about trading cars. He estimates he will still have to borrow $25,000 to pay for his new car. How large will Prof. Finance's monthly car loan payment be if he can get a 5-year (60 equal monthly payments) car loan from the university's credit union at 6.2 percent?

5-46. (*Nonannual compounding using a calculator*) Bowflex's television ads say you can get a fitness machine that sells for $999 for $33 a month for 36 months. What rate of interest are you paying on this Bowflex loan?

5-47. (*Nonannual compounding using a calculator*) Ford's current incentives include 4.9 percent financing for 60 months or $1,000 cash back for a Mustang. Let's assume Suzie Student wants to buy the premium Mustang convertible, which costs $25,000, and she has no down payment other than the cash back from Ford. If she chooses the $1,000 cash back, Suzie can borrow from the VTech Credit Union at 6.9 percent for 60 months (Suzie's credit isn't as good as Prof. Finance's). What will Suzie Student's monthly payment be under each option? Which option should she choose?

5-48. (*Nonannual compounding using a calculator*) Ronnie Rental plans to invest $1,000 at the end of each quarter for 4 years into an account that pays 6.4 percent compounded quarterly. He will use this money as a down payment on a new home at the end of the 4 years. How large will his down payment be 4 years from today?

5-49. (*Nonannual compounding using a calculator*) Dennis Rodman has a $5,000 debt balance on his Visa card that charges 12.9 percent compounded monthly. Dennis's current minimum monthly payment is 3 percent of his debt balance, which is $150. How many months (round up) will it take Dennis to pay off his credit card if he pays the current minimum payment of $150 at the end of each month?

5-50. (*Nonannual compounding using a calculator*) Should we have bet the kids' college fund at the dog track? In the downturn of 2008–2009 investors suffered substantial declines on tax-sheltered college savings plans (called 529 plans) around the country. Let's look at one specific case of a college professor (let's call him Prof. ME) with two young children. Two years ago Prof. ME invested $160,000 hoping to have $420,000 available 12 years later when the first child started college. However, the account's balance is now only $140,000. Let's figure out what is needed to get Prof. ME's college savings plan back on track.

   a. What was the original annual rate of return needed to reach Prof. ME's goal when he started the fund 2 years ago?
   b. Now with only $140,000 in the fund and 10 years remaining until his first child starts college, what annual rate of return would the fund have to earn to reach Prof. ME's $420,000 goal if he adds nothing to the account?
   c. Shocked by his experience of the past 2 years, Prof. ME feels the college mutual fund has invested too much in stocks. He wants a low-risk fund in order to ensure he has the necessary $420,000 in 10 years, and he is willing to make end-of-the-month deposits to the fund as well. He later finds a fund that promises to pay a guaranteed return of 6 percent compounded monthly. Prof. ME decides to transfer the $140,000 to this new fund and make the necessary monthly deposits. How large of a monthly deposit must Prof. ME make into this new fund to meet his $420,000 goal?
   d. Now Prof. ME gets sticker shock from the necessary monthly deposit he has to make into the guaranteed fund in the preceding question. He decides to invest the $140,000 today and $500 at the end of each month for the next 10 years into a fund consisting of 50 percent stock and 50 percent bonds and hope for the best. What annual rate of return would the fund have to earn in order to reach Prof. ME's $420,000 goal?

5-51. (*Complex annuity*) Upon graduating from college 35 years ago, Dr. Nick Riviera was already thinking of retirement. Since then he has made deposits into his retirement fund on a quarterly basis in the amount of $300. Nick has just completed his final payment and is at last ready to retire. His retirement fund has earned 9% interest compounded quarterly.

   a. How much has Nick accumulated in his retirement account?
   b. In addition to all this, 15 years ago, Nick received an inheritance check for $20,000 from his beloved uncle. He decided to deposit the entire amount into his retirement fund. What is his current balance in the fund?

5-52. (*Solving for r in an annuity*) Your folks just called and would like some advice from you. An insurance agent just called them and offered them the opportunity to purchase an annuity for $21,074.25 that will pay them $3,000 per year for 20 years, but they don't have the slightest idea what return they would be making on their investment of $21,074.25. What rate of return will they be earning?

5-53. (*Complex annuity and future value*) Milhouse, 22, is about to begin his career as a rocket scientist for a NASA contractor. Being a rocket scientist, Milhouse knows that he should begin saving for retirement immediately. Part of his inspiration came from reading an article on Social Security in *Newsweek*, where he saw that the ratio of workers paying taxes to retirees collecting checks will drop dramatically in the future. In fact the ratio was 8.6 workers for every retiree in 1955; today the ratio is 3.3, and it will drop to 2 workers for every retiree in 2040. Milhouse's retirement plan pays 9 percent interest annually and allows him to make equal yearly contributions. Upon retirement Milhouse plans to buy a new boat, which he estimates will cost him $300,000 in 43 years (he plans to retire at age 65). He also estimates that in order to live comfortably he will require a yearly income of $80,000 for each year after he retires. Based on family history, Milhouse expects to live until age 80 (that is, he would like to receive 15 payments of $80,000 at the end of each year). When he retires, Milhouse will purchase his boat in one lump sum and place the remaining balance into an account, which pays 6% interest, from which he will withdraw his $80,000 per year. If Milhouse's first contribution is made 1 year from today, and his last is made the day he retires, how much money must he contribute each year to his retirement fund?

5-54. (*Future value*) Bob Terwilliger received $12,345 for his services as financial consultant to the mayor's office of his hometown of Springfield. Bob says that his consulting work was his civic duty and that he should not receive any compensation. So, he has invested his paycheck into an account paying 3.98 percent annual interest and left the account in his will to the city of Springfield on the condition that the city could not collect any money from the account for 200 years. How much money will the city receive from Bob's generosity in 200 years?

5-55. (*Solving for r*) Kirk Van Houten, who has been married for 23 years, would like to buy his wife an expensive diamond ring with a platinum setting on their 30-year wedding anniversary. Assume that the cost of the ring will be $12,000 in 7 years. Kirk currently has $4,510 to invest. What annual rate of return must Kirk earn on his investment to accumulate enough money to pay for the ring?

5-56. (*Solving for n*) Jack asked Jill to marry him, and she has accepted under one condition: Jack must buy her a new $330,000 Rolls-Royce Phantom. Jack currently has $45,530 that he may invest. He has found a mutual fund that pays 4.5% annual interest in which he will place the money. How long will it take Jack to win Jill's hand in marriage?

5-57. (*Present value*) Ronen Consulting has just realized an accounting error which has resulted in an unfunded liability of $398,930 due in 28 years. Toni Flanders, the company's CEO, is scrambling to discount the liability to the present to assist in valuing the firm's stock. If the appropriate discount rate is 7 percent, what is the present value of the liability?

Mini Case

For your job as the business reporter for a local newspaper, you are given the task of putting together a series of articles that explain the power of the time value of money to your readers. Your editor would like you to address several specific questions in addition to demonstrating for the readership the use of time value of money techniques by applying them to several problems. What would be your response to the following memorandum from your editor?

> To: Business Reporter
> From: Perry White, Editor, *Daily Planet*
> Re: Upcoming Series on the Importance and Power of the Time Value of Money

In your upcoming series on the time value of money, I would like to make sure you cover several specific points. In addition, before you begin this assignment, I want to make sure we are all reading from the same script, as accuracy has always been the cornerstone of the *Daily Planet*. In this regard, I'd like a response to the following questions before we proceed:

a. What is the relationship between discounting and compounding?
b. What is the relationship between the present value factor and the annuity present value factor?
c. 1. What will $5,000 invested for 10 years at 8 percent compounded annually grow to?
   2. How many years will it take $400 to grow to $1,671 if it is invested at 10 percent compounded annually?
   3. At what rate would $1,000 have to be invested to grow to $4,046 in 10 years?
d. Calculate the future sum of $1,000, given that it will be held in the bank for 5 years and earn 10 percent compounded semiannually.
e. What is an annuity due? How does this differ from an ordinary annuity?
f. What is the present value of an ordinary annuity of $1,000 per year for 7 years discounted back to the present at 10 percent? What would be the present value if it were an annuity due?
g. What is the future value of an ordinary annuity of $1,000 per year for 7 years compounded at 10 percent? What would be the future value if it were an annuity due?
h. You have just borrowed $100,000, and you agree to pay it back over the next 25 years in 25 equal end-of-year payments plus 10 percent compound interest on the unpaid balance. What will be the size of these payments?
i. What is the present value of a $1,000 perpetuity discounted back to the present at 8 percent?

j. What is the present value of a $1,000 annuity for 10 years, with the first payment occurring at the end of year 10 (that is, ten $1,000 payments occurring at the end of year 10 through year 19), given a discount rate of 10 percent?

k. Given a 10 percent discount rate, what is the present value of a perpetuity of $1,000 per year if the first payment does not begin until the end of year 10?

Self-Test Solutions

SS-1. This is a compound interest problem in which you must first find the future value of $25,000 growing at 8 percent compounded annually for 3 years and then allow that future value to grow for an additional 3 years at 10 percent. First, the value of the $25,000 after 3 years growing at 8 percent is

$$FV_3 = PV(1 + r)^n$$
$$FV_3 = \$25,000(1 + 0.8)^3$$
$$FV_3 = \$31,492.80$$

Thus, after 3 years you have $31,492.80. Now this amount is allowed to grow for 3 years at 10 percent. Plugging this into equation (1), with $PV = \$31,492.80$, $r = 10$ percent, and $n = 3$ years, we solve for FV_3.

$$FV_3 = \$31,492.80(1 + 0.10)^3$$
$$FV_3 = \$41,916.92$$

Thus, after 6 years the $25,000 will have grown to $41,916.92.

SS-2. This loan amortization problem is actually just a present-value-of-an-annuity problem in which we know the values of r, n, and PV and are solving for PMT. In this case the value of r is 13 percent, n is 10 years, and PV is $30,000. Substituting these values into equation (4) we find

$$\$30,000 = PMT\left[\frac{1 - (1 + 0.13)^{-10}}{0.13}\right]$$

$$\$5,528.69 = PMT$$

Determine the value of $25,000 growing at 8 percent for 3 years:

CALCULATOR SOLUTION

Data Input	Function Key
3	N
8	I/Y
25,000	PV
0	PMT

Function Key	Answer
CPT	
FV	−31,492.80

STEP 2
Determine the value of the $31,492.80, calculated in step 1, growing at 10 percent for 3 years.

CALCULATOR SOLUTION

Data Input	Function Key
3	N
10	I/Y
31,492.80	PV
0	PMT

Function Key	Answer
CPT	
FV	−41,916.92

CALCULATOR SOLUTION

Data Input	Function Key
10	N
13	I/Y
30,000	PV
0	FV

Function Key	Answer
CPT	
PMT	−5,528.69

The Meaning and Measurement of Risk and Return

From Chapter 6 of *Foundations of Finance*, 7/e. Arthur J. Keown. John D. Martin. J. William Petty. Copyright © 2011 by Pearson Education.
Published by Prentice Hall. All rights reserved.

The Meaning and Measurement of Risk and Return

Learning Objectives

After reading this chapter, you should be able to:

 Define and measure **the expected rate of return of an individual investment.**

 Define and measure **the riskiness of an individual investment.**

 Compare **the historical relationship between risk and rates of return in the capital markets.**

 Explain **how diversifying investments affects the riskiness and expected rate of return of a portfolio or combination of assets.**

Explain **the relationship between an investor's required rate of return on an investment and the riskiness of the investment.**

One of the most important concepts in finance is *risk and return,* which is the total focus of our third principle of finance—**Risk Requires a Reward.** You only have to consider what happened in the capital markets, especially stocks, from late 2007 to early 2009 to see the overwhelming presence of risk and returns. For example, if you had been so unfortunate as to buy a portfolio of stocks consisting of the Standard & Poor's 500 in October 2007 and sold in February 2009, you would have lost 53 percent of your money. Even worse, if you had held Bank of America stock during that time period, you would have lost 94 percent of your money! However, if you had been so astute as to buy Bank of America stock in February 2009 and sold four months later in June 2009, you would have earned a whopping 333 percent return on your investment. Even investing in the S&P stocks would have earned you 29 percent on your investment—not bad for a few months.

Clearly, owning stocks in recent times has not been for the faint of heart, where in a single day you could have earned as much as five percent on your investment, or lost even more. The market crash and extreme volatility in stock prices in 2008 and 2009 are what Nassim Nicholas Taleb would call a black swan—a highly improbable event that has a massive impact.[1] As a consequence, our confidence in forecasting the future has been undermined. Furthermore, our lives have been impacted and future plans delayed. We are much more cognizant of the financial risks that we face, both individually and in business.

---

[1]In his book *The Black Swan: The Impact of the Highly Improbable* (New York: Random House, 2007), Nassim Nicholas Taleb uses the analogy of a black swan, which represents a highly unlikely event. Until black swans were discovered in Australia, everyone assumed that all swans were white. Thus, for Taleb, the black swan symbolizes an event that no one thinks possible.

In this chapter, we will help you understand the nature of risk and how risk *should* relate to expected returns on investments. We will look back beyond the past few years to see what we can learn about long-term historical risk-and-return relationships. These are topics that should be of key interest to us all in this day and age.

The need to recognize risk in financial decisions has already been apparent in earlier chapters. In this book, we referred to the discount rate, or the interest rate, as the opportunity cost of funds, but we did not look at the reasons why that rate might be high or low. For example, we did not explain why in June 2009 you could buy bonds issued by General Electric that promised to pay a 6.3 percent rate of return, or why you could buy Dow Chemical bonds that would give you an 8.7 percent rate of return, provided that both firms make the payments to the investors as promised.

In this chapter, we learn that risk is an integral force underlying rates of return. To begin our study, we define expected return and risk and offer suggestions about how these important concepts of return and risk can be measured quantitatively. We also compare the historical relationship between risk and rates of return. We then explain how diversifying investments can affect the expected return and riskiness of those investments. We also consider how the riskiness of an investment should affect the required rate of return on an investment.

Let's begin our study by looking at what we mean by the expected rate of return and how it can be measured.

©Nell Redmond/AP Wide World Photos

 REMEMBER YOUR PRINCIPLES

Principle This chapter has one primary objective, that of helping you understand **Principle 3: Risk Requires a Reward**.

Expected Return Defined and Measured

The expected benefits, or returns, an investment generates come in the form of cash flows. Cash flow, not accounting profit, is the relevant variable the financial manager uses to measure returns. This principle holds true regardless of the type of security, whether it is a debt instrument, preferred stock, common stock, or any mixture of these (such as convertible bonds).

To begin our discussion about an asset's expected rate of return, let's first understand how to compute an **historical** or **realized rate of return** on an investment. It may also be called a **holding-period return**. For instance, consider the dollar return you would have earned had you purchased a share of Apple stock on April 1, 2009 for $104.50 and sold one month later on May 1 for $125.80. The dollar return from your investment would have been $21.30 ($21.30 = $125.80 − $104.50), assuming that the company paid no dividend. In addition to the dollar gain, we can calculate the rate of return as a percentage. It is useful to summarize the return on an investment in terms of a percentage because that way we can see the return per dollar invested which is independent of how much we actually invest.

The rate of return earned from the investment in Apple can be calculated as the ratio of the dollar return of $21.30 divided by your $104.50 investment in the stock at the beginning of the month, or 20.4 percent (0.204 = $21.30 ÷ $104.50).

Define and measure the expected rate of return of an individual investment.

holding-period return (historical or realized rate of return) the rate of return earned on an investment, which equals the dollar gain divided by the amount invested.

We can formalize the return calculations using equations (1) and (2):

Holding-Period Dollar Gain would be:

$$\text{Holding-period dollar gain, DG} = \text{Price}_{\text{end of period}} + \frac{\text{cash distribution}}{\text{(dividend)}} - \text{Price}_{\text{beginning of period}} \quad (1)$$

and for the holding-period rate of return

$$\text{Rate of return, } r = \frac{\text{dollar gain}}{P_{\text{beginning of period}}} = \frac{P_{\text{end of period}} + \text{Dividend} - P_{\text{beginning of period}}}{P_{\text{beginning of period}}} \quad (2)$$

The method we have just used to compute the holding-period return on our investment in Apple tells us the return we actually earned during an historical time period. However, the risk–return trade-off that investors face on a day-to-day basis is based *not* on realized rates of return, but on what the investor *expects* to earn on an investment in the future. We can think of the rate of return that will ultimately be realized from making a risky investment in terms of a range of possible return outcomes, much like the distribution of grades for this class at the end of the term. To describe this range of possible returns, it is customary to use the average of the different possible returns. We refer to the average of the possible rates of return as the investment's **expected rate of return**.

Accurately measuring expected future cash flows is not easy in a world of uncertainty. To illustrate, assume you are considering an investment costing $10,000, for which the future cash flows from owning the security depend on the state of the economy, as estimated in Table 1.

In any given year, the investment could produce any one of three possible cash flows, depending on the particular state of the economy. With this information, how should we select the cash flow estimate that means the most for measuring the investment's expected rate of return? One approach is to calculate an *expected* cash flow. The expected cash flow is simply the weighted average of the *possible* cash flow outcomes such that the weights are the probabilities of the various states of the economy occurring. Stated as an equation:

expected rate of return The arithmetic mean or average of all possible outcomes where those outcomes are weighted by the probability that each will occur.

$$\text{Expected cash flow, } \overline{CF} = \begin{pmatrix} \text{cash flow} & & \text{probability} \\ \text{in state 1} & \times & \text{of state 1} \\ (CF_1) & & (Pb_1) \end{pmatrix} + \begin{pmatrix} \text{cash flow} & & \text{probability} \\ \text{in state 2} & \times & \text{of state 2} \\ (CF_2) & & (Pb_2) \end{pmatrix}$$

$$+ \begin{pmatrix} \text{cash flow} & & \text{probability} \\ \text{in state 3} & \times & \text{of state 3} \\ (CF_3) & & (Pb_3) \end{pmatrix} \quad (3)$$

> ### REMEMBER YOUR PRINCIPLES
> **Principle** Remember that future cash flows, not reported earnings, determine the investor's rate of return. That is, **Principle 1: Cash Flow Is What Matters**.

For the present illustration:

$$\text{Expected cash flow} = (0.2)(\$1,000) + (0.3)(\$1,200) + (0.5)(\$1,400)$$
$$= \$1,260$$

In addition to computing an expected dollar return from an investment, we can also calculate an expected rate of return

State of the Economy	Probability of the States[a]	Cash Flows from the Investment	Percentage Returns (Cash Flow ÷ Investment Cost)
Economic recession	20%	$1,000	10% ($1,000 ÷ $10,000)
Moderate economic growth	30%	1,200	12% ($1,200 ÷ $10,000)
Strong economic growth	50%	1,400	14% ($1,400 ÷ $10,000)

TABLE 1 Measuring the Expected Return of an Investment

[a]The probabilities assigned to the three possible economic conditions have to be determined subjectively, which requires managers to have a thorough understanding of both the investment cash flows and the general economy.

CAN YOU DO IT?

COMPUTING EXPECTED CASH FLOW AND EXPECTED RETURN

You are contemplating making a $5,000 investment that would have the following possible outcomes in cash flow each year. What is the expected value of the future cash flows and the expected rate of return?

PROBABILITY	Rate of Return	CASH FLOW
0.30	7%	$350
0.50	13%	625
0.20	18%	900

Expected Value = (.30 x 350) +(0.50*625) +(0.20 * 900) = $105 +$312.50 + $180=$597.50
Cash Flow
Expected Rate of Return = (.30 x 7) + (0.50 x 13) + (0.20 x18) = .02 +. 07 +0.04 = .13 or 13%

earned on the $10,000 investment. Similar to the expected cash flow, the expected rate of return is *a weighted average of all the possible returns, weighted by the probability that each return will occur*. As the last column in Table 1 shows, the $1,400 cash inflow, assuming strong economic growth, represents a 14 percent return ($1,400 ÷ $10,000). Similarly, the $1,200 and $1,000 cash flows result in 12 percent and 10 percent returns, respectively. Using these percentage returns in place of the dollar amounts, the expected rate of return can be expressed as follows:

$$\text{Expected rate of return}, \bar{r} = \left(\begin{array}{c} \text{rate of return} \\ \text{for state 1} \\ (r_1) \end{array} \times \begin{array}{c} \text{probability} \\ \text{of state 1} \\ (Pb_1) \end{array} \right) + \left(\begin{array}{c} \text{rate of return} \\ \text{for state 2} \\ (r_2) \end{array} \times \begin{array}{c} \text{probability} \\ \text{of state 2} \\ (Pb_2) \end{array} \right)$$

$$+ \left(\begin{array}{c} \text{rate of return} \\ \text{for state 3} \\ (r_3) \end{array} \times \begin{array}{c} \text{probability} \\ \text{of state 3} \\ (Pb_3) \end{array} \right) \tag{4}$$

In our example:

$\bar{r} = (0.2)(10\%) + (0.3)(12\%) + (0.5)(14\%) = 12.6\%$

With our concept and measurement of expected returns, let's consider the other side of the investment coin: risk.

Concept Check

1. When we speak of "benefits" from investing in an asset, what do we mean?
2. Why is it difficult to measure future cash flows?
3. Define *expected rate of return*.

Risk Defined and Measured

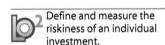

Define and measure the riskiness of an individual investment.

Because we live in a world where events are uncertain, the way we see risk is vitally important in almost all dimensions of our life. The Greek poet and statesman Solon, writing in the sixth century B.C., put it this way:

> There is risk in everything that one does, and no one knows where he will make his landfall when his enterprise is at its beginning. One man, trying to act effectively, fails to foresee something and falls into great and grim ruination, but to another man, one who is acting ineffectively, a god gives good fortune in everything and escape from his folly.[2]

Solon would have given more of the credit to Zeus than we would for the outcomes of our ventures. However, his insight reminds us that little is new in this world, including the

---

[2]Translated by Arthur W. H. Adkins from the Greek text of Solon's poem "Prosperity, Justice, and the Hazards of Life," in M. L. West, ed., *Iambi et Elegi Graeci ante Alexandrum Cantati*, vol. 2 (Oxford: Clarendon Press, 1972).

DID YOU GET IT?
COMPUTING EXPECTED CASH FLOW AND EXPECTED RETURN

PROBABILITY	POSSIBLE		EXPECTED	
	CASH FLOW	RETURN	CASH FLOW	RETURN
0.30	$350	7.0%	$105.00	2.1%
0.50	625	12.5%	312.50	6.3%
0.20	900	18.0%	180.00	3.6%
Expected cash flow and rate of return			$597.50	12.0%

The possible returns are equal to the possible cash flows divided by the $5,000 investment. The expected cash flow and return are equal to the possible cash flows and possible returns multiplied by the probabilities.

need to acknowledge and compensate as best we can for the risks we encounter. In fact, the significance of risk and the need for understanding what it means in our lives is noted by Peter Bernstein in the following excerpt:

> What is it that distinguishes the thousands of years of history from what we think of as modern times? The answer goes way beyond the progress of science, technology, capitalism, and democracy.
>
> The distant past was studded with brilliant scientists, mathematicians, inventors, technologists, and political philosophers. Hundreds of years before the birth of Christ, the skies had been mapped, the great library of Alexandria built, and Euclid's geometry taught. Demand for technological innovation in warfare was as insatiable then as it is today. Coal, oil, iron, and copper have been at the service of human beings for millennia, and travel and communication mark the very beginnings of recorded civilization.
>
> The revolutionary idea that defines the boundary between modern times and the past is the mastery of risk: the notion that the future is more than a whim of the gods and that men and women are not passive before nature. Until human beings discovered a way across that boundary, the future was a mirror of the past or the murky domain of oracles and soothsayers who held a monopoly over knowledge of anticipated events.[3]

In our study of risk, we want to consider these questions:

1. What is risk?
2. How do we know the amount of risk associated with a given investment; that is, how do we measure risk?
3. If we choose to diversify our investments by owning more than one asset, as most of us do, will such diversification reduce the riskiness of our combined portfolio of investments?

Without intending to be trite, risk means different things to different people, depending on the context and on how they feel about taking chances. For the student, risk is the possibility of failing an exam or the chance of not making his or her best grades. For the coal miner or the oil field worker, risk is the chance of an explosion in the mine or at the well site. For the retired person, risk means perhaps not being able to live comfortably on a fixed income. For the entrepreneur, risk is the chance that a new venture will fail.

risk potential variability in future cash flows.

While certainly acknowledging these different kinds of risk, we limit our attention to the risk inherent in an investment. In this context, **risk** is the *potential variability in future cash flows*. The wider the range of possible events that can occur, the greater the risk.[4] If we think about it, this is a relatively intuitive concept.

---

[3]Peter Bernstein, *Against the Gods: The Remarkable Story of Risk.* John Wiley & Sons, Inc., New York, 1996, p. 1.
[4]When we speak of possible events, we must not forget that it is the highly unlikely event that we cannot anticipate that may have the greatest impact on the outcome of an investment. So, we evaluate investment opportunities based on the best information available, but there may be a *black swan* that we cannot anticipate.

To help us grasp the fundamental meaning of risk within this context, consider two possible investments:

1. The first investment is a U.S. Treasury bill, a government security that matures in 90 days and promises to pay an annual return of 3 percent. If we purchase and hold this security for 90 days, we are virtually assured of receiving no more and no less than 3 percent on an annualized basis. For all practical purposes, the risk of loss is nonexistent.

2. The second investment involves the purchase of the stock of a local publishing company. Looking at the past returns of the firm's stock, we have made the following estimate of the annual returns from the investment:

CHANCE OF OCCURRENCE	RATE OF RETURN ON INVESTMENT
1 chance in 10 (10% chance)	0%
2 chances in 10 (20% chance)	5%
4 chances in 10 (40% chance)	15%
2 chances in 10 (20% chance)	25%
1 chance in 10 (10% chance)	30%

Investing in the publishing company could conceivably provide a return as high as 30 percent if all goes well, or no return (0 percent) if everything goes against the firm. However, in future years, both good and bad, we could expect a 15 percent return on average.[5]

$$\text{Expected return} = (0.10)(0\%) + (0.20)(5\%) + (0.40)(15\%) + (0.20)(25\%)$$
$$+ (0.10)(30\%)$$
$$= 15\%$$

Comparing the Treasury bill investment with the publishing company investment, we see that the Treasury bill offers an expected 3 percent annualized rate of return, whereas the publishing company has an expected rate of return of 15 percent. However, our investment in the publishing firm is clearly more "risky"—that is, there is greater uncertainty about the final outcome. Stated somewhat differently, there is a greater variation or dispersion of possible returns, which in turn implies greater risk.[6] Figure 1 shows these differences graphically in the form of discrete probability distributions.

FIGURE 1 The Probability Distribution of the Returns on Two Investments

[5]We assume that the particular outcome or return earned in 1 year does *not* affect the return earned in the subsequent year. Technically speaking, the distribution of returns in any year is assumed to be independent of the outcome in any prior year.

[6]How can we possibly view variations above the expected return as risk? Should we even be concerned with the positive deviations above the expected return? Some would say "no," viewing risk as only the negative variability in returns from a predetermined minimum acceptable rate of return. However, as long as the distribution of returns is symmetrical, the same conclusions will be reached.

Although the return from investing in the publishing firm is clearly less certain than for Treasury bills, quantitative measures of risk are useful when the difference between two investments is not so evident. We can quantify the risk of an investment by computing the variance in the possible investment returns and its square root, the **standard deviation** (σ). For the case where there are n possible returns (i.e., states of the economy) we calculate the variance as follows:

$$
\begin{aligned}
\text{Variance in} \atop \text{rates of return} \atop (\sigma^2) = &\left[\left(\begin{array}{c}\text{rate of return} \\ \text{for state 1} \\ (r_1)\end{array} - \begin{array}{c}\text{expected rate} \\ \text{of return} \\ \bar{r}\end{array}\right)^2 \times \begin{array}{c}\text{probability} \\ \text{of state 1} \\ (Pb_1)\end{array}\right] \\
&+ \left[\left(\begin{array}{c}\text{rate of return} \\ \text{for state 2} \\ (r_2)\end{array} - \begin{array}{c}\text{expected rate} \\ \text{of return} \\ \bar{r}\end{array}\right)^2 \times \begin{array}{c}\text{probability} \\ \text{of state 2} \\ (Pb_2)\end{array}\right] \\
&+ \cdots + \left[\left(\begin{array}{c}\text{rate of return} \\ \text{for state } n \\ (r_n)\end{array} - \begin{array}{c}\text{expected rate} \\ \text{of return} \\ \bar{r}\end{array}\right)^2 \times \begin{array}{c}\text{probability} \\ \text{of state } n \\ (Pb_n)\end{array}\right]
\end{aligned}
$$

(5)

For the publishing company's common stock, we calculate the standard deviation using the following five-step procedure:

STEP 1 Calculate the expected rate of return of the investment, which was calculated above to be 15%.

STEP 2 Subtract the expected rate of return of 15% from each of the possible rates of return and square the difference.

STEP 3 Multiply the squared differences calculated in step 2 by the probability that those outcomes will occur.

STEP 4 Sum all the values calculated in step 3 together. The sum is the variance of the distribution of possible rates of return. Note that the variance is actually the *average squared difference between the possible rates of return and the expected rate of return.*

STEP 5 Take the square root of the variance calculated in step 4 to calculate the standard deviation of the distribution of possible rates of return.

Table 2 illustrates the application of this process, which results in an estimated standard deviation for the common stock investment of 9.2%. This compared to the Treasury bill investment, which is risk free, has a standard deviation of 0%. The more risky the investment, the higher is its standard deviation.

TABLE 2 Measuring the Variance and Standard Deviation of the Publishing Company Investment					
State of the World	Rate of Return	Chance or Probability		Step 2	Step 3
A	B $(r - \bar{r}) \times$	C	D = B × C	E = $(B - \bar{r})^2$	F = E × C
1	0%	0.10	0%	225%	22.5%
3	5%	0.20	1%	100%	20.0%
4	15%	0.40	6%	0%	0%
4	25%	0.20	5%	100%	20.0%
5	30%	0.10	3%	225%	22.5%

Step 1: Expected Return ($\bar{r}$) = ⟶ 15%

Step 4: Variance = ⟶ 85%

Step 5: Standard Deviation = ⟶ 9.2%

CAN YOU DO IT?

COMPUTING THE STANDARD DEVIATION

In the preceding "Can You Do It?" we computed the expected cash flow of $597.50 and the expected return of 12 percent on a $5,000 investment. Now let's calculate the standard deviation of the returns. The probabilities of possible returns are given as follows:

PROBABILITY	RETURNS
0.30	7.0%
0.50	12.5%
0.20	18.0%

Alternatively, we could use equation (5) to calculate the standard deviation in investment returns as follows:

$$\sigma = \left[\begin{array}{l} (\ 0\% - 15\%)^2(.10) + (\ 5\% - 15\%)^2(.20) \\ + (15\% - 15\%)^2(.40) + (25\% - 15\%)^2(.20) \\ + (30\% - 15\%)^2(.10) \end{array} \right]^{\frac{1}{2}}$$

$$= \sqrt{85\%} = 9.22\%$$

Although the standard deviation of returns provides us with a quantitative measure of an asset's riskiness, how should we interpret the result? What does it mean? Is the 9.22 percent standard deviation for the publishing company investment good or bad? First, we should remember that statisticians tell us that two-thirds of the time, an event will fall within one standard deviation of the expected value (assuming the distribution is normally distributed; that is, it is shaped like a bell). Thus, given a 15 percent expected return and a standard deviation of 9.22 percent for the publishing company investment, we can reasonably anticipate that the actual returns will fall between 5.78 percent and 24.22 percent (15% ± 9.22%) two-thirds of the time. In other words, there is not much certainty with this investment.

A second way of answering the question about the meaning of the standard deviation comes by comparing the investment in the publishing firm against other investments. Obviously the attractiveness of a security with respect to its return and risk cannot be determined in isolation. Only by examining other available alternatives can we reach a conclusion about a particular investment's risk. For example, if another investment, say, an investment in a firm that owns a local radio station, has the same expected return as the publishing company, 15 percent, but with a standard deviation of 7 percent, we would consider the risk associated with the publishing firm, 9.22 percent, to be excessive. In the technical jargon of modern portfolio theory, the radio station investment is said to "dominate" the publishing firm investment. In common sense terms, this means that the radio station investment has the same expected return as the publishing company investment, but is less risky.

FINANCE AT WORK

A DIFFERENT PERSPECTIVE OF RISK

The first Chinese symbol shown here represents danger; the second stands for opportunity. The Chinese define risk as the combination of danger and opportunity. Greater risk, according to the Chinese, means we have greater opportunity to do well, but also greater danger of doing badly.

ETHICS IN FINANCIAL MANAGEMENT

"I SHOULD HAVE SAID NO"

At 66, Aaron Beam is getting on with his life. Six years ago Beam made headlines by admitting that he cooked the books at Health-South Corp., the Birmingham, Alabama-based provider of inpatient and outpatient rehabilitation services that he co-founded.

Released after three months in a minimum-security prison, Beam retreated to his small hometown of Loxley, Alabama. Having sold his $3 million dream home to pay restitution and legal fees, Beam now lives modestly and mows lawns for a living. But he is also developing another career: educational speaker.

In a recent interview with Beam, Edward Teach reports the following conversation:

Most CFOs can probably tell stories about the CEOs they've worked with, but in your case it sounds like an especially difficult relationship.
Unless you were there and experienced it, it's hard to understand. You couldn't tell [Scrushy] no on anything. I have seen him so mad over minor things that I actually feared for my physical safety. I often joke with students that if Richard Scrushy and Hannibal Lecter were in a fight, I would bet on Richard Scrushy.

How did the fraud begin?
By 1994 or 1995 we were a *Fortune* 500 company and the largest company in Alabama; we had 40,000 employees in all 50 states. But as we matured, it got more and more difficult to make our numbers. You can't keep growing at 20% to 30% every year on the bottom line. To keep the Street from lowering its estimates, we started lowering our reserves for bad debts; when we did acquisitions we would change the estimates of the companies we were acquiring so we could apply those estimates to our earnings as we went forward.

We committed fraud in the summer of 1996, when we could no longer change estimates to make earnings. We thought we could make a lot of entries small enough that the auditors wouldn't detect them. So one night, during the second quarter of 1996, I said, "OK, let's do it," and we credited revenue that did not exist and we debited assets that did not exist.

You kept committing fraud until you quit in 1997. How did you feel during that time?
I felt rotten. It was terrible. My hope was that after we had done it once, we wouldn't have to do it again. But after doing it for four

quarters, I felt like it wasn't going to end, so that's when I left. We had dug ourselves [into] a hole.

Weston Smith finally blew the whistle. Do you regret not having done so yourself?
The correct thing I should have done was, at the critical point when we weren't going to make our numbers, I should have said no [to any illegal actions]. If I got fired, I got fired. Once you actually commit fraud and have blood on your hands, getting out of the trap is very difficult.

Today you travel to business schools and talk to students about your experience at HealthSouth. What do you hope to accomplish?
I'm trying to turn a big negative into a positive, because there is such a need for ethics in the business world today, and I'm in a unique position to talk about it. If we can teach college students that they're going to face these kinds of temptations every day in the business world, we can make a difference.

What's life like for you now?
It's actually pretty good, even though I basically have no wealth now. I'm just back to being an ordinary guy. I went back to college and took a two-year certificate program in turf management. I have a lawn-service business—it's one man and a lawn mower. I'm cutting grass and doing public speaking and working on a book about my experiences.

Are you at peace with yourself?
I am. My marriage survived through it all. People seem to respect what I'm doing in my speaking. It's sad, though, and I tell people this: I was a founder of one of the most successful health-care companies in the history of the United States. Today HealthSouth is trading on the New York Stock Exchange and doing well. But I won't be remembered for that. I will be remembered as one of the guys who committed the fraud. That hurts, and it hurt my family a lot. But, you know, you heal over time, and I'm OK today.

Source: Edward Teach, "I Should Have Said No," *CFO Magazine*, June 1, 2009, pp. 34–36.

What if we compare the investment in the publishing company with one in a quick oil-change franchise, an investment in which the expected rate of return is an attractive 24 percent but the standard deviation is estimated at 13 percent? Now what should we do? Clearly, the oil-change franchise has a higher expected rate of return, but it also has a larger standard deviation. In this example, we see that the real challenge in selecting the better investment comes when one investment has a higher expected rate of return but also exhibits greater risk. *Here the final choice is determined by our attitude toward risk, and there is no single right answer.* You might select the publishing company, whereas I might choose the oil-change investment, and neither of us would be wrong. We would simply be expressing our tastes and preferences about risk and return.

DID YOU GET IT?
COMPUTING THE STANDARD DEVIATION

DEVIATION (POSSIBLE RETURN − 12% EXPECTED RETURN)	DEVIATION SQUARED	PROBABILITY	PROBABILITY × DEVIATION SQUARED
−5.0%	0.25%	0.30	0.075%
0.5%	0.0025%	0.50	0.00125%
6.0%	0.36%	0.20	0.072%
Sum of squared deviations × probability (variance)			0.14825%
Standard deviation			3.85%

Concept Check

1. How is risk defined?

2. How does the standard deviation help us measure the riskiness of an investment?

3. Does greater risk imply a bad investment?

Rates of Return: The Investor's Experience

 Compare the historical relationship between risk and rates of return in the capital markets.

So far, we have mostly used hypothetical examples of expected rates of return and risk; however, it is also interesting to look at returns that investors have actually received on different types of securities. For example, Ibbotson Associates publishes the long-term historical annual rates of return for the following types of investments beginning in 1926 and continuing to the present:

1. Common stocks of large companies
2. Common stocks of small firms
3. Long-term corporate bonds
4. Long-term U.S. government bonds
5. Intermediate-term U.S. government bonds
6. U.S. Treasury bills (short-term government securities)

Before comparing these returns, we should think about what to expect. First, we would intuitively expect a Treasury bill (short-term government securities) to be the least risky of the six portfolios. Because a Treasury bill has a short-term maturity date, the price is less volatile (less risky) than the price of an intermediate- or long-term government security. In turn, because there is a chance of default on a corporate bond, which is essentially nonexistent for government securities, a long-term government bond is less risky than a long-term corporate bond. Finally, the common stocks of large companies are more risky than corporate bonds, with small-company stocks being more risky than large-firm stocks.

With this in mind, we could reasonably expect different rates of return to the holders of these varied securities. If the market rewards an investor for assuming risk, the average annual rates of return should increase as risk increases.

A comparison of the annual rates of return for the six respective portfolios for the years 1926 to 2008 is provided in Figure 2. Four aspects of these returns are included: (1) the nominal average annual rate of return; (2) the standard deviation of the returns, which measures the volatility, or riskiness, of the returns; (3) the real average annual rate of return, which is the nominal return less the inflation rate; and (4) the risk premium, which represents the additional return received beyond the risk-free rate (Treasury bill rate) for assuming risk. Looking at the first two columns of nominal average annual returns and standard deviations, we get a good overview of the risk–return relationships that have existed over the 83 years ending in 2008. In every case, there has been a positive relationship between risk and return, with Treasury bills being least risky and small-company stocks being most risky.

FINANCE AT WORK

HARD LESSONS

When Anthony Dombrowik was promoted from controller to CFO of the Red Lion Hotel Group in 2008, he knew the role would be challenging. What he didn't know was that his first year would essentially be a trial-by-fire, requiring him to navigate through some of the most daunting times ever faced by American business. During Dombrowik's first 16 months on the job, Red Lion's revenues dropped some 13% with no recovery in sight. The company cut 10% of its workforce, including finance staffers, and combed its operations for any and all cost-cutting ideas, even switching to cheaper guest-room soaps. Dombrowik is thankful that none of the commercial mortgage-backed securities (CMBS) that finance the bulk of Red Lion's business have come due recently—there's no chance of rolling them over when they do—but soon he will have to find a new source of outside funding. At the same time, he is looking for opportunity in the ashes, hoping to grow the business by acquiring or franchising distressed hotel properties that may come up for sale.

Since September 2008, when the bankruptcy of Lehman Brothers triggered the near-meltdown of the nation's financial system, the CFO's role was reshaped in new and sometimes unnerving ways. Thanks to the post-September credit crunch and steep falloff in consumer demand, thousands of finance chiefs like Dombrowik have restructured their businesses, executed layoffs, hoarded cash, and begged for financing. Many such actions are standard operating procedure in tough times, and some will be reversed when the economy finally turns around. But [the most recent] recession—the longest and nastiest since the Great Depression—[promised] to leave a lasting impact on business in general and corporate finance in particular.

Indeed, more than 85 percent of finance executives responding to a *CFO Magazine* survey said they don't expect their companies to return to business as usual after the economy recovers. They predict that substantial adjustments will be necessary, whether that means shuttering business units, responding to new competitive challenges, or dealing with new (and generally unwelcome) regulation.

Ironically, even though the vast majority anticipate what some refer to as a "new normal," nearly half expected their current business model to serve the company well going forward; a substantial number, however, expected their firm's strategy to change once they can shift their attention away from short-term survival.

One thing is clear: No CFO is likely to forget the hard lessons he or she has learned in areas like cash management, forecasting, risk, and human capital. "Those who lived through the Depression were forever more frugal, and I think you'll see something similar this time in the business world," says Dombrowik. He for one is planning to retain as much of Red Lion's recent cost-cutting as possible when demand picks up again (although the soaps will likely be upgraded).

Source: Alix Stuart, "Hard Lessons," *CFO Magazine,* September 1, 2009, pp. 42–44.

The return information in Figure 2 clearly demonstrates that only common stock has in the long run served as an inflation hedge and provided any substantial risk premium. However, it is equally apparent that the common stockholder is exposed to a sizable amount of risk, as is demonstrated by the 20.6 percent standard deviation for large-company stocks and

FIGURE 2 Historical Rates of Return

Securities	Nominal Average Annual Returns	Standard Deviation of Returns	Real Average Annual Returns[a]	Risk Premium[b]
Large-company stocks	11.7%	20.6%	8.6%	7.9%
Small-company stocks	16.4%	33.0%	13.3%	14.6%
Corporate bonds	6.2%	8.4%	3.1%	2.4%
Government bonds	6.1%	9.4%	3.0%	2.3%
U.S. Treasury bills	3.8%	3.1%	0.7%	0.0%
Inflation	3.1%	4.2%		

[a]The real return equals the nominal returns less the inflation rate of 3.1 percent.
[b]The risk premium equals the nominal security return than the average risk-free rate (Treasury bills) of 3.8 percent.

the 33 percent standard deviation for small-company stocks. In fact, in the 1926 to 2008 time frame, common shareholders of large firms received negative returns in 23 of the 83 years, compared with only 1 (1938) in 83 years for Treasury bills.

Concept Check

1. What is the additional compensation for assuming greater risk called?
2. In Figure 2, which rate of return is the risk-free rate? Why?

Risk and Diversification

 Explain how diversifying investments affects the riskiness and expected rate of return of a portfolio or combination of assets.

More can be said about risk, especially about its nature, when we own more than one asset in our investment portfolio. Let's consider for the moment how risk is affected if we diversify our investment by holding a variety of securities.

Let's assume that you graduated from college in December 2008. Not only did you get the good job you had hoped for, but you also finished the year with a little nest egg—not enough to take that summer fling to Europe like some of your college friends but a nice surplus. Besides, you suspected that they used credit cards to go anyway. So, you made two stock investments with your nest egg—one in Harley Davidson and one in Starbucks. (As the owner of a Harley Softail motorcycle, you've had a passion for riding since your high school days. And you give Starbucks credit for helping you get through many long study sessions.) You then focused on your career and seldom thought about your investments. Your first extended break from work came June 2009. After a lazy Saturday morning, you decided to get on the Internet to see how your investments did over the previous several months. You bought Starbucks for $9, and the stock was now trading at almost $15. "Not bad," you thought. But then the bad news—Harley-Davidson was selling for $16, compared to the $20 that you paid for the stock.

Clearly, what we have described about Harley Davidson and Starbucks were events unique to these two companies, and as we would expect, investors reacted accordingly; that is, the value of the stock changed in light of the new information. Although we might have wished we had owned only Starbucks stock at the time, most of us would prefer to avoid such uncertainties; that is, we are risk averse. Instead, we would like to reduce the risk associated with our investment portfolio, without having to accept a lower expected return. Good news: It is possible by diversifying your portfolio!

Diversifying Away the Risk

If we diversify our investments across different securities rather than invest in only one stock, the variability in the returns of our portfolio should decline. The reduction in risk will occur if the stock returns within our portfolio do not move precisely together over time—that is, if they are not perfectly correlated. Figure 3 shows graphically what we could

FIGURE 3 Variability of Returns Compared with Size of Portfolio

expect to happen to the variability of returns as we add additional stocks to the portfolio. The reduction occurs because some of the volatility in returns of a stock are unique to that security. The unique variability of a single stock tends to be countered by the uniqueness of another security. However, we should not expect to eliminate all risk from our portfolio. In practice, it would be rather difficult to cancel all the variations in returns of a portfolio, because stock prices have some tendency to move together. Thus, we can divide the total risk (total variability) of our portfolio into two types of risk: (1) **company-unique risk**, or **unsystematic risk**, and (2) **market risk**, or **systematic risk**. Company-unique risk might also be called **diversifiable risk**, in that it *can be diversified away*. Market risk is **nondiversifiable risk**; it *cannot be eliminated through random diversification*. These two types of risk are shown graphically in Figure 3. Total risk declines until we have approximately 20 securities, and then the decline becomes very slight.

The remaining risk, which would typically be about 40 percent of the total risk, is the portfolio's systematic, or market, risk. At this point, our portfolio is highly correlated with all securities in the marketplace. Events that affect our portfolio now are not so much unique events as changes in the general economy, major political events, and sociological changes. Examples include changes in interest rates in the economy, changes in tax legislation that affect all companies, or increasing public concern about the effect of business practices on the environment. Our measure of risk should, therefore, measure how responsive a stock or portfolio is to changes in a market portfolio, such as the New York Stock Exchange or the S&P 500 Index.[7]

Measuring Market Risk

To help clarify the idea of systematic risk, let's examine the relationship between the common stock returns of Google and the returns of the S&P 500 Index.

The monthly returns for Google and the S&P 500 Index for the 12 months ending May 2009 are presented in Table 3 and Figure 4. These *monthly returns*, or **holding-period returns**, as they are often called, are calculated as follows.[8]

$$\text{Monthly holding return} = \frac{\text{Price}_{\text{end of month}} - \text{Price}_{\text{beginning of month}}}{\text{Price}_{\text{beginning of month}}}$$

$$= \frac{\text{Price}_{\text{end of month}}}{\text{Price}_{\text{beginning of month}}} - 1 \tag{6}$$

For instance, the holding-period return for Google and the S&P 500 Index for March 2009 is computed as follows:

$$\text{The Google return} = \frac{\text{stock price at end of March 2009}}{\text{stock price at end of February 2009}} - 1$$

$$= \frac{\$395.97}{\$348.06} - 1 = 0.138 = 13.8\%$$

$$\text{The S\&P 500 Index return} = \frac{\text{index value at end of March 2009}}{\text{index value at end of February 2009}} - 1$$

$$= \frac{\$872.81}{\$797.87} - 1 = 0.0939 = 9.4\%$$

company-unique risk see unsystematic risk.

unsystematic risk the risk related to an investment return that can be eliminated through diversification. Unsystematic risk is the result of factors that are unique to the particular firm. Also called company-unique risk or diversifiable risk.

market risk see systematic risk.

systematic risk (1) the risk related to an investment return that cannot be eliminated through diversification. Systematic risk results from factors that affect all stocks. Also called market risk or nondiversifiable risk. (2) The risk of a project from the viewpoint of a well-diversified shareholder. This measure takes into account that some of the project's risk will be diversified away as the project is combined with the firm's other projects, and, in addition, some of the remaining risk will be diversified away by shareholders as they combine this stock with other stocks in their portfolios.

diversifiable risk see Unsystematic risk.

nondiversifiable risk see Systematic risk.

holding-period return the return an investor would receive from holding a security for a designated period of time. For example, a monthly holding-period return would be the return for holding a security for a month.

[7]The New York Stock Exchange Index is an index that reflects the performance of all stocks listed on the New York Stock Exchange. The Standard & Poor's (S&P) 500 Index is similarly an index that measures the combined stock-price performance of the companies that constitute the 500 largest companies in the United States, as designated by Standard & Poor's.

[8]For simplicity's sake, we are ignoring the dividend that the investor receives from the stock as part of the total return. In other words, letting D_t equal the dividend received by the investor in month t, the holding-period return would more accurately be measured as

$$r_1 = \frac{P_t + D_t}{P_{t-1}} - 1 \tag{7}$$

TABLE 3 Monthly Holding-Period Returns, Google versus the S&P 500 Index, June 2008 through May 2009

Month and Year	Google Price	Google Returns (%)	S&P 500 Index Price	S&P 500 Index Returns (%)
2008				
May	$526.42		$1,280.00	
June	473.75	−10.0%	1,267.38	−1.0%
July	463.29	−2.2%	1,282.83	1.2%
August	400.52	−13.5%	1,164.74	−9.2%
September	359.36	−10.3%	968.75	−16.8%
October	292.96	−18.5%	896.24	−7.5%
November	307.65	5.0%	903.25	0.8%
December	338.53	10.0%	825.88	−8.6%
2009				
January	337.99	−0.2%	735.09	−11.0%
February	348.06	3.0%	797.87	8.5%
March	395.97	13.8%	872.81	9.4%
April	417.23	5.4%	919.14	5.3%
May	426.56	2.2%	942.87	2.6%
Average return		−1.3%		−2.2%
Standard deviation		9.9%		8.3%

At the bottom of Table 3, we have also computed the averages of the returns for the 12 months, for both Google and the S&P 500 Index, and the standard deviation for these returns. Because we are using historical return data, we assume each observation has an equal probability of occurrence. Thus, the average holding-period return is found by summing the returns and dividing by the number of months; that is,

$$\text{Average holding period return} = \frac{\text{return in month 1} + \text{return in month 2} + \cdots + \text{return in last month}}{\text{number of monthly returns}}$$

(8)

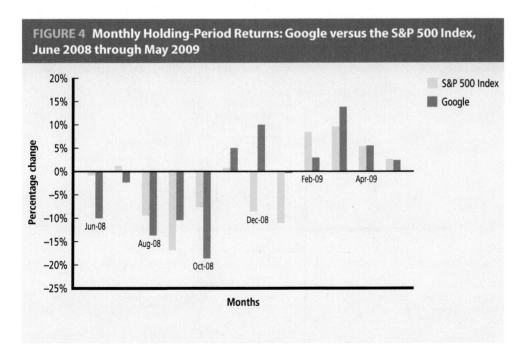

FIGURE 4 Monthly Holding-Period Returns: Google versus the S&P 500 Index, June 2008 through May 2009

and the standard deviation is computed as follows:

Standard
deviation

$$= \sqrt{\frac{(\text{return in month 1} - \text{average return})^2 + (\text{return in month 2} - \text{average return})^2 + \cdots (\text{return in last month} - \text{average return})^2}{\text{number of monthly returns} - 1}}$$

(9)

In looking at Table 3 and Figure 4, we notice the following things about Google's holding-period returns over the 12 months ending in May 2009.

1. Google's owners experienced significant negative monthly holding-period returns, mostly from June through October 2008, losing 1.3 percent on average per month for the entire 12-month period. During the same time period, the general market, as represented by the Standard & Poor's 500 Index, declined 2.2 percent on average each month. Remember that the returns in Table 3 are historical or realized, and not expected. No investor would invest if she expected to lose money in an investment. But in a world of risk, your returns may not match your expectations. In fact, referring back to Figure 1, we see that over the long term (83 years to be exact) investors in large companies earned almost a 1 percent monthly return. What will happen in the future, no one can say. Hopefully, the old "normal" will return.

2. The second bad news is the high volatility of the returns, which is a measure of the risk. As shown at the bottom of Table 3, Google's standard deviation is 9.9 percent, compared to 8.3 percent for the S&P 500 Index. Both these numbers are high relative to the average monthly returns. These results, which are again based on the second half of 2008 and the first half of 2009, are far higher than in previous years, especially for the S&P 500 Index. For example, the 8.3 percent for the S&P 500 Index compares to about 2 percent during 2005–2006. So not only did values decline during 2008 and 2009, but the fluctuations of the returns from month to month have been high. Negative historical returns and high volatility—not exactly an investor's idea of fun.

3. We should also notice the tendency, although far from perfect, of Google's stock price to increase when the value of the S&P 500 Index increases and vice versa. This was the case in 10 of the 12 months. That is, there is a moderate positive relationship between Google's stock returns and the S&P 500 Index returns.

With respect to our third observation, that there is a relationship between the stock returns of Google and the S&P 500 Index, it is helpful to see this relationship by graphing Google's

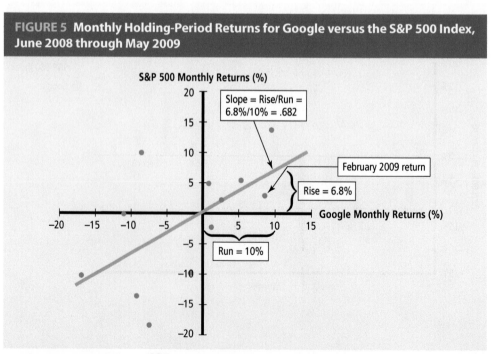

FIGURE 5 Monthly Holding-Period Returns for Google versus the S&P 500 Index, June 2008 through May 2009

returns against the S&P 500 Index returns. We provide such a graph in Figure 5. In the figure, we have plotted Google's returns on the vertical axis and the returns for the S&P 500 Index on the horizontal axis. Each of the 12 dots in the figure represents the returns of Google and the S&P 500 Index for a particular month. For instance, the returns for February 2009 for Google and the S&P 500 Index were 3.0 percent and 8.5 percent, respectively, which are noted in the figure.

In addition to the dots in the graph, we have drawn a line of "best fit," which we call the **characteristic line**. *The slope of the characteristic line measures the average relationship between a stock's returns and those of the S&P 500 Index*: or stated differently, *the slope of the line indicates the average movement in a stock's price in response to a movement in the S&P 500 Index price.* We can estimate the slope of the line visually by fitting a line that appears to cut through the middle of the dots. We then compare the rise (increase of the line on the vertical axis) to the run (increase on the horizontal axis). Alternatively, we can enter the return data into a financial calculator or Excel spreadsheet, which will calculate the slope based on statistical analysis. For Google, the slope of the line is 0.68, which means that on average that as the market returns (S&P 500 Index returns) increase or decrease 1 percent, the return for Google on average increases or decreases 0.68 percentage points.

We can also think of the 0.68 slope of the characteristic line as indicating that Google's returns are 0.68 times as volatile on average as those of the overall market (S&P 500 Index). This slope has come to be called **beta** (β) in investor jargon, and it *measures the average relationship between a stock's returns and the market's returns.* It is a term you will see almost any time you read an article written by a financial analyst about the riskiness of a stock.

Looking once again at Figure 5, we see that the dots (returns) are scattered all about the characteristic line—most of the returns do not fit neatly on the characteristic line. That is, the average relationship may be 0.68, but the variation in Google's returns is only partly explained by the stock's average relationship with the S&P 500 Index. There are other driving forces unique to Google that also affect the firm's stock returns. (Earlier, we called this company-unique risk.) If we were, however, to diversify our holdings and own, say, 20 stocks with betas of 0.68, we could essentially eliminate the variation about the characteristic line. That is, we would remove almost all the volatility in returns, except for that caused by the general market, which is represented by the slope of the line in Figure 5. If we plotted the returns of our 20-stock portfolio against the S&P 500 Index, the points in our new graph would fit nicely along a straight line with a slope of 0.68, which means that the beta (β) of the portfolio is also 0.68. The new graph would look something like the one shown in Figure 6. In other words, by diversifying our portfolio, we can essentially eliminate the variations

characteristic line the line of "best fit" through a series of returns for a firm's stock relative to the market's returns. The slope of the line, frequently called beta, represents the average movement of the firm's stock returns in response to a movement in the market's returns.

beta the relationship between an investment's returns and the market's returns. This is a measure of the investment's nondiversifiable risk.

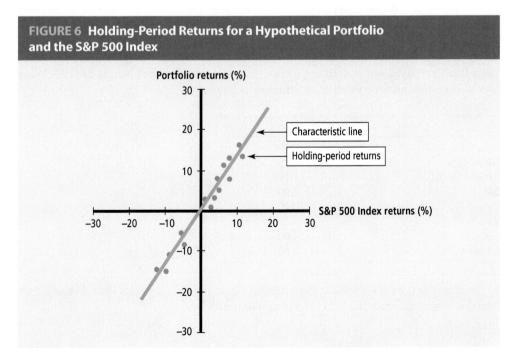

FIGURE 6 Holding-Period Returns for a Hypothetical Portfolio and the S&P 500 Index

CAN YOU DO IT?

ESTIMATING BETA

Below, we provide the end-of-month prices for McDonald's stock and the Standard & Poor's 500 Index for November 2008 through May 2009. Given the information, compute the following both for McDonald's and the S&P 500: (1) the monthly holding-period returns, (2) the average monthly returns, and (3) the standard deviation of the returns. Next, graph the holding-period returns of McDonald's on the vertical axis against the holding-period returns of the S&P 500 on the horizontal axis. Draw a line on your graph similar to what we did in Figure 5 to estimate the average relationship between the stock returns of McDonald's and the returns of the overall market as represented by the S&P 500. What is the approximate slope of your line? What does this tell you?

(In working this problem, it would be easier if you used an Excel spreadsheet including the slope function.

	MCDONALDS CORP.	S&P 500
Nov-08	$57.73	$896.24
Dec-08	61.11	903.25
Jan-09	51.19	825.88
Feb-09	52.05	735.09
Mar-09	53.64	797.87
Apr-09	57.31	872.81
May-09	57.06	919.14

about the characteristic line, leaving only the variation in returns for a company that comes from variations in the general market returns.

So beta (β)—the slope of the characteristic line—is a measure of a firm's market risk or systematic risk, which is the risk that remains for a company even after we have diversified our portfolio. It is this risk—and only this risk—that matters for investors who have broadly diversified portfolios.

Although we have said that beta is a measure of a stock's systematic risk, how should we interpret a specific beta? For instance, when is a beta considered low and when is it considered high? In general, a stock with a beta of zero has no systematic risk; a stock with a beta of 1 has systematic or market risk equal to the "typical" stock in the marketplace; and a stock with a beta exceeding 1 has more market risk than the typical stock. Most stocks, however, have betas between 0.60 and 1.60.

We should also realize that calculating beta is not an exact science. The final estimate of a firm's beta is heavily dependent on one's methodology. For instance, it matters whether you use 24 months in your measurement or 60 months, as most professional investment companies do. Take our computation of Google's beta. We said Google's beta is 0.68 but Value Line, a well-known investment service, has estimated Google's beta to be 0.90. Value Line's beta estimates for a number of firms are as follows:

	BETAS
Coca-Cola	0.70
ExxonMobil	0.75
General Electric	1.15
IBM	0.90
Merck	0.70
Nike	0.90
PepsiCo	0.60
WalMart	0.60

To this point, we have talked about measuring an individual stock's beta. We will now consider how to measure the beta for a portfolio of stocks.

Measuring a Portfolio's Beta

What if we were to diversify our portfolio, as we have just suggested, but instead of acquiring stocks with the same beta as Google (0.68), we buy 8 stocks with betas of 1.0 and 12 stocks with betas of 1.5. What would the beta of our portfolio become? As it works out, the **portfolio beta** is merely the average of the individual stock betas. It is a *weighted average of the individual securities' betas, with the weights being equal to the proportion of the portfolio invested in each security.* Thus, the beta (β) of a portfolio consisting of n stocks is equal to

portfolio beta the relationship between a portfolio's returns and the market returns. It is a measure of the portfolio's nondiversifiable risk.

$$
\begin{aligned}
\text{Portfolio}\atop\text{beta} = &\left(\begin{array}{c}\text{percentage of}\\\text{portfolio invested}\\\text{in asset 1}\end{array} \times \begin{array}{c}\text{beta for}\\\text{asset 1'}\\(\beta_1)\end{array}\right)\\
+ &\left(\begin{array}{c}\text{percentage of}\\\text{portfolio invested}\\\text{in asset 2}\end{array} \times \begin{array}{c}\text{beta for}\\\text{asset 2'}\\(\beta_2)\end{array}\right) + \cdots\\
+ &\left(\begin{array}{c}\text{percentage of}\\\text{portfolio invested}\\\text{in asset } n\end{array} \times \begin{array}{c}\text{beta for}\\\text{asset } n\\(\beta_n)\end{array}\right)
\end{aligned}
\tag{10}
$$

So, assuming we bought equal amounts of each stock in our new 20-stock portfolio, the beta would simply be 1.3, calculated as follows:

$$
\text{Portfolio beta} = \left(\frac{8}{20} \times 1.0\right) + \left(\frac{12}{20} \times 1.50\right) = 1.3
$$

Thus, whenever the general market increases or decreases 1 percent, our new portfolio's returns would change 1.3 percent on average, which means that our new portfolio has more systematic, or market, risk than the market has as a whole.

We can conclude that the beta of a portfolio is determined by the betas of the individual stocks. If we have a portfolio consisting of stocks with low betas, then our portfolio will have a low beta. The reverse is true as well. Figure 7 presents these situations graphically.

Before leaving the subject of risk and diversification, we want to share a study that demonstrates the effects of diversifying our investments, not just across different stocks but also across different types of securities.

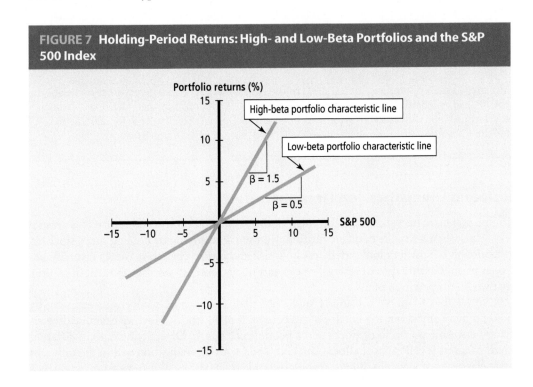

FIGURE 7 Holding-Period Returns: High- and Low-Beta Portfolios and the S&P 500 Index

DID YOU GET IT?

ESTIMATING BETA

The holding-period returns, average monthly returns, and the standard deviations for McDonald's and the S&P 500 data are as follows:

	MCDONALDS CORP.		S&P 500	
	PRICES	RETURNS	PRICES	RETURNS
Nov-08	$57.73		$896.24	
Dec-08	61.11	5.85%	903.25	0.78%
Jan-09	51.19	−16.23%	825.88	−8.57%
Feb-09	52.05	1.68%	735.09	−10.99%
Mar-09	53.64	3.05%	797.87	8.54%
Apr-09	57.31	6.84%	872.81	9.39%
May-09	57.06	−0.44%	919.14	5.31%
Average return		0.13%		0.74%
Standard deviation		8.45%		8.73%

The graph would appear as follows:

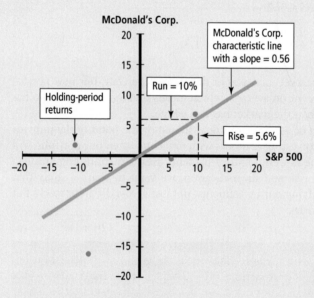

The average relationship between McDonald's stock returns and the S&P 500's returns as estimated is 0.56, where the rise of the line is 5.6 relative to a run (horizontal axis) of 10 (0.56 = 5.6/10). If our estimates fairly represent the relationships, then McDonald's stock returns are less volatile than the market's returns. When the market rises (or falls) 1 percent, McDonald's stock will rise (or fall) 0.56 percent. (We should, however, be hesitant to draw any firm conclusions here, given the limited number of return observations.)

Risk and Diversification Demonstrated

To this point, we have described the effect of diversification on risk and return in a general way. Also, when we spoke of diversification, we were diversifying by holding more stocks in our portfolio. Now let's look briefly on how risk and return change as we (1) diversify between two different types of assets—stocks and bonds, and (2) increase the length of time that we hold a portfolio of assets.

Notice that when we previously spoke about diversification, we were diversifying by holding more stock, but the portfolio still consisted of all stocks. Now we examine diversifying between a portfolio of stocks and a portfolio of bonds. Diversifying among different kinds of assets is called **asset allocation**, compared with diversification within the different asset classes, such as stocks, bonds, real estate, and commodities. We know from experience

asset allocation identifying and selecting the asset classes appropriate for a specific investment portfolio and determining the proportions of those assets within the portfolio.

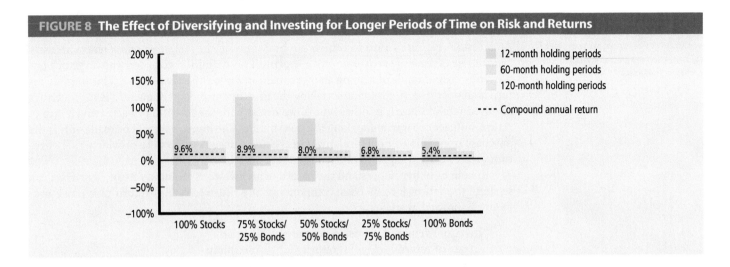

FIGURE 8 **The Effect of Diversifying and Investing for Longer Periods of Time on Risk and Returns**

that the benefit we receive from diversifying is far greater through effective asset allocation than from astutely selecting individual stocks to include with an asset category.

Figure 8 presents the range of rolling returns for several mixtures of stocks and bonds depending on whether we held the investments 12 months, 60 months, or 120 months between 1926 and 2008. For the 12-month holding period, we would have purchased the investment at the beginning of each year and sold at the end of each year, repeating this process every year from 1926 to 2008. Then for the 60 months, we would have invested at the beginning of the year and held the investment for 60 months. In other words, we invested at the beginning of 1926 and sold at the end 1930, then did the same for 1927–1931, repeating the process for all 60-month periods all the way through 2008. Finally, we would have invested at the beginning of each year, holding each investment for 120 months.

As we observe in Figure 8, moving from an all-stock portfolio to a mixture of stocks and bonds and finally to an all-bond portfolio reduces the variability of returns (our measure for risk) significantly along with declining average rates of return. Stated differently, if we want to increase our expected returns, we must assume more risk. That is, there is a clear relationship between risk and return. Reminds us of **Principle 3: Risk Requires a Reward**.

P3
Principle

Equally important, how long we hold our investments matters greatly when it comes to reducing risk. As we move from 12 months to 60 months, and finally to 120 months, we see the range of return falling sharply, especially when we move from 12-month holding periods to 60-month holding periods. As a side note, notice that there has never been a time between 1926 and 2008 when an investor lost money if she held an all-stock portfolio—the most risky portfolio—for ten years. In other words, *the market rewards the patient investor.*

In the next section, we complete our study of risk and returns by connecting risk—market or systematic risk—to the investor's *required* rate of return. After all, although risk is an important issue, it is primarily important in its effect on the investor's required rate of return.

Concept Check

1. Give specific examples of systematic and unsystematic risk. How many different securities must be owned to essentially diversify away unsystematic risk?

2. What method is used to measure a firm's market risk?

3. After reviewing Figure 5, explain the difference between the plotted dots and the firm's characteristic line. What must be done to eliminate the variations?

The Investor's Required Rate of Return

 5 Explain the relationship between the investor's required rate of return on an investment and the riskiness of the investment.

In this section, we examine the concept of the investor's required rate of return, especially as it relates to the riskiness of an asset, and then we see how the required rate of return might be measured.

The Required Rate of Return Concept

required rate of return minimum rate of return necessary to attract an investor to purchase or hold a security.

An investor's **required rate of return** can be defined as the *minimum rate of return necessary to attract an investor to purchase or hold a security*. This definition considers the investor's opportunity cost of funds of making an investment in *the next-best investment*. This forgone return is an opportunity cost of undertaking the investment and, consequently, is the investor's required rate of return. In other words, we invest with the intention of achieving a rate of return sufficient to warrant making the investment. The investment will be made only if the purchase price is low enough relative to expected future cash flows to provide a rate of return greater than or equal to our required rate of return.

To help us better understand the nature of an investor's required rate of return, we can separate the return into its basic components: the risk-free rate of return plus a risk premium. Expressed as an equation:

$$\text{Investor's required rate of return} = \text{risk-free rate of return} + \text{risk premium} \tag{11}$$

risk-free rate of return the rate of return on risk-free investments. The interest rates on short-term U.S. government securities are commonly used to measure this rate.

risk premium the additional return expected for assuming risk.

The **risk-free rate of return** is the *required rate of return, or discount rate, for riskless investments*. Typically, our measure for the risk-free rate of return is the U.S. Treasury bill rate. The **risk premium** is the *additional return we must expect to receive for assuming risk*. As the level of risk increases, we will demand additional expected returns. Even though we may or may not actually receive this incremental return, we must have reason to expect it; otherwise, why expose ourselves to the chance of losing all or part of our money?

EXAMPLE 1

Assume you are considering the purchase of a stock that you believe will provide a 14 percent return over the next year. If the expected risk-free rate of return, such as the rate of return for 90-day Treasury bills, is 5 percent, then the risk premium you are demanding to assume the additional risk is 9 percent (14% − 5%).

Measuring the Required Rate of Return

We have seen that (1) systematic risk is the only relevant risk—the rest can be diversified away, and (2) the required rate of return, k, equals the risk-free rate plus a risk premium. We will now examine how we can estimate investors' required rates of return.

capital asset pricing model (CAPM) an equation stating that the expected rate of return on a project is a function of (1) the risk-free rate, (2) the investment's systematic risk, and (3) the expected risk premium for the market portfolio of all risky securities.

The finance profession has had difficulty in developing a practical approach to measure an investor's required rate of return; however, financial managers often use a method called the **capital asset pricing model (CAPM)**. The capital asset pricing model is *an equation that equates the expected rate of return on a stock to the risk-free rate plus a risk premium for the stock's systematic risk*. Although certainly not without its critics, the CAPM provides an intuitive approach for thinking about the return that an investor should require on an investment, given the asset's systematic or market risk.

Equation (11) above provides the natural starting point for measuring the investor's required rate of return and sets us up for using the CAPM. Rearranging this equation to solve for the risk premium we have

$$\text{Risk premium} = \text{investor's required rate of return, } r - \text{risk-free rate of return } r_f \tag{12}$$

which simply says that the risk premium for a security equals the investor's required return less the risk-free rate existing in the market. For example, if the required return is 15 percent, and the risk-free rate is 5 percent, the risk premium is 10 percent. Also, if the required return for the market portfolio is 12 percent, and the risk-free rate is 5 percent, the risk premium

FINANCE AT WORK

DOES BETA ALWAYS WORK?

At the start of 1998, Apple Computer was in deep trouble. As a result, its stock price fluctuated wildly—far more than other computer firms, such as IBM. However, based on the capital asset pricing model (CAPM) and its measure of beta, the required return of Apple's investors would have been only 8 percent, compared with 12 percent for IBM's stockholders. Equally interesting, when Apple's situation improved in the spring of that year, and its share price became less volatile, Apple's investors, at least according to the CAPM, would have required a rate of return of 11 percent—a 3 percentage point increase from the earlier required rate of return. That is not what intuition would suggest should have happened.

So what should we think? Just when Apple's future was most in doubt and its shares most volatile, its beta was only 0.47, suggesting that Apple's stock was only half as volatile as the overall stock market. In reality, beta is meaningless here. The truth is that Apple was in such a dire condition that its stock price simply "decoupled" itself from the stock market. So, as IBM and its peer stock prices moved up and down with the rest of the market, Apple shares reacted solely to news about the company, without

regard for the market's movements. The stock's beta thus created the false impression that Apple shares were more stable than the stock market.

The lesson here is that beta may at times be misleading when used with individual companies. Instead, its use is far more reliable when applied to a portfolio of companies. If a firm that was interested in acquiring Apple Computer in 1998, for instance, had used the beta in computing the required rate of return for the acquisition, it would without a doubt have overvalued Apple.

So does that mean that CAPM is worthless? No, not as long as company-unique risk is not the main driving force in a company's stock price movements or if investors are able to diversify away specific company risk. Then they would bid up the price of such shares until they reflected only market risk. For example, a mutual fund that specializes in "distressed stocks" might purchase a number of "Apple Computer-type companies," each with its own problems, but for different reasons. For such investors, betas work pretty well. Thus, the moral of the story is to exercise common sense and judgment when using a beta.

---

for the market would be 7 percent. This 7 percent risk premium would apply to any security having systematic (nondiversifiable) risk equivalent to the general market, or a beta (β) of 1.

In this same market, a security with a beta (β) of 2 should provide a risk premium of 14 percent, or twice the 7 percent risk premium existing for the market as a whole. Hence, in general, the appropriate required rate of return for a given security should be determined by

$$
\begin{aligned}
\text{Required return on security, } r &= \text{risk free rate of return, } r_f \\
&+ \text{beta for security, } \beta \times \left(\text{required return on the market portfolio, } r_m - \text{risk-free rate of return, } r_f \right)
\end{aligned}
\tag{13}
$$

Equation (13) is the CAPM. This equation designates the risk–return trade-off existing in the market, where risk is measured in terms of beta. Figure 9 graphs the CAPM as the **security market line**.[9] The security market line is *the graphic representation of the CAPM. It is the line that shows the appropriate required rate of return given a stock's systematic risk.*

security market line the return line that reflects the attitudes of investors regarding the minimum acceptable return for a given level of systematic risk associated with a security.

---

[9]Two key assumptions are made in using the security market line. First, we assume that the marketplace where securities are bought and sold is highly efficient. Market efficiency indicates that the price of an asset responds quickly to new information, thereby suggesting that the price of a security reflects all available information. As a result, the current price of a security is considered to represent the best estimate of its future price. Second, the model assumes that a perfect market exists. A perfect market is one in which information is readily available to all investors at a nominal cost. Also, securities are assumed to be infinitely divisible, with any transaction costs incurred in purchasing or selling a security being negligible. Furthermore, investors are assumed to be single-period wealth maximizers who agree on the meaning and significance of the available information. Finally, within the perfect market, all investors are *price takers*, which simply means that a single investor's actions cannot affect the price of a security. These assumptions are obviously not descriptive of reality. However, from the perspective of positive economics, the mark of a good theory is the accuracy of its predictions, not the validity of the simplifying assumptions that underlie its development.

157

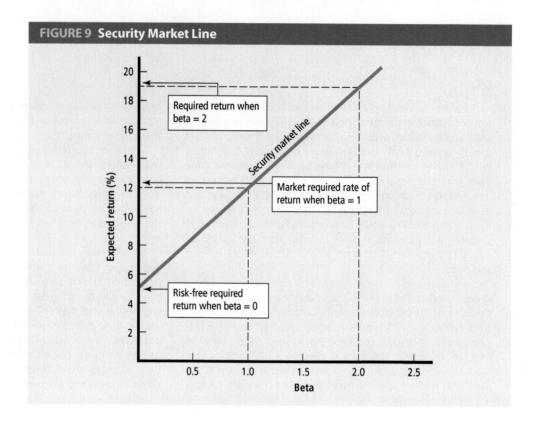

FIGURE 9 Security Market Line

As presented in this figure, securities with betas equal to 0, 1, and 2 should have required rates of return as follows:

If $\beta = 0$: required rate of return $= 5\% + 0(12\% - 5\%) = 5\%$

If $\beta = 1$: required rate of return $= 5\% + 1(12\% - 5\%) = 12\%$

If $\beta = 2$: required rate of return $= 5\% + 2(12\% - 5\%) = 19\%$

where the risk-free rate is 5 percent, and the required return for the market portfolio is 12 percent.

> ### REMEMBER YOUR PRINCIPLES
>
> **Principle** The conclusion of the matter is that **Principle 3** is alive and well. It tells us, **Risk Requires a Reward**. That is, there is a risk–return trade-off in the market.

Concept Check

1. How does opportunity cost affect an investor's required rate of return?
2. What are the two components of the investor's required rate of return?
3. How does beta fit into factoring the risk premium in the CAPM equation?
4. Assuming the market is efficient, what is the relationship between a stock's price and the security market line?

CAN YOU DO IT?

COMPUTING A REQUIRED RATE OF RETURN

Determine a fair expected (or required) rate of return for a stock that has a beta of 1.25 when the risk-free rate is 5 percent, and the expected market return is 9 percent.

DID YOU GET IT?
COMPUTING A REQUIRED RATE OF RETURN

The appropriate rate of return would be:

Required return = risk-free rate + [beta × (market return − risk-free rate)]

$$= 5\% + [1.25 \times (9\% - 5\%)]$$

$$= 10\%$$

Summary

In this book, we referred to the discount rate as the interest rate, or the opportunity cost of funds. At that point, we considered a number of important factors that influence interest rates, including the price of time, expected or anticipated inflation, the risk premium related to maturity (liquidity), and the variability of future returns. In this chapter, we have returned to our study of rates of return and looked ever so carefully at the relationship between risk and rates of return.

In a world of uncertainty, we cannot make forecasts with certitude. Thus, we must speak in terms of *expected* events. The expected return on an investment may therefore be stated as a weighted average of all possible returns, weighted by the probability that each will occur.

Risk for our purposes is the variability of returns and can be measured by the standard deviation. Ibbotson Associates have provided us with annual rates of return earned on different types of security investments as far back as 1926. They summarize among other things, the annual returns for six portfolios of securities made up of

1. Common stocks of large companies
2. Common stocks of small firms
3. Long-term corporate bonds
4. Long-term U.S. government bonds
5. Intermediate-term U.S. government bonds
6. U.S. Treasury bills

A comparison of the annual rates of return for these respective portfolios for the years 1926 to 2008 shows a positive relationship between risk and return, with Treasury bills being least risky and common stocks of small firms being most risky. From the data, we are able to see the benefit of diversification in terms of improving the return–risk relationship. Also, the data clearly demonstrate that only common stock has in the long run served as an inflation hedge, and that the risk associated with common stock can be reduced if investors are patient in receiving their returns.

We made an important distinction between nondiversifiable risk and diversifiable risk. We concluded that the only relevant risk, given the opportunity to diversify our portfolio, is a security's nondiversifiable risk, which we called by two other names: systematic risk and market-related risk.

The capital asset pricing model provides an intuitive framework for understanding the risk–return relationship. The CAPM suggests that investors determine an appropriate required rate of return, depending upon the amount of systematic risk inherent in a security. This minimum acceptable rate of return is equal to the risk-free rate plus a risk premium for assuming risk.

 Define and measure the expected rate of return of an individual investment.

 Define and measure the riskiness of an individual investment.

 Compare the historical relationship between risk and rates of return in the capital markets.

 Explain how diversifying investments affects the riskiness and expected rate of return of a portfolio or combination of assets.

 Explain the relationship between the investor's required rate of return on an investment and the riskiness of the investment.

Key Terms

Asset allocation	Expected rate of return
Beta	Holding-period return
Capital asset pricing model (CAPM)	Market risk
Characteristic line	Nondiversifiable risk
Company-unique risk	Portfolio beta
Diversifiable risk	Required rate of return

Risk	Standard deviation
Risk-free rate of return	Systematic risk
Risk premium	Unsystematic risk
Security market line	

Review Questions

All Review Questions and Study Problems are available in MyFinanceLab.

6-1. a. What is meant by the investor's required rate of return?

    b. How do we measure the riskiness of an asset?

    c. How should the proposed measurement of risk be interpreted?

6-2. What is (a) unsystematic risk (company-unique or diversifiable risk) and (b) systematic risk (market or nondiversifiable risk)?

6-3. What is a beta? How is it used to calculate r, the investor's required rate of return?

6-4. What is the security market line? What does it represent?

6-5. How do we measure the beta of a portfolio?

6-6. If we were to graph the returns of a stock against the returns of the S&P 500 Index, and the points did not follow a very ordered pattern, what could we say about that stock? If the stock's returns tracked the S&P 500 returns very closely, then what could we say?

6-7. Over the past 8 decades, we have had the opportunity to observe the rates of return and the variability of these returns for different types of securities. Summarize these observations.

6-8. What effect will diversifying your portfolio have on your returns?

Self-Test Problems

(The solutions to the following problems are found at the end of the chapter.)

ST-1. (*Expected return and risk*) Universal Corporation is planning to invest in a security that has several possible rates of return. Given the following probability distribution of returns, what is the expected rate of return on the investment? Also compute the standard deviations of the returns. What do the resulting numbers represent?

PROBABILITY	RETURN
0.10	−10%
0.20	5%
0.30	10%
0.40	25%

ST-2. (*Capital asset pricing model*) Using the CAPM, estimate the appropriate required rate of return for the three stocks listed here, given that the risk-free rate is 5 percent, and the expected return for the market is 17 percent.

STOCK	BETA
A	0.75
B	0.90
C	1.40

ST-3. (*Average expected return and risk*) Given the holding-period returns shown here, calculate the average returns and the standard deviations for the Kaifu Corporation and for the market.

MONTH	KAIFU CORP.	MARKET
1	4%	2%
2	6	3
3	0	1
4	2	−1

ST-4. (*Holding-period returns*) From the price data that follow, compute the holding-period returns for periods 2 through 4.

PERIOD	STOCK PRICE
1	$10
2	13
3	11
4	15

ST-5. (*Security market line*)

   a. Determine the expected return and beta for the following portfolio:

STOCK	PERCENTAGE OF PORTFOLIO	BETA	EXPECTED RETURN
1	40%	1.00	12%
2	25	0.75	11
3	35	1.30	15

   b. Given the foregoing information, draw the security market line and show where the securities fit on the graph. Assume that the risk-free rate is 8 percent and that the expected return on the market portfolio is 12 percent. How would you interpret these findings?

Study Problems

6-1. (*Expected rate of return and risk*) Carter Inc. is evaluating a security. One-year Treasury bills are currently paying 9.1 percent. Calculate the investment's expected return and its standard deviation. Should Carter invest in this security?

PROBABILITY	RETURN
0.15	6%
0.30	9%
0.40	10%
0.15	15%

6-2. (*Expected rate of return and risk*) Summerville Inc. is considering an investment in one of two common stocks. Given the information that follows, which investment is better, based on the risk (as measured by the standard deviation) and return of each?

COMMON STOCK A		COMMON STOCK B	
PROBABILITY	RETURN	PROBABILITY	RETURN
0.30	11%	0.20	−5%
0.40	15%	0.30	6%
0.30	19%	0.30	14%
		0.20	22%

6-3. (*Required rate of return using CAPM*)

   a. Compute a fair rate of return for Intel common stock, which has a 1.2 beta. The risk-free rate is 6 percent, and the market portfolio (New York Stock Exchange stocks) has an expected return of 16 percent.

   b. Why is the rate you computed a fair rate?

6-4. (*Estimating beta*) From the graph in the margin relating the holding-period returns for Aram Inc. to the S&P 500 Index, estimate the firm's beta.

Holding-period returns
Aram Inc.

6-5. (*Capital asset pricing model*) Levine Manufacturing Inc. is considering several investments. The rate on Treasury bills is currently 6.75 percent, and the expected return for the market is 12 percent. What should be the required rates of return for each investment (using the CAPM)?

SECURITY	BETA
A	1.50
B	0.90
C	0.70
D	1.15

6-6. (*Capital asset pricing model*) MFI Inc. has a beta of 0.86. If the expected market return is 11.5 percent and the risk-free rate is 7.5 percent, what is the appropriate required return of MFI (using the CAPM)?

6-7. (*Capital asset pricing model*) The expected return for the general market is 12.8 percent, and the risk premium in the market is 4.3 percent. Tasaco, LBM, and Exxos have betas of 0.864, 0.693, and 0.575, respectively. What are the corresponding required rates of return for the three securities?

6-8. (*Computing holding-period returns*)

a. From the price data here, compute the holding-period returns for Jazman and Solomon for periods 2 through 4.

PERIOD	JAZMAN	SOLOMON
1	$9	$27
2	11	28
3	10	32
4	13	29

b. How would you interpret the meaning of a holding-period return?

6-9. (*Measuring risk and rates of return*)

a. Given the holding-period returns shown here, compute the average returns and the standard deviations for the Zemin Corporation and for the market.

MONTH	ZEMIN CORP.	MARKET
1	6%	4%
2	3	2
3	−1	1
4	−3	−2
5	5	2
6	0	2

b. If Zemin's beta is 1.54 and the risk-free rate is 8 percent, what would be an appropriate required return for an investor owning Zemin? (*Note:* Because the returns of Zemin Corporation are based on monthly data, you will need to annualize the returns to make them compatible with the risk-free rate. For simplicity, you can convert from monthly to yearly returns by multiplying the average monthly returns by 12.)

c. How does Zemin's historical average return compare with the return you believe to be a fair return, given the firm's systematic risk?

6-10. (*Portfolio beta and security market line*) You own a portfolio consisting of the stocks below:

STOCK	PERCENTAGE OF PORTFOLIO	BETA	EXPECTED RETURN
1	20%	1.00	16%
2	30	0.85	14
3	15	1.20	20
4	25	0.60	12
5	10	1.60	24

The risk-free rate is 7 percent. Also, the expected return on the market portfolio is 15.5 percent.

a. Calculate the expected return of your portfolio. (*Hint:* The expected return of a portfolio equals the weighted average of the individual stocks' expected returns, where the weights are the percentage invested in each stock.)

b. Calculate the portfolio beta.

c. Given the foregoing information, plot the security market line on paper. Plot the stocks from your portfolio on your graph.

d. From your plot in part c, which stocks appear to be your winners and which ones appear to be losers?

e. Why should you consider your conclusion in part d to be less than certain?

6-11. (*Expected return, standard deviation, and capital asset pricing model*) The following are the end-of-month prices for both the Standard & Poor's 500 Index and Hewlett-Packard's common stock.

a. Using the data here, calculate the holding-period returns for each of the months.

	HEWLETT-PACKARD	S&P 500 INDEX
2008		
May	$ 46.55	$ 1,400.38
June	43.81	1,280.00
July	44.39	1,267.38
August	46.49	1,282.83
September	45.90	1,164.74
October	38.00	968.75
November	35.02	896.24
December	36.10	903.25
2009		
January	34.57	825.88
February	28.88	735.09
March	31.99	797.87
April	35.90	872.81
May	34.28	919.14

b. Calculate the average monthly return and the standard deviation for both the S&P 500 and Hewlett-Packard.

c. Develop a graph that shows the relationship between the Hewlett-Packard stock returns and the S&P 500 Index. (Show the Hewlett-Packard returns on the vertical axis and the S&P 500 Index returns on the horizontal axis as done in Figure 5.)

d. From your graph, describe the nature of the relationship between Hewlett-Packard stock returns and the returns for the S&P 500 Index.

6-12. (*Standard deviation*) Given the following probabilities and returns for Mik's Corporation, find the standard deviation.

PROBABILITY	RETURNS
0.40	7%
0.25	4%
0.15	18%
0.20	10%

6-13. Assume you have the following portfolio.

	STOCK WEIGHT	BETA
Apple	38%	1.50
Green Mountain Coffee	15%	1.44
Disney	27%	1.15
Target	20%	1.20

What is the portfolio's beta?

6-14. (*Holding period dollar gain and return*) Suppose you purchased 16 shares of Disney stock for $24.22 per share on May 1, 2009. On September 1 of the same year, you sold 12 shares of the stock for $25.68. Calculate the holding-period dollar gain for the shares you sold, assuming no dividend was distributed, and the holding-period rate of return.

6-15. Go to www.moneychimp.com. Select the link "Volatility." Complete the retirement planning calculator, making the assumptions that you believe are appropriate for you. Then go to the Monte Carlo simulation calculator. Assume that you invest in large-company common stocks during your working years and then invest in long-term corporate bonds during retirement. Use the nominal average returns and standard deviations shown in Figure 2. What did you learn?

6-16. Go to www.cgi.money.cnn.com/tools. Choose "Asset Allocator." Answer the questions and click "Calculate." Try different options and see how the calculator suggests you allocate your investments.

6-17. Access http://finance.yahoo.com. On the left side of the page, scroll down to and select "Investing" and then choose "Education." Next select "Glossary" and find "Expected Return" and "Expected Value." What did you learn from the definitions of these terms?

6-18. Go to www.investopedia.com/university/beginner, where there is an article on "Investing 101: A Tutorial for Beginning Investors." Read the article and explain what it says about risk tolerance.

Mini Case

Note: Although not absolutely necessary, you are advised to use a computer spreadsheet to work the following problem.

a. Use the price data from the table that follows for the Standard & Poor's 500 Index, Walmart, and Target to calculate the holding-period returns for the 24 months from July 2007 through June 2009.

MONTH	S&P 500	WALMART	TARGET
Jun-07	1,503.35	46.32	61.86
Jul-07	1,455.27	44.24	58.91
Aug-07	1,473.99	42.22	64.28
Sep-07	1,526.75	42.24	61.98
Oct-07	1,549.38	43.75	59.83
Nov-07	1,481.14	46.35	58.62
Dec-07	1,468.36	46.20	48.88
Jan-08	1,378.55	49.32	54.17
Feb-08	1,330.63	48.21	51.56
Mar-08	1,322.70	51.45	49.67
Apr-08	1,385.59	56.63	52.07
May-08	1,400.38	56.63	52.43
Jun-08	1,280.00	55.12	45.68
Jul-08	1,267.38	57.50	44.44
Aug-08	1,282.83	58.17	52.26
Sep-08	1,164.74	58.98	48.35
Oct-08	968.75	54.96	39.54
Nov-08	896.24	55.03	33.44
Dec-08	903.25	55.45	34.21
Jan-09	825.88	46.60	30.91
Feb-09	735.09	48.70	28.20
Mar-09	797.87	51.82	34.25
Apr-09	872.81	50.13	41.10
May-09	919.14	49.74	39.30
June-09	946.21	48.68	39.00

b. Calculate the average monthly holding-period returns and the standard deviation of these returns for the S&P 500 Index, Walmart, and Target.

c. Plot (1) the holding-period returns for Walmart against the Standard & Poor's 500 Index, and (2) the Target holding-period returns against the Standard & Poor's 500 Index. (Use Figure 5 as the format for your graph.)

d. From your graphs in part c, describe the nature of the relationship between the stock returns for Walmart and the returns for the S&P 500 Index. Make the same comparison for Target.

e. Assume that you have decided to invest one-half of your money in Walmart and the remainder in Target. Calculate the monthly holding-period returns for your two-stock portfolio. (*Hint:* The monthly return for the portfolio is the average of the two stocks' monthly returns.)

f. Plot the returns of your two-stock portfolio against the Standard & Poor's 500 Index as you did for the individual stocks in part c. How does this graph compare to the graphs for the individual stocks? Explain the difference.

g. The following table shows the returns on an *annualized* basis that were realized from holding long-term government bonds for the same period. Calculate the average *monthly* holding-period returns and the standard deviations of these returns. (*Hint:* You will need to convert the annual returns to monthly returns by dividing each return by 12 months.)

MONTH AND YEAR	ANNUALIZED RATE OF RETURN (%)
Jul-07	5.00%
Aug-07	4.67%
Sep-07	4.52%
Oct-07	4.53%
Nov-07	4.15%
Dec-07	4.10%
Jan-08	3.74%
Feb-08	3.74%
Mar-08	3.51%
Apr-08	3.68%
May-08	3.88%
Jun-08	4.10%
Jul-08	4.01%
Aug-08	3.89%
Sep-08	3.69%
Oct-08	3.81%
Nov-08	3.53%
Dec-08	2.42%
Jan-09	2.52%
Feb-09	2.87%
Mar-09	2.82%
Apr-09	2.93%
May-09	3.29%
Jun-09	3.18%

h. Now assuming that you have decided to invest equal amounts of money in Walmart, Target, and long-term government securities, calculate the monthly returns for your three-asset portfolio. What is the average return and the standard deviation?

i. Make a comparison of the average returns and the standard deviations for all the individual assets and the two portfolios that we designed. What conclusions can be reached by your comparison?

j. According to Standard & Poor's, the betas for Walmart and Target are 0.59 and 1.02, respectively. Compare the meaning of these betas relative to the standard deviations calculated above.

k. Assume that the current treasury bill rate is 4.5 percent and that the expected market return is 10 percent. Given the betas for Walmart and Target in part j, estimate an appropriate rate of return for the two firms.

Self-Test Solutions

SS-1.

(A) PROBABILITY	(B) RETURN	EXPECTED RETURN ($\bar{r}$)	WEIGHTED DEVIATION
$P(r)$	(r)	$(A) \times (B)$	$(r - \bar{r})^2 P(r)$
0.10	−10%	−1%	52.9%
0.20	5	1	12.8
0.30	10	3	2.7
0.40	25	10	57.6
		$\bar{r} = 13\%$	$\sigma^2 = 126.0\%$
			$\sigma = 11.22\%$

From our studies in statistics, we know that if the distribution of returns were normal, then Universal could expect a return of 13 percent, with a 67 percent possibility that this return would vary up or down by 11.22 percent between 1.78 percent (13% − 11.22%) and 24.22 percent (13% + 11.22%). However, it is apparent from the probabilities that the distribution is not normal.

SS-2.

Stock A: 5% + 0.75 (17% − 5%) = 14.0%

Stock B: 5% + 0.90 (17% − 5%) = 15.8%

Stock C: 5% + 1.40 (17% − 5%) = 21.8%

SS-3.

KAIFU		MARKET	
Average return:	$\dfrac{4\% + 6\% + 0\% + 2\%}{4} = 3\%$	Average return:	$\dfrac{2\% + 3\% + 1\% - 1\%}{4} = 1.25\%$
Standard deviation:	$\sqrt{\dfrac{[(4\% - 3\%)^2 + (6\% - 3\%)^2 + (0\% - 3\%)^2 + (2\% - 3\%)^2]}{4 - 1}} = 2.58\%$	Standard deviation:	$\sqrt{\dfrac{[(2\% - 1.25\%)^2 + (3\% - 1.25\%)^2 + (1\% - 1.25\%)^2 + (-1\% - 1.25\%)^2]}{4 - 1}} = 1.71\%$

SS-4.

TIME	STOCK PRICE	HOLDING-PERIOD RETURN
1	$10	
2	13	($13 ÷ $10) − 1 = 30.0%
3	11	($11 ÷ $13) − 1 = −15.4%
4	15	($15 ÷ $11) − 1 = 36.4%

SS-5. a. Portfolio expected return:

$(0.4 \times 12\%) + (0.25 \times 11\%) + (0.35 \times 15\%) = 12.8\%$

Portfolio beta:

$(0.4 \times 1) + (0.25 \times 0.75) + (0.35 \times 1.3) = 1.04$

b.

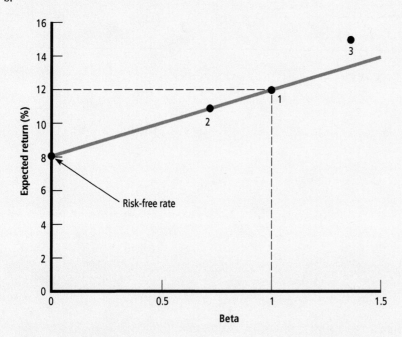

Stocks 1 and 2 seem to be right in line with the security market line, which suggest that they are earning a fair return, given their systematic risk. Stock 3, on the other hand, is earning more than a fair return (above the security market line). We might be tempted to conclude that security 3 is undervalued. However, we may be seeing an illusion; it is possible to mis-specify the security market line by using bad estimates in our data.

The Valuation and Characteristics of Bonds

From Chapter 7 of *Foundations of Finance*, 7/e. Arthur J. Keown. John D. Martin. J. William Petty. Copyright © 2011 by Pearson Education. Published by Prentice Hall. All rights reserved.

The Valuation and Characteristics of Bonds

Learning Objectives

After reading this chapter, you should be able to:

1. Distinguish **between different kinds of bonds.**

2. Explain **the more popular features of bonds.**

3. Define **the term** *value* **as used for several different purposes.**

4. Explain **the factors that determine value.**

5. Describe **the basic process for valuing assets.**

6. Estimate **the value of a bond.**

7. Compute **a bondholder's expected rate of return.**

8. Explain **three important relationships that exist in bond valuation.**

If you have ever shopped at Neiman Marcus, you know it sells only very high-quality products, which for many of us means *expensive*.

For many years Neiman Marcus' stock had been traded on the New York Stock Exchange, but that ended in 2005, when a private investment group, including Texas Pacific Group and Warburg Pincus LLC, bought the firm for $5.1 billion. To buy the stock, the investors borrowed a lot of money to finance the purchase, and then they provided the equity financing to complete it. In this type of financing arrangement, known as a *leveraged buyout*, or LBO, the new owners work with the firm's managers to make it more efficient and then eventually sell it to other investors or take the firm public. By 2005, LBOs were taking on significantly more debt than in the past to make their purchases. Consequently, the owners of these firms were finding it more difficult to sell the companies or to take them public. So, they began paying themselves large dividends, which meant that there was less money available to service the companies' debt.

In announcing the sale, Richard A. Smith, Neiman Marcus' CEO and chairman of the board, remarked, "This transaction provides outstanding shareholder value and represents an endorsement of the excellent performance of our entire team." But although Smith considered the sale to be a good deal for the firm's stockholders, the firm's bondholders, who had loaned the company money, were not happy.

In the Neiman Marcus case, the bondholders made an unusual demand of the shareholders: For the interest they were to be paid as part of the buyout, they agreed to accept new bonds rather than cash—a provision known as a *payment in kind*, or PIK. But they insisted that Neiman Marcus must not pay any dividends to the new shareholders with the money that was saved by the trade, or PIK.

Although the PIK provision does provide, as CFO James Skinner notes, "a security blanket in case of financial stress," the fact is, bondholders did not want to see shareholders rewarded at their expense. "You want to make sure there's enough cash available to pay debt [rather than see it] go out to the equity holders," observed Paul Scanlon, a manager at Putnam Investments, which bought more than $13 million of the bonds.

"LBO activity has firmly established its place atop the list of bondholder concerns," wrote the authors of a Morgan Stanley report. Given the increasingly aggressive terms of the deals, they added, "All we need is Michael Douglas to squeeze back into his bespoke suit, his Gucci loafers, and release *Wall Street II*, and we'll know the end of the LBO boom can't be far behind."

Source: Adapted from Ronald Fink, "Bondholder Backlash," *CFO Magazine*, February 01, 2006, pp. 51–55, and www.neimanmarcusgroup.com

Scott Olson/Getty Images

Knowing the fair value or price of an asset is no easy matter. The *Maxims* by the French writer La Rouchefoucauld, written over 3 centuries ago, still speak to us: "The greatest of all gifts is the power to estimate things at their true worth."

Understanding how to value financial securities is essential if managers are to meet the objective of maximizing the value of the firm. If they are to maximize the investors' value, they must know what drives the value of an asset. Specifically, they need to understand how bonds and stocks are valued in the marketplace; otherwise, they cannot act in the best interest of the firm's investors.

A bond is one form of a company's long-term debt. In this chapter, we begin by identifying the different kinds of bonds. We next look at the features or characteristics of most bonds. We then examine the concepts of and procedures for valuing an asset and apply these ideas to valuing bonds.

We now begin our study by considering the different kinds of bonds.

Types of Bonds

A **bond** is a *type of debt or long-term promissory note, issued by the borrower, promising to pay its holder a predetermined and fixed amount of interest per year and the face value of the bond at maturity.* However, there is a wide variety of such creatures. Just to mention a few, we have

Debentures	Eurobonds
Subordinated debentures	Convertible bonds
Mortgage bonds	

The following sections briefly explain each of these types of bonds.

Debentures

The term **debenture** applies to *any unsecured long-term debt*. Because these bonds are unsecured, the earning ability of the issuing corporation is of great concern to the bondholder.

Distinguish between different kinds of bonds.

bond a long-term (10-year or more) promissory note issued by the borrower, promising to pay the owner of the security a predetermined, fixed amount of interest each year.

debenture any unsecured long-term debt.

They are also viewed as being more risky than secured bonds and, as a result, must provide investors with a higher yield than secured bonds provide. Often the firm issuing debentures attempts to provide some protection to the holder of the debenture by agreeing not to issue more secured long-term debt that would further tie up the firm's assets. To the issuing firm, the major advantage of debentures is that no property has to be secured by them. This allows the firm to issue debt and still preserve some future borrowing power.

Subordinated Debentures

unsecured —no collateral also long term.

subordinated debenture a debenture that is subordinated to other debentures in terms of its payments in case of insolvency.

Many firms have more than one issue of debentures outstanding. In this case a hierarchy may be specified, in which some debentures are given *subordinated standing in case of insolvency*. The claims of the **subordinated debentures** are honored only after the claims of secured debt and unsubordinated debentures have been satisfied.

Mortgage Bonds

collateral

mortgage bond a bond secured by a lien on real property.

A **mortgage bond** is a *bond secured by a lien on real property*. Typically, the value of the real property is greater than that of the mortgage bonds issued. This provides the mortgage bondholders with a margin of safety in the event the market value of the secured property declines. In the case of foreclosure, *trustees*, who represent the bondholders and act on their behalf, have the power to sell the secured property and use the proceeds to pay the bondholders. The bond trustee, usually a banking institution or trust company, oversees the relationship between the bondholder and the issuing firm, protecting the bondholder and seeing that the terms of the indenture are carried out. In the event that the proceeds from this sale do not cover the bonds, the bondholders become general creditors, similar to debenture bondholders, for the unpaid portion of the debt.

Eurobonds

Eurobond a bond issued in a country different from the one in which the currency of the bond is denominated; for example, a bond issued in Europe or Asia by an American company that pays interest and principal to the lender in U.S. dollars.

Currency of bond is different from where bond is issued.

Eurobonds are not so much a different type of security. They are simply securities, in this case *bonds, issued in a country different from the one in which the currency of the bond is denominated*. For example, a bond that is issued in Europe or in Asia by an American company and that pays interest and principal to the lender in U.S. dollars would be considered a Eurobond. Thus, even if the bond is not issued in Europe, it merely needs to be sold in a country different from the one in which the bond's currency is denominated to be considered a Eurobond.

The primary attractions of Eurobonds to borrowers, aside from favorable rates, are the relative lack of regulation (Eurobonds are not registered with the Securities and Exchange Commission [SEC]), less-rigorous disclosure requirements than those of the SEC, and the speed with which they can be issued. Interestingly, not only are Eurobonds not registered with the SEC, but they may not be offered to U.S. citizens and residents.

Convertible Bonds

convertible bond a debt security that can be converted into a firm's stock at a prespecified price.

Convertible bonds are debt securities that can be converted into a firm's stock at a prespecified price. For instance, you might have a convertible bond with a face, or par, value of $1,000 that pays 6 percent interest, or $60, each year. The bond matures in 5 years, at which time the company must pay the $1,000 par value to the bondholder. However, at the time the bond was issued, the firm gave the bondholder the option of either collecting the $1,000 or receiving shares of the firm's stock at a conversion price of $50. In other words, the bondholder would receive 20 shares (20 = $1,000 par value ÷ $50 conversion price). What would you do if you were the bondholder? If the stock were selling for more than $50, then you would want to give up the $1,000 par value and take the stock. Thus, it's the investor's choice either to take the $1,000 promised when the bond was issued or to convert the bond into the firm's stock.

Consider Ingersoll Rand Company, a diversified equipment manufacturer. In 2009, the firm issued $300 million of 5-percent convertible debt. The bonds can be converted at any time into Ingersoll Rand common stock at a conversion price of $17.94 per share. Because the par value for each bond is $1,000, a bondholder can convert one bond into 55.74 shares (55.74 shares = $1,000 ÷ $17.94 price per share.) This option allows the investor to be repaid the $1,000 par value or to convert into stock if the total value of the stock exceeds $1,000. Thus,

FINANCE AT WORK

ALCOA: HOW TO RAISE $1.5 BILLION AHEAD OF WEAK EARNINGS

March 16, 2009, was a day of bad news for investors. Alcoa warned of a first-quarter loss, cut its quarterly dividend to three cents a share from 17 cents and told investors it wanted to raise $1.1 billion in the capital markets to help it prepare for a long downturn in its business and pay back debt that was coming due soon. The stock fell 8.7 percent on the following day.

Still, the company wanted to raise the cash quickly, regardless of whether or not there was an overhang of bad news. "These windows are short, and when you have these few days, you have to act. I think the market has become more accustomed to the volatility. People are now so used to seeing volatility that news flow is impacting them less," said a person familiar with the deal.

Alcoa and its underwriters (Morgan Stanley, Credit Suisse Group, Citigroup, and Barclays Capital) settled on a two-pronged approach, selling stock and convertible bonds. In the end, Alcoa sold $900 million of stock and $500 million of convertible debt.

The key to getting the financing done was speed: a two-day boot camp of meetings and phone calls with investors. With the aluminum industry suffering, management emphasized that Alcoa would be a survivor and talked up the company's financial and economic position compared with peers. The executives told investors a bottom was near for the aluminum sector and particularly for plunging aluminum prices, which are near historical lows. At the same time, they maintained that demand is delayed and due to rise. In short, their "pitch" held that things were so bad that they had to get better.

With the credit markets showing signs of thawing and the stock market hitting 12-year lows in March, companies decided to sell more bonds to pay off their existing debt. But Alcoa opted for a large equity offering because it didn't want to endanger its balance sheet by piling on more debt, according to people familiar with the company's plans. "Alcoa decided to take some dilution on equity and open up the options a bit more," one person said. In addition, the company paid significantly lower fees to the underwriters to sell stock than it would for a debt offering on which it also would be shelling out interest payments.

The company pitched the offering as a chance for investors who had sold their holdings in the downturn of last year to get back in at relatively low prices.

Alcoa also had a little bit of luck on its side: As the deal was being priced, aluminum prices showed the biggest one-day uptick in more than a year, with a 7-percent boost based on optimism from research analysts.

Perhaps the biggest surprise was the success of the convertible debt. Underwriters had planned to sell only about $250 million of bonds that would convert to stock in five years. But they saw pressing investor demand for more as convertible bonds prepare to become one of the most sought-after securities by investors looking to put money to work. That demand enabled underwriters to trim the coupon payment—or interest rate—to 5.25% from 6%, reducing the cost to the company.

Source: http://blogs.wsj.com/deals/2009/03/25/alcoa-how-to-raise-15-billion-ahead-of-weak-earnings/tab/print/, accessed June 25, 2009.

with convertible bonds, the investor gets to participate in the upside if the company does well. For instance, three months after the bonds were issued, the firm's stock was selling for $27. If you had been an investor, you could have converted the bonds into 55.74 shares of stock, which would be worth about $1,500. Not bad for three months.

Now that you have an understanding of the kinds of bonds firms might issue, let's look at some of the characteristics and terminology of bonds.

Concept Check

1. How do debentures, subordinated debentures, and mortgage bonds differ with regard to their risk? How would investors respond to the varying types of risk?

2. How is a Eurobond different from a bond issued in Asia that is denominated in dollars?

3. Why would a convertible bond increase much more in value than a bond that is not convertible?

Terminology and Characteristics of Bonds

 Explain the more popular features of bonds.

Before valuing bonds, we first need to understand the terminology related to bonds. Then we will be better prepared to determine the value of a bond.

When a firm or nonprofit institution needs financing, one source is bonds. As already noted, this type of financing instrument is simply a long-term promissory note, issued by the borrower, promising to pay its holder a predetermined and fixed amount of interest each year. Some of the more important terms and characteristics that you might hear about bonds are as follows:

Claims on assets and income   Call provision
Par value   Indenture
Coupon interest rate   Bond ratings
Maturity

Let's consider each in turn.

Claims on Assets and Income

In the case of insolvency, claims of debt, including bonds, are generally honored before those of both common stock and preferred stock. In general, if the interest on bonds is not paid, the bond trustees can classify the firm as insolvent and force it into bankruptcy. Thus, the bondholders' claim on income is more likely to be honored than that of the common stockholders, whose dividends are paid at the discretion of the firm's management. However, different types of debt can have a hierarchy among themselves as to the order of their claims on assets.

Par Value

par value on the face of a bond, the stated amount that the firm is to repay upon the maturity date.

The **par value** of a bond is its *face value, which is returned to the bondholder at maturity*. In general, corporate bonds are issued in denominations of $1,000, although there are some exceptions to this rule. Also, when bond prices are quoted, either by financial managers or in the financial press, prices are generally expressed as a percentage of the bond's par value. For example, a Time-Warner Cable bond was recently quoted as selling for $116.72. That does not mean you can buy the bond for $116.72. It means that this bond is selling for 116.72 percent of its par value of $1,000. Hence, the market price of this bond is actually $1,167.20. At maturity in 2019 the bondholder will receive $1,000.

Coupon Interest Rate

coupon interest rate the interest rate contractually owed on a bond as a percent of its par value.

The **coupon interest rate** on a bond indicates the *percentage of the par value of the bond that will be paid out annually in the form of interest*. Thus, regardless of what happens to the price of a bond with an 8 percent coupon interest rate and a $1,000 par value, it will pay out $80 annually in interest until maturity ($0.08 \times \$1,000 = \$80$). For the Time-Warner Cable bonds, the coupon rate is 8.25 percent; thus an investor owning the bonds would receive 8.25 percent of its par value of $1,000, or $82.50 ($82.50 = 0.0825 \times \$1,000$) per year. The investor receives a fixed dollar income each year from the interest; thus, these bonds are called **fixed-rate bonds**.

fixed-rate bond a bond that pays a fixed amount of interest to the investor each year.

zero coupon bond a bond issued at a substantial discount from its $1,000 face value and that pays little or no interest.

Occasionally, a firm will issue bonds that have zero or very low coupon rates, thus the name **zero coupon bonds**. Instead of paying interest, the company sells the bonds at a substantial discount below the $1,000 par or face value. Thus, the investor receives a large part (or all with zero coupon bonds) of the return from the appreciation of the bond value as it moves in time to maturity. For example, Amgen, the biotech company, issued $3.95 billion face value bonds with a coupon rate of only 1/8th of 1 percent. Thus, the investors would hardly receive any interest income. But the bonds were issued to the investors at $500 for each $1,000 face value bond. Investors who purchased these bonds for $500 could hold them until they mature and would then receive the $1,000 par value.

Maturity

maturity the length of time until the bond issuer returns the par value to the bondholder and terminates the bond.

The **maturity** of a bond indicates *the length of time until the bond issuer returns the par value to the bondholder and terminates or redeems the bond.*

Call Provision

callable bond (redeemable bond) an option available to a company issuing a bond whereby the issuer can call (redeem) the bond before it matures. This is usually done if interest rates decline below what the firm is paying on the bond.

call protection period a prespecified time period during which a company cannot recall a bond.

If a company issues bonds and then later the prevailing interest rate declines, the firm may want to pay off the bonds early and then issue new bonds with a lower interest rate. To do so, the bond must be **callable**, or **redeemable**; otherwise, the firm cannot force the bondholder to accept early payment. The issuer, however, usually must pay the bondholders a premium, such as 1 year's interest. Also, there frequently is a **call protection period** where the firm cannot call the bond for a prespecified time period.

Indenture

An **indenture** is the *legal agreement between the firm issuing the bonds and the trustee who represents the bondholders*. The indenture provides the specific terms of the loan agreement, including a description of the bonds, the rights of the bondholders, the rights of the issuing firm, and the responsibilities of the trustee. This legal document may run 100 pages or more in length, with the majority of it devoted to defining protective provisions for the bondholder.

Typically, the restrictive provisions included in the indenture attempt to protect the bondholders' financial position relative to that of other outstanding securities. Common provisions involve (1) prohibiting the sale of the firm's accounts receivable, (2) limiting common stock dividends, (3) restricting the purchase or sale of the firm's fixed assets, and (4) setting limits on additional borrowing by the firm. Not allowing the sale of accounts receivable is specified because such sales would benefit the firm's short-run liquidity position at the expense of its future liquidity position. Common stock dividends may not be allowed if the firm's liquidity falls below a specified level, or the maximum dividend payout might be limited to some fraction, say, 50 or 60 percent of earnings. Fixed-asset restrictions generally require permission before they can be liquidated or used as collateral on new loans. Constraints on additional borrowing usually involve limiting the amount and type of additional long-term debt that can be issued. All these restrictions have one thing in common: They attempt to prohibit actions that would improve the status of other securities at the expense of bonds, and to protect the status of bonds from being weakened by any managerial action.

indenture the legal agreement between the firm issuing bonds and the bond trustee who represents the bondholders, providing the specific terms of the loan agreement.

Bond Ratings

John Moody first began to rate bonds in 1909. Since that time three rating agencies—Moody's, Standard & Poor's, and Fitch Investor Services—have provided ratings on corporate bonds. These ratings involve a judgment about the future risk potential of the bonds. Although they deal with expectations, several historical factors seem to play a significant role in their determination. Bond ratings are favorably affected by (1) a greater reliance on equity as opposed to debt in financing the firm, (2) profitable operations, (3) a low variability in past earnings, (4) large firm size, and (5) little use of subordinated debt. In turn, the rating a bond receives affects the interest rate demanded on the bond by the investors. The poorer the bond rating, the higher the interest rate demanded by investors. (Table 1 describes these ratings.) Thus, bond ratings are extremely important for the financial

> **REMEMBER YOUR PRINCIPLES**
> **Principle** When we say that a lower bond rating means a higher interest rate charged by the investors (bondholders), we are observing an application of **Principle 3: Risk Requires a Reward**.

TABLE 1	Standard & Poor's Corporate Bond Ratings
AAA	This is the highest rating assigned by Standard & Poor's for debt obligation and indicates an extremely strong capacity to pay principal and interest.
AA	Bonds rated AA also qualify as high-quality debt obligations. Their capacity to pay principal and interest is very strong, and in the majority of instances, they differ from AAA issues only by a small degree.
A	Bonds rated A have a strong capacity to pay principal and interest, although they are somewhat more susceptible to the adverse effects of changes in circumstances and economic conditions.
BBB	Bonds rated BBB are regarded as having an adequate capacity to pay principal and interest. Whereas they normally exhibit adequate protection parameters, adverse economic conditions or changing circumstances are more likely to lead to a weakened capacity to pay principal and interest for bonds in this category than for bonds in the A category.
BB B CCC CC	Bonds rated BB, B, CCC, and CC are regarded, on balance, as predominantly speculative with respect to the issuer's capacity to pay interest and repay principal in accordance with the terms of the obligation. BB indicates the lowest degree of speculation and CC the highest. Although such bonds will likely have some quality and protective characteristics, these are outweighed by large uncertainties or major risk exposures to adverse conditions.
C	The rating C is reserved for income bonds on which no interest is being paid.
D	Bonds rated D are in default, and payment of principal and/or interest is in arrears.
Plus (+) or Minus (−): To provide more detailed indications of credit quality, the ratings from AA to BB may be modified by the addition of a plus or minus sign to show relative standing within the major rating categories.	

Source: Adapted from www.standardandpoors.com, December 2005.

FINANCE AT WORK

CLEAR CHANNEL RATING IS CUT

In early 2009, faced with a decrease in advertising revenues, Clear Channel Communications eliminated about 9 percent of its workforce. On March 9, 2009, Moody's Investors Service downgraded the media conglomerate's credit rating four notches. The following is an article that appeared in the *Wall Street Journal* on March 10, 2009.

Moody's Investors Service slashed Clear Channel Communications Inc.'s credit rating by four notches Monday, and said the downgrade reflected the "high probability" that the company will break its financial covenants this year.

The covenants call for a ratio of secured debt to earnings before interest, taxes, depreciation and amortization of no more than 9.5 times. As of the end of 2008, that ratio was at 6.39 times, compared with six times at the end of September.

Moody's analyst Neil Begley wrote that "compliance will be very challenging" and "a debt restructuring will be likely." Clear Channel,

the country's largest radio and outdoor advertising company, declined to comment. Clear Channel bonds due in 2018 traded at about 10 cents on the dollar Monday.

Moody's current rating for the company is Caa3, two notches away from Moody's lowest rating.

Bishop Cheen, an analyst at Wachovia Capital Markets LLC, agrees that the company will fall out of compliance, but not until 2010. While the company seems safely within its limit for now, its radio and billboard advertising is deteriorating at a rapid clip.

The company took on $15.7 billion in connection with its privatization, which closed last year. Last month, it tapped an additional $1.6 billion of a $2 billion credit facility, spooking the markets. Many investors believed that Clear Channel was drawing down the facility while it still could.

Source: Sarah McBride, "Clear Channel Rating is Cut," *Wall Street Journal*, March 10, 2009, pg. B2.

---

junk bond any bond rated BB or below.

manager. They provide an indicator of default risk that in turn affects the interest rate that must be paid on borrowed funds.

Toward the bottom end of the rating spectrum, we have **junk bonds**, which are high-risk debt with *ratings of BB or below* by Moody's and Standard & Poor's. The lower the rating, the higher the chance of default. The lowest rating is CC for Standard & Poor's and Ca for Moody's. Originally, the term "junk bonds" was used to describe firms with sound financial histories that were facing severe financial problems and suffering from poor credit ratings. Junk bonds are also called **high-yield bonds** because of the high interest rates they pay the investor. Typically, they have an interest rate of between 3 and 5 percent more than AAA-grade long-term debt.

high-yield bond see Junk bond.

We are now ready to think about bond valuation. To begin, we must first clarify precisely what we mean by value. Next, we need to understand the basic concepts of valuation and the process for valuing an asset. Then we may apply these concepts to valuing a bond and to valuing stocks.

REMEMBER YOUR PRINCIPLES

Principle Some have thought junk bonds were fundamentally different from other securities, but they are not. They are bonds with a great amount of risk and, therefore, promise high expected returns. Thus, **Principle 3: Risk Requires a Reward**.

Concept Check

book value (1) the value of an asset as shown on the firm's balance sheet. It represents the historical cost of the asset rather than its current market value or replacement cost. (2) The depreciated value of a company's assets (original cost less accumulated depreciation) less outstanding liabilities.

1. What are some of the important features of a bond? Which features determine the cash flows associated with a bond?

2. What restrictions are typically included in an indenture in order to protect the bondholder?

3. How does the bond rating affect an investor's required rate of return? What actions could a firm take to receive a more favorable rating?

Define the term *value* as used for several different purposes.

Defining Value

The term *value* is often used in different contexts, depending on its application. **Book value** is the *value of an asset as shown on a firm's balance sheet*. It represents the historical cost of the asset rather than its current worth. For instance, the book value of a company's common stock is the amount the investors originally paid for the stock and, therefore, the amount the firm received when the stock was issued.

Liquidation value is the *dollar sum that could be realized if an asset were sold individually and not as part of a going concern*. For example, if a firm's operations were discontinued and its assets were divided up and sold, the sales price would represent the asset's liquidation value.

The **market value** of an asset is the *observed value for the asset in the marketplace*. This value is determined by supply and demand forces working together in the marketplace, whereby buyers and sellers negotiate a mutually acceptable price for the asset. For instance, the market price for Harley-Davidson's common stock on June 20, 2009, was $25 per share. This price was reached by a large number of buyers and sellers working through the New York Stock Exchange. In theory, a market price exists for all assets. However, many assets have no readily observable market price because trading seldom occurs. For instance, the market price for the common stock of Vision Research Organization, a recent start-up firm in Dallas, Texas, would be more difficult to establish than the market value of Harley-Davidson's common stock.

The **intrinsic, or economic, value** of an asset—also called the **fair value**—is the *present value of the asset's expected future cash flows*. This value is the amount an investor should be willing to pay for the asset given the amount, timing, and riskiness of its future cash flows. Once the investor has estimated the intrinsic value of a security, this value could be compared with its market value when available. If the intrinsic value is greater than the market value, then the security is undervalued in the eyes of the investor. Should the market value exceed the investor's intrinsic value, then the security is overvalued.

We hasten to add that if the securities market is working efficiently, the market value and the intrinsic value of a security will be equal. Whenever a security's intrinsic value differs from its current market price, the competition among investors seeking opportunities to make a profit will quickly drive the market price back to its intrinsic value. Thus, we may define an **efficient market** as one in which *the values of all securities at any instant fully reflect all available public information*, which results in the market value and the intrinsic value being the same. If the markets are efficient, it is extremely difficult for an investor to make extra profits from an ability to predict prices.

The idea of market efficiency has been the backdrop for an intense battle between professional investors and university professors. The academic community has contended that someone throwing darts at the list of securities in the *Wall Street Journal* could do as well as a professional money manager. Market professionals retort that academicians are grossly mistaken in this view. The war has been intense but also one that the student of finance should find intriguing.

> **liquidation value** the dollar sum that could be realized if an asset were sold.

> **market value** the value observed in the marketplace.

> **intrinsic, or economic, value** the present value of an asset's expected future cash flows. This value is the amount the investor considers to be fair value, given the amount, timing, and riskiness of future cash flows.

> **fair value** the present value of an asset's expected future cash flows.

> **efficient market** market where the values of all securities fully recognize all available public information.

> **REMEMBER YOUR PRINCIPLES**
>
> **Principle** The fact that investors have difficulty identifying stocks that are undervalued relates to **Principle 4: Market Prices Are Generally Right**. In an efficient market, the price reflects all available public information about the security and, therefore, it is priced fairly.

Concept Check

1. Explain the different types of value.
2. Why should the market value equal the intrinsic value?

What Determines Value?

Explain the factors that determine value.

For our purposes, *the value of an asset is its intrinsic value or the present value of its expected future cash flows*, when these cash flows are discounted back to the present using the investor's required rate of return. This statement is true for valuing all assets, and it serves as the basis of almost all that we do in finance. Thus, value is affected by three elements:

1. The amount and timing of the asset's expected cash flows
2. The riskiness of these cash flows
3. The investor's required rate of return for undertaking the investment

The first two factors are characteristics of the asset. The third one, the required rate of return, is the minimum rate of return necessary to attract an investor to purchase or hold a

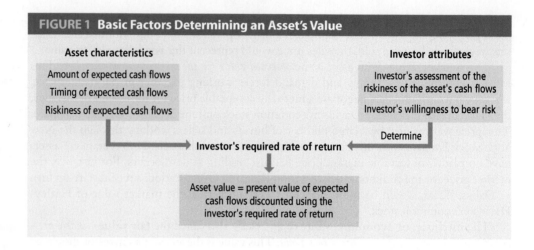

FIGURE 1 Basic Factors Determining an Asset's Value

Asset characteristics

Amount of expected cash flows
Timing of expected cash flows
Riskiness of expected cash flows

Investor attributes

Investor's assessment of the riskiness of the asset's cash flows
Investor's willingness to bear risk

Determine

Investor's required rate of return

Asset value = present value of expected cash flows discounted using the investor's required rate of return

---

REMEMBER YOUR PRINCIPLES

Principle Our discussions should remind us of three of our principles that help us understand finance:

Principle 3: Risk Requires a Reward.
Principle 2: Money Has a Time Value.
Principle 1: Cash Flow Is What Matters.

Determining the economic worth or value of an asset always relies on these three principles. Without them, we would have no basis for explaining value. With them, we can know that the amount and timing of cash, not earnings, drive value. Also, we must be rewarded for taking risk; otherwise, we will not invest.

security. This rate of return is determined by *the rates of return available on similar investments*, or is called the opportunity cost of funds. This rate must be high enough to compensate the investor for risk perceived in the asset's future cash flows.

Figure 1 depicts the basic factors involved in valuation. As the figure shows, finding the value of an asset involves the following steps:

1. Assessing the asset's characteristics, which include the amount and timing of the expected cash flows and the riskiness of these cash flows
2. Determining the investor's required rate of return, which embodies the investor's attitude about assuming risk and the investor's perception of the riskiness of the asset
3. Discounting the expected cash flows back to the present, using the investor's required rate of return as the discount rate

Thus, intrinsic value is a function of the cash flows yet to be received, the riskiness of these cash flows, and the investor's required rate of return.

Concept Check

1. What are the three important elements of asset valuation?

5 Describe the basic process for valuing assets.

Valuation: The Basic Process

The valuation process can be described as follows: It is assigning value to an asset by calculating the present value of its expected future cash flows using the investor's required rate of return as the discount rate. The investor's required rate of return, r, is determined by the level of the risk-free rate of interest and risk premium that the investor feels is necessary compensation. Therefore, a basic asset valuation model can be defined mathematically as follows:

$$\text{Asset value} = \frac{\text{Cash flow in year 1}}{\left(1 + \begin{array}{c}\text{required}\\\text{rate of return}\end{array}\right)^1} + \frac{\text{Cash flow in year 2}}{\left(1 + \begin{array}{c}\text{required}\\\text{rate of return}\end{array}\right)^2} + \cdots + \frac{\text{Cash flow in year } n}{\left(1 + \begin{array}{c}\text{required}\\\text{rate of return}\end{array}\right)^n}$$

CAN YOU DO IT?

COMPUTING AN ASSET'S VALUE

You purchased an asset that is expected to provide $5,000 cash flow per year for 4 years. If you have a 12 percent required rate of return, what is the value of the asset for you?

Or stated in symbols, we have:

$$V = \frac{C_1}{(1 + r)^1} + \frac{C_2}{(1 + r)^2} + \cdots + \frac{C_n}{(1 + r)^n} \qquad (1)$$

where V = the intrinsic value, or present value, of an asset producing expected future cash flows, C_t, in years 1 through n

C_t = cash flow to be received at time t

r = the investor's required rate of return

Using equation (1), there are three basic steps in the valuation process:

Step 1. Estimate the C_t in equation (1), which is the amount and timing of the future cash flows the security is expected to provide.

Step 2. Determine r, the investor's required rate of return.

Step 3. Calculate the intrinsic value, V, as the present value of expected future cash flows discounted at the investor's required rate of return.

Equation (1), which measures the present value of future cash flows, is the basis of the valuation process. It is the most important equation in this chapter because all the remaining equations in this chapter are merely reformulations of this one equation. If we understand equation (1), all the valuation work we do, and a host of other topics as well, will be much clearer in our minds.

With the foregoing principles of valuation as our foundation, let's now look at how bonds are valued.

Valuing Bonds

 Estimate the value of a bond.

The value of a bond is the present value of both the future interest to be received and the par or maturity value of the bond. It's that simple.

The process for valuing a bond, as depicted in Figure 2, requires knowing three essential elements: (1) the amount and timing of the cash flows to be received by the investor, (2) the time to maturity of the bond, and (3) the investor's required rate of return. The amount of cash flows is dictated by the periodic interest to be received and by the par value to be paid at maturity. Given these elements, we can compute the value of the bond, or the present value.

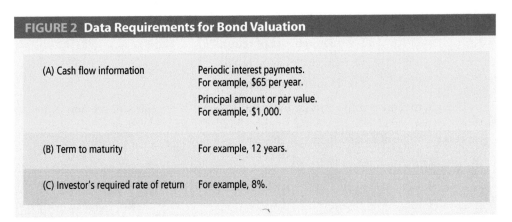

FIGURE 2 Data Requirements for Bond Valuation

(A) Cash flow information	Periodic interest payments. For example, $65 per year. Principal amount or par value. For example, $1,000.
(B) Term to maturity	For example, 12 years.
(C) Investor's required rate of return	For example, 8%.

EXAMPLE 1

Consider a bond issued by Walmart with a maturity date of 2013 and a stated annual coupon rate of 4.55 percent.[1] In December 2009, with 4 years left to maturity, investors owning the bonds were only requiring a 2.48 percent rate of return. We can calculate the value of the bonds to these investors using the following three-step valuation procedure:

Step 1. Estimate the amount and timing of the expected future cash flows. Two types of cash flows are received by the bondholder:

a. Annual interest payments equal to the coupon rate of interest times the face value of the bond. In this example, the bond's coupon interest rate is 4.55 percent; thus, the annual interest payment is $45.50 = 0.0455 \times $1,000$. Assuming that 2009 interest payments have already been made, these cash flows will be received by the bondholder in each of the 4 years before the bond matures (2010 through 2013 = 4 years).

b. The face value of $1,000 to be received in 2013.

To summarize, the cash flows received by the bondholder are as follows:

YEARS	1	2	3	4
	$45.50	$45.50	$45.50	$ 45.50
				$1,000.00
				$1,045.50

Step 2. Determine the investor's required rate of return by evaluating the riskiness of the bond's future cash flows. A 2.48 percent required rate of return for the bondholders is given. However, we should recall that an investor's required rate of return is equal to a rate earned on a risk-free security plus a risk premium for assuming risk.

Step 3. Calculate the intrinsic value of the bond as the present value of the expected future interest and principal payments discounted at the investor's required rate of return.

In general, the present value of a bond is found as follows:

$$\text{Bond value} = V_b = \frac{\$ \text{ interest in year 1}}{(1 + \text{required rate of return})^1}$$

$$+ \frac{\$ \text{ interest in year 2}}{(1 + \text{required rate of return})^2}$$

$$+ \frac{\$ \text{ interest in year 3}}{(1 + \text{required rate of return})^3}$$

$$+ \cdots$$

$$+ \frac{\$ \text{ interest in year } n}{(1 + \text{required rate of return})^n}$$

$$+ \frac{\$ \text{ maturity value of bond}}{(1 + \text{required rate of return})^n} \tag{2a}$$

Using I_t to represent the interest payment in year t, M to represent the bond's maturity (or par) value, and r_b to equal the bondholder's required rate of return, we can express the value of a bond maturing in year n as follows:

$$V_b = \frac{\$I_1}{(1 + r_b)^1} + \frac{\$I_2}{(1 + r_b)^2} + \frac{\$I_3}{(1 + r_b)^3} + \cdots + \frac{\$I_n}{(1 + r_b)^n} + \frac{\$M}{(1 + r_b)^n} \tag{2b}$$

(continued on next page)

[1]Walmart pays interest to its bondholders on a semiannual basis on June 15 and December 15. However, for the moment, assume the interest is to be received annually. The effect of semiannual payments is examined shortly.

DID YOU GET IT?

COMPUTING AN ASSET'S VALUE

The value of an asset generating $5,000 per year for 4 years, given a 12 percent required rate of return, would be $15,186.75. Using a TI BA II Plus calculator, we find the answer as follows:

CALCULATOR SOLUTION

Data Input	Function Key
12	I/Y
4	N
−5,000	+/− PMT
0	FV

Function Key	Answer
CPT	
PV	15,186.75

If an investor owns an asset that pays $5,000 in cash flows each year for 4 years, he would earn exactly his required rate of return of 12 percent if he paid $15,186.75 today.

Notice that equation (2b) is a restatement of equation (1), where now the cash flows are represented by the interest received each period and the par value of the bond when it matures. In either equation, the value of an asset is the present value of its future cash flows.

The equation for finding the value of the Walmart bonds would be as follows:

$$V_b = \frac{\$45.50}{(1 + 0.0248)^1} + \frac{\$45.50}{(1 + 0.0248)^2} + \frac{\$45.50}{(1 + 0.0248)^3} + \frac{\$45.50}{(1 + 0.0248)^4} + \frac{\$1,000}{(1 + 0.0248)^4}$$

Finding the value of the Walmart bonds can be represented graphically as follows:

YEAR	0	1	2	3	4
Dollars received at end of year		$45.50	$45.50	$45.50	$ 45.50 +$1,000.00 $1,045.50
Present value	$1,077.91				

Using a TI BA II Plus financial calculator, we find the value of the bond to be $1,077.91, as calculated in the margin.[2] Thus, if investors consider 2.48 percent to be an appropriate required rate of return in view of the risk level associated with Walmart bonds, paying a price of $1,077.91 would satisfy their return requirement.

We can also solve for the value of Walmart's bonds using a spreadsheet. The solution using Excel appears as follows:

CALCULATOR SOLUTION

Data Input	Function Key
4	N
2.48	I/Y
−45.50	+/− PMT
1000	+/− FV

Function Key	Answer
CPT	
PV	1,077.91

	A	B	C	D
1	Required rate of return	Rate	2.48%	
2	Years left to maturity	Nper	4	
3	Annual interest payment	Pmt	−45.50	
4	Future value	FV	−1,000	
5	Present value	PV	$1,077.91	
6				
7		Equation:		
8		=PV(Rate,Nper,Pmt,FV) = PV(C1,C2,C3,C4)		
9				
10				

[2]Note that we are using the TI BA II Plus.

CAN YOU DO IT?

COMPUTING A BOND'S VALUE

La Fiesta Restaurants issued bonds that have a 6 percent coupon interest rate. Interest is paid annually. The bonds mature in 12 years. If your required rate of return is 8 percent, what is the value of a bond to you?

Concept Check

1. What two factors determine an investor's required rate of return?

2. How does the required rate of return affect a bond's value?

In the preceding Walmart illustration, the interest payments were assumed to be paid annually. However, companies typically pay interest to bondholders semiannually. For example, Walmart actually pays a total of $45.50 per year, but disburses the interest semiannually ($22.75 each June 15 and December 15).

Several steps are involved in adapting equation (2b) for semiannual interest payments.[3] First, thinking in terms of *periods* instead of years, a bond with a life of n years paying interest semiannually has a life of $2n$ periods. In other words, a 4-year bond ($n = 4$) that remits its interest on a semiannual basis actually makes 8 payments. Although the number of periods has doubled, the *dollar* amount of interest being sent to the investors for each period and the bondholders' required rate of return are half of the equivalent annual figures. I_t becomes $I_t/2$ and r_b is changed to $r_b/2$; thus, for semiannual compounding, equation (2b) becomes

$$V_b = \frac{\$I_1/2}{\left(1+\dfrac{r_b}{2}\right)^1} + \frac{\$I_2/2}{\left(1+\dfrac{r_b}{2}\right)^2} + \frac{\$I_3/2}{\left(1+\dfrac{r_b}{2}\right)^3} + \cdots + \frac{\$I_n/2}{\left(1+\dfrac{r_b}{2}\right)^{2n}} + \frac{\$M}{\left(1+\dfrac{r_b}{2}\right)^{2n}} \tag{3}$$

We can now compute the value of the Walmart bonds, recognizing that interest is being paid semiannually. We simply change the number of periods from 4 years to 8 semiannual periods and the required rate of return from 2.48 percent annually to 1.24 percent per semiannual period and divide interest payment by 2 to get $22.75. The value of the bond would now be $1,078.36.

This solution can be found using a calculator as shown in the margin or a spreadsheet that would look as follows:

CALCULATOR SOLUTION

Data Input	Function Key
$2n \rightarrow 2 \times 4 \rightarrow 8$	N
$2.48 \div 2 \rightarrow 1.24$	1/Y
$22.75	+/− PMT
1000	+/− FV

Function Key	Answer
CPT	
PV	1,078.36

	A	B	C	D	E
1	Required rate of return	Rate	1.24%		
2	Years left to maturity	Nper	8		
3	Annual interest payment	Pmt	−22.75		
4	Future value	FV	−1,000		
5	Present value	PV	$1,078.36		
6					
7		Equation:			
8		=PV(Rate,Nper,Pmt,FV) = PV(C1,C2,C3,C4)			
9					
10					
11					

[3]The logic for calculating the value of a bond that pays interest semiannually is similar to the material presented earlier in the book, where compound interest with nonannual periods was discussed.

DID YOU GET IT?

COMPUTING A BOND'S VALUE

The LaFiesta bond with a 6 percent coupon rate pays $60 in interest per year ($60 = 0.06 coupon rate × $1,000 par value). Thus, you would receive $60 per year for 12 years plus the $1,000 in par value in year 12. Assuming an 8 percent required rate of return, the value of the bond would be $849.28.

CALCULATOR SOLUTION

Data Input	Function Key
8	I/Y
12	N
60	+/− PMT
1,000	+/− FV

Function Key	Answer
CPT	
PV	849.28

If an investor owns a bond that pays $60 in interest each year for 12 years, she would earn exactly her required rate of return of 8 percent if she paid $849.28 today.

Concept Check

1. How do semiannual interest payments affect the asset valuation equation?

Now that we know how to value a bond, we will next examine a bondholder's rate of return from investing in a bond, or what is called bond yields.

Bond Yields

Compute a bond's expected rate of return.

There are two calculations used to measure the rate of return a bondholder receives from owning a bond: the yield to maturity and the current yield.

Yield to Maturity

Theoretically, each bondholder could have a different required rate of return for a particular bond. However, the financial manager is interested only in the expected rate of return that is implied by the market prices of the firm's bonds, or what we call the yield to maturity.

To measure the bondholder's **expected rate of return**, $\bar{r}_b$, we would find the *discount rate that equates the present value of the future cash flows (interest and maturity value) with the current market price of the bond.*[4] It is also the *rate of return the investor will earn if the bond is held to maturity*, thus the name **yield to maturity**. So, when referring to bonds, the terms *expected rate of return* and *yield to maturity* are often used interchangeably.

To illustrate this concept, consider the Brister Corporation's bonds, which are selling for $1,100. The bonds carry a coupon interest rate of 9 percent and mature in 10 years. (Remember, the coupon rate determines the interest payment—coupon rate × par value.)

To determine the expected rate of return ($\bar{r}_b$) implicit in the current market price, we need to find the rate that discounts the anticipated cash flows back to a present value of $1,100, the current market price (P_0) for the bond.

expected rate of return (1) the discount rate that equates the present value of the future cash flows (interest and maturity value) of a bond with its current market price. It is the rate of return an investor will earn if the bond is held to maturity. (2) The rate of return the investor expects to receive on an investment by paying the existing market price of the security.

yield to maturity The rate of return a bondholder will receive if the bond is held to maturity. (It is equivalent to the expected rate of return.)

[4]When we speak of computing an expected rate of return, we are not describing the situation very accurately. Expected rates of return are ex ante (before the fact) and are based on "expected and unobservable future cash flows" and, therefore, can only be "estimated."

The expected return for the Brister Corporation bondholders is 7.54 percent, which can be found as presented in the margin by using the TI BA II Plus calculator, or by using a computer spreadsheet, as follows:

	A	B	C	D	E
1	Years left to maturity	Nper	10		
2	Annual interest payment	Pmt	90		
3	Present value	PV	−1,100		
4	Future value	FV	1,000		
5	Required rate of return	Rate	7.54%		
6					
7		Equation:			
8		=RATE(Nper,Pmt,PV,FV) = RATE(C1,C2,C3,C4)			
9					
10					

Current Yield

The **current yield** on a bond refers to the *ratio of the annual interest payment to the bond's current market price.* If, for example, we have a bond with an 8 percent coupon interest rate, a par value of $1,000, and a market price of $700, it would have a current yield of 11.4 percent:

$$\text{Current yield} = \frac{\text{annual interest payment}}{\text{current market price of the bond}} \tag{4}$$

In our example

$$\text{Current yield} = \frac{0.08 \times \$1,000}{\$700} = \frac{\$80}{\$700} = 0.114 = 11.4\%$$

We should understand that the current yield, although frequently quoted in the popular press, is an incomplete picture of the expected rate of return from holding a bond. The current yield indicates the cash income that results from holding a bond in a given year, but it fails to recognize the capital gain or loss that will occur if the bond is held to maturity. As such, it is not an accurate measure of the bondholder's expected rate of return.

Explain three important relationships that exist in bond valuation.

Bond Valuation: Three Important Relationships

We have now learned to find the value of a bond (V_b), given (1) the amount of interest payments (I_t), (2) the maturity value (M), (3) the length of time to maturity (n periods), and (4) the investor's required rate of return, r_b. We also know how to compute the expected rate of return ($\bar{r}_b$), which also happens to be the current interest rate on the bond, given (1) the current market value (P_0), (2) the amount of interest payments (I_t), (3) the maturity value (M), and (4) the length of time to maturity (n periods). We now have the basics. But let's go further in our understanding of bond valuation by studying several important relationships:

1. The value of a bond is inversely related to changes in the investor's present required rate of return. In other words, as interest rates increase (decrease), the value of the bond decreases (increases).

    To illustrate, assume that an investor's required rate of return for a given bond is 12 percent. The bond has a par value of $1,000 and annual interest payments of $120, indicating a 12 percent coupon interest rate ($120 ÷ $1,000 = 12%). Assuming a 5-year maturity date, the bond would be worth $1,000, computed as follows:

$$V_b = \frac{\$I_1}{(1 + r_b)^1} + \cdots + \frac{\$I_n}{(1 + r_b)^n} + \frac{\$M}{(1 + r_b)^n}$$

In our example

$$V_b = \frac{\$120}{(1 + 0.12)^1} + \frac{\$120}{(1 + 0.12)^2} + \frac{\$120}{(1 + 0.12)^3} + \frac{\$120}{(1 + 0.12)^4} + \frac{\$120}{(1 + 0.12)^5} + \frac{\$1,000}{(1 + 0.12)^5}$$

Using a calculator, we find the value of the bond to be $1,000.

CALCULATOR SOLUTION

Data Input	Function Key
12	I/Y
5	N
120	+/− PMT
1,000	+/− FV

Function Key	Answer
CPT	
PV	1,000

If, however, the investors' required rate of return increases from 12 percent to 15 percent, the value of the bond would decrease to $899.44, computed as follows:

CALCULATOR SOLUTION

Data Input	Function Key
15	I/Y
5	N
120	+/− PMT
1,000	+/− FV

Function Key	Answer
CPT	
PV	899.44

On the other hand, if the investor's required rate of return decreases to 9 percent, the bond would increase in value to $1,116.69.

CALCULATOR SOLUTION

Data Input	Function Key
9	I/Y
5	N
120	+/− PMT
1,000	+/− FV

Function Key	Answer
CPT	
PV	1,116.69

This inverse relationship between the investor's required rate of return and the value of a bond is presented in Figure 3. Clearly, as investors demand a higher rate of return, the value of a bond decreases: The higher rate of return can be achieved only by paying less for the bond. Conversely, a lower required rate of return yields a higher market value for the bond.

DID YOU GET IT?

COMPUTING THE YIELD TO MATURITY AND CURRENT YIELD

The Argon bonds pay $50 in interest per year ($50 = 0.05 coupon rate × $1,000 par value) for the duration of the bond, or for 8 years. The investor will then receive $1,000 at the bond's maturity. Given a market price of $925, the yield to maturity would be 6.2 percent.

CALCULATOR SOLUTION

Data Input	Function Key
8	N
925	PV
50	+/− PMT
1,000	+/− FV

Function Key	Answer
CPT	
I/Y	6.22

$$\text{Current yield} = \frac{\text{annual interest payment}}{\text{current market price of the bond}}$$

$$= \frac{\$50}{\$925} = 0.0541 = 5.41\%$$

If an investor paid $925 for a bond that pays $50 in interest each year for 8 years, along with the $1,000 par value in the eighth year, he would earn exactly 6.2 percent on the investment.

Changes in bond prices represent an element of uncertainty for the bond investor. If the current interest rate (required rate of return) changes, the price of a bond also fluctuates. An increase in interest rates causes the bondholder to incur a loss in market value. Because future interest rates and the resulting bond value cannot be predicted with certainty, a bond investor is exposed to the *risk of changing values as interest rates vary*. This risk has come to be known as **interest rate risk**.

interest rate risk the variability in a bond's value caused by changing interest rates.

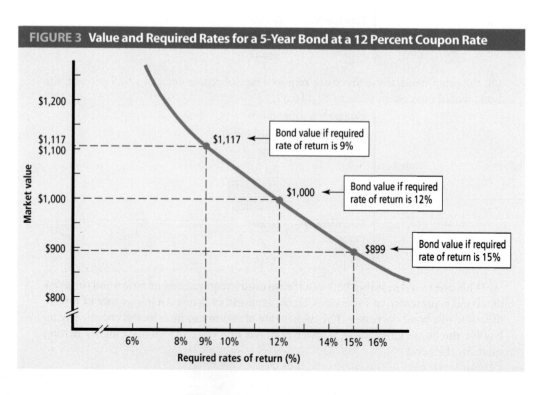

FIGURE 3 Value and Required Rates for a 5-Year Bond at a 12 Percent Coupon Rate

2. The market value of a bond will be less than the par value if the required rate of return of investors is above the coupon interest rate; but it will be valued above par value if the required rate of return of investors is below the coupon interest rate.

Using the previous example, we observed that

◆ The bond has a *market value* of $1,000, equal to the par, or maturity, value, when the required rate of return demanded by investors equals the 12 percent coupon interest rate. In other words, if

required rate = coupon rate, then *market value = par value*
   12%   =   12%,   then $1,000 = $1,000

◆ When the required rate is 15 percent, which exceeds the 12 percent coupon rate, the market value of the bond falls below par value to $899.44; that is, if

required rate > coupon rate, then *market value < par value*
   15%   >   12%,   then $899.44 < $1,000

In this case the *bond sells at a discount below par value*; thus, it is called a **discount bond**.

> **discount bond** a bond that sells at a discount, or below par value.

◆ When the required rate is 9 percent, or less than the 12 percent coupon rate, the market value, $1,116.69, exceeds the bond's par value. In this instance, if

required rate < coupon rate, then *market value > par value*
   9%   <   12%,   then $1,116.69 > $1,000

The *bond is now selling at a premium above par value*; thus, it is a **premium bond**.

> **premium bond** a bond that is selling above its par value.

3. Long-term bonds have greater interest rate risk than do short-term bonds.

As already noted, a change in current interest rates (the required rate of return) causes an inverse change in the market value of a bond. However, the impact on value is greater for long-term bonds than it is for short-term bonds.

In Figure 3 we observed the effect of interest rate changes on a 5-year bond paying a 12 percent coupon interest rate. What if the bond did not mature until 10 years from today instead of 5 years? Would the changes in market value be the same? Absolutely not. The changes in value would be more significant for the 10-year bond. For example, what if the current interest rates increase from 9 percent to 12 percent and then to 15 percent? In this case, a 10-year bond's value would drop more sharply than a 5-year bond's value would. The values for both the 5-year and the 10-year bonds are shown here.

	MARKET VALUE FOR A 12% COUPON-RATE BOND MATURING IN	
REQUIRED RATE	**5 YEARS**	**10 YEARS**
9%	$1,116.69	$1,192.53
12%	1,000.00	1,000.00
15%	899.44	849.44

The reason long-term bond prices fluctuate more than short-term bond prices in response to interest rate changes is simple. Assume an investor bought a 10-year bond yielding a 12 percent interest rate. If the current interest rate for bonds of similar risk increased to 15 percent, the investor would be locked into the lower rate for 10 years. If, on the other hand, a shorter term bond had been purchased—say, one maturing in 2 years—the investor would have to accept the lower return for only 2 years and not the full 10 years. At the end of year 2, the investor would receive the maturity value of $1,000 and could buy a bond offering the higher 15 percent rate for the remaining 8 years. Thus, interest rate risk is determined, at least in part, by the length of time an investor is required to commit to an investment.

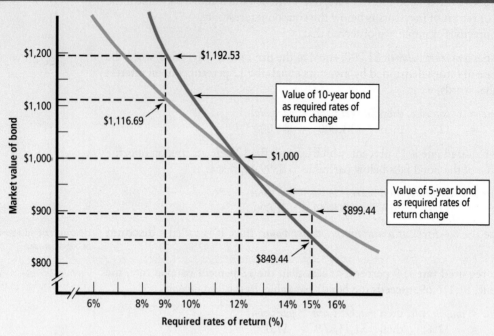

FIGURE 4 The Market Values of a 5-Year and a 10-Year Bond at Different Required Rates of Return

Using these values and the required rates, we can graph the changes in values for the two bonds relative to different interest rates. These comparisons are provided in Figure 4. The figure clearly illustrates that the price of a long-term bond (say, 10 years) is more responsive or sensitive to interest rate changes than the price of a short-term bond (say, 5 years). However, the holder of a long-term bond can take some comfort from the fact that long-term interest rates are usually not as volatile as short-term rates. If the short-term rate changed 1 percentage point, for example, it would not be unusual for the long-term rate to change only 0.3 percentage points.

Concept Check

1. Why does a bond sell at a discount when the coupon rate is lower than the required rate of return and vice versa?

2. As interest rates increase, why does the price of a long-term bond decrease more than a short-term bond?

Summary

Distinguish between different kinds of bonds.

Understanding how to compute the value of a security underlies much of what we do in finance. Only if we know what matters to our investors can we maximize the firm's value.

There is a variety of types of bonds, including:

Debentures	Eurobonds
Subordinated debentures	Convertible bonds
Mortgage bonds	

Explain the more popular features of bonds.

Some of the more popular terms and characteristics used to describe bonds include the following:

Claims on assets and income	Call provision
Par value	Indenture
Coupon interest rate	Bond ratings
Maturity	

Value is defined differently depending on the context. But for us, value is the present value of future cash flows expected to be received from an investment, discounted at the investor's required rate of return.

Define the term *value* as used for several different purposes.

Three basic factors determine an asset's value: (1) the amount and timing of future cash flows, (2) the riskiness of the cash flows, and (3) the investor's attitude about the risk.

The valuation process can be described as follows: It is assigning value to an asset by calculating the present value of its expected future cash flows using the investor's required rate of return as the discount rate. The investor's required rate of return, r, equals the risk-free rate of interest plus a risk premium to compensate the investor for assuming risk.

Explain the factors that determine value.

The value of a bond is the present value of both future interest to be received and the par or maturity value of the bond.

Describe the basic process for valuing assets.

To measure the bondholder's expected rate of return, we find the discount rate that equates the present value of the future cash flows (interest and maturity value) with the current market price of the bond. The expected rate of return for a bond is also the rate of return the investor will earn if the bond is held to maturity, or the yield to maturity. We may also compute the current yield as the annual interest payment divided by the bond's current market price, but this is not an accurate measure of a bondholder's expected rate of return.

Estimate the value of a bond.

Certain key relationships exist in bond valuation, these being:

1. A decrease in interest rates (the required rates of return) will cause the value of a bond to increase; by contrast, an interest rate increase will cause a decrease in value. The change in value caused by changing interest rates is called interest rate risk.

Compute a bond's expected rate of return.

2. If the required rate of return (current interest rate):
   a. Equals the coupon interest rate, the bond will sell at par, or maturity value.
   b. Exceeds the bond's coupon rate, the bond will sell below par value, or at a discount.
   c. Is less than the bond's coupon rate, the bond will sell above par value, or at a premium.

3. A bondholder owning a long-term bond is exposed to greater interest rate risk than one owning a short-term bond.

Explain three important relationships that exist in bond valuation.

Key Terms

Bond

Book value

Callable bond (redeemable bond)

Call protection period

Convertible bond

Coupon interest rate

Current yield

Debenture

Discount bond

Efficient market

Eurobond

Expected rate of return

Fair value

Fixed-rate bond

High-yield bond

Indenture

Interest rate risk

Intrinsic, or economic, value

Junk bond

Liquidation value

Market value

Maturity

Mortgage bond

Par value

Premium bond

Subordinated debenture

Yield to maturity

Zero coupon bond

Review Questions

All Review Questions and Study Problems are available in MyFinanceLab.

7-1. Distinguish between debentures and mortgage bonds.

7-2. Define (a) Eurobonds, (b) zero coupon bonds, and (c) junk bonds.

7-3. Describe the bondholder's claim on the firm's assets and income.

7-4. a. How does a bond's par value differ from its market value?

    b. Explain the difference between a bond's coupon interest rate, current yield, and required rate of return.

7-5. What factors determine a bond's rating? Why is the rating important to the firm's manager?

7-6. What are the basic differences between book value, liquidation value, market value, and intrinsic value?

7-7. What is a general definition of the intrinsic value of an asset?

7-8. Explain the three factors that determine the intrinsic, or economic, value of an asset.

7-9. Explain the relationship between the required rate of return and the value of a security.

7-10. Define the expected rate of return to bondholders.

Self-Test Problems

(The solution to the following problems are found at the end of the chapter.)

ST-1. (*Bond valuation*) Trico bonds have an annual coupon rate of 8 percent and a par value of $1,000 and will mature in 20 years. If you require a return of 7 percent, what price would you be willing to pay for the bond? What happens if you pay *more* for the bond? What happens if you pay *less* for the bond?

ST-2. (*Bond valuation*) Sunn Co.'s bonds, maturing in 7 years, pay 8 percent interest on a $1,000 face value. However, interest is paid semiannually. If your required rate of return is 10 percent, what is the value of the bond? How would your answer change if the interest were paid annually?

ST-3. (*Bondholders' expected rate of return*) Sharp Co. bonds are selling in the market for $1,045. These 15-year bonds pay 7 percent interest annually on a $1,000 par value. If they are purchased at the market price, what is the expected rate of return?

Study Problems

7-1. (*Bond valuation*) You own a 20-year, $1,000 par value bond paying 7 percent interest annually. The market price of the bond is $875, and your required rate of return is 10 percent.

    a. Compute the bond's expected rate of return.

    b. Determine the value of the bond to you, given your required rate of return.

    c. Should you sell the bond or continue to own it?

7-2. (*Bond valuation*) Calculate the value of a bond that will mature in 14 years and has a $1,000 face value. The annual coupon interest rate is 7 percent, and the investor's required rate of return is 10 percent.

7-3. (*Bond valuation*) At the beginning of the year, you bought a $1,000 par value corporate bond with a 6 percent annual coupon rate and a 10-year maturity date. When you bought the bond, it had an expected yield to maturity of 8 percent. Today the bond sells for $1,060.

    a. What did you pay for the bond?

    b. If you sold the bond at the end of the year, what would be your one-period return on the investment?

7-4. (*Bond valuation*) Shelly Inc. bonds have a 10 percent coupon rate. The interest is paid semiannually, and the bonds mature in 8 years. Their par value is $1,000. If your required rate of return is 8 percent, what is the value of the bond? What is the value if the interest is paid annually?

7-5. (*Bond relationship*) Crawford Inc. has two bond issues outstanding, both paying the same annual interest of $85, called Series A and Series B. Series A has a maturity of 12 years, whereas Series B has a maturity of 1 year.

    a. What would be the value of each of these bonds when the going interest rate is (1) 5 percent, (2) 8 percent, and (3) 12 percent? Assume that there is only one more interest payment to be made on the Series B bonds.

    b. Why does the longer-term (12-year) bond fluctuate more when interest rates change than does the shorter-term (1-year) bond?

7-6. (*Bondholders' expected rate of return*) The market price is $900 for a 10-year bond ($1,000 par value) that pays 8 percent interest (4 percent semiannually). What is the bond's expected rate of return?

7-7. (*Bondholders' expected rate of return*) You own a bond that has a par value of $1,000 and matures in 5 years. It pays a 9 percent annual coupon rate. The bond currently sells for $1,200. What is the bond's expected rate of return?

7-8. (*Bond valuation*) ExxonMobil 20-year bonds pay 9 percent interest annually on a $1,000 par value. If bonds sell at $945, what is the bonds' expected rate of return?

7-9. (*Bondholders' expected rate of return*) Zenith Co.'s bonds mature in 12 years and pay 7 percent interest annually. If you purchase the bonds for $1,150, what is your expected rate of return?

7-10. (*Bond valuation*) National Steel 15-year, $1,000 par value bonds pay 8 percent interest annually. The market price of the bonds is $1,085, and your required rate of return is 10 percent.

    a. Compute the bond's expected rate of return.
    b. Determine the value of the bond to you, given your required rate of return.
    c. Should you purchase the bond?

7-11. (*Bond valuation*) You own a bond that pays $100 in annual interest, with a $1,000 par value. It matures in 15 years. Your required rate of return is 12 percent.

    a. Calculate the value of the bond.
    b. How does the value change if your required rate of return (1) increases to 15 percent or (2) decreases to 8 percent?
    c. Explain the implications of your answers in part b as they relate to interest rate risk, premium bonds, and discount bonds.
    d. Assume that the bond matures in 5 years instead of 15 years. Recompute your answers in part b.
    e. Explain the implications of your answers in part d as they relate to interest rate risk, premium bonds, and discount bonds.

7-12. (*Bond valuation*) New Generation Public Utilities issued a bond with a $1,000 par value that pays $80 in annual interest. It matures in 20 years. Your required rate of return is 7 percent.

    a. Calculate the value of the bond.
    b. How does the value change if your required rate of return (1) increases to 10 percent or (2) decreases to 6 percent?
    c. Explain the implications of your answers in part b as they relate to interest rate risk, premium bonds, and discount bonds.
    d. Assume that the bond matures in 10 years instead of 20 years. Recompute your answers in part b.
    e. Explain the implications of your answers in part d as they relate to interest rate risk, premium bonds, and discount bonds.

7-13. (*Bond valuation—zero coupon*) The Logos Corporation is planning on issuing bonds that pay no interest but can be converted into $1,000 at maturity, 7 years from their purchase. To price these bonds competitively with other bonds of equal risk, it is determined that they should yield 9 percent, compounded annually. At what price should the Logos Corporation sell these bonds?

7-14. (*Bond valuation*) You are examining three bonds with a par value of $1,000 (you receive $1,000 at maturity) and are concerned with what would happen to their market value if interest rates (or the market discount rate) changed. The three bonds are

    Bond A—a bond with 3 years left to maturity that has a 10 percent annual coupon interest rate, but the interest is paid semiannually.
    Bond B—a bond with 7 years left to maturity that has a 10 percent annual coupon interest rate, but the interest is paid semiannually.
    Bond C—a bond with 20 years left to maturity that has a 10 percent annual coupon interest rate, but the interest is paid semiannually.

What would be the value of these bonds if the market discount rate were

    a. 10 percent per year compounded semiannually?
    b. 4 percent per year compounded semiannually?
    c. 16 percent per year compounded semiannually?
    d. What observations can you make about these results?

7-15. (*Yield to maturity*) Assume the market price of a 5-year bond for Margaret Inc. is $900, and it has a par value of $1000. The bond has an annual interest rate of 6 percent that is paid semi-annually. What is the yield to maturity of the bond?

7-16. (*Current yield*) Assume you have a bond with a semiannual interest payment of $35, a par value of $1000, and a current market price of $780. What is the current yield of the bond?

7-17. (*Yield to maturity*) An 8-year bond for Katy Corporation has a market price of $700 and a par value of $1,000. If the bond has an annual interest rate of 6 percent, but pays interest semiannually, what is the bond's yield to maturity?

7-18. (*Expected rate of return*) Assume you own a bond with a market value of $820 that matures in 7 years. The par value of the bond is $1,000. Interest payments of $30 are paid semiannually. What is your expected rate of return on the bond?

7-19. (*Yield to maturity*) You own a 10-year bond that pays 6 percent interest annually. The par value of the bond is $1,000 and the market price of the bond is $900. What is the yield to maturity of the bond?

7-20. (*Bondholders' expected rate of return*) You purchased a bond for $1,100. The bond has a coupon rate of 8 percent, which is paid semiannually. It matures in 7 years and has a par value of $1,000. What is your expected rate of return?

Mini Case

Here are data on $1,000 par value bonds issued by Microsoft, Ford, and Xerox at the end of 2008. Assume you are thinking about buying these bonds as of January 2009. Answer the following questions:

a. Calculate the values of the bonds if your required rates of return are as follows: Microsoft, 6 percent; Ford, 15 percent; Xerox, 10 percent; where

	MICROSOFT	FORD	XEROX
Coupon interest rate	5.25%	7.125%	8.0%
Years to maturity	30	25	16

b. At the end of 2008, the bonds were selling for the following amounts:

Microsoft	$1,009.00
Ford	$ 610.00
Xerox	$ 805.00

What were the expected rates of return for each bond?

c. How would the value of the bonds change if (1) your required rate of return (r_b) increased 2 percentage points or (2) decreased 2 percentage points?

d. Explain the implications of your answers in part b in terms of interest rate risk, premium bonds, and discount bonds.

e. Should you buy the bonds? Explain.

Self-Test Solutions

SS-1.

$$\text{Value } (V_b) = \frac{\$80}{(1.07)^1} + \frac{\$80}{(1.07)^2} + \cdots + \frac{\$80}{(1.07)^{20}} + \frac{\$1000}{(1.07)^{20}}$$

Using a financial calculator, we find the value of the bond to be $1,105.94:

CALCULATOR SOLUTION	
Data Input	Function Key
7	I/Y
20	N
80	+/− PMT
1,000	+/− FV
Function Key	Answer
CPT	
PV	1,105.94

If you pay more for the bond, your required rate of return will not be satisfied. In other words, by paying an amount for the bond that exceeds $1,105.94, the expected rate of return for the bond is less than the required rate of return. If you have the opportunity to pay less for the bond, the expected rate of return exceeds the 7 percent required rate of return.

SS-2. If interest is paid semiannually:

$$\text{Value } (V_b) = \frac{\$40}{(1.05)^1} + \cdots + \frac{\$40}{(1.05)^{14}} + \frac{\$1,000}{(1.05)^{14}}$$

The value of the bond would be $901.01:

CALCULATOR SOLUTION

Data Input	Function Key
5	I/Y
14	N
40	+/− PMT
1,000	+/− FV

Function Key	Answer
CPT	
PV	901.01

If interest is paid annually:

$$\text{Value } (V_b) = \frac{\$80}{(1.10)^1} + \cdots + \frac{\$80}{(1.10)^7} + \frac{\$1,000}{(1.10)^7}$$

The value of the bond would be $902.63:

CALCULATOR SOLUTION

Data Input	Function Key
10	I/Y
7	N
80	+/− PMT
1,000	+/− FV

Function Key	Answer
CPT	
PV	902.63

SS-3. Finding the bond's yield to maturity, the expected rate of return is based on the following equation:

$$\$1,045 = \frac{\$70}{(1 + \bar{r}_b)^1} + \cdots + \frac{\$70}{(1 + \bar{r}_b)^{15}} + \frac{\$1,000}{(1 + \bar{r}_b)^{15}}$$

Using a financial calculator, we find the yield to maturity to be 6.52 percent:

CALCULATOR SOLUTION

Data Input	Function Key
15	N
70	+/− PMT
1000	+/− FV
1045	PV

Function Key	Answer
CPT	
I/Y	6.52

193

The Valuation and Characteristics of Stock

From Chapter 8 of *Foundations of Finance*, 7/e. Arthur J. Keown. John D. Martin. J. William Petty. Copyright © 2011 by Pearson Education. Published by Prentice Hall. All rights reserved.

The Valuation and Characteristics of Stock

Learning Objectives

After reading this chapter, you should be able to:

1. **Identify** the basic characteristics of preferred stock.

2. **Value** preferred stock.

3. **Identify** the basic characteristics of common stock.

4. **Value** common stock.

5. **Calculate** a stock's expected rate of return.

Some companies believe that a good name can be their most important asset—and actually boost the stock price. For example, a print ad by United Technologies Corp. looked deceptively like an assembly diagram for a model helicopter. Study it more closely, however, and you'll notice that the color schematic of UTC's Sikorsky S-92 copter is embedded with messages aimed at Wall Street.

Text near the engine trumpets 40 percent lower maintenance costs than comparable helicopters and a "health and usage system" that ensures the S-92 "always operates at peak performance." Next to a view of the cockpit, you learn that the thermal imaging system lets rescuers find people they can't see. Other text notes fuel efficiency that allows "more rescues per gallon" and paint with few compounds that harm the environment. "You don't have to understand everything we do to profit from it," crows the tagline. The underlying theme: UTC is a great investment because it is a leader in innovation and eco-friendly technologies that help the bottom line.

More research went into crafting those messages than you might imagine. The $49 billion Hartford conglomerate has long been frustrated that the strengths of its individual brands may be well known, but as for the publicly traded parent, investor surveys showed "most view us as some sleepy Northeast company," says UTC Communications Vice-President Nancy T. Lintner.

So UTC turned to a tiny consulting firm named Communications Consulting Worldwide, led by sociologist Pamela Cohen and former Ernst & Young strategist Jonathan Low, pioneers in the nascent study of how public perceptions affect a company's stock price. A CCW team spent months processing a bewildering amount of assorted data UTC had amassed over the years. It included studies tracking consumer perceptions of its brands, employee satisfaction, views of stock analysts and investors, corporate press releases, thousands of newspaper and magazine articles, and two years' worth of UTC financial information and daily stock movements. After feeding the data into an elaborate computer model, Cohen and Low concluded that 27 percent of UTC's stock market value was attributable to intangibles like its reputation.

The duo determined the way to drive up the stock was to make investors more aware of UTC's environmental responsibility, innovation, and employee training—points the company had not stressed publicly. To make sure investors got the message, UTC plastered the Sikorsky S-92 ads and others like it featuring an Otis elevator, a Pratt & Whitney jet engine, and a hybrid bus with UTC Power fuel cells, on four commuter train stations in Connecticut towns with high concentrations of financiers. "The work we did with CCW guided the development of our ad strategy," says Lintner. "We're very happy with the results."

Many investment pros scoff at suggestions they can be influenced by image manipulation. And to most CEOs, corporate image is not something to fret about—at least, not until a crisis erupts, like an options scandal, employee class action, or ecological disaster. Even when execs try to be proactive, it's often by gut. Want to be viewed as a good corporate citizen? Order up a PR blitz on your charity work or efforts to go green. Eager to land on a magazine's most-admired list? Gin up a strategy to game the selection process.

But a more sophisticated understanding of the power of perception is starting to take hold among savvy corporations. More and more are finding that the way in which the outside world expects a company to behave and perform can be its most important asset. Indeed, a company's reputation for being able to deliver growth, attract top talent, and avoid ethical mishaps can account for much of the 30 percent to 70 percent gap between the book value of most companies and their market capitalizations. And while the value of a reputation is vastly less tangible than property, revenue, or cash, more experts are arguing it is possible not only to quantify it but even to predict how image changes in specific areas will harm or hurt the share price.

Of course, spin alone can't create a lasting public image. A company's message must be grounded in reality, and its reputation is built over years. And if there is a negative image based on a poor record of reliability, safety, or labor relations, "please don't hire a PR company to fix it," says strategy professor Phil Rosenzweig of Switzerland's International Institute for Management Development. "Correct the underlying problem first." The biggest driver of a company's reputation and stock performance is, after all, its financial results, notes Rosenzweig, author of *The Halo Effect*, a book that details how quickly reputations can turn.

Regardless of our conclusion about the merits of image management, the fact remains that managers care deeply about their company's stock price, frequently believing that their stock is undervalued. In this chapter, we will be studying the basic characteristics of stock, both preferred and common stock. We will then examine how stocks are valued and how we can determine the market's rate of return for a given stock.

In this book, we developed a general concept about valuation, and economic value was defined as the present value of the expected future cash flows generated by an asset. We then applied that concept to valuing bonds.

Source: Adapted from "What Price Reputation?" *Business Week*, July 9, 2007, http://www.businessweek.com/magazine/content/07_28/b4042050.htm, accessed June 30, 2009.

We continue our study of valuation in this chapter, but we now give our attention to valuing stocks, both preferred stock and common stock. As already noted at the outset of our study of finance and on several occasions since, the financial manager's objective should be to maximize the value of the firm's common stock. Thus, we need to understand what determines stock value. Also, only with an understanding of valuation can we compute a firm's cost of capital, a concept essential to making effective capital investment decisions.

Preferred Stock

Identify the basic characteristics of preferred stock.

preferred stock a hybrid security with characteristics of both common stock and bonds. Preferred stock is similar to common stock in that it has no fixed maturity date, the nonpayment of dividends does not bring on bankruptcy, and dividends are not deductible for tax purposes. Preferred stock is similar to bonds in that dividends are limited in amount.

Preferred stock is often referred to as a *hybrid security* because it has *many characteristics of both common stock and bonds*. Preferred stock is similar to common stock in that (1) it has no fixed maturity date, (2) if the firm fails to pay dividends, it does not bring on bankruptcy, and (3) dividends are not deductible for tax purposes. On the other hand, preferred stock is similar to bonds in that dividends are fixed in amount.

The amount of the preferred stock dividend is generally fixed either as a dollar amount or as a percentage of the par value. For example, Georgia Pacific has preferred stock outstanding that pays an annual dividend of $53, whereas AT&T has some 6⅜ percent preferred stock outstanding. The AT&T preferred stock has a par value of $25; hence, each share pays 6.375 percent × $25, or $1.59 in dividends annually.

To begin, we first discuss several features associated with almost all preferred stock. Then we take a brief look at methods of retiring preferred stock. We close by learning how to value preferred stock.

The Characteristics of Preferred Stock

Although each issue of preferred stock is unique, a number of characteristics are common to almost all issues. Some of these more frequent traits include

- Multiple series of preferred stock
- Preferred stock's claim on assets and income
- Cumulative dividends
- Protective provisions
- Convertibility
- Retirement provisions

All these features are presented in the discussion that follows.

Multiple Series   If a company desires, it can issue more than one series of preferred stock, and each series can have different characteristics. In fact, it is quite common for firms that issue preferred stock to issue more than one series. These issues can be differentiated in that some are convertible into common stock and others are not, and they have varying protective provisions in the event of bankruptcy. For instance, the Xerox Corporation has a Series B and Series C preferred stock.

Claim on Assets and Income   Preferred stock has priority over common stock with regard to claims on assets in the case of bankruptcy. The preferred stock claim is honored after that of bonds and before that of common stock. Multiple issues of preferred stock may be given an order of priority. Preferred stock also has a claim on income before common stock. That is, the firm must pay its preferred stock dividends before it pays common stock dividends. Thus, in terms of risk, preferred stock is safer than common stock because it has a prior claim on assets and income. However, it is riskier than long-term debt because its claims on assets and income come after those of debt, such as bonds.

Cumulative Dividends   Most preferred stocks carry a **cumulative feature** that *requires all past, unpaid preferred stock dividends be paid before any common stock dividends are declared.* The purpose is to provide some degree of protection for the preferred shareholder.

Protective Provisions   In addition to the cumulative feature, protective provisions are common to preferred stock. These **protective provisions** generally *allow for voting rights in the event of nonpayment of dividends, or they restrict the payment of common stock dividends if the preferred stock payments are not met or if the firm is in financial difficulty.* For example, consider the stocks of Tenneco Corporation and Reynolds Metals. The Tenneco preferred stock has a protective provision that provides preferred stockholders with voting rights whenever six quarterly dividends are in arrears. At that point the preferred shareholders are given the power to elect a majority of the board of directors. The Reynolds Metals preferred stock includes a protective provision that precludes the payment of common stock dividends during any period in which the preferred stock payments are in default. Both provisions offer preferred stockholders protection beyond that provided by the cumulative provision and further reduce their risk. Because of these protective provisions, preferred stockholders do not require as high a rate of return. That is, they will accept a lower dividend payment.

Convertibility   Much of the preferred stock that is issued today is **convertible preferred stock**; that is, *at the discretion of the holder, the stock can be converted into a predetermined number of shares of common stock.* In fact, today about one-third of all preferred stock issued has a convertibility feature. The convertibility feature is, of course, desirable to the investor and, thus, reduces the cost of the preferred stock to the issuer.

Can chose to remain as bond holder or change to stocks.
It decreases the risk for stockholders.

Retirement Provisions   Although preferred stock does not have a set maturity date associated with it, issuing firms generally provide for some method of retiring the stock, usually in the form of a call provision or a sinking fund. A **call provision** *entitles a company to repurchase its preferred stock from holders at stated prices over a given time period.* In fact, the Securities and Exchange Commission discourages firms from issuing preferred stock without some call provision. For example, Wyeth, a large pharmaceutical and health care products company, published the following news release:

> **Madison, N.J., April 23, 2009**—Wyeth (NYSE: WYE) announced today that it will fully redeem all of its outstanding Convertible Preferred Stock, effective on July 15, 2009 (the "Redemption Date"). As of April 22, 2009, there were 8,896 shares of Convertible Preferred Stock outstanding.
>
> The redemption price for each share of Convertible Preferred Stock is $60.08, which includes an amount equal to all accrued but unpaid dividends up to, and including, the Redemption Date.

The call feature on preferred stock usually requires buyers to pay an initial premium of approximately 10 percent above the par value or issuing price of the preferred stock. Then, over time, the call premium generally decreases. By setting the initial call price above the initial issue price and allowing it to decline slowly over time, the firm protects the investor from an early call that carries no premium. A call provision also allows the issuing firm to plan the retirement of its preferred stock at predetermined prices.

A **sinking-fund provision** *requires the firm to periodically set aside an amount of money for the retirement of its preferred stock.* This money is then used to purchase the preferred stock in the open market or to call the stock, whichever method is cheaper. For instance, the Xerox Corporation has two preferred stock issues, one that has a 7-year sinking-fund provision and another with a 17-year sinking-fund provision.

Valuing Preferred Stock

 Value preferred stock.

As already explained, the owner of preferred stock generally receives a constant dividend from the investment in each period. In addition, most preferred stocks are perpetuities (nonmaturing). In this instance, finding the value (present value) of preferred stock, (V_{ps}), with a level cash-flow stream continuing indefinitely, may best be explained by an example.

> ### EXAMPLE 1
>
> Consider Xerox's Series C preferred stock issue. In similar fashion to valuing bonds, we use a three-step valuation procedure.
>
> **STEP 1** Estimate the amount and timing of the receipt of the future cash flows the preferred stock is expected to provide. Xerox's preferred stock pays an annual dividend of $6.25. The shares do not have a maturity date; that is, they are a perpetuity.
>
> **STEP 2** Evaluate the riskiness of the preferred stock's future dividends and determine the investor's required rate of return. The investor's required rate of return is assumed to equal 5 percent for the Xerox preferred stock.[1]
>
> **STEP 3** Calculate the economic, or intrinsic, value of the Xerox share of preferred stock, which is the present value of the expected dividends discounted at the investor's required rate of return. The valuation model for a share of preferred stock, V_{ps}, is therefore defined as follows:
>
> $$V_{ps} = \frac{\text{dividend in year 1}}{(1 + \text{required rate of return})^1} \tag{1}$$
>
> $$+ \frac{\text{dividend in year 2}}{(1 + \text{required rate of return})^2}$$
>
> $$+ \cdots + \frac{\text{dividend in infinity}}{(1 + \text{required rate of return})^\infty}$$
>
> $$= \frac{D_1}{(1 + r_{ps})^1} + \frac{D_2}{(1 + r_{ps})^2} + \cdots + \frac{D_\infty}{(1 + r_{ps})^\infty}$$
>
> Because the dividends in each period are equal for preferred stock, equation (1) can be reduced to the following relationship:[2]
>
> $$V_{ps} = \frac{\text{annual dividend}}{\text{required rate of return}} = \frac{D}{r_{ps}} \tag{2}$$

$V_{ps} = \frac{\$6.25}{0.05} = \$125$

---

[1] In this book, we learned about measuring an investor's required rate of return.

[2] To verify this result, we begin with equation (1):

$$V_{ps} = \frac{D_1}{(1 + r_{ps})^1} + \frac{D_2}{(1 + r_{ps})^2} + \cdots + \frac{D_n}{(1 + r_{ps})^n}$$

If we multiply both sides of this equation by $(1 + r_{ps})$, we have

$$V_{ps}(1 + r_{ps}) = D_1 + \frac{D_2}{(1 + r_{ps})} + \cdots + \frac{D_n}{(1 + r_{ps})^{n-1}} \tag{1i}$$

Subtracting (1) from (1i) yields

$$V_{ps}(1 + r_{ps} - 1) = D_1 - \frac{D_n}{(1 + r_{ps})^n} \tag{1ii}$$

As n approaches infinity, $D_n/(1 + r_{ps})^n$ approaches zero. Consequently,

$$V_{ps}\, r_{ps} = D_1 \text{ and } V_{ps} = \frac{D_1}{r_{ps}} \tag{1iii}$$

Because $D_1 = D_2 = \cdots = D_n$, we need not designate the year. Therefore,

$$V_{ps} = \frac{D}{r_{ps}} \tag{2}$$

FINANCE AT WORK

READING A STOCK QUOTE IN THE WALL STREET JOURNAL

Following is a section of the *Wall Street Journal* that gives the quotes on July 29, 2009, for some of the stocks traded on the New York Stock Exchange that day.

The stocks listed include familiar companies—such as General Dynamics, General Electric (GE), and General Mills—that are listed in the *Wall Street Journal* on a daily basis.

To help us understand how we read the quotes, consider General Electric.

- The 52-week *high* column shows General Electric stock reached a high of 30.39 ($30.39) during the past year.
- The 52-week *low* column shows that General Electric sold at a low of 5.73 ($5.73) during the past year.

- The *stock* (General Electric) and *div* column give the corporation's name and the amount of dividend that General Electric paid its stockholders in the last year; $0.40 per share.
- *Yld*% (3.3) is the stock's dividend yield—the amount of the dividend divided by the day's closing price (0.40 ÷ 12.26).
- *PE* (9) gives the current market price (12.26) divided by the firm's earnings per share.
- The amount of General Electric stock traded on July 29, 2009, is represented in the *Volume* column, or 76,116,275.
- The previous day's closing price is subtracted from the closing price (*close*) of $12.26 for July 29, 2009, for a net change (*Net Chg*) of −0.26.

52 WEEKS							
HI	LO	STOCK (DIV)	YLD%	PE	VOLUME	CLOSE	NET CHG
94.41	35.28	General Dynamics	2.8	9	3,427,486	54.55	0.81
30.39	5.73	General Electric 0.40	3.3	9	76,116,275	12.26	−0.26
20.52	6.40	General Maritime 2.00	22.4	12	979,772	8.94	−0.28
72.01	46.37	General Mills 1.88	3.2	16	1,633,649	59.08	
16.68	1.84	General Steel Holdings			568,207	4.75	−0.23
38.74	10.37	Genesco		16	262,004	20.23	−0.41

(Notice the large differences between the 52-week high and low prices. This gives us a small glimpse of the significance of the stock market declines in 2008.)

Note: You can also see stock quotes on the *Wall Street Journal* website at http://online.wsj.com/mdc/public/page/2_3024-NYSE.html?mod=mdc_uss_pglnk.

Equation (2) represents the present value of an infinite stream of cash flows, when the cash flows are the same each year. We can determine the value of the Xerox preferred stock, using equation (2), as follows:

$$V_{ps} = \frac{D}{r_p} = \frac{\$6.25}{0.05} = \$125.00$$

In summary, the value of a preferred stock is the present value of all future dividends. But because most preferred stocks are nonmaturing—the dividends continue to infinity—we rely on a shortcut for finding value as represented by equation (2).

Concept Check

1. What features of preferred stock are different from bonds?
2. What provisions are available to protect a preferred stockholder?
3. What cash flows associated with preferred stock are included in the valuation model equation (1)? Why is the valuation model simplified in equation (2)?

CAN YOU DO IT?

VALUING PREFERRED STOCK

If a preferred stock pays 4 percent on its par, or stated, value of $100, and your required rate of return is 7 percent, what is the stock worth to you?

3 Identify the basic characteristics of common stock.

common stock shares that represent the ownership in a corporation.

(Ownership of firm)

Common Stock

Common stock is *a certificate that indicates ownership in a corporation*. In effect, bondholders and preferred stockholders can be viewed as creditors, whereas the common stockholders are the true owners of the firm. Common stock does not have a maturity date but exists as long as the firm does. Common stock also does not have an upper limit on its dividend payments. Dividend payments must be declared each period (usually quarterly) by the firm's board of directors. In the event of bankruptcy, the common stockholders, as owners of the corporation, will not receive any payment until the firm's creditors, including the bondholders and preferred shareholders, have been paid. Next we look at several characteristics of common stock. Then we focus on valuing common stock.

The Characteristics of Common Stock

We now examine common stock's claim on income and assets, its limited liability feature, and holders' voting and preemptive rights.

Claim on Income As the owners of a creditors, the common shareholders have the right to the residual income after creditors and preferred stockholders have been paid. This income may be paid directly to the shareholders in the form of dividends or retained within the firm and reinvested in the business. Although it is obvious the shareholder benefits immediately from the distribution of income in the form of dividends, the reinvestment of earnings also benefits the shareholder. Plowing back earnings into the firm should result in an increase in the value of the firm, its earning power, future dividends, and, ultimately, an increase in the value of the stock. In effect, residual income is distributed directly to shareholders in the form of dividends or indirectly in the form of capital gains (value increases) on their common stock.

The right to residual income has advantages and disadvantages for the common stockholder. The advantage is that the potential return is limitless. Once the claims of the senior securities, such as bonds and preferred stock, have been satisfied, the remaining income flows to the common stockholders in the form of dividends or capital gains. The disadvantage is that if the bond and preferred stock claims on income totally absorb earnings, common shareholders receive nothing. In years when earnings fall, it is the common shareholders who suffer first.

Claim on Assets Just as common stock has a residual claim on income, it also has a residual claim on assets in the case of liquidation. Unfortunately, when bankruptcy does occur, the claims of the common shareholders generally go unsatisfied because debt holders and preferred stockholders have first and second claims on the assets. This residual claim on assets adds to the risk of common stock. Thus, although common stocks have historically

FINANCE AT WORK

DOES STOCK BY ANY OTHER NAME SMELL AS SWEET?

All publicly traded stocks have ticker symbols, or abbreviations used to identify them. During 2005–2006, Harley-Davidson Inc.'s investor-relations personnel thought about changing their firm's stock ticker symbol, HDI. It wasn't exactly evocative of the motorcycle maker's image, and there was something better available: HOG (biker-slang for a Harley motorcycle). Interestingly, after Harley-Davidson adopted the new symbol in mid-August 2006, its shares gained nearly 16 percent in 5 weeks, compared with about 4 percent for the Standard & Poor's 500 Index.

It wasn't the first time a stock had risen after adopting a catchy ticker symbol. Counterintuitive as it may seem, research suggests that companies with clever symbols do better than other companies. Any suggestion of a cause-and-effect relationship may be hokum, but tickers that make investors chuckle—think Sotheby's BID, Advanced Medical Optics Inc.'s EYE, or PORK for Premium Standard Farms Inc.—also may make them richer, at least for a time. In one study, researchers at Princeton University found that companies with pronounceable symbols do better soon after an IPO than companies with symbols that can't be said as a word. In another study, researchers found that a portfolio of stocks with clever ticker symbols returned 23.6 percent compounded annually during the years 1990–2004, compared with 12.3 percent for a hypothetical index of all NYSE and Nasdaq stocks. The clever stocks included such well-known stocks as Anheuser Busch Cos. (BUD) and Southwest Airlines Co. (LUV), along with companies eventually delisted or acquired, such as

Grand Havana Enterprises Inc. (PUFF) and Lion Country Safari (GRRR).

Some companies are more deliberate in aligning their ticker symbol with their brand. Yum Brands Inc., which runs restaurant chains including KFC, Pizza Hut, and Long John Silver's, actually changed its name in 2002, in part, to reflect its ticker symbol, YUM. The company, formerly known as Tricon Global Restaurants Inc., is trying to attract individual investors by advertising its name and ticker symbol at events such as the Kentucky Derby.

"It's easy for people to remember and puts a smile on their face," said Virginia Ferguson, a Yum spokeswoman. With a share price of $53.01, the stock is up about 230 percent from its 1997 debut price of $16, adjusted for splits, and has risen 68 percent since the name change to Yum Brands.

Michael Cooper, an associate professor of finance at the University of Utah, who has studied investor behavior, said that both papers were "intriguing," but that he would need to see further study before accepting the results.

The researchers themselves say it probably wouldn't behoove investors to make decisions based on their studies. "We certainly don't recommend that people make trading decisions based on our findings," said one researcher. "Rather, our findings suggest that economic models should take psychological factors into account if they are designed to faithfully capture how the markets operate in practice."

Source: Adapted from Jennifer Valentino, "Does Stock by Any Other Name Smell as Sweet?" *Wall Street Journal*, September 28, 2006, P. C1.

provided a large return, averaging 10 percent annually since the late 1920s, there is also a higher risk associated with common stock.

Limited Liability   Although the common shareholders are the actual owners of the corporation, their *liability in the case of bankruptcy is limited to the amount of their investment*. The advantage is that investors who might not otherwise invest their funds in the firm become willing to do so. This **limited liability** feature aids the firm in raising funds.

> **limited liability** a protective provision whereby the investor is not liable for more than the amount he or she has invested in the firm.

Voting Rights   The common stock shareholders are entitled to elect the board of directors and are, in general, the only security holders given a vote. Common shareholders have the right not only to elect the board of directors but also to approve any change in the corporate charter. A typical change might involve the authorization to issue new stock or to accept a merger proposal. Voting for directors and charter changes occurs at the corporation's annual meeting. Although shareholders can vote in person, the majority generally vote by proxy. A **proxy** *gives a designated party the temporary power of attorney to vote for the signee at the corporation's annual meeting*. The firm's management generally solicits proxy votes, and, if the shareholders are satisfied with the firm's performance, has little problem securing them. However, in times of financial distress or when managerial takeovers are threatened, **proxy fights**—*battles between rival groups for proxy votes*—occur.

> **proxy** a means of voting in which a designated party is provided with the temporary power of attorney to vote for the signee at the corporation's annual meeting.

> **proxy fight** a battle between rival groups for proxy votes in order to control the decisions made in a stockholders' meeting.

Although each share of common stock carries the same number of votes, the voting procedure is not always the same from company to company. The two procedures commonly used are majority and cumulative voting. Under **majority voting**, *each share of stock allows the*

> **majority voting** voting in which each share of stock allows the shareholder one vote, and each position on the board of directors is voted on separately. As a result, a majority of shares has the power to elect the entire board of directors.

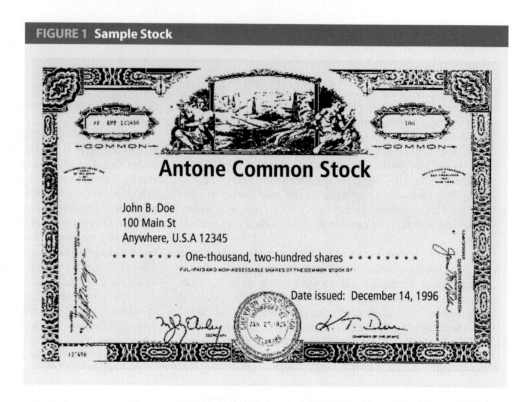

FIGURE 1 Sample Stock

Antone Common Stock

John B. Doe
100 Main St
Anywhere, U.S.A 12345

* * * * * * * One-thousand, two-hundred shares * * * * * * *

FULL-PAID AND NON-ASSESSABLE SHARES OF THE COMMON STOCK OF

Date issued: December 14, 1996

shareholder one vote, and each position on the board of directors is voted on separately. Because each member of the board of directors is elected by a simple majority, a majority of shares has the power to elect the entire board of directors.

With **cumulative voting**, *each share of stock allows the stockholder a number of votes equal to the number of directors being elected*. The shareholder can then cast all of his or her votes for a single candidate or split them among the various candidates. The advantage of a cumulative voting procedure is that it gives minority shareholders the power to elect a director.

In theory, the shareholders pick the corporate board of directors, generally through proxy voting, and the board of directors, in turn, picks the management. In reality, shareholders are offered a slate of nominees selected by management from which to choose. The end result is that management effectively selects the directors, who then may have more allegiance to the managers than to the shareholders. This sets up the potential for agency problems in which a divergence of interests between managers and shareholders is allowed to exist, with the board of directors not monitoring the managers on behalf of the shareholders as they should.

Preemptive Rights The **preemptive right** *entitles the common shareholder to maintain a proportionate share of ownership in the firm*. When new shares are issued, common shareholders have the first right of refusal. If a shareholder owns 25 percent of the corporation's stock, then he or she is entitled to purchase 25 percent of the new shares. *Certificates issued to the shareholders giving them an option to purchase a stated number of new shares of stock at a specified price during a 2- to 10-week period* are called **rights**. These rights can be exercised (generally at a price set by management below the common stock's current market price), allowed to expire, or sold in the open market.

---

cumulative voting voting in which each share of stock allows the shareholder a number of votes equal to the number of directors being elected. The shareholder can then cast all of his or her votes for a single candidate or split them among the various candidates.

preemptive right the right entitling the common shareholder to maintain his or her proportionate share of ownership in the firm.

right a certificate issued to common stockholders giving them an option to purchase a stated number of new shares at a specified price during a 2- to 10-week period.

 Value common stock.

Valuing Common Stock

Like bonds and preferred stock, a common stock's value is equal to the present value of all future cash flows—dividends in this case—expected to be received by the stockholder. However, in contrast to preferred stock dividends, common stock does not provide the investor with a predetermined, constant dividend. For common stock, the dividend is based on the profitability of the firm and its decision to pay dividends or to retain the profits for reinvestment. As a consequence, dividend streams tend to increase with the growth in corporate earnings. Thus, the growth of future dividends is a prime distinguishing feature of common stock.

The Growth Factor in Valuing Common Stock What is meant by the term *growth* when used in the context of valuing common stock? A company can grow in a variety of ways. It can become larger by borrowing money to invest in new projects. Likewise, it can issue new stock for expansion. Managers can also acquire another company to merge with the existing firm, which would increase the firm's assets. Although it can accurately be said that the firm has grown, the original stockholders may or may not participate in this growth. Growth is realized through the infusion of new capital. The firm size clearly increases, but unless the original investors increase their investment in the firm, they will own a smaller portion of the expanded business.

Another means of growing is **internal growth**, which requires that *managers retain some or all of the firm's profits for reinvestment in the firm*, resulting in the growth of future earnings and, hopefully, the value of the common stock. This process underlies the essence of potential growth for the firm's current stockholders and is the only relevant growth for our purposes of valuing a firm's common shares.[3]

> **internal growth** a firm's growth rate resulting from reinvesting the company's profits rather than distributing them as dividends. The growth rate is a function of the amount retained and the return earned on the retained funds.

EXAMPLE 2

To illustrate the nature of internal growth, assume that the return on equity for PepsiCo is 16 percent.[4] If PepsiCo decides to pay all the profits out in dividends to its stockholders, the firm will experience no growth internally. It might become larger by borrowing more money or issuing new stock, but internal growth will come only through the retention of profits. If, on the other hand, PepsiCo retains all of the profits, the stockholders' investment in the firm would grow by the amount of profits retained, or by 16 percent. If, however, PepsiCo keeps only 50 percent of the profits for reinvestment, the common shareholders' investment would increase only by half of the 16 percent return on equity, or by 8 percent. We can express this relationship by the following equation:

$$g = ROE \times pr$$

where g = the growth rate of future earnings and the growth in the common stockholders' investment in the firm

ROE = the return on equity (net income/common book value)

pr = *the company's percentage of profits retained*, called the **profit-retention rate**[5]

Therefore, if only 25 percent of the profits were retained by PepsiCo, we would expect the common stockholders' investment in the firm and the value of the stock price to increase, or grow, by 4 percent; that is,

$$g = 16\% \times 0.25 = 4\%$$

> **profit-retention rate** the company's percentage of profits retained.

In summary, common stockholders frequently rely on an increase in the stock price as a source of return. If the company is retaining a portion of its earnings for reinvestment, future profits and dividends should grow. This growth should be reflected by an increase in the market price of the common stock in future periods. Therefore, both types of return (dividends and price appreciation) must be recognized in valuing common stock.

---

[3]We are not arguing that the existing common stockholders never benefit from the use of external financing; however, such benefit is nominal if capital markets are efficient.

[4]The return on equity is the accounting rate of return on the common shareholders' investment in the company and is computed as follows:

$$\text{Return on equity} = \frac{\text{net income}}{(\text{common stock} + \text{retained earnings})}$$

[5]The retention rate is also equal to (1 − the percentage of profits paid out in dividends). *The percentage of profits paid out in dividends* is often called the **dividend-payout ratio**.

> **dividend-payout ratio** dividends as a percentage of earnings.

CAUTIONARY TALE

FORGETTING PRINCIPLE 4—MARKET PRICES ARE GENERALLY RIGHT

Principle 4 tells us that Market Prices Are Generally Right. But there are always investors who think they can outsmart the market by statistical analysis. Jason Zweig describes some of the more "creative," or should we say foolish, attempts to beat the market.

> The Super Bowl market indicator holds that stocks will do well after a team from the old National Football League wins the Super Bowl. The Pittsburgh Steelers, an original NFL team, won this year, and the market is up as well. Unfortunately, the losing Arizona Cardinals also are an old NFL team.
>
> The "Sell in May and go away" rule advises investors to get out of the market after April and get back in after October. With the market up 17 percent since April 30 [less than 10 weeks], that rule isn't looking so good at this point.
>
> Meanwhile, dozens—probably hundreds—of Web sites hawk "proprietary trading tools" and analytical "models" based on factors with cryptic names like McMillan oscillators or floors and ceilings.
>
> There is no end to such rules. But there isn't much sense to most of them either. An entertaining new book, *Nerds on Wall Street*, by

the veteran quantitative money manager David Leinweber, dissects the shoddy thinking that underlies most of these techniques.

> The stock market generates such vast quantities of information that, if you plow through enough of it for long enough, you can always find some relationship that appears to generate spectacular returns—by coincidence alone. This sham is known as "data mining."
>
> Every year, billions of dollars pour into data-mined investing strategies. No one knows if these techniques will work in the real world. Their results are hypothetical—based on "back-testing," or a simulation of what would have happened if the manager had actually used these techniques in the past, typically without incurring any fees, trading costs or taxes.
>
> Those assumptions are completely unrealistic, of course. But data-mined numbers can be so irresistible that, as Mr. Leinweber puts it, "they are one of the leading causes of the evaporation of money. . . ."

Source: Adapted from Jason Zweig, "Data Mining Isn't a Good Bet For Stock-Market Predictions," *Wall Street Journal*, August 8–9, 2009, p. C1.

Example of compounding interest.

Dividend Valuation Model The value of a common stock when defining value as the present value of future dividends relies on the same basic equation that we used with preferred stock [equation (1)], with the exception that we are using the required rate of return of common stockholders, r_{cs}. That is,

$$V_{cs} = \frac{D_1}{(1 + r_{cs})^1} + \frac{D_2}{(1 + r_{cs})^2} + \cdots + \frac{D_n}{(1 + r_{cs})^n} + \cdots + \frac{D_\infty}{(1 + r_{cs})^\infty} \tag{3}$$

Equation (3) indicates that we are discounting the dividend at the end of the first year, D_1, back 1 year; the dividend in the second year, D_2, back 2 years; the dividend in the nth year back n years; and the dividend in infinity back an infinite number of years. The required rate of return is r_{cs}. In using equation (3), note that the value of the stock is established

CAN YOU DO IT?

MEASURING JOHNSON & JOHNSON'S GROWTH RATE

In 2008, Johnson & Johnson had a return on equity of 19.47 percent, as computed to the right. The firm's earnings per share was $4.63 and it paid $1.87 in dividends per share. If these relationships hold in the future, what will be the firm's internal growth rate?

$$\text{Return on equity (ROE)} = \frac{\text{net income}}{\text{common stock} + \text{retained earnings}}$$

$$= \frac{\$12,849}{\$66,499}$$

$$= 19.47\%$$

at the beginning of the year, say January 1, 2010. The most recent past dividend, D_0, would have been paid the previous day, December 31, 2009. Thus, if we purchased the stock on January 1, the first dividend would be received in 12 months, on December 31, 2010, which is represented by D_1.

Fortunately, equation (3) can be reduced to a much more manageable form if dividends grow each year at a constant rate, g. The constant-growth, common-stock valuation equation can be presented as follows:[6]

$$\text{Common stock value} = \frac{\text{dividend in year 1}}{\text{required rate of return} - \text{growth rate}} \quad (4)$$

$$V_{cs} = \frac{D_1}{r_{cs} - g}$$

[handwritten margin note: If it ask for value It means intrinsic value. slide: $D_0 = \$100$ $k_{es} = 17\%$ $g = 10\%$ $D_1 = \$1.10$]

In other words, the intrinsic value (present value) of a share of common stock whose dividends grow at a constant annual rate can be calculated using equation (4). Although the interpretation of this equation might not be intuitively obvious, simply remember that it solves for the present value of the future dividend stream growing at a rate, g, to infinity, assuming that r_{cs} is greater than g.

EXAMPLE 3

Consider the valuation of a share of common stock that paid a $2 dividend at the end of last year and is expected to pay a cash dividend every year from now to infinity. Each year the dividends are expected to grow at a rate of 10 percent. Based on an assessment of the riskiness of the common stock, the investor's required rate of return is 15 percent. Using this information, we would compute the value of the common stock as follows:

1. Because the $2 dividend was paid last year, we must compute the next dividend to be received, that is, D_1, where

$$D_1 = D_0 (1 + g)$$

$$= \$2(1 + 0.10)$$

$$= \$2.20$$

---

[6]When common stock dividends grow at a constant rate of g every year, we can express the dividend in any year in terms of the dividend paid at the end of the previous year, D_0. For example, the expected dividend year 1 hence is simply $D_0(1 + g)$. Likewise, the dividend at the end of t years is $D_0(1 + g)^t$. Using this notation, the common-stock valuation equation in (3) can be rewritten as follows:

$$V_{cs} = \frac{D_0 (1 + r_{cs})^1}{(1 + g)^1} + \frac{D_0 (1 + g)^2}{(1 + r_{cs})^2} + \cdots + \frac{D_0 (1 + g)^n}{(1 + r_{cs})^n} + \cdots + \frac{D_0 (1 + g)^\infty}{(1 + r_{cs})^\infty} \quad (3i)$$

If both sides of equation (3i) are multiplied by $(1 + r_{cs})/(1 + g)$ and then equation (4) is subtracted from the product, the result is

$$\frac{V_{cs} (1 + r_{cs})}{1 + g} - V_{cs} = D_0 - \frac{D_0 (1 + g)^\infty}{(1 + r_{cs})^\infty} \quad (3ii)$$

If $r_{cs} > g$, which normally should hold, $[D_0(1 + g)(1 + r_{cs}^\infty)]$ approaches zero. As a result,

$$\frac{V_{cs} (1 + r_{cs})}{1 + g} - V_{cs} = D_0$$

$$V_{cs}\left(\frac{1 + r_{cs}}{1 + g}\right) - V_{cs}\left(\frac{1 + g}{1 + g}\right) = D_0$$

$$V_{cs}\left[\frac{(1 + r_{cs}) - (1 + g)}{1 + g}\right] = D_0 \quad (3iii)$$

$$V_{cs} (r_{cs} - g) = D_0 (1 + g)$$

$$V_{cs} = \frac{D_1}{r_{cs} - g}$$

[handwritten margin note: Alternative Get present value of dividend and " " of price To get intrinsic value]

DID YOU GET IT?

MEASURING JOHNSON & JOHNSON'S GROWTH RATE

To compute Johnson & Johnson's internal growth rate, we must know (1) the firm's return on equity, and (2) what percentage of the earnings are being retained and reinvested in the business—that is, used to grow the business.

The return on equity was computed to be 19.47 percent. We then calculate the percentage of the profits that is being retained as follows:

$$\text{Percentage of profits retained} = 1 - \frac{\text{dividends per share}}{\text{earnings per share}}$$

$$= 1 - \frac{\$1.87}{\$4.63}$$

$$= 1 - 0.404$$

$$= 0.596 = 59.6\%$$

Thus, Johnson & Johnson is paying out 40.4 percent of its earnings, which means it is retaining 59.6 percent.

Then we compute the internal growth rate as follows:

$$\text{Internal growth rate} = \text{return on equity} \times \text{percentage of earnings retained}$$

$$= 19.47\% \times 59.6\%$$

$$= 11.6\%$$

The ability of a firm to grow is critical to its future, but only if the firm has attractive opportunities in which to invest. Also, there must be a way to finance the growth, which can occur by borrowing more, issuing stock, or not distributing the profits to the owners (not paying dividends). The last option is called internal growth. Johnson & Johnson was able to grow internally by almost 12 percent by earning 19.47 percent on the equity's investment and retaining about 60 percent of the profits in the business.

2. Now, using equation (4),

$$V_{cs} = \frac{D_1}{r_{cs} - g}$$

$$= \frac{\$2.20}{0.15 - 0.10}$$

$$= \$44$$

We have argued that the value of a common stock is equal to the present value of all future dividends, which is without question a fundamental premise of finance. In practice, however, managers, along with many security analysts, often talk about the relationship between stock value and earnings, rather than dividends. We would encourage you to be very cautious in using earnings to value a stock. Even though it may be a popular practice,

CAN YOU DO IT?

CALCULATING COMMON STOCK VALUE

The Abraham Corporation paid $1.32 in dividends per share *last year*. The firm's projected growth rate is 6 percent for the foreseeable future. If the investor's required rate of return for a firm with Abraham's level of risk is 10 percent, what is the value of the stock?

significant available evidence suggests that investors look to the cash flows generated by the firm, not the earnings, for value. A firm's value truly is the present value of the cash flows it produces.

Concept Check

1. What features of common stock indicate ownership in the corporation versus preferred stock or bonds?
2. In what two ways does a shareholder benefit from ownership?
3. How does internal growth versus the infusion of new capital affect the original shareholders?
4. Describe the process for common stock valuation.

> **REMEMBER YOUR PRINCIPLES**
>
> **Principle** Valuing common stock is no different from valuing preferred stock; only the pattern of the cash flows changes. Thus, the valuation of common stock relies on the same three principles that were used in valuing preferred stock:
>
> **Principle 1: Cash Flow Is What Matters.**
>
> **Principle 2: Money Has a Time Value.**
>
> **Principle 3: Risk Requires a Reward.**
>
> Determining the economic worth, or value, of an asset always relies on these three principles. Without them, we would have no basis for explaining value. With them, we can know that the amount and timing of cash, not earnings, drives value. Also, we must be rewarded for taking risk; otherwise, we will not invest.

The Expected Rate of Return of Stockholders

5 Calculate a stock's expected rate of return.

The expected rate of return, or yield to maturity, on a bond is the return the bondholder expects to receive on the investment by paying the existing market price for the security. This rate of return is of interest to the financial manager because it tells the manager about investors' expectations. The same can be said for the financial manager needing to know the expected rate of return of the firm's stockholders, which is the topic of this section.

The Expected Rate of Return of Preferred Stockholders

To compute the expected rate of return of preferred stockholders, we use the valuation equation for preferred stock. Earlier, equation (2) specified the value of a preferred stock, V_{ps}, as

$$V_{ps} = \frac{\text{annual dividend}}{\text{required rate of return}} = \frac{D}{r_{ps}}$$

Solving equation (2) for r_{ps}, we have

$$r_{ps} = \frac{\text{annual dividend}}{\text{preferred stock value}} = \frac{D}{V_{ps}}$$

(5)

[Handwritten notes:]
Unknown is discount rate.
Expected rate of return.
$P_{ps} = V_{ps} = \frac{\text{Dividend}}{K_{ps}}$
$K_{ps} = \frac{\text{Dividend}}{\text{Price}_{ps}} = \frac{55}{\$75} = 6.67\%$

DID YOU GET IT?

CALCULATING COMMON STOCK VALUE

Abraham's stock value would be $35:

$$\text{Value} = \frac{\text{dividend year 1}}{\text{required rate of return} - \text{growth rate}}$$

$$= \frac{\$1.32 \times (1 + .06)}{0.10 - 0.06} = \frac{\$1.40}{0.04} = \$35$$

So the value of a common stock, much like preferred stock, is the present value of all future dividends. However, unlike preferred stock, common stock dividends are assumed to increase as the firm's profits increase. So the dividend is growing over time. And with a bit of calculus—keep the faith, baby—we can find the stock value by taking the dividend that is expected to be received at the end of the coming year and dividing it by the investor's required rate of return less the assumed constant growth rate. When we do, we have the present value of the dividends, which is the value of the stock.

Thus, the *required* rate of return of preferred stockholders simply equals the stock's annual dividend divided by the stock's intrinsic value. We can also use this equation to solve for a preferred stock's *expected* rate of return, $\bar{r}_{ps}$, as follows:[7]

$$\bar{r}_{ps} = \frac{\text{annual dividend}}{\text{preferred stock market price}} = \frac{D}{P_{ps}} \tag{6}$$

Note that we have merely substituted the current market price, P_{ps}, for the intrinsic value, V_{ps}. The expected rate of return, $\bar{r}_{ps}$, therefore, equals the annual dividend relative to the price the stock is currently selling for, P_{ps}. Thus, the **expected rate of return, $\bar{r}_{ps}$, is the rate of return the investor can expect to earn from the investment if it is bought at the current market price.**

For example, if the present market price of the preferred stock is $50, and it pays a $3.64 annual dividend, the expected rate of return implicit in the present market price is

$$\bar{r}_{ps} = \frac{D}{P_{ps}} = \frac{\$3.64}{\$50} = 7.28\%$$

Therefore, investors (who pay $50 per share for a preferred security that is paying $3.64 in annual dividends) are expecting a 7.28 percent rate of return.

expected rate of return The rate of return investors expect to receive on an investment by paying the current market price of the security.

The Expected Rate of Return of Common Stockholders

The valuation equation for common stock was defined earlier in equation (3) as

$$\text{Common stock value} = \frac{\text{dividend in year 1}}{(1 + \text{required rate of return})^1}$$

$$+ \frac{\text{dividend in year 2}}{(1 + \text{required rate of return})^2}$$

$$+ \cdots + \frac{\text{dividend in year infinity}}{(1 + \text{required rate of return})^\infty}$$

$$V_{cs} = \frac{D_1}{(1 + r_{cs})^1} + \frac{D_2}{(1 + r_{cs})^2} + \cdots + \frac{D_\infty}{(1 + r_{cs})^\infty}$$

Owing to the difficulty of discounting to infinity, we made the key assumption that the dividends, D_t, increase at a constant annual compound growth rate of g. If this assumption is valid, equation (4) was shown to be equivalent to

$$\text{Common stock value} = \frac{\text{dividend in year 1}}{\text{required rate of return} - \text{growth rate}}$$

$$V_{cs} = \frac{D_1}{r_{cs} - g}$$

Thus, V_{cs} represents the maximum value that investors having a required rate of return of r_{cs} would pay for a security having an anticipated dividend in year 1 of D_1 that is expected to grow in future years at rate g. Solving equation (4) for r_{cs}, we can compute the common stockholders' required rate of return as follows:[8]

$$r_{cs} = \frac{D_1}{V_{cs}} + g \tag{7}$$

dividend yield

annual growth rate

[7]We will use $\bar{r}$ to represent a security's *expected* rate of return versus r for investors' *required* rate of return.
[8]At times the expected dividend at year-end (D_1) is not given. Instead, we might only know the most recent dividend (paid yesterday), that is, D_0. If so, equation (4) must be restated as follows:

$$V_{cs} = \frac{D_1}{(r_{cs} - g)} = \frac{D_0(1 + g)}{(r_{cs} - g)}$$

According to this equation, the required rate of return is equal to the dividend yield plus a growth factor. Although the growth rate, g, applies to the growth in the company's dividends, given our assumptions, the stock's value can also be expected to increase at the same rate. For this reason, g represents the annual percentage growth in the stock value. In other words, the required rate of return of investors is satisfied by their receiving dividends *and* capital gains, as reflected by the expected percentage growth rate in the stock price.

As was done for preferred stock earlier, we may revise equation (7) to measure a common stock's *expected* rate of return, $\bar{r}_{cs}$. Replacing the intrinsic value, V_{cs}, in equation (7) with the stock's current market price, P_{cs}, we may express the stock's expected rate of return as follows:

$$\bar{r}_{cs} = \frac{\text{dividend in year 1}}{\text{market price}} + \text{growth rate} = \frac{D_1}{P_{cs}} + g \tag{8}$$

Historically, most of the returns on stocks come from price appreciation, or capital gains, with a smaller part of the return coming from dividends, with 2008–2009 being the exception. The Standard & Poor's 500 Index, for example, returned a 10 percent annual return on average since 1926. But the dividend yield (dividend ÷ stock price) accounted for only about 2–3 percent of the return. The remaining 7–8 percent resulted from price appreciation.

As a final note, we should understand that the *expected* rate of return implied by a given market price equals the *required* rate of return for investors at the margin. For these investors, the expected rate of return is just equal to their required rate of return and, therefore, they are willing to pay the current market price for the security. These investors' required rate of return is of particular significance to the financial manager because it represents the cost of new financing to the firm.

Concept Check

1. In computing the required rate of return for common stock, why should the growth factor be added to the dividend yield?
2. How does an efficient market affect the required and expected rates of return?

Summary

Identify the basic characteristics of preferred stock.

Valuation is an important process in financial management. An understanding of valuation, both the concepts and procedures, supports the financial officer's objective of maximizing the value of the firm.

Preferred stock has no fixed maturity date, and the dividends are fixed in amount. Some of the more common characteristics of preferred stock include the following:

- There are multiple classes of preferred stock.
- Preferred stock has a priority claim on assets and income over common stock.
- Any dividends, if not paid as promised, must be paid before any common stock dividends may be paid; that is, they are cumulative.
- Protective provisions are included in the contract with the shareholder to reduce the investor's risk.
- Some preferred stocks are convertible into common stock shares.

In addition, there are provisions frequently used to retire an issue of preferred stock, such as the ability of the firm to call its preferred stock or to use a sinking-fund provision.

Value preferred stock.

Value is the present value of future cash flows discounted at the investor's required rate of return. Although the valuation of any security entails the same basic principles, the procedures used in each situation vary. For example, we learned that valuing a bond involves calculating the present value of the future interest to be received plus the present value of the principal returned to the investor at the maturity of the bond.

For securities with cash flows that are constant in each year but with no specified maturity, such as preferred stock, the present value equals the dollar amount of the annual dividend divided by the investor's required rate of return; that is,

$$\text{Preferred stock value} = \frac{\text{annual dividend}}{\text{required rate of return}}$$

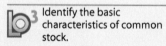

Identify the basic characteristics of common stock.

Common stock involves ownership in the corporation. In effect, bondholders and preferred stockholders can be viewed as creditors, whereas common stockholders are the owners of the firm. Common stock does not have a maturity date but exists as long as the firm does. Nor does common stock have an upper limit on its dividend payments. Dividend payments must be declared by the firm's board of directors before they are issued. In the event of bankruptcy, the common stockholders, as owners of the corporation, cannot exercise claims on assets until the firm's creditors, including its bondholders and preferred shareholders, have been satisfied. However, common stockholders' liability is limited to the amount of their investment.

The common stockholders are entitled to elect the firm's board of directors and are, in general, the only security holders given a vote. Common shareholders also have the right to approve any change in the company's corporate charter. Although each share of stock carries the same number of votes, the voting procedure is not always the same from company to company.

The preemptive right entitles the common shareholder to maintain a proportionate share of ownership in the firm.

When future dividends are expected to increase at a constant growth rate, the value of the common stock may be given by the following equation:

Value common stock.

$$\text{Common stock value} = \frac{\text{dividend in year 1}}{\text{required rate of return} - \text{growth rate}}$$

Growth here relates to *internal* growth only—growth achieved by retaining part of the firm's profits and reinvesting them in the firm—as opposed to growth achieved by issuing new stock or acquiring another firm.

Growth in and of itself does not mean that a firm is creating value for its stockholders. Only if profits are reinvested at a rate of return greater than the investor's required rate of return will growth result in increased stockholder value.

The expected rate of return on a security is the required rate of return of investors who are willing to pay the present market price for the security, but no more. This rate of return is important to the financial manager because it equals the required rate of return of the firm's investors.

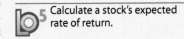

Calculate a stock's expected rate of return.

The expected rate of return for preferred stock is computed as follows:

$$\text{Expected return, preferred stock} = \frac{\text{annual dividend}}{\text{market price}}$$

The expected rate of return for common stock is calculated as follows:

$$\text{Expected return, common stock} = \frac{\text{dividend in year 1}}{\text{market price}} + \text{growth rate}$$

Key Terms

Call provision

Common stock

Convertible preferred stock

Cumulative feature

Cumulative voting

Dividend-payout ratio

Expected rate of return

Internal growth

Limited liability

Majority voting

Preemptive right

Preferred stock

Profit-retention rate

Protective provisions

Proxy

Proxy fight

Right

Sinking-fund provision

Review Questions

All Review Questions and Study Problems are available in MyFinanceLab.

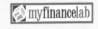

8-1. Why is preferred stock referred to as a hybrid security? It is often said to combine the worst features of common stock and bonds. What is meant by this statement?

8-2. Because preferred stock dividends in arrears must be paid before common stock dividends, should they be considered a liability and appear on the right-hand side of the balance sheet?

8-3. Why would a preferred stockholder want the stock to have a cumulative dividend feature and protective provisions?

8-4. Why is preferred stock frequently convertible? Why is it callable?

8-5. Compare valuing preferred stock and common stock.

8-6. Define investors' expected rate of return.

8-7. State how investors' expected rate of return is computed.

8-8. The common stockholders receive two types of return from their investment. What are they?

Self-Test Problems

(The solutions to the following problems are found at the end of the chapter.)

ST-1. (*Preferred stock valuation*) What is the value of a preferred stock when the dividend rate is 16 percent on a $100 par value? The appropriate discount rate for a stock of this risk level is 12 percent.

ST-2. (*Preferred stockholder expected return*) You own 250 shares of Dalton Resources preferred stock, which currently sells for $38.50 per share and pays annual dividends of $3.25 per share.

    a. What is your expected return?

    b. If you require an 8 percent return, given the current price, should you sell or buy more stock?

ST-3. (*Preferred stock valuation*) The preferred stock of Armlo pays a $2.75 dividend. What is the value of the stock if your required return is 9 percent?

ST-4. (*Common stock valuation*) Crosby Corporation common stock paid $1.32 in dividends last year and is expected to grow indefinitely at an annual 7 percent rate. What is the value of the stock if you require an 11 percent return?

ST-5. (*Common stockholder expected return*) Blackburn & Smith common stock currently sells for $23 per share. The company's executives anticipate a constant growth rate of 10.5 percent and an end-of-year dividend of $2.50.

    a. What is your expected rate of return?

    b. If you require a 17 percent return, should you purchase the stock?

Study Problems

8-1. (*Preferred stock expected return*) You are planning to purchase 100 shares of preferred stock and must choose between Stock A and Stock B. Stock A pays an annual dividend of $4.50 and is currently selling for $35. Stock B pays an annual dividend of $4.25 and is selling for $36. If your required return is 12 percent, which stock should you choose?

8-2. (*Measuring growth*) The Fisayo Corporation wants to achieve a steady 7 percent growth rate. If it can achieve a 12 percent return on equity, what percentage of earnings must Fisayo retain for investment purposes?

8-3. (*Common stock valuation*) Dalton Inc. has an 11.5 percent return on equity and retains 55 percent of its earnings for reinvestment purposes. It recently paid a dividend of $3.25 and the stock is currently selling for $40.

    a. What is the growth rate for Dalton Inc.?

    b. What is the expected return for Dalton's stock?

    c. If you require a 13 percent return, should you invest in the firm?

8-4. (*Common stock valuation*) Bates Inc. pays a dividend of $1 and is currently selling for $32.50. If investors require a 12 percent return on their investment from buying Bates stock, what growth rate would Bates Inc. have to provide the investors?

8-5. (*Preferred stock valuation*) What is the value of a preferred stock when the dividend rate is 14 percent on a $100 par value? The appropriate discount rate for a stock of this risk level is 12 percent.

8-6. (*Preferred stockholder expected return*) Solitron preferred stock is selling for $42.16 per share and pays $1.95 in dividends. What is your expected rate of return if you purchase the security at the market price?

8-7. (*Preferred stockholder expected return*) You own 200 shares of Somner Resources preferred stock, which currently sells for $40 per share and pays annual dividends of $3.40 per share.

    a. What is your expected return?

    b. If you require an 8 percent return, given the current price, should you sell or buy more stock?

8-8. (*Common stock valuation*) You intend to purchase Marigo common stock at $50 per share, hold it 1 year, and then sell it after a dividend of $6 is paid. How much will the stock price have to appreciate for you to satisfy your required rate of return of 15 percent?

8-9. (*Common stockholder expected return*) Made-It common stock currently sells for $22.50 per share. The company's executives anticipate a constant growth rate of 10 percent and an end-of-year dividend of $2.

   a. What is your expected rate of return if you buy the stock for $22.50?

   b. If you require a 17 percent return, should you purchase the stock?

8-10. (*Common stock valuation*) Header Motor Inc. paid a $3.50 dividend last year. At a constant growth rate of 5 percent, what is the value of the common stock if the investors require a 20 percent rate of return?

8-11. (*Measuring growth*) Given that a firm's return on equity is 18 percent and management plans to retain 40 percent of earnings for investment purposes, what will be the firm's growth rate?

8-12. (*Common stockholder expected return*) The common stock of Zaldi Co. is selling for $32.84 per share. The stock recently paid dividends of $2.94 per share and has a projected constant growth rate of 9.5 percent. If you purchase the stock at the market price, what is your expected rate of return?

8-13. (*Common stock valuation*) Honeywag common stock is expected to pay $1.85 in dividends next year, and the market price is projected to be $42.50 per share by year-end. If investors require a rate of return of 11 percent, what is the current value of the stock?

8-14. (*Common stockholder expected return*) The market price for Hobart common stock is $43 per share. The price at the end of 1 year is expected to be $48, and dividends for next year should be $2.84. What is the expected rate of return?

8-15. (*Preferred stock valuation*) Pioneer preferred stock is selling for $33 per share in the market and pays a $3.60 annual dividend.

   a. What is the expected rate of return on the stock?

   b. If an investor's required rate of return is 10 percent, what is the value of the stock for that investor?

   c. Should the investor acquire the stock?

8-16. (*Common stock valuation*) The common stock of NCP paid $1.32 in dividends last year. Dividends are expected to grow at an 8 percent annual rate for an indefinite number of years.

   a. If NCP's current market price is $23.50 per share, what is the stock's expected rate of return?

   b. If your required rate of return is 10.5 percent, what is the value of the stock for you?

   c. Should you make the investment?

8-17. (*Preferred stock valuation*) Calculate the value of a preferred stock that pays a dividend of $6 per share if your required rate of return is 12 percent.

8-18. (*Measuring growth*) Pepperdine Inc.'s return on equity is 16 percent, and the management plans to retain 60 percent of earnings for investment purposes. What will be the firm's growth rate?

8-19. (*Preferred stock expected return*) You are planning to purchase 100 shares of preferred stock and must choose between stock in Kristen Corporation and Titus Corporation. Your required rate of return is 9 percent. If the stock in Kristen pays a dividend of $2 and is selling for $23 and the stock in Titus pays a dividend of $3.25 and is selling for $31, which stock should you choose?

8-20. (*Preferred stockholder expected return*) You own 150 shares of James Corporation preferred stock at a market price of $22 per share. James pays dividends of $1.55. What is your expected rate of return? If you have a required rate of return of 9 percent, should you buy more stock?

8-21. (*Preferred stock expected return*) You are considering the purchase of 150 shares of preferred stock. Your required return is 11 percent. If the stock is currently selling for $40 and pays a dividend of $5.25, should you purchase the stock?

8-22. (*Common stockholder expected return*) If you purchased 125 shares of common stock that pays an end-of-year dividend of $3, what is your expected rate of return if you purchased the stock for $30 per share? Assume the stock is expected to have a constant growth rate of 7 percent.

8-23. (*Preferred stockholder expected return*) You are considering the purchase of Davis stock at a market price of $36.72 per share. Assume the stock pays an annual dividend of $2.33. What would be your expected return? Should you purchase the stock if your required return is 8 percent?

8-24. (*Common stockholder expected return*) Daisy executives anticipate a growth rate of 12 percent for the company's common stock. The stock is currently selling for $42.65 per share and pays an end-of-year dividend of $1.45. What is your expected rate of return if you purchase the stock for its current market price of $42.65?

Mini Case

You have finally saved $10,000 and are ready to make your first investment. You have the three following alternatives for investing that money:

- Capital Cities ABC, Inc. bonds with a par value of $1,000, that pays an 8.75 percent on its par value in interest, sells for $1,314, and matures in 12 years.
- Southwest Bancorp preferred stock paying a dividend of $2.50 and selling for $25.50.
- Emerson Electric common stock selling for $36.75, with a par value of $5. The stock recently paid a $1.32 dividend and the firm's earnings per share has increased from $1.49 to $3.06 in the past five years. The firm expects to grow at the same rate for the foreseeable future.

Your required rates of return for these investments are 6 percent for the bond, 7 percent for the preferred stock, and 15 percent for the common stock. Using this information, answer the following questions.

    a. Calculate the value of each investment based on your required rate of return.
    b. Which investment would you select? Why?
    c. Assume Emerson Electric's managers expect an earnings downturn and a resulting decrease in growth of 3 percent. How does this affect your answers to parts a and b?
    d. What required rates of return would make you indifferent to all three options?

Self-Test Solutions

SS-1. Value $(V_{ps}) = \dfrac{0.16 \times \$100}{0.12}$

$= \dfrac{\$16}{0.12}$

$= \$133.33$

SS-2.   a. Expected return $= \dfrac{\text{dividend}}{\text{market price}} = \dfrac{\$3.25}{\$38.50} = 0.0844 = 8.44\%$

    b. Given your 8 percent required rate of return, the stock is worth $40.62 to you:

$\text{Value} = \dfrac{\text{dividend}}{\text{required rate of return}} = \dfrac{\$3.25}{0.08} = \$40.63$

Because the expected rate of return (8.44%) is greater than your required rate of return (8%) or because the current market price ($38.50) is less than $40.63, the stock is undervalued and you should buy.

SS-3. Value $(V_{ps}) = \dfrac{\text{dividend}}{\text{required rate of return}} = \dfrac{\$2.75}{0.09} = \$30.56$

SS-4. Value $(V_{cs}) = \dfrac{\text{last year dividend }(1 + \text{growth rate})}{\text{required rate of return} - \text{growth rate}}$

$= \dfrac{\$1.32(1.07)}{0.11 - 0.07}$

$= \$35.31$

SS-5. a. Expected rate of return $(\bar{r}_{cs}) = \dfrac{\text{dividend in year 1}}{\text{market price}} + \text{growth rate}$

$$\bar{r}_{cs} = \frac{\$2.50}{\$23.00} + 0.105 = 0.2137$$

$$\bar{r}_{cs} = 21.37\%$$

b. $V_{cs} = \dfrac{\$2.50}{0.17 - 0.105} = \$38.46$

The expected rate of return exceeds your required rate of return, which means that the value of the security to you is greater than the current market price. Thus, you should buy the stock.

The Cost of Capital

From Chapter 9 of *Foundations of Finance*, 7/e. Arthur J. Keown. John D. Martin. J. William Petty. Copyright © 2011 by Pearson Education.
Published by Prentice Hall. All rights reserved.

The Cost of Capital

Learning Objectives

After reading this chapter, you should be able to:

1 Describe **the concepts underlying the firm's cost of capital (technically, its weighted average cost of capital) and the purpose for its calculation.**

2 Calculate **the after-tax cost of debt, preferred stock, and common equity.**

3 Calculate **a firm's weighted average cost of capital.**

4 Describe **the procedure used by PepsiCo to estimate the cost of capital for a multidivisional firm.**

5 Use **the cost of capital to evaluate new investment opportunities.**

6 Calculate **equivalent interest rates for different countries.**

On November 4, 2008, ExxonMobil Corp. (XOM) announced the biggest quarterly and annual earnings for any U.S. company, ever! The earnings were $4.83 billion for the third quarter of 2008. But is ExxonMobil creating value for its shareholders? The key to answering this question rests not just on the level of the firm's earnings but also on (i) how large an investment has been made in the company in order to produce these earnings and (ii) how risky the firm's investors perceive the company's investments to be. In other words, we need to know two things: What *rate* of return did the company earn on its invested capital, and what is the *market's required rate of return* on that invested capital (the company's cost of capital)?

The firm's cost of capital provides an estimate of just how much return the firm's combined investors expect from the company. Estimating a firm's cost of capital is very intuitive in theory but can be somewhat tedious in practice. In theory, what is required is the following: One, identifying all of the firm's sources of capital and their relative importance (that is, what fraction of the firm's invested capital comes from each source). Two, estimating the market's required rate of return for each source of capital the firm uses. Three, calculating an average of the required rates of return for each source of capital where the required rate of return for each source has been weighted by its contribution to the total capital invested in the firm.

The cost of capital is not only important when evaluating the company's overall performance, but is also used when evaluating individual investment decisions made by the firm. For example, when ExxonMobil is considering the development of a new oil production property in Nigeria, the company needs to estimate just how much return is needed to justify the investment. Similarly, when it is considering a chemical plant in Southeast Asia or Louisiana, the company's analysts need a benchmark return to compare to the investment's expected return. The cost of capital provides this benchmark.

Not to hold you in suspense any longer, ExxonMobil Corp. earned a whopping 36 percent rate of return on the firm's book assets and a 15 percent rate of return on the market value of the firm's investments. Given that the firm had to earn less than 10 percent to satisfy all of its investors (both equity and debt), it created a lot of value for its investors even in the midst of a worsening financial crisis. In this chapter, we investigate how to estimate the cost of funds to the firm. We will refer to the combined cost of borrowed money and money invested in the company by the firm's stockholders as the weighted average cost of capital or simply the firm's cost of capital.

Having studied the connection between risk and investor required rates of return and specifically, investor required rates of return for bondholders and stockholders, we are now ready to consider required rates of return for the firm as a whole. That is, just as the individuals that lend the firm money (bondholders) and those that invest in its stock have their individual required rates of return, we can also think about a combined required rate of return for the firm as a whole. This required rate of return for the firm is a blend of the required rates of return of all investors that we will estimate using a weighted average of the individual rates of return called the firm's **weighted average cost of capital** or simply the firm's cost of capital. Just like any cost of doing business, the firm must earn at least this cost if it is to create value for its owners.

In this chapter, we discuss the fundamental determinants of a firm's cost of capital and the rationale for its calculation and use. This entails developing the logic for estimating the cost of debt capital, preferred stock, and common stock.

weighted average cost of capital a composite of the individual costs of financing incurred by each capital source. A firm's weighted cost of capital is a function of (1) the individual costs of capital, and (2) the capital structure mix.

The Cost of Capital: Key Definitions and Concepts

 Describe the concepts underlying the firm's cost of capital (technically, its weighted average cost of capital) and the purpose for its calculation.

Opportunity Costs, Required Rates of Return, and the Cost of Capital

The firm's cost of capital is sometimes referred to as the firm's opportunity cost of capital. The term *opportunity cost* comes from the study of economics and is defined as the cost of making a choice in terms of the next best opportunity that is foregone. For example, the opportunity cost of taking a part-time job at Starbucks (SBUX) is the lost wages from the on-campus job you would have taken otherwise. Similarly, when a firm chooses to invest money it has raised from investors, it is in essence deciding not to return the money to the investors. Thus, the opportunity cost of investing the money is the cost the firm incurs by keeping the money and not returning it to the investors which is the firm's cost of capital.

CAN YOU DO IT?

DETERMINING HOW FLOTATION COSTS AFFECT THE COST OF CAPITAL

McDonald's Corporation sold a portion of its ownership interest in its rapidly growing fast-food Mexican restaurant Chipotle in January of 2006 for $22.00 per share. If the investor's required rate of return on these shares was 18 percent, and McDonald's incurred transaction costs totaling $2.00 per share, what was the cost of capital to McDonald's after adjusting for the effects of the transaction costs?

Is the investor's required rate of return the same thing as the cost of capital? Not exactly. Two factors drive a wedge between the investor's required rate of return and the cost of capital to the firm.

1. **Taxes.** When a firm borrows money to finance the purchase of an asset, the interest expense is deductible for federal income tax calculations. Consider a firm that borrows at 9 percent and then deducts its interest expense from its revenues before paying taxes at a rate of 34 percent. For each dollar of interest it pays, the firm reduces its taxes by $0.34. Consequently, the actual cost of borrowing to the firm is only 5.94% [0.09 − (0.34 × 0.09) = 0.09(1 − 0.34) = 0.0594, or 5.94%].

2. **Transaction costs.** Here we are referring to the costs the firm incurs *when it raises funds by issuing a particular type of security.* These are sometimes called flotation costs. For example, if a firm sells new shares for $25 per share but incurs transaction costs of $5 per share, then the cost of capital for the new common equity is increased. Assume that the investor's required rate of return is 15 percent for each $25 share; then 0.15 × $25 = $3.75 must be earned each year to satisfy the investor's required return. However, the firm has only $20 to invest, so the cost of capital (*k*) is calculated as the rate of return that must be earned on the $20 net proceeds that will produce a return of $3.75; that is,

$$\$20k = \$25 \times 0.15 = \$3.75$$

$$k = \frac{\$3.75}{\$20.00} = 0.1875, \text{ or } 18.75\%$$

We will have more to say about both these considerations when we discuss the costs of the individual sources of capital to the firm shortly.

The Firm's Financial Policy and the Cost of Capital

financial policy the firm's policies regarding the sources of financing it plans to use and the particular mix (proportions) in which they will be used.

A firm's **financial policy**—that is, *the policies regarding the sources of finances it plans to use and the particular mix (proportions) in which they will be used*—governs its use of debt and equity financing. The particular mixture of debt and equity that the firm uses can impact the firm's cost of capital. However, in this chapter, we assume that the firm maintains a fixed financial policy that is reflected in a fixed debt–equity ratio.

Concept Check

1. How is an investor's required rate of return related to an opportunity cost?
2. How do flotation costs impact the firm's cost of capital?

Determining the Costs of the Individual Sources of Capital

LO2 Calculate the after-tax cost of debt, preferred stock, and common equity.

In order to attract new investors, companies have created a wide variety of financing instruments or securities. In this chapter, we stick to three basic types: debt, preferred stock, and common stock. In calculating the respective cost of financing using each of these types of securities, we estimate the investor's required rate of return after properly adjusting for any transaction or flotation costs. In addition, because we will be discounting after-tax cash flows, we adjust our cost of capital for the effects of corporate taxes. In summary, the cost of a particular source of capital is equal to the investor's required rate of return after adjusting for the effects of both flotation costs and corporate taxes.

The Cost of Debt

In this book we learned that the value of a bond can be described in terms of the present value of the bond's future interest and principal payments. For example, if the bond has three years until maturity and pays interest annually, its value can be expressed as follows:

$$\text{Bond price} = \frac{\text{interest paid in year 1}}{\left(1 + \text{bondholder's required rate of return } (r_d)\right)^1} + \frac{\text{interest paid in year 2}}{\left(1 + \text{bondholder's required rate of return } (r_d)\right)^2}$$

$$+ \frac{\text{interest paid in year 3}}{\left(1 + \text{bondholder's required rate of return } (r_d)\right)^3} + \frac{\text{principal}}{\left(1 + \text{bondholder's required rate of return } (r_d)\right)^3} \quad (1)$$

Earlier in this book, we used the above bond price equation to estimate the bondholder's required rate of return. This required rate of return is commonly referred to as the bond's yield to maturity.

Since firms must pay flotation costs when they sell bonds, the net proceeds per bond received by the firm is less than the market price of the bond. Consequently, the cost of debt capital (k_d) is higher than the bondholder's required rate of return and is calculated using equation (2) as follows:

$$\text{Net proceeds per bond} = \frac{\text{interest paid in year 1}}{\left(1 + \text{cost of debt capital or } k_d\right)^1} + \frac{\text{interest paid in year 2}}{\left(1 + \text{cost of debt capital or } k_d\right)^2}$$

$$+ \frac{\text{interest paid in year 3}}{\left(1 + \text{cost of debt capital or } k_d\right)^3} + \frac{\text{principal}}{\left(1 + \text{cost of debt capital or } k_d\right)^3} \quad (2)$$

Note that the adjustment for flotation costs simply involves replacing the market price of the bond with the net proceeds per bond received by the firm after paying these costs. The result of this adjustment is that the discount rate that solves equation (2) is now the firm's cost of debt financing before adjusting for the effect of corporate taxes—that is, the before-tax cost of debt (k_d). The final adjustment we make is to account for the fact that interest is tax deductible. Thus, the after-tax cost of debt capital is simply the before-tax cost of debt (k_d) times one minus the corporate tax rate.

DID YOU GET IT?
DETERMINING HOW FLOTATION COSTS AFFECT THE COST OF CAPITAL

If the required rate of return on the shares was 18 percent, and the shares sold for $22.00 with $2.00 in transaction costs incurred per share, then the cost of equity capital for Chipotle Mexican Grill is found by grossing up the investor's required rate of return as follows:

$$\text{Cost of equity capital} = \frac{\text{investor's required rate of return}}{(1 - \% \text{ flotation costs})} = \frac{18\%}{1 - \left(\dfrac{\$2.00}{\$22.00}\right)} = 19.80\%$$

Incidentally, although the shares were sold to the public for $22.00 per share, they doubled to $44.00 by the end of the day after being traded in the secondary market.

> ### EXAMPLE 1
>
> Synopticom Inc. plans a bond issue for the near future and wants to estimate its current cost of debt capital. After talking with the firm's investment banker, the firm's chief financial officer has determined that a 20-year maturity bond with a $1,000 face value and 8 percent coupon (paying $8\% \times \$1{,}000 = \$80$ per year in interest) can be sold to investors for $908.32. As we illustrated earlier, equation (1) can be generalized to solve for the investor's required rate of return (r_d) for a 20-year bond. In this instance the bond pays 20 annual interest payments of $80 plus a $1,000 principal amount in the 20th year; that is,
>
> $$\$908.32 = \frac{\$80}{(1 + r_d)^1} + \frac{\$80}{(1 + r_d)^2} + \frac{\$80}{(1 + r_d)^3} + \cdots + \frac{\$80}{(1 + r_d)^{19}} + \frac{\$80 + \$1{,}000}{(1 + r_d)^{20}}$$
>
> In this case, Synopticom's creditors require a 9 percent rate of return. The cost of capital to the firm is higher than 9 percent, however, because the firm will have to pay flotation costs of $58.32 per bond when it issues the securities. The flotation costs reduce the net proceeds to Synopticom to $850. Substituting into equation (2), we find that the before-tax cost of capital for the bond issue (k_d) is 9.73 percent, that is,
>
> $$\$850.00 = \frac{\$80}{(1 + k_d)^1} + \frac{\$80}{(1 + k_d)^2} + \frac{\$80}{(1 + k_d)^3} + \cdots + \frac{\$80}{(1 + k_d)^{19}} + \frac{\$80 + \$1{,}000}{(1 + k_d)^{20}}$$
>
> Once again, we can solve equation (2) using a financial calculator, as we illustrate in the margin.
>
> One final adjustment is necessary to obtain the firm's after-tax cost of debt capital. Assuming that Synopticom is in the 34 percent corporate income tax (T_c) bracket, we estimate the after-tax cost of debt capital as follows:
>
> $$\text{After-tax cost of debt} = \text{before-tax cost of debt} \times \left(1 - \frac{\text{corporate}}{\text{tax rate}} \right)$$
>
> $$= 9.73\%(1 - 0.34) = 6.422\%$$

CALCULATOR SOLUTION

Data Input	Function Key
20	N
−850	PV
80	PMT
1000	FV

Function Key	Answer
CPT I/Y	9.73

The Cost of Preferred Stock

You may recall that the price of a share of preferred stock is equal to the present value of the constant stream of preferred stock dividends, i.e.,

$$\frac{\text{Price of a share of}}{\text{preferred stock}} = \frac{\text{preferred stock dividend}}{\text{required rate of return of the preferred stockholder } (r_{ps})} \tag{3}$$

If we can observe the price of the share of preferred stock and we know the preferred stock dividend, we can calculate the preferred stockholder's required rate of return as follows:

$$\frac{\text{Required rate of return}}{\text{of the preferred stockholder } (r_{ps})} = \frac{\text{preferred stock dividend}}{\text{price of a share of preferred stock}} \tag{4}$$

Once again, because flotation costs are usually incurred when new preferred shares are sold, the investor's required rate of return is less than the cost of preferred capital to the firm. To calculate the cost of preferred stock, we must adjust the required rate of return to reflect these flotation costs. We replace the price of a preferred share in equation (4) with the net proceeds per share from the sale of new preferred shares. The resulting formula can be used to calculate the cost of preferred stock to the firm.

$$\text{Cost of preferred stock } (k_{ps}) = \frac{\text{preferred stock dividend}}{\text{net proceeds per preferred share}} \tag{5}$$

Note that the net proceeds per share are equal to the price per share of preferred stock minus flotation cost per share of newly issued preferred stock.

What about corporate taxes? In the case of preferred stock, no tax adjustment must be made because, unlike interest payments, preferred dividends are not tax deductible.

EXAMPLE 2

El Paso Edison has issued preferred stock that pays an annual dividend of $4.25 per share. On November 23, 2009, the stock closed at $58.50. Assume that if the firm were to sell an issue of preferred stock with the same characteristics as its outstanding issue, it would incur flotation costs of $1.375 per share and the shares would sell for their November 23, 2009, closing price. What is El Paso Edison's cost of preferred stock?

Substituting into equation (5), we get the following cost of preferred stock for El Paso Edison:

$$k_{ps} = \frac{\$4.25}{(\$58.50 - \$1.375)} = 0.0744, \text{ or } 7.44\%$$

Note that there is no adjustment for taxes because preferred dividends are not tax deductible—that is, preferred dividends are paid after corporate taxes, unlike bond interest, which is paid with before-tax dollars.

The Cost of Common Equity

Common equity is unique in two respects. First, the cost of common equity is more difficult to estimate than the cost of debt or cost of preferred stock because the common stockholder's required rate of return is not observable. For example, there is no stated coupon rate or set dividend payment they receive. This results from the fact that common stockholders are the residual owners of the firm, which means that their return is equal to what is left of the firm's earnings after paying the firm's bondholders their contractually set interest and principal payments and the preferred stockholders their promised dividends. Second, common equity can be obtained either from the retention and reinvestment of firm earnings or through the sale of new shares. The costs associated with each of these sources are different from one another because the firm does not incur any flotation costs when it retains earnings, but it does incur costs when it sells new common shares.

We discuss two methods for estimating the common stockholder's required rate of return, which is the foundation for our estimate of the firm's cost of equity capital. These methods are based on the dividend growth model and the capital asset pricing model.

The Dividend Growth Model

Recall that the value of a firm's common stock is equal to the present value of all future dividends. When dividends are expected to grow at a rate g forever, and g is less than the investor's required rate of return, k_{cs}, then the value of a share of common stock, P_{cs}, can be written as

$$P_{cs} = \frac{D_1}{k_{cs} - g} \tag{6}$$

where D_1 is the dividend expected to be received by the firm's common shareholders 1 year hence. The expected dividend is simply the current dividend (D_0) multiplied by 1 plus the annual rate of growth in dividends (that is, $D_1 = D_0(1 + g)$). The investor's required rate of return then is found by solving equation (6) for k_{cs}.

$$k_{cs} = \frac{D_1}{P_{cs}} + g \tag{7}$$

CAN YOU DO IT?

CALCULATING THE COST OF DEBT FINANCING

General Auto Parts Corporation recently issued a 2-year bond with a face value of $20 million and a coupon rate of 5.5 percent per year (assume interest is paid annually). The subsequent cash flows to General Auto Parts were as follows:

	TODAY	YEAR 1	YEAR 2
Principal	$18 million	($0.00 million)	($20 million)
Interest		($0.99 million)	($0.99 million)
Total	$18 million	($0.99 million)	($20.99 million)

What was the cost of capital to General Auto Parts for the debt issue?

CAN YOU DO IT?

CALCULATING THE COST OF PREFERRED STOCK FINANCING

Carson Enterprises recently issued $25 million in preferred stock at a price of $2.50 per share. The preferred shares carry a 10 percent dividend, or $0.25 per share (assume that it is paid annually). After paying all the fees and costs associated with the preferred issue the firm realized $2.25 per share issued.
   What was the cost of capital to Carson Enterprises from the preferred stock issue?

Note that k_{cs} is the investor's required rate of return for investing in the firm's stock. It also serves as our estimate of the cost of equity capital, where new equity capital is obtained by retaining a part of the firm's current-period earnings. Recall that common equity financing can come from one of two sources: the retention of earnings or the sale of new common shares. When the firm retains earnings, it doesn't incur any flotation costs; thus, the investor's required rate of return is the same as the firm's cost of new equity capital in this instance.

If the firm issues new shares to raise equity capital, then it incurs flotation costs. Once again we adjust the investor's required rate of return for flotation costs by substituting the net proceeds per share, NP_{cs}, for the stock price, P_{cs}, in equation (7) to estimate the cost of new common stock, k_{ncs}.

$$k_{ncs} = \frac{D_1}{NP_{cs}} + g \tag{8}$$

EXAMPLE 3

The Talbot Corporation's common shareholders anticipate receiving a $2.20 per share dividend next year, based on the fact that they received $2 last year and expect dividends to grow 10 percent next year. Furthermore, analysts predict that dividends will continue to grow at a rate of 10 percent into the foreseeable future. Given that the firm's stock is trading for $50 per share, we can calculate the investor's required rate of return (and the cost of retained earnings) as follows:

$$k_{cs} = \frac{D_1}{P_{cs}} + g = \frac{\$2.20}{\$50.00} + 0.10 = 0.144, \text{ or } 14.4\%$$

DID YOU GET IT?
CALCULATING THE COST OF DEBT FINANCING

General Auto Parts Corporation receives $18 million from the sale of the bonds (after paying flotation costs) and is required to make principal plus interest payments at the end of the next 2 years. The total cash flows (both the inflow and the outflows) are summarized below:

	TODAY	YEAR 1	YEAR 2
Principal	$18 million	($0.00 million)	($20 million)
Interest		($0.99 million)	($0.99 million)
Total	$18 million	($0.99 million)	($20.99 million)

We can estimate the before-tax cost of capital from the bond issue by solving for k_d in the following bond valuation equation:

$$\text{Net bond proceeds}_{today} = \frac{\text{interest paid in year 1}}{(1 + k_d)^1} + \frac{\text{interest paid in year 2}}{(1 + k_d)^2} + \frac{\text{principal paid in year 2}}{(1 + k_d)^2}$$

$$\$18,000,000 = \frac{\$990,000}{(1 + k_d)^1} + \frac{\$990,000}{(1 + k_d)^2} + \frac{\$20,000,000}{(1 + k_d)^2}$$

$$k_d = 10.77\%$$

DID YOU GET IT?
CALCULATING THE COST OF PREFERRED STOCK FINANCING

Carson Enterprises sold its shares of preferred stock for net proceeds of $2.25 a share, and each share entitles the holder to a $0.25 cash dividend every year. Because the dividend payment is constant for all future years, we can calculate the cost of capital raised by the sale of preferred stock (k_{ps}) as follows:

$$\text{Cost of preferred stock } (k_{ps}) = \frac{\text{preferred stock dividend}}{\text{net proceeds per preferred share}} = \frac{\$0.25}{\$2.25} = 11.11\%$$

Should Talbot decide to issue new common stock, then it would incur a cost of $7.50 per share, or 15 percent of the current stock price. The resulting cost of new common equity capital would be

$$k_{ncs} = \frac{D_1}{NP_{cs}} + g = \frac{\$2.20}{\$50 - \$7.50} + 0.10 = 0.1518, \text{ or } 15.18\%$$

Thus, Talbot faces two costs of capital with respect to common equity. If it uses retained earnings, then the cost of capital to the firm is 14.4 percent, and if it issues new common stock, the corresponding cost is 15.18 percent. This difference will prove to be important later when we calculate the overall or weighted average cost of capital for the firm.

Issues in Implementing the Dividend Growth Model

The principal advantage of the dividend growth model as a basis for calculating the firm's cost of capital as it relates to common stock is the model's simplicity. To estimate an investor's required rate of return, the analyst needs only to observe the current dividend and stock price and to estimate the rate of growth in future dividends. The primary drawback relates to the applicability or appropriateness of the valuation model. That is, the dividend growth model is based on the fundamental assumption that dividends are expected to grow at a constant rate g forever. To avoid this assumption, analysts frequently utilize more complex valuation models in which dividends are expected to grow for, say, 5 years at one rate and then grow at a lower rate from year 6 forward. We do not consider these more complex models here.

Even if the constant growth rate assumption is acceptable, we must arrive at an estimate of that growth rate. We could estimate the rate of growth in historical dividends ourselves or go to published sources of growth rate expectations. Investment advisory services such as Value Line provide their own analysts' estimates of earnings growth rates (generally spanning up to 5 years), and the Institutional Brokers' Estimate System (I/B/E/S) collects and publishes earnings per share forecasts made by more than 1,000 analysts for a broad list of stocks. These estimates are helpful but still require the careful judgment of an analyst in their use because they relate to earnings (not dividends) and extend only 5 years into the future (not forever, as required by the dividend growth model). Nonetheless, these estimates provide a useful guide to making your initial dividend growth rate estimate.

The Capital Asset Pricing Model

Recall that the capital asset pricing model (CAPM) provides a basis for determining the investor's expected or required rate of return from investing in a firm's common stock. The model depends on three things:

1. The risk-free rate, r_f
2. The systematic risk of the common stock's returns relative to the market as a whole, or the stock's beta coefficient, β
3. The market-risk premium, which is equal to the difference in the expected rate of return for the market as a whole, that is, the expected rate of return for the "average security" minus the risk-free rate, or in symbols, $r_m - r_f$

Using the CAPM, the investor's required rate of return can be written as follows:

$$k_c = r_f + \beta(r_m - r_f) \tag{9}$$

EXAMPLE 4

Talbot Corporation's common stock has a beta coefficient of 1.40. Furthermore, the risk-free rate is currently 3.75 percent, and the expected rate of return on the market portfolio of all risky assets is 12 percent. Using the CAPM from equation (9), we can estimate Talbot's cost of equity as follows:

$$k_c = r_f + \beta(r_m - r_f)$$
$$= 0.0375 + 1.4(0.12 - 0.0375) = 0.153, \text{ or } 15.3\%$$

Note that the required rate of return we have estimated is the cost of retained earnings because no transaction costs are considered.

Issues in Implementing the CAPM

The CAPM approach has two primary advantages when it comes to calculating a firm's cost of capital as it relates to common stock. First, the model is simple and easy to understand and implement. The model variables are readily available from public sources, with the possible exception of beta coefficients for small firms and/or privately held firms. Second, because the model does not rely on dividends or any assumption about the growth rate in dividends, it can be applied to companies that do not currently pay dividends or are not expected to experience a constant rate of growth in dividends.

CAN YOU DO IT?

CALCULATING THE COST OF NEW COMMON STOCK USING THE DIVIDEND GROWTH MODEL

In March of 2010, the Mayze Corporation sold an issue of common stock in a public offering. The shares sold for $100 per share. Mayze's dividend in 2009 was $8 per share, and analysts expect that the firm's earnings and dividends will grow at a rate of 6 percent per year for the foreseeable future. What is the common stock investor's required rate of return (and the cost of retained earnings)?

Although the shares sold for $100 per share, Mayze received net proceeds from the issue of only $95 per share. The difference represents the flotation cost paid to the investment banker.

What is your estimate of the cost of new equity for Mayze using the dividend growth model?

CAN YOU DO IT?

CALCULATING THE COST OF COMMON STOCK USING THE CAPM

The Mayze Corporation issued common stock in March 2010, for $100 per share. However, before the issue was made, the firm's chief financial officer (CFO) asked one of his financial analysts to estimate the cost of the common stock financing using the CAPM. The analyst looked on Yahoo! Finance and got an estimate of 0.90 for the firm's beta coefficient. She also consulted online sources to get the current yield on a 10-year U.S. Treasury bond, which was 5.5 percent. The final estimate she needed to complete her calculation of the cost of equity using the CAPM was the market-risk premium, or the difference in the expected rate of return on all equity securities and the rate of return on the 10-year U.S. Treasury bond. After a bit of research she decided that the risk premium should be based on a 12 percent expected rate of return for the market portfolio and the 5.5 percent rate on the Treasury bond.

What is your estimate of the cost of common stock for Mayze using the CAPM?

Of course, using the CAPM requires that we obtain estimates of each of the three model variables—r_f, β, and $(r_m - r_f)$. Let's consider each in turn. First, the analyst has a wide range of U.S. government securities on which to base an estimate of the risk-free rate (r_f). Treasury securities with maturities from 30 days to 20 years are readily available. Unfortunately, the CAPM offers no guidance about the appropriate choice. In fact, the model itself assumes that there is but one risk-free rate, and it corresponds to a one-period return (the length of the period is not specified, however). Consequently, we are left to our own judgment about which maturity we should use to represent the risk-free rate. For applications of the cost of capital involving long-term capital expenditure decisions, it seems reasonable to select a risk-free rate of comparable maturity. So, if we are calculating the cost of capital to be used as the basis for evaluating investments that will provide returns over the next 20 years, it seems appropriate to use a risk-free rate corresponding to a U.S. Treasury bond of comparable maturity.

Second, estimates of security beta (β) coefficients are available from a wide variety of investment advisory services, including Merrill Lynch and Value Line, among others. Alternatively, we could collect historical stock market returns for the company of interest as well as a general market index (such as the Standard and Poor's 500 Index) and estimate the stock's beta as the slope of the relationship between the two return series. However, because beta estimates are widely available for a large majority of publicly traded firms, analysts frequently rely on published sources for betas.

Finally, estimating the market-risk premium can be accomplished by looking at the history of stock returns and the premium earned over (under) the risk-free rate of interest. In this book, we reported a summary of the historical returns earned on risk-free securities and common stocks. We saw that on average over the past 70 years, common stocks have earned a premium of roughly 5.5 percent over long-term government bonds. Thus, for our purposes, we will utilize this estimate of the market-risk premium $(r_m - r_f)$ when estimating the investor's required rate of return on equity using the CAPM.

FINANCE AT WORK

IPOS: SHOULD A FIRM GO PUBLIC?

When a privately owned company decides to distribute its shares to the general public, it goes through a process known as an initial public offering (IPO). There are a number of advantages to having a firm's shares traded in the public equity market, including the following:

- **New capital is raised.** When the firm sells its shares to the public, it acquires new capital that can be invested in the firm.
- **The firm's owners gain liquidity of their share holdings.** Publicly traded shares are more easily bought and sold, so the owners can more easily liquidate all or part of their investment in the firm.
- **The firm gains future access to the public capital market.** Once a firm has raised capital in the public markets, it is easier to go back a second and third time.
- **Being a publicly traded firm can benefit the firm's business.** Public firms tend to enjoy a higher profile than their privately held counterparts. This may make it easier to make sales and attract vendors to supply goods and services to the firm.

However, all is not rosy as a publicly held firm. There are a number of potential disadvantages, including the following:

- **Reporting requirements can be onerous.** Publicly held firms are required to file periodic reports with the Securities and Exchange Commission (SEC). This is not only onerous in terms of the time and effort required, but also some business owners feel they must reveal information to their competitors that could be potentially damaging.

- **The private equity investors now must share any new wealth with the new public investors.** Once the firm is a publicly held company, the new shareholders share on an equal footing with the company founders the good (and bad) fortune of the firm.
- **The private equity investors lose a degree of control over the organization.** Outsiders gain voting control over the firm to the extent that they own its shares.
- **An IPO is expensive.** A typical firm may spend 15 to 25 percent of the money raised on expenses directly connected to the IPO. This cost is increased further if we consider the cost of lost management time and disruption of business associated with the IPO process.
- **Exit of the company's owners is usually limited.** The company's founders may want to sell their shares through the IPO, but this is not allowed for an extended period of time following the IPO. Therefore, this is not usually a good mechanism for cashing out the company founders.
- **Everyone involved faces legal liability.** The IPO participants are jointly and severally liable for each others' actions. This means that they can be sued for any omissions from the IPO's prospectus should the market valuation fall below the IPO offering price.

Carefully weighing the financial consequences of each of these advantages and disadvantages can provide a company's owners (and managers) with some basis for answering the question of whether they want to become a public corporation.

Other Sources: Professor Ivo Welch's Web site: welch.som.yale.edu provides a wealth of information concerning IPOs.

In addition to the historical average market-risk premium, we can also utilize surveys of professional economists' opinions regarding future premiums.[1] For example, in a survey conducted in 1998 by Yale economist Ivo Welch, the median 30-year market-risk premium for all survey participants was 7 percent. When the survey was repeated in 2000, the corresponding market-risk premium had fallen to 5 percent. These results suggest two things. First, the market-risk premium is not fixed. It varies through time with the general business cycle. In addition, it appears that using a market-risk premium somewhere between 5 percent and 7 percent is reasonable when estimating the cost of capital using the capital asset pricing model.

Concept Check

1. Define the cost of debt, preferred equity, and common equity financing.
2. The cost of common equity financing is more difficult to estimate than the costs of debt and preferred equity. Explain why.
3. What is the dividend growth model, and how is it used to estimate the cost of common equity financing?
4. Describe the capital asset pricing model and how it can be used to estimate the cost of common equity financing.
5. What practical problems are encountered in using the CAPM to estimate common equity capital cost?

[1]The results reported here come from Ivo Welch, "Views of Financial Economists on the Equity Premium and on Professional Controversies," *Journal of Business* 73–74 (October 2000): pp. 501–537; and Ivo Welch, "The Equity Premium Consensus Forecast Revisited," Cowles Foundation Discussion Paper No. 1325 (September 2001).

230

The Weighted Average Cost of Capital

3 Calculate a firm's weighted average cost of capital.

Now that we have calculated the individual costs of capital for each of the sources of financing the firm might use, we turn to the combination of these capital costs into a single weighted average cost of capital. To estimate the weighted average cost of capital, we need to know the cost of each of the sources of capital used and the capital structure mix. We use the term **capital structure** to refer to *the proportions of each source of financing used by the firm*. Although a firm's capital structure can be quite complex, we focus our examples on the three basic sources of capital: bonds, preferred stock, and common equity.

capital structure the mix of long-term sources of funds used by the firm. This is also called the firm's capitalization. The relative total (percentage) of each type of fund is emphasized.

In words, we calculate the weighted average cost of capital for a firm that uses only debt and common equity using the following equation:

$$\begin{matrix}\text{Weighted} \\ \text{average cost} \\ \text{of capital}\end{matrix} = \left(\begin{matrix}\text{after-tax} \\ \text{cost of} \\ \text{debt}\end{matrix} \times \begin{matrix}\text{proportion} \\ \text{of debt} \\ \text{financing}\end{matrix}\right) + \left(\begin{matrix}\text{cost of} \\ \text{equity}\end{matrix} \times \begin{matrix}\text{proportion} \\ \text{of equity} \\ \text{financing}\end{matrix}\right) \quad (10)$$

For example, if a firm borrows money at 6 percent after taxes, pays 10 percent for equity, and raises its capital in equal proportions from debt and equity, its weighted average cost of capital is 8 percent—that is,

Weighted average cost of capital = $[0.06 \times 0.5] + [0.10 \times 0.5] = 0.08$ or 8%

In practice, the calculation of the cost of capital is more complex than this example. For one thing, firms often have multiple debt issues with different required rates of return, and they also use preferred equity as well as common equity financing. Furthermore, when common equity capital is raised, it is sometimes the result of retaining and reinvesting the firm's earnings and, at other times, it involves a new stock offering. Of course, in the case of retained earnings, the firm does not incur the costs associated with selling new common stock. This means that equity from retained earnings is less costly than a new stock offering. In the examples that follow, we address each of these complications.

DID YOU GET IT?
CALCULATING THE COST OF NEW COMMON STOCK USING THE DIVIDEND GROWTH MODEL

We can estimate the cost of equity capital using the dividend growth model by substituting into the following equation:

$$\text{Cost of new common stock } (k_{ncs}) = \frac{\text{expected dividend next year } (D_1)}{\text{net proceeds per share } (NP_{cs})} + \text{dividend growth rate } (g) = \frac{\$8.00}{\$95.00} + 0.06 = 14.42\%$$

DID YOU GET IT?
CALCULATING THE COST OF COMMON STOCK USING THE CAPM

The CAPM can be used to estimate the investor's required rate of return as follows:

$$\begin{matrix}\text{Cost of} \\ \text{common equity}(k_{cs})\end{matrix} = \left(\begin{matrix}\text{risk-free} \\ \text{rate of interest } (r_f)\end{matrix}\right) + \left(\begin{matrix}\text{Mayze's beta} \\ \text{coefficient } (\beta)\end{matrix}\right) \times \left[\begin{matrix}\text{expected market} \\ \text{rate of return } (r_m)\end{matrix} - \left(\begin{matrix}\text{risk-free} \\ \text{rate of interest } (r_f)\end{matrix}\right)\right]$$

Making the appropriate substitutions, we get the following estimate of the investor's required rate of return using the CAPM model:

Cost of common equity $(k_{cs}) = 0.055 + 0.90 \times (0.12 - 0.055) = 0.1135$ or 11.35%

Capital Structure Weights

The reason we calculate a cost of capital is that it enables us to evaluate one or more of the firm's investment opportunities. Remember that the cost of capital should reflect the riskiness of the project being evaluated, so a firm should calculate multiple costs of capital when it makes investments in multiple divisions or business units having different risk characteristics. Thus, for the calculated cost of capital to be meaningful, it must correspond directly to the riskiness of the particular project being analyzed. That is, in theory the cost of capital should reflect the particular way in which the funds are raised (the capital structure used) and the systemic risk characteristics of the project. Consequently, the correct way to calculate capital structure weights is to use the actual dollar amounts of the various sources of capital actually used by the firm.[2]

In practice, *the mixture of financing sources used by a firm will vary from year to year.* For this reason, many firms find it expedient to use target capital structure proportions when calculating the firm's weighted average cost of capital. For example, a firm might use its target mix of 40 percent debt and 60 percent equity to calculate its weighted average cost of capital even though, in that particular year, it raised the majority of its financing requirements by borrowing. Similarly, it would continue to use the target proportions in the subsequent year, when it might raise the majority of its financing needs by reinvesting earnings or issuing new stock.

Calculating the Weighted Average Cost of Capital

The weighted average cost of capital, k_{wacc}, is simply a weighted average of all the capital costs incurred by the firm. Table 1 illustrates the procedure used to estimate k_{wacc} for a firm that has debt, preferred stock, and common equity in its target capital structure mix. Two possible scenarios are described in the two panels. First, in Panel A the firm is able to finance all of its target capital structure requirements for common equity using retained earnings. Second, in Panel B the firm must use a new equity offering to raise the equity capital it requires. For example, if the firm has set a 75 percent target for equity financing and has current earnings of $750,000, then it can raise up to $750,000/0.75 = $1,000,000 in new financing before it has to sell new equity. For $1,000,000 or less in capital spending, the firm's weighted average cost of capital would be calculated using the cost of equity from retained earnings (following Panel A of Table 1). For more than $1,000,000 in new capital, the cost of capital would rise to reflect the impact of the higher cost of using new common stock (following Panel B of Table 1).

TABLE 1 Calculating the Weighted Average Cost of Capital

PANEL A: COMMON EQUITY RAISED BY RETAINED EARNINGS			
		Capital Structure	
Source of Capital	Weights	× Cost of Capital	= Product
Bonds	w_d	$k_d(1 - T_c)$	$w_d \times k_d(1 - T_c)$
Preferred stock	w_{ps}	k_{ps}	$w_{ps} \times k_{ps}$
Common equity			
Retained earnings	w_{cs}	k_{cs}	$w_{cs} \times k_{cs}$
Sum =	100%	Sum =	k_{wacc}

PANEL B: COMMON EQUITY RAISED BY SELLING NEW COMMON STOCK			
		Capital Structure	
Source of Capital	Weights	× Cost of Capital	= Product
Bonds	w_d	$k_d(1 - T_c)$	$w_d \times k_d(1 - T_c)$
Preferred stock	w_{ps}	k_{ps}	$w_{ps} \times k_{ps}$
Common equity			
Common stock	w_{ncs}	k_{ncs}	$w_{ncs} \times k_{ncs}$
Sum =	100%	Sum =	k_{wacc}

[2]There are instances when we will want to calculate the cost of capital for the firm as a whole. In this case, the appropriate weights to use are based on the market value of the various capital sources used by the firm. Market values rather than book values properly reflect the sources of financing used by a firm at any particular point in time. However, when a firm is privately owned, it is not possible to get market values of its securities, and book values are often used.

EXAMPLE 5

Ash Inc.'s capital structure and estimated capital costs are found in Table 2. Note that the sum of the capital structure weights must equal 100 percent if we have properly accounted for all sources of financing and in the correct amounts. For example, Ash plans to invest a total of $3 million in common equity to fund a $5 million investment. Because Ash has earnings equal to the $3,000,000 it needs in new equity financing, the entire amount of new equity will be raised by retaining earnings.

We calculate the weighted average cost of capital following the procedure described in Panel A of Table 1 and using the information found in Table 2. The resulting calculations are found in Panel A of Table 3, in which Ash Inc.'s weighted average cost of capital for up to $5,000,000 in new financing is found to be 12.7 percent.

If Ash needs more than $5,000,000, it will not have any retained earnings to provide the additional equity capital. Thus, to maintain its desired 60 percent equity financing proportion, Ash will now have to issue common stock that costs 18 percent.

Panel B of Table 3 contains the calculation of Ash's weighted average cost of capital for more than $5,000,000. The resulting cost is 13.9 percent.

In practice, many firms calculate only one cost of capital, using a cost of equity capital that ignores the transaction costs associated with raising new equity capital. In essence, they would use the capital cost calculated for Ash in Panel A of Table 3, regardless of the level of new financing for the year. Although this is technically incorrect, it is an understandable practice given the inexactness of the estimates of equity capital cost and the relatively small differences that result from the adjustment.

TABLE 2 Capital Structure and Capital Costs for Ash Inc.

Source of Capital	Amount of Funds Raised ($)	Percentage of Total	After-Tax Cost of Capital
Bonds	1,750,000	35%	7%
Preferred stock	250,000	5%	13%
Retained earnings	3,000,000	60%	16%
Total	5,000,000	100%	

TABLE 3 The Weighted Average Cost of Capital for Ash Inc.

PANEL A: COST OF CAPITAL FOR $0 TO $5,000,000 IN NEW CAPITAL

Source of Capital	Capital Structure Weights	Cost of Capital	Product
Bonds	35%	7%	2.45%
Preferred stock	5%	13%	0.65%
Retained earnings	60%	16%	9.60%
Total	100%	$k_{wacc} =$	12.70%

PANEL B: COST OF CAPITAL FOR MORE THAN $5,000,000

Source of Capital	Capital Structure Weights	Cost of Capital	Product
Bonds	35%	7%	2.45%
Preferred stock	5%	13%	0.65%
New common stock	60%	18%	10.80%
Total	100%	$k_{wacc} =$	13.90%

CAUTIONARY TALE

FORGETTING PRINCIPLE 3: RISK REQUIRES A REWARD

What happens to a firm's cost of capital when the capital market that the firm depends on for financing simply stops working? Investment banking firm Goldman Sachs discovered the answer to this question the hard way. In 2008, as potential lenders became very nervous about the future of the economy, the credit markets from which Goldman Sachs borrowed money on a regular basis simply stopped functioning. The effect of this shutdown was that Goldman Sachs no longer had access to cheap short-term debt financing. And this meant the firm was at greater risk of financial distress. This high risk of firm failure caused its equity holders to demand a much higher rate of return and thus, Goldman Sachs's cost of equity financing skyrocketed.

Ultimately, faced with a crisis, Goldman arranged for a $10 billion loan from the U.S. Government's Troubled Asset Relief Fund (TARP) and obtained a $5 billion equity investment from famed investor Warren Buffett. The combined effects of these actions stabilized the firm's financial situation and lowered the firm's cost of capital dramatically. Goldman Sachs and Morgan Stanley are the only two large investment banking firms to survive the financial crisis.

So what can Goldman Sachs learn from this experience? Debt financing, and in particular short-term debt financing, may offer higher returns in the short run, but this use of financial leverage comes with a significant increase in risk to the equity holders, and this translates to higher costs of equity financing for the firm.

Concept Check

1. A firm's capital structure and its target capital structure proportions are important determinants of a firm's weighted average cost of capital. Explain.

2. Explain in words the calculation of a firm's weighted average cost of capital. What exactly are we averaging and what do the weights represent?

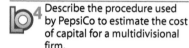
Describe the procedure used by PepsiCo to estimate the cost of capital for a multidivisional firm.

Calculating Divisional Costs of Capital: PepsiCo Inc.

If a firm operates in multiple industries, each with its own particular risk characteristics, should it use different capital costs for each division? **Principle 1** suggests that the financial manager should recognize these risk differences in estimating the cost of capital to use in each division. This is exactly what PepsiCo did before February 1997, when it was operating in three basic industries.

CAN YOU DO IT?

CALCULATING THE WEIGHTED AVERAGE COST OF CAPITAL

In the fall of 2009, Grey Manufacturing was considering a major expansion of its manufacturing operations. The firm has sufficient land to accommodate the doubling of its operations, which will cost $200 million. To raise the needed funds Grey's management has decided to simply mimic the firm's present capital structure as follows:

SOURCE OF CAPITAL	AMOUNT OF FUNDS RAISED ($)	PERCENTAGE OF TOTAL	AFTER-TAX COST OF CAPITAL*
Debt	$ 80,000,000	40%	5.20%
Common stock	120,000,000	60%	14.50%
Total	$200,000,000	100%	

What is your estimate of Grey's weighted average cost of capital?

*You may assume that these after-tax costs of capital have been appropriately adjusted for any transaction costs incurred when raising the funds.

FINANCE AT WORK

THE PILLSBURY COMPANY ADOPTS EVA WITH A GRASSROOTS EDUCATION PROGRAM

A key determinant of the success of any incentive-based program is employee buy-in. If employees simply view a new performance measurement and reward system as "just another" reporting requirement, the program will have little impact on their behavior and, consequently, little effect on the firm's operating performance. In addition, if a firm's employees do not understand the measurement system, it is very likely that it will be distrusted and may even have counterproductive effects on the firm's performance.

So how do you instill in your employees the notion that your performance measurement and reward system does indeed lead to the desired result? Pillsbury took a unique approach to the problem by using a simulation exercise in which the value of applying the principles of Economic Value Added (EVA®) could be learned by simulating the operations of a hypothetical factory. Employees used the simulation to follow the value-creation process from the factory's revenue, to net operating profit after taxes, to the weighted average cost of capital. The results were gratifying. One Pillsbury manager noted, "you saw the lights go on in people's eyes" as employees realized, "Oh, this really does impact my work environment."

Briggs and Stratton used a similar training program to instill the basic principles of EVA in its employees. Its business-simulation example was even more basic than the Pillsbury factory. Briggs and Stratton used a convenience store's operations to teach line workers the importance of controlling waste, utilizing assets fully, and managing profit margins. Stern Stewart and Company, which coined the term *EVA*, has also developed a training tool, the EVA Training Tutor.™ The EVA Training Tutor addresses four basic issues using CD-ROM technology:

- Why is creating shareholder wealth an important corporate and investor goal?
- What is the best way to measure wealth and business success?
- Which business strategies have created wealth, and which have failed?
- What can you do to create wealth and increase the stock price of your company?

The educational programs described briefly here are examples of how major corporations are seeing the need to improve the financial literacy of their employees to make the most of their human and capital resources.

Sources: Adapted from George Donnelly, "Grassroots EVA," CFO.com (May 1, 2000), www.cfo.com and The EVA Training Tutor™ (Stern Stewart and Company).

PepsiCo went to great lengths to estimate the cost of capital for each of its three major operating divisions (restaurants, snack foods, and beverages).[3] We briefly summarize the basic elements of the calculations involved in these estimates, including the cost of debt financing, the cost of common equity, the target capital structure weights, and the weighted average cost of capital.

Table 4 contains the estimates of the after-tax cost of debt for each of PepsiCo's three divisions and assuming a 38 percent tax rate. Table 5 contains the estimates of the cost of

TABLE 4 Estimating PepsiCo's Cost of Debt

	Pretax Cost of Debt	×	(1 − Tax Rate)	=	After-Tax Cost of Debt
Restaurants	8.93%	×	0.62	=	5.54%
Snack foods	8.43%	×	0.62	=	5.23%
Beverages	8.51%	×	0.62	=	5.28%

TABLE 5 The Cost of Equity Capital for PepsiCo's Operating Divisions

	Risk-Free Rate	+	Beta	×	(Expected Market Return − Risk-Free Rate)	=	Cost of Equity
Restaurants	7.28%	+	1.17	×	(11.48% − 7.28%)	=	12.19%
Snack foods	7.28%	+	1.02	×	(11.48% − 7.28%)	=	11.56%
Beverages	7.28%	+	1.07	×	(11.48% − 7.28%)	=	11.77%

[3]PepsiCo spun off its restaurants division in February 1997. However, the example used here was based on the company before the spin-off.

DID YOU GET IT?

CALCULATING THE WEIGHTED AVERAGE COST OF CAPITAL

The weighted average cost of capital (WACC) for Grey Manufacturing can be calculated using the following table:

SOURCE OF CAPITAL	PERCENTAGE OF TOTAL CAPITAL	AFTER-TAX COST OF CAPITAL	PRODUCT
Debt	40%	5.20%	2.0800%
Common stock	60%	14.50%	8.7000%
		WACC =	10.7800%

Consequently, we estimate Grey's WACC to be 10.78%.

TABLE 6 PepsiCo's Weighted Average Cost of Capital for Each of Its Operating Divisions

	Cost of Equity Times the Target Equity Ratio	+	After-Tax Cost of Debt Times the Target Debt Ratio	=	Weighted Average Cost of Capital
Restaurants	(12.19%)(0.70)	+	(5.54%)(0.30)	=	10.20%
Snack foods	(11.56%)(0.80)	+	(5.23%)(0.20)	=	10.29%
Beverages	(11.77%)(0.74)	+	(5.28%)(0.26)	=	10.08%

equity capital for each of PepsiCo's three operating divisions using the CAPM. We will not explain the intricacies of their method for estimating divisional betas, except to say that they make use of beta estimates for a number of competitor firms from each of the operating divisions, which involves making appropriate adjustments for differences in the use of financial leverage across the competitor firms used in the analysis.[4]

The weighted average cost of capital for each of the divisions is estimated in Table 6 using the capital costs estimated in Tables 4 and 5 and using PepsiCo's target capital structure weights for each operating division. Note that the weighted average costs of capital for all three divisions fall within a very narrow range, between 10.08 percent and 10.29 percent.

Concept Check

1. Why should firms that own and operate multiple businesses with very different risk characteristics use business-specific or divisional costs of capital?
2. Describe the process used to estimate the divisional costs of capital for PepsiCo.

Table 7 contains a summary of the formulas you need to estimate the weighted average cost of capital. If divisional costs of capital are to be estimated, then we must apply these formulas individually to each division because the opportunity costs of capital sources and the financing mix (proportions) used can differ, as we have just seen in the PepsiCo example.

[4]This method of using betas from comparable firms is sometimes referred to as the pure play method, because the analyst seeks independent beta estimates for firms engaged in only one business (i.e., restaurants or beverages). The betas for these pure play companies are then used to estimate the beta for a business or division.

TABLE 7 A Summary of Cost of Capital Formulas

1. The After-Tax Cost of Debt, $k_d(1 - T_c)$

   a) Calculate the before-tax cost of debt, k_d, as follows:

   $$\text{Net proceeds } (NP_d) = \frac{\text{interest (year 1)}}{(1 + \text{cost of debt capital } (k_d))^1} + \frac{\text{interest (year 2)}}{(1 + k_d)^2} + \frac{\text{principal}}{(1 + k_d)^2} \quad (2)$$

   b) Calculate the after-tax cost of debt as follows:

   after-tax cost of debt $= k_d(1 - T_c)$

   where T_c is the corporate tax rate.

2. The Cost of Preferred Stock, k_{ps}

   $$k_{ps} = \frac{\text{preferred stock dividend}}{\text{net proceeds per share of preferred stock } (NP_{ps})} \quad (5)$$

   where NP_{ps} is the net proceeds per share of new preferred stock sold after flotation costs.

3. The Cost of Common Equity

   a) Method 1: dividend growth model

   Calculate the cost of internal common equity (retained earnings), k_{cs}, as follows:

   $$k_{cs} = \frac{D_1}{P_{cs}} + g \quad (7)$$

   where D_1 is the expected dividend for the next year, P_{cs} is the current price of the firm's common stock, and g is the rate of growth in dividends per year.

   Calculate the cost of external common equity (new stock offering), k_{ncs}, as follows:

   $$k_{ncs} = \frac{D_1}{NP_{cs}} + g \quad (8)$$

   where NP_{cs} is the net proceeds to the firm after flotation costs per share of stock sold.

   b) Method 2: capital asset pricing model, k_c

   $$k_c = r_f + \beta(r_m - r_f) \quad (9)$$

   where the risk-free rate is k_{rf}; the systemic risk of the common stock's returns relative to the market as a whole, or the stock's beta coefficient, is β; and the market-risk premium, which is equal to the difference in the expected rate of return for the market as a whole (i.e., the expected rate of return for the "average security") minus the risk-free rate, is $k_m - k_{rf}$.

4. The Weighted Average Cost of Capital

$$\begin{pmatrix} \text{Weighted} \\ \text{average cost} \\ \text{of capital} \end{pmatrix} = \left(\begin{matrix} \text{after-tax} \\ \text{cost of} \\ \text{debt} \end{matrix} \times \begin{matrix} \text{proportion} \\ \text{of debt} \\ \text{financing} \end{matrix} \right) + \left(\begin{matrix} \text{cost of} \\ \text{equity} \end{matrix} \times \begin{matrix} \text{proportion} \\ \text{of equity} \\ \text{financing} \end{matrix} \right) \quad (10)$$

Note that we are simply calculating a weighted average of the costs of each of the firm's sources of capital where the weights reflect the firm's relative use of each source.

Using a Firm's Cost of Capital to Evaluate New Capital Investments

5 Use the cost of capital to evaluate new investment opportunities.

If a firm has traditionally used a single cost of capital for all projects undertaken within each of several operating divisions (or companies) with very different risk characteristics, then the company will likely encounter resistance from the high-risk divisions if it changes to a divisional cost of capital structure. Consider the case of the hypothetical firm Global Energy, whose divisional costs of capital are illustrated in Figure 1. Global Energy is an integrated oil company that engages in a wide range of hydrocarbon-related businesses, including exploration and development, pipelines, and refining. Each of these businesses has its unique set of risks. In Figure 1 we see that the overall, or enterprise-wide, cost of capital for Global Energy is 11 percent, reflecting an average of the firm's divisional costs of capital, ranging from a low of 8 percent for pipelines up to 18 percent for exploration and development.

At present Global Energy is using a cost of capital of 11 percent to evaluate its new investment proposals from all three operating divisions. This means that exploration and

FINANCE AT WORK

WEIGHTED AVERAGE COSTS OF CAPITAL ESTIMATES: 1993–2005

The value-based management consulting firm Stern Stewart estimates the WACC for the 1,000 largest U.S. firms each year as part of its analysis of their performance. In the 2004 performance review (based on 2003 data) the average WACC across all 1,000 firms was 7.5%, and the median was 7.4%. The maximum WACC was 14% compared to a minimum of only 4.2%. The following list contains the WACC estimates for a sample of well-known firms for 5-year intervals spanning 1993–2005:

COMPANY NAME	2005	2003	1998	1993
Walmart Stores	5.8%	6.2%	6.6%	7.5%
Coca-Cola Co.	5.9%	6.4%	6.6%	7.6%
ExxonMobil Corp.	6.1%	7.0%	7.3%	8.0%
General Electric Co.	6.9%	7.3%	7.7%	8.6%
American Express	8.6%	8.0%	8.4%	9.5%
Procter & Gamble Co.	7.2%	7.4%	8.2%	9.1%
United Parcel Service Inc.	7.4%	7.8%	8.1%	9.2%
Johnson & Johnson	7.8%	8.2%	8.4%	9.3%
Lilly (Eli) & Co.	7.6%	8.0%	8.4%	9.5%
Merck & Co.	7.6%	8.0%	8.5%	9.6%
Amgen Inc.	9.6%	10.0%	10.4%	11.4%
Dell Computer Corp.	10.3%	10.8%	11.1%	11.9%
Hewlett-Packard	10.1%	10.8%	11.4%	12.1%
International Business Machines Corp.	10.8%	11.3%	11.7%	12.8%
Cisco Systems Inc.	12.0%	12.2%	13.0%	14.0%
Microsoft Corp.	11.7%	11.8%	12.5%	13.6%
Intel Corp.	13.2%	13.7%	14.0%	14.8%
Average	8.7%	9.1%	9.5%	10.5%
Aaa Corporate Bond Yield	4.8%	5.63%	6.23%	7.00%
Average WACC - Aaa Bond Yield	3.9%	3.48%	3.31%	3.50%

The average WACC across this sample of firms declines over the period from 12.5 percent down to 9.1 percent. This decline is attributable to the general decline in interest rates (note that the Aaa corporate bond yield declined from 7 percent in 1993 down to 4.8 in 2005 such that the spread of WACC over the Aaa bond yield is relatively flat).

In addition, the WACC estimates are consistent across the period, with Walmart exhibiting the lowest WACC and Intel Corp. the highest.

Source: WACC estimates were taken from the Stern Stewart Annual Performance Ranking for 2006.

FIGURE 1 Global Energy Divisional Costs of Capital
Using a company-wide cost of capital for a multidivisional firm results in systematic overinvestment in high-risk projects and underinvestment in low-risk projects.

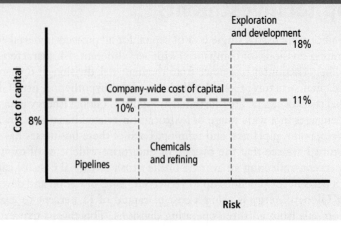

development projects earning as little as 11 percent are being accepted even though the capital market dictates that projects of this risk should earn 18 percent. Thus, Global Energy overinvests in high-risk projects. Similarly, the company will underinvest in its two lower-risk divisions, where the company-wide cost of capital is used.

Now consider the prospect of moving to division costs of capital and the implications this might have for the three divisions. Specifically, the managers of the exploration and development division are likely to see this as an adverse move for them because it will surely cut the level of new investment capital flowing into their operations. In contrast, the managers of the remaining two divisions will see the change as good news because, under the company-wide cost of capital system, they have been rejecting projects earning more than their market-based costs of capital (8 percent and 10 percent for pipelines and refining, respectively) but less than the company's 11 percent cost of capital.

Concept Check

1. What are the implications for a firm's capital investment decisions of using a company-wide cost of capital when the firm has multiple operating divisions that each have unique risk attributes and capital costs?

2. If a firm has decided to move from a situation in which it uses a company-wide cost of capital to divisional costs of capital, what problems is it likely to encounter?

Finance and the Multinational Firm: Why Do Interest Rates Differ Between Countries?[5]

 6 Calculate equivalent interest rates for different countries.

If borrowers and lenders can freely obtain money in one country and invest it in another, why are interest rates not the same the world over? Stated somewhat differently, if capital markets are fully integrated and money flows to the highest rate of interest, it would seem that the forces of competition would make interest rates the same for a borrower with a given amount of risk.

Let's consider a hypothetical example to see how this might work. Assume that a U.S. firm can borrow 1,000 yen in Japan for 5 percent interest, paying back 1,050 yen in 1 year. Alternatively, the U.S. firm can borrow an equivalent amount in the United States and pay 15.5 percent interest. Why the big difference? Is capital 10.5 percent cheaper in Japan, and if so, why don't U.S. firms simply switch to the Japanese capital market for their funds? The answer, as we will now illustrate, lies in the differences in the anticipated rates of inflation for Japan versus the United States.

Although it was not obvious in the preceding example, we assumed a zero rate of inflation for the Japanese economy and a 10 percent rate of inflation for the U.S. economy.

CAN YOU DO IT?

EVALUATING INTEREST RATE PARITY ACROSS COUNTRIES

The rate of interest on a 1-year Treasury bill was 5 percent at the end of 2007, and the corresponding rate of interest on a 1-year note issued by the Brazilian government was 18 percent. The international Fisher effect states that the real rate of interest is the same in both countries.

If the real rate is equal to 2 percent, what are the rates of inflation in the two countries? What is the ratio of 1 plus the nominal rates of interest in the two countries? What is the corresponding ratio of 1 plus the rate of inflation in the two countries?

---

[5]This section is from W. Carl Kester and Timothy A. Luehrman, "What Makes You Think U.S. Capital Is So Expensive?" *Journal of Applied Corporate Finance* (Summer 1992): pp. 29–41. Reprinted with permission.

DID YOU GET IT?

EVALUATING INTEREST RATE PARITY ACROSS COUNTRIES

The international Fisher theory of interest rate parity states that the real rate of interest should be the same across countries but nominal rates across countries will differ as a result of differential rates of anticipated inflation. Thus, for the U.S.–Brazil example, we estimate the ratio of 1 plus the nominal rates of interest as follows (where the U.S. is in the numerator):

$$\frac{(1 + 0.05)}{(1 + 0.18)} = 0.8898$$

Using the Fisher model to estimate the rates of inflation impounded in the nominal rates of interest for the United States and Brazil, and where the real rate is assumed to be 2 percent in both countries, we get estimated inflation for the United States equal to 2.94 percent and 15.69 percent for Brazil. The ratio of 1 plus these two rates of inflation then equals:

$$\frac{(1 + 0.0294)}{(1 + 0.1569)} = 0.8898$$

With a zero anticipated rate of inflation, the nominal rate of interest in Japan (the rate we see quoted in the financial press) is equal to the real rate of 5 percent.[6] Under these assumptions, the nominal rate in the United States can be calculated using the Fisher model as follows:

$$\text{U.S. nominal rate of interest} = (1 + \text{real rate, U.S.})(1 + \text{inflation rate, U.S.}) - 1$$

$$= (1.05)(1.10) - 1 = 0.155, \text{ or } 15.5\%$$

To understand the reason for the different interest rates in Japan and the United States, we must extend the Fisher model to its international counterpart.

Rearranging terms, we get the following relationship between nominal interest rates in the domestic and foreign country and the differences in anticipated inflation in the two countries:

$$r_{n,b} - r_{n,f} = i_b - i_f \tag{11}$$

Economists have formalized the relationship between interest rates of different countries in the interest rate parity theorem. This theorem is as follows:

$$\frac{(1 + r_{n,b})}{(1 + r_{n,f})} = \frac{E_1}{E_0} \tag{12}$$

where $r_{n,b}$ is the domestic one-period rate of interest, $r_{n,f}$ is the corresponding rate of interest in a foreign country, E_0 and E_1 are the exchange rates corresponding to the current period (i.e., the spot exchange rate) and one period hence (i.e., the one-period forward exchange rate).

Thus, differences in observed nominal rates of interest should equal differences in the expected rates of inflation between the two countries. This means that when we compare the interest rates for similar loans in two countries and they are not the same, we should immediately suspect that the expected rates of inflation for the two economies differ by an amount roughly equal to the interest rate differential.

To illustrate, let's consider the previous example, in which the domestic one-period interest rate $(r_{n,b})$ is 15.5 percent, the Japanese rate of interest $(r_{n,f})$ is 5 percent, the spot exchange ratio (E_0) is \$1 to 1 yen, and the forward exchange rate (E_1) is \$1.10 to 1 yen. Substituting into equation (12) produces the following result:

$$\frac{(1 + 0.155)}{(1 + 0.05)} = \frac{1.1}{1} = 1.10$$

---

[6]The real rate of interest is simply the rate of interest that is earned where the expected rate of inflation is zero.

The key thing to note here is that nominal interest rates are tied to exchange rates, and, as we learned earlier, differences in nominal rates of interest are tied to expected rates of inflation.

Why would we expect the interest rate parity relationship to hold? The answer lies in the fact that there are investors who stand ready to engage in arbitrage (trading) to enforce this relationship (within the bounds of transaction costs). Formally, we rely on the fundamental dictum of an efficient market (the law of one price). Very simply, the exchange-adjusted prices of identical loans must be within transaction costs of equality or the opportunity exists for traders to buy the low-cost loan and sell the higher-priced loan for a profit.

Summary

In this book we learned about the connection between risk and investor required rates of return. Moreover, in previous chapters we calculated investor required rates of return for bondholders and stockholders. We combined these individual costs of funds from borrowed and owners into a single cost of capital for the firm as a whole. This required rate of return for the firm is a blend of the required rates of return of all investors that we will estimate using a weighted average of the individual rates of return called the firm's weighted average cost of capital or simply the firm's cost of capital. Just like any cost of doing business, the firm must earn at least this cost if it is to create value for its owners.

 Describe the concepts underlying the firm's cost of capital (technically, its weighted average cost of capital) and the purpose for its calculation.

The investor's required rate of return must be adjusted for the flotation costs incurred in selling new securities to get an estimate of the firm's cost of capital. For debt or bonds the after-tax cost of capital is calculated as follows:

 Calculate the after-tax cost of debt, preferred stock, and common equity.

$$\text{Net proceeds per bond} = \frac{\text{interest paid in year 1}}{\left(1 + \dfrac{\text{cost of debt capital or } k_d}{}\right)^1} + \frac{\text{interest paid in year 2}}{\left(1 + \dfrac{\text{cost of debt capital or } k_d}{}\right)^2}$$

$$+ \frac{\text{interest paid in year 3}}{\left(1 + \dfrac{\text{cost of debt capital or } k_d}{}\right)^3} + \frac{\text{principal}}{\left(1 + \dfrac{\text{cost of debt capital or } k_d}{}\right)^3} \qquad (2)$$

After solving equation (2) for the cost of debt, k_d, we adjust this before-tax cost of financing to an after-tax cost by multiplying it by one minus the corporate tax rate.

The cost of preferred stock financing (k_{ps}) is calculated as follows:

$$\text{Cost of preferred stock } (k_{ps}) = \frac{\text{preferred stock dividend}}{\text{net proceeds per preferred share}} \qquad (5)$$

The after-tax cost of common equity can be calculated in one of two ways. The first involves the use of the dividend growth model of stock valuation introduced, i.e.,

$$\text{Cost of common stock } (k_{cs}) = \frac{\text{common stock dividend for year 1 } (D_1)}{\text{price of common stock}}$$

$$+ \frac{\text{growth rate in dividends } (g)}{} \qquad (8)$$

The second method for estimating the cost of common equity involves the use of the capital asset pricing model (CAPM), which we first discussed. There we learned that the CAPM provides a basis for evaluating investors' required rates of return on common equity, r_m, using three variables:

1. The risk-free rate, r_f
2. The systematic risk of the common stock's returns relative to the market as a whole, or the stock's beta coefficient, β

3. The market-risk premium, which is equal to the difference in the expected rate of return for the market as a whole—that is, the expected rate of return for the "average security" minus the risk-free rate, $r_m - r_f$

The CAPM is written as follows:

$$k_c = r_f + \beta(r_m - r_f) \tag{9}$$

 3 Calculate a firm's weighted average cost of capital.

We found that all of the variables on the right side of equation (9) could be obtained from public sources for larger, publicly traded firms. However, for privately held firms, the CAPM is more difficult to apply in the estimation of investor-required rates of return.

The firm's weighted average cost of capital, k_{wacc}, can be defined as follows:

$$k_{wacc} = w_d k_d(1 - T_c) + w_{ps} k_{ps} + w_{cs} k_{cs} + w_{ncs} k_{ncs} \tag{10}$$

where the terms in equation (10) are defined as follows:

k_{wacc} = the weighted average cost of capital
w_d = the weight associated with debt financing (i.e., proportion of the total capital that is financed using debt)
w_{ps} = the weight associated with preferred stock financing (i.e., the proportion of the total capital that is financed using preferred stock)
w_{cs} = the weight associated with common stock financing resulting from the retention of firm earnings (i.e., the proportion of the total capital that is financed by retaining and reinvesting earnings)
w_{ncs} = the weight associated with new common stock financing (i.e., the proportion of the total capital that is financed through the sale of common stock)
k_d = the cost of debt financing
k_{ps} = the cost of preferred stock financing
k_{cs} = the cost of common stock financing through the retention of earnings
k_{ncs} = the cost of common stock financing through the sale of a new issue of common stock
T_c = the corporate tax rate

Note that the w terms represent the market value weights associated with the firm's use of each of its sources of financing. We are calculating a weighted average of the costs of each of the firm's sources of capital where the weights reflect the firm's relative use of each source.

The weights used to calculate k_{wacc} should theoretically reflect the market values of each capital source as a fraction of the total market value of all capital sources (i.e., the market value of the firm). However, the analyst frequently finds the use of market value weights is impractical, either because the firm's securities are not publicly traded or because all capital sources are not used in proportion to their makeup of the firm's target capital structure in every financing episode. In these instances, we found that the weights should be the firm's long-term target financial mix.

 4 Describe the procedure used by PepsiCo to estimate the cost of capital for a multidivisional firm.

The firm's weighted average cost of capital will reflect the operating or business risk of the firm's present set of investments and the financial risk attendant upon the way in which those assets are financed. Therefore, this cost of capital estimate is useful only for evaluating new investment opportunities that have similar business and financial risks. Remember that the primary determinant of the cost of capital for a particular investment is the risk of the investment itself, not the source of the capital. Multidivisional firms such as PepsiCo resolve this problem by calculating a different cost of capital for each of their major operating divisions.

 5 Use the cost of capital to evaluate new investment opportunities.

If borrowers and lenders can freely choose where they borrow and lend money, why aren't interest rates the same all over the world? The answer lies in differences in the anticipated rates of inflation between countries. In fact, the international Fisher effect states that the differences in the rates of interest charged for the same loan in two different countries is equal to the difference in the anticipated rates of inflation in the countries. So, rates of interest are equal around the world only after we account for differences in rates of inflation between countries. Of course, the international Fisher effect does not hold exactly due to political and other risk considerations that can serve to restrict capital flow between countries. However, the Fisher effect does provide a useful starting point for understanding why there are differences in interest rates throughout the world.

6 Calculate equivalent interest rates for different countries.

Key Terms

Capital structure
Financial policy

Weighted average cost
of capital

Review Questions

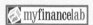

All Review Questions and Study Problems are available in MyFinanceLab.

9-1. Define the term *cost of capital*.

9-2. Why do we calculate a firm's weighted average cost of capital?

9-3. In computing the cost of capital, which sources of capital do we consider?

9-4. How does a firm's tax rate affect its cost of capital? What is the effect of the flotation costs associated with a new security issue?

9-5. a. Distinguish between internal common equity and new common stock.

    b. Why is a cost associated with internal common equity?

    c. Describe the two approaches that could be used in computing the cost of common equity.

9-6. What might we expect to see in practice in the relative costs of different sources of capital?

Self-Test Problems

(The solutions to the following problems are provided at the end of the chapter.)

ST-1. (*Individual or component costs of capital*) Compute the cost for the following sources of financing:

    a. A $1,000 par value bond with a market price of $970 and a coupon interest rate of 10 percent. Flotation costs for a new issue would be approximately 5 percent. The bonds mature in 10 years and the corporate tax rate is 34 percent.

    b. A preferred stock selling for $100 with an annual dividend payment of $8. The flotation cost will be $9 per share. The company's marginal tax rate is 30 percent.

    c. Retained earnings totaling $4.8 million. The price of the common stock is $75 per share, and the dividend per share was $9.80 last year. The dividend is not expected to change in the future.

    d. New common stock when the most recent dividend was $2.80. The company's dividends per share should continue to increase at an 8 percent growth rate into the indefinite future. The market price of the stock is currently $53; however, flotation costs of $6 per share are expected if the new stock is issued.

ST-2. (*Weighted average cost of capital*) The capital structure for the Carion Corporation is provided here. The company plans to maintain its debt structure in the future. If the firm has a 5.5 percent after-tax cost of debt, a 13.5 percent cost of preferred stock, and an 18 percent cost of common stock, what is the firm's weighted average cost of capital?

CAPITAL STRUCTURE ($000)	
Bonds	$1,083
Preferred stock	268
Common stock	3,681
	$5,032

ST-3. (*Weighted average cost of capital*) ABBC Inc. operates a very successful chain of yogurt and coffee shops spread across the southwestern part of the United States and needs to raise funds for its planned expansion into the Northwest. The firm's balance sheet at the close of 2009 appeared as follows:

Cash	$ 2,010,000		
Accounts receivable	4,580,000		
Inventories	1,540,000	Long-term debt	$ 8,141,000
Net property, plant, and equipment	32,575,000	Common equity	32,564,000
Total assets	$40,705,000	Total debt and equity	$40,705,000

At present the firm's common stock is selling for a price equal to 2.5 times its book value, and the firm's bonds are selling at par. The company's management estimates that the market requires an

18 percent return on its common stock, the firm's bonds command a yield to maturity of 8 percent, and the firm faces a tax rate of 35 percent. At the end of the previous year ABBC's common stock was selling for a price of 2.5 times its book value, and its bonds were trading near their par value.

   a. What does ABBC's capital structure look like?

   b. What is ABBC's weighted average cost of capital?

   c. If ABBC's stock price were to rise such that it sold at 3.5 times book value and the cost of equity fell to 15 percent, what would the firm's weighted average cost of capital be (assuming the cost of debt and tax rate do not change)?

ST-4. (*Divisional costs of capital and investment decisions*) Belton Oil and Gas Inc. is a Houston-based independent oil and gas firm. In the past Belton's managers have used a single firmwide cost of capital of 13 percent to evaluate new investments. However, the firm has long recognized that its exploration and production division is significantly more risky than the pipeline and transportation division. In fact, comparable firms to Belton's E&P division have equity betas of about 1.7, whereas distribution companies typically have equity betas of only 0.8. Given the importance of getting the cost of capital estimate as close to correct as possible, the firm's chief financial officer has asked you to prepare cost of capital estimates for each of the two divisions. The requisite information needed to accomplish your task is contained here:

◆ The cost of debt financing is 7 percent before taxes of 35 percent. However, if the E&P division were to borrow based on its projects alone, the cost of debt would probably be 9 percent, and the pipeline division could borrow at 5.5 percent. You may assume these costs of debt are after any flotation costs the firm might incur.

◆ The risk-free rate of interest on long-term U.S. Treasury bonds is currently 4.8 percent, and the market-risk premium has averaged 7.3 percent over the past several years.

◆ The E&P division adheres to a target debt ratio of 10 percent, whereas the pipeline division utilizes 40 percent borrowed funds.

◆ The firm has sufficient internally generated funds such that no new stock will have to be sold to raise equity financing.

   a. Estimate the divisional costs of capital for the E&P and pipeline divisions.

   b. What are the implications of using a company-wide cost of capital to evaluate new investment proposals in light of the differences in the costs of capital you estimated previously?

Study Problems

9-1. (*Individual or component costs of capital*) Compute the cost of the following:

   a. A bond that has $1,000 par value (face value) and a contract or coupon interest rate of 11 percent. A new issue would have a flotation cost of 5 percent of the $1,125 market value. The bonds mature in 10 years. The firm's average tax rate is 30 percent and its marginal tax rate is 34 percent.

   b. A new common stock issue that paid a $1.80 dividend last year. The par value of the stock is $15, and earnings per share have grown at a rate of 7 percent per year. This growth rate is expected to continue into the foreseeable future. The company maintains a constant dividend–earnings ratio of 30 percent. The price of this stock is now $27.50, but 5 percent flotation costs are anticipated.

   c. Internal common equity when the current market price of the common stock is $43. The expected dividend this coming year should be $3.50, increasing thereafter at a 7 percent annual growth rate. The corporation's tax rate is 34 percent.

   d. A preferred stock paying a 9 percent dividend on a $150 par value. If a new issue is offered, flotation costs will be 12 percent of the current price of $175.

   e. A bond selling to yield 12 percent after flotation costs, but before adjusting for the marginal corporate tax rate of 34 percent. In other words, 12 percent is the rate that equates the net proceeds from the bond with the present value of the future cash flows (principal and interest).

9-2. (*Cost of equity*) Salte Corporation is issuing new common stock at a market price of $27. Dividends last year were $1.45 and are expected to grow at an annual rate of 6 percent forever. Flotation costs will be 6 percent of market price. What is Salte's cost of equity?

9-3. (*Cost of debt*) Belton is issuing a $1,000 par value bond that pays 7 percent annual interest and matures in 15 years. Investors are willing to pay $958 for the bond. Flotation costs will be 11 percent of market value. The company is in an 18 percent tax bracket. What will be the firm's after-tax cost of debt on the bond?

9-4. (*Cost of preferred stock*) The preferred stock of Julian Industries sells for $36 and pays $3.00 in dividends. The net price of the security after issuance costs is $32.50. What is the cost of capital for the preferred stock?

9-5. (*Cost of debt*) The Zephyr Corporation is contemplating a new investment to be financed 33 percent from debt. The firm could sell new $1,000 par value bonds at a net price of $945. The coupon interest rate is 12 percent, and the bonds would mature in 15 years. If the company is in a 34 percent tax bracket, what is the after-tax cost of capital to Zephyr for bonds?

9-6. (*Cost of preferred stock*) Your firm is planning to issue preferred stock. The stock sells for $115; however, if new stock is issued, the company would receive only $98. The par value of the stock is $100, and the dividend rate is 14 percent. What is the cost of capital for the stock to your firm?

9-7. (*Cost of internal equity*) Pathos Co.'s common stock is currently selling for $23.80. Dividends paid last year were $0.70. Flotation costs on issuing stock will be 10 percent of market price. The dividends and earnings per share are projected to have an annual growth rate of 15 percent. What is the cost of internal common equity for Pathos?

9-8. (*Cost of equity*) The common stock for the Bestsold Corporation sells for $58. If a new issue is sold, the flotation costs are estimated to be 8 percent. The company pays 50 percent of its earnings in dividends, and a $4 dividend was recently paid. Earnings per share 5 years ago were $5. Earnings are expected to continue to grow at the same annual rate in the future as during the past 5 years. The firm's marginal tax rate is 34 percent. Calculate the cost of (a) internal common equity and (b) external common equity.

9-9. (*Cost of debt*) Sincere Stationery Corporation needs to raise $500,000 to improve its manufacturing plant. It has decided to issue a $1,000 par value bond with a 14 percent annual coupon rate and a 10-year maturity. The investors require a 9 percent rate of return.

    a. Compute the market value of the bonds.

    b. What will the net price be if flotation costs are 10.5 percent of the market price?

    c. How many bonds will the firm have to issue to receive the needed funds?

    d. What is the firm's after-tax cost of debt if its average tax rate is 25 percent and its marginal tax rate is 34 percent?

9-10. (*Cost of debt*)

    a. Rework problem 9-9 as follows: Assume an 8 percent coupon rate. What effect does changing the coupon rate have on the firm's after-tax cost of capital?

    b. Why is there a change?

9-11. (*Divisional costs of capital*) LPT Inc. is an integrated oil company headquartered in Dallas, Texas. The company has three operating divisions: oil exploration and production (commonly referred to as E&P), pipelines, and refining. Historically, LPT did not spend a great deal of time thinking about the opportunity costs of capital for each of its divisions and used a company-wide weighted average cost of capital of 14 percent for all new capital investment projects. Recent changes in its businesses have made it abundantly clear to LPT's management that this is not a reasonable approach. For example, investors demand a much higher expected rate of return for exploration and production ventures than for pipeline investments. Although LPT's management agrees, in principle at least, that different operating divisions should face an opportunity cost of capital that reflects their individual risk characteristics, they are not in agreement about whether a move toward divisional costs of capital is a good idea based on practical considerations.

    a. Pete Jennings is the chief operating officer for the E&P division, and he is concerned that going to a system of divisional costs of capital may restrain his ability to undertake very promising exploration opportunities. He argues that the firm really should be concerned about finding those opportunities that offer the highest possible rate of return on invested capital. Pete contends that using the firm's scarce capital to take on the most promising projects would lead to the greatest increase in shareholder value. Do you agree with Pete? Why or why not?

    b. The pipeline division manager, Donna Selma, has long argued that charging her division the company-wide cost of capital of 14 percent severely penalizes her opportunities to increase shareholder value. Do you agree with Donna? Explain.

9-12. (*Weighted average cost of capital*) Crawford Enterprises is a publicly held company located in Arnold, Kansas. The firm began as a small tool and die shop but grew over its 35-year life to become a leading supplier of metal fabrication equipment used in the farm tractor industry. At the close of 2009 the firm's balance sheet appeared as follows:

Cash	$ 540,000		
Accounts receivable	4,580,000		
Inventories	7,400,000	Long-term debt	$12,590,000
Net property, plant, and equipment	18,955,000	Common equity	18,885,000
Total assets	$31,475,000	Total debt and equity	$31,475,000

At present the firm's common stock is selling for a price equal to its book value, and the firm's bonds are selling at par. Crawford's managers estimate that the market requires a 15 percent return on its common stock, the firm's bonds command a yield to maturity of 8 percent, and the firm faces a tax rate of 34 percent.

    a. What is Crawford's weighted average cost of capital?

    b. If Crawford's stock price were to rise such that it sold at 1.5 times book value, causing the cost of equity to fall to 13 percent, what would the firm's cost of capital be (assuming the cost of debt and tax rate do not change)?

9-13. (*Divisional costs of capital and investment decisions*) In May of this year Newcastle Mfg. Company's capital investment review committee received two major investment proposals. One of the proposals was put forth by the firm's domestic manufacturing division, and the other came from the firm's distribution company. Both proposals promise internal rates of return equal to approximately 12 percent. In the past Newcastle has used a single firmwide cost of capital to evaluate new investments. However, managers have long recognized that the manufacturing division is significantly more risky than the distribution division. In fact, comparable firms in the manufacturing division have equity betas of about 1.6, whereas distribution companies typically have equity betas of only 1.1. Given the size of the two proposals, Newcastle's management feels it can undertake only one, so it wants to be sure that it is taking on the more promising investment. Given the importance of getting the cost of capital estimate as close to correct as possible, the firm's chief financial officer has asked you to prepare cost of capital estimates for each of the two divisions. The requisite information needed to accomplish your task is contained here:

   ◆ The cost of debt financing is 8 percent before taxes of 35 percent. You may assume this cost of debt is after any flotation costs the firm might incur.

   ◆ The risk-free rate of interest on long-term U.S. Treasury bonds is currently 4.8 percent, and the market-risk premium has averaged 7.3 percent over the past several years.

   ◆ Both divisions adhere to target debt ratios of 40 percent.

   ◆ The firm has sufficient internally generated funds such that no new stock will have to be sold to raise equity financing.

    a. Estimate the divisional costs of capital for the manufacturing and distribution divisions.

    b. Which of the two projects should the firm undertake (assuming it cannot do both due to labor and other nonfinancial restraints)? Discuss.

Mini Case

The balance sheet that follows indicates the capital structure for Nealon Inc. Flotation costs are (a) 15 percent of market value for a new bond issue, and (b) $2.01 per share for preferred stock. The dividends for common stock were $2.50 last year and are projected to have an annual growth rate of 6 percent. The firm is in a 34 percent tax bracket. What is the weighted average cost of capital if the firm's finances are in the following proportions?

TYPE OF FINANCING	PERCENTAGE OF FUTURE FINANCING
Bonds (8%, $1,000 par, 16-year maturity)	38%
Preferred stock (5,000 shares outstanding,	
$50 par, $1.50 dividend)	15%
Common equity	47%
Total	100%

a. Market prices are $1,035 for bonds, $19 for preferred stock, and $35 for common stock. There will be sufficient internal common equity funding (i.e., retained earnings) available such that the firm does not plan to issue new common stock. Calculate the firm's weighted average cost of capital.

b. In part a we assumed that Nealon would have sufficient retained earnings such that it would not need to sell additional common stock to finance its new investments. Consider the situation now, when Nealon's retained earnings anticipated for the coming year are expected to fall short of the equity requirement of 47 percent of new capital raised. Consequently, the firm foresees the possibility that new common shares will have to be issued. To facilitate the sale of shares, Nealon's investment banker has advised management that they should expect a price discount of approximately 7 percent, or $2.45 per share. Under these terms, the new shares should provide net proceeds of about $32.55. What is Nealon's cost of equity capital when new shares are sold, and what is the weighted average cost of the added funds involved in the issuance of new shares?

Self-Test Solutions

The following notations are used in this group of problems:

k_d = the before-tax cost of debt

k_{ps} = the cost of preferred stock

k_{cs} = the cost of internal common equity

k_{ncs} = the cost of new common stock

T_c = the marginal tax rate

D_t = the dollar dividend per share, where D_0 is the most recently paid dividend and D_1 is the forthcoming dividend

P_0 = the market price of a security

NP_0 = the value of security less any flotation costs incurred in issuing the security

SS-1.

a. $$\$921.50 = \sum_{t=1}^{n} \frac{\$100}{(1 + k_d)^t} + \frac{\$1,000}{(1 + k_d)^{10}}$$

RATE	VALUE
11%	$940.90
k_d%	$921.50
12%	$887.00

$19.40

$53.90

$$k_d = 0.11 + \left(\frac{\$19.40}{\$53.90}\right)0.01 = 0.1136 = 11.36\%$$

$$k_{d(1-t)} = 11.36\%(1 - 0.34) = 7.50\%$$

b. $k_{ps} = \dfrac{D}{NP_0}$

$$k_{ps} = \frac{\$8}{\$100 - \$9} = 0.0879 = 8.79\%$$

c. $k_{cs} = \dfrac{D_1}{P_0} + g$

$$k_{cs} = \frac{\$9.80}{\$75} + 0\% = 0.1307 = 13.07\%$$

d. $k_{ncs} = \dfrac{D_1}{NP_0} + g$

$$k_{ncs} = \frac{\$2.80(1 + 0.08)}{\$53 - \$6} + 0.08 = 0.1443 = 14.43\%$$

SS-2.

Carion Corporation—Weighted Cost of Capital

	CAPITAL STRUCTURE	WEIGHTS	INDIVIDUAL COST	WEIGHTED COSTS
Bonds	$1,083	0.2152	5.5%	1.18%
Preferred stock	268	0.0533	13.5%	0.72%
Common stock	3,681	0.7315	18.0%	13.17%
	$5,032	1.0000		15.07%

SS-3. Given:

Cash	$ 2,010,000		
Accounts receivable	4,580,000		
Inventories	1,540,000	Long-term debt	$ 8,141,000
Net property, plant, and equipment	32,575,000	Common equity	32,564,000
Total assets	$40,705,000	Total debt and equity	$40,705,000
Cost of debt financing	8%		
Cost of equity	18%		
Tax rate	35%		
Market-to-book ratio	2.50		

a. *What does ABBC's capital structure look like?* Note that because the market-to-book ratio (market value of equity to book value of equity) is 2.5, the market value of the firm's equity is 2.5 × $32,564,000, or $81,410,000. The market value of debt is assumed to equal its book value. Thus,

COMPONENT	MARKET VALUE BALANCE SHEET	PROPORTION	AFTER-TAX COST	PRODUCT
Long-term debt	$ 8,141,000	9%	4.88%	0.44%
Common equity	81,410,000	91%	18.00%	16.38%
	$89,551,000			16.82%

b. *What is ABBC's weighted average cost of capital?* Based on the above calculations, the answer is 16.8 percent.

c. *If ABBC's stock price were to rise such that it sold at 3.5 times book value and the cost of equity fell to 15 percent, what would the firm's weighted average cost of capital be (assuming the cost of debt and tax rate do not change)?*

Cost of debt financing	8%
Cost of equity	15%
Tax rate	35%
Market-to-book ratio	3.50

COMPONENT	MARKET VALUE BALANCE SHEET	PROPORTION	AFTER-TAX COST	PRODUCT
Long-term debt	$ 8,141,000	7%	5.20%	0.36%
Common equity	113,974,000	93%	15.00%	13.95%
	$122,115,000			14.31%

SS-4. Given:

	E&P DIVISION	PIPELINE DIVISION
Equity beta	1.7	0.8
Tax rate	35.0%	35.0%
Cost of debt	9.0%	5.5%
Debt ratio	10.0%	40.0%
Risk-free rate	4.8%	
Market-risk premium	7.3%	

a.

EXPLORATION AND DEVELOPMENT DIVISION			
COMPONENT	PROPORTION	AFTER-TAX COST	PRODUCT
Debt	10.0%	5.9%	0.6%
Equity	90.0%	17.2%	15.5%
			16.1%

PIPELINE DIVISION			
COMPONENT	PROPORTION	AFTER-TAX COST	PRODUCT
Debt	40.0%	3.6%	1.4%
Equity	60.0%	10.6%	6.4%
			7.8%

b. The very dramatic differences in the two divisional cost of capital estimates underscore the importance of carefully analyzing the capital costs that correspond as closely as possible to the riskiness of the use for which the funds are being requested. For example, using a 13 percent cost of capital for the firm as a whole leads to accepting E&P projects that fall well below the true cost of raising funds for these types of investments (16.1 percent). Similarly, using the 13 percent company-wide cost of capital will result in the rejection of value-enhancing investments that earn in excess of the 7.8 percent cost of capital that is appropriate to the pipeline division.

Capital-Budgeting Techniques and Practice

From Chapter 10 of *Foundations of Finance*, 7/e. Arthur J. Keown. John D. Martin. J. William Petty. Copyright © 2011 by Pearson Education.
Published by Prentice Hall. All rights reserved.

Capital-Budgeting Techniques and Practice

Learning Objectives

After reading this chapter, you should be able to:

1. **Discuss** the difficulty encountered in finding profitable projects in competitive markets and the importance of the search.

2. **Determine** whether a new project should be accepted or rejected using the payback period, the net present value, the profitability index, and the internal rate of return.

3. **Explain** how the capital-budgeting decision process changes when a dollar limit is placed on the capital budget.

4. **Discuss** the problems encountered in project ranking.

5. **Explain** the importance of ethical considerations in capital-budgeting decisions.

6. **Discuss** the trends in the use of different capital-budgeting criteria.

7. **Explain** how foreign markets provide opportunities for finding new capital-budgeting projects.

Back in 1955, the Walt Disney Company changed the face of entertainment when it opened Disneyland, its first theme park in Anaheim, California, at a cost of $17.5 million. Since then Disney has opened theme parks in Orlando, Florida; Tokyo, Japan; Paris, France, and in September 2005, 香港迪士尼樂園, or Hong Kong Disneyland, was opened. This $3.5 billion project, with much of that money provided by the Hong Kong government, was opened in the hopes of reaching what has largely been an untapped Chinese market. For Disney, a market this size was simply too large to pass up.

Hong Kong Disneyland opened spectacularly, with more than 250,000 annual flowering plants, 15,000 canopy trees, plenty of rides and attractions, and, as its centerpiece, Sleeping Beauty's castle, complete with its trademark blue-pointed turret. To boost visitors, more attractions, including the Pirates of the Caribbean, It's a Small World, Peter Pan's Flight, Big Thunder Mountain Railroad, and the Haunted Mansion, were all added. Still, Hong Kong Disneyland cannot be termed a success, steadily losing money since it opened.

For Disney, keeping its theme parks and resorts division healthy is extremely important because this division accounts for over one-quarter of the company's revenues. Certainly, there are opportunities for Disney in China; with a population of 1.26 billion people, it accounts for 20 percent of the entire world's total population and Hong Kong Disneyland was supposed to provide Disney with a foothold in the potentially lucrative market in China. While Hong Kong Disneyland has not lived up to Disney's expectations, Disney has not given up and in 2009 a proposal by Disney to build Shanghai Disneyland, scheduled to open by 2014, received approval from the central government. Learning from its mistakes in Hong Kong, Disney's new proposed park would be much larger and easier for Chinese families to visit.

Sunnymok/ChinaFotoPress/Newscom

To say the least, with an investment of close to $6 billion, the outcome of this decision will have a major effect on Disney's future. Whether this was a good or bad decision, only time will tell. The question we will ask in this chapter is: How did Disney go about making this decision to enter the Chinese market and build Hong Kong Disneyland and, after losing money on its Hong Kong venture, how did it go about making the decision to build Shanghai Disneyland? The answer is that the company did it using the decision criteria we will examine in this chapter.

This chapter is actually the first of two chapters dealing with the process of decision making with respect to making investments in fixed assets—that is, should a proposed project be accepted or rejected? We will refer to this process as capital budgeting. In this chapter we will look at the methods used to evaluate new projects. In deciding whether to accept a new project, we will focus on free cash flows. Free cash flows represent the benefits generated from accepting a capital-budgeting proposal. We will assume we know what level of free cash flows is generated by a project and will work on determining whether that project should be accepted. Later on in this book, we will examine what a free cash flow is and how we measure it. We will also look at how risk enters into this process.

Finding Profitable Projects

 Discuss the difficulty encountered in finding profitable projects in competitive markets and the importance of the search.

Without question it is easier to *evaluate profitable projects or investments in fixed assets, a process referred to as* **capital budgeting**, than it is to find them. In competitive markets, generating ideas for profitable projects is extremely difficult. The competition is brisk for new profitable projects, and once they have been uncovered, competitors generally rush in, pushing down prices and profits. For this reason a firm must have a systematic strategy for generating capital-budgeting projects based on these ideas. Without this flow of new projects and ideas, the firm cannot grow or even survive for long. Instead, it will be forced to live off the profits from existing projects with limited lives. So where do these ideas come from for new products, or for ways to improve existing products or make them more profitable? The answer is from inside the firm—from everywhere inside the firm, in fact.

Typically, a firm has a research and development (R&D) department that searches for ways of improving existing products or finding new products. These ideas may come from

capital budgeting the process of decision making with respect to investments made in fixed assets—that is, should a proposed project be accepted or rejected.

within the R&D department or may be based on referral ideas from executives, sales personnel, anyone in the firm, or even customers. For example, at Ford Motor Company before the 1990s, ideas for product improvements had typically been generated in Ford's R&D department. Unfortunately, this strategy was not enough to keep Ford from losing much of its market share to Japanese competitors. In an attempt to cut costs and improve product quality, Ford moved from strict reliance on an R&D department to seeking the input of employees at all levels for new ideas. Bonuses are now provided to workers for their cost-cutting suggestions, and assembly-line personnel who can see the production process from a hands-on point of view are now brought into the hunt for new projects. The effect on Ford has been positive and it helped Ford avoid the bankruptcy problems that befell GM and Chrysler. Although not all suggested projects prove to be profitable, many new ideas generated from within the firm turn out to be good ones.

Another way an existing product can be applied to a new market is illustrated by Kimberly-Clark, the manufacturer of Huggies disposable diapers. The company took its existing diaper product line, made the diapers more waterproof, and began marketing them as disposable swim pants called Little Swimmers. Sara Lee Hosiery boosted its market by expanding its offerings to appeal to more customers and more customer needs. For example, Sara Lee Hosiery introduced Sheer Energy pantyhose for support, Just My Size pantyhose aimed at larger-women sizes, and Silken Mist pantyhose in shades better suited for African American women.

Big investments such as these go a long way toward determining the future of the company, but they don't always work as planned. Just look at Burger King's development of its new french fries. It looked like a slam dunk great idea. Burger King took an uncooked french fry and coated it with a layer of starch that made it crunchier and kept it hot longer. The company spent over $70 million on the new fries, and even gave away 15 million orders on a "Free Fryday." Unfortunately, the product didn't go down with consumers, and Burger King was left to eat the loss. Given the size of the investment we're talking about, you can see why such a decision is so important.

Concept Check

1. Why is it so difficult to find an exceptionally profitable project?

2. Why is the search for new profitable projects so important?

CAUTIONARY TALE

FORGETTING PRINCIPLE 3: RISK REQUIRES A REWARD AND PRINCIPLE 4: MARKET PRICES ARE GENERALLY RIGHT

In the world of investing, you win some, you lose some. A common misconception is that high-risk investments always provide high returns. In fact, there are no guarantees. That's why consistently high returns paid year in and year out from a fund known for its exclusivity and its double-digit rates of return should have given investors pause.

In December of 2008 an investor in the fund, quoted in *Time* magazine, wrote, "All we knew was that my wife's entire family had been in the fund for decades and lived well on the returns, which ranged from 15% to 22%. It was all very secretive and tough to get into, which, looking back, was a brilliant strategy to lure suckers."

The fund in question is the one we now know as the Ponzi scheme orchestrated by Bernard "Bernie" Madoff. A Ponzi scheme is an investment that pays returns to investors from the money they originally invested along with money provided by new investors, rather than any profits earned. A Ponzi scheme is destined to collapse because the payments made exceed any earnings from the investment. Madoff's scam is considered to be the biggest Wall Street fraud ever attempted. Prosecutors estimate the size of the scam as somewhere between $50 billion to $54.8 billion.

In efficient markets, high returns are extremely difficult to achieve in good and bad years. Harry Markopolos, who once worked for one of Madoff's competitors, long suspected that Madoff's returns were simply too good to be true and wrote letters for at least a decade to the Securities and Exchange Commission trying to persuade them to investigate Madoff. As Markopolos observed, one thing that we know from efficient markets is that if an investment promises a return that looks too good to be true, it probably is.

Source: Robert Chew, "How I Got Screwed by Bernie Madoff," *Time*, December 15, 2008, http://www.time.com/time/business/article/0,8599,1866398,00.html.

Capital-Budgeting Decision Criteria

As we explained, when deciding whether to accept a new project, we focus on cash flows because cash flows represent the benefits generated from accepting a capital-budgeting proposal. In this chapter we assume a given cash flow is generated by a project and work on determining whether that project should be accepted.

We consider four commonly used criteria for determining the acceptability of investment proposals. The first one is the least sophisticated in that it does not incorporate the time value of money into its calculations; the other three do take it into account. For the time being, the problem of incorporating risk into the capital-budgeting decision is ignored. In addition, we assume that the appropriate discount rate, required rate of return, or cost of capital is given.

The Payback Period — *Does not include the time value of money*

The **payback period** is the *number of years needed to recover the initial cash outlay related to an investment*. Because this criterion measures how quickly the project will return its original investment, it deals with free cash flows, which measure the true timing of the benefits, rather than accounting profits. Unfortunately, it also ignores the time value of money and does not discount these free cash flows back to the present. Rather, the accept/reject criterion centers on whether the project's payback period is less than or equal to the firm's maximum desired payback period. For example, if a firm's maximum desired payback period is 3 years, and an investment proposal requires an initial cash outlay of $10,000 and yields the following set of annual cash flows, what is its payback period? Should the project be accepted?→ *NO*

payback period the number of years it takes to recapture a project's initial outlay.

How quickly the project will return its original investment.

YEAR	FREE CASH FLOW
1	$2,000
2	4,000
3	3,000
4	3,000
5	9,000

> 6,000
— 9,000
— 12,000

In this case, after 3 years the firm will have recaptured $9,000 on an initial investment of $10,000, leaving $1,000 of the initial investment to be recouped. During the fourth year $3,000 will be returned from this investment, and, assuming it will flow into the firm at a constant rate over the year, it will take one-third of the year ($1,000/$3,000) to recapture the remaining $1,000. Thus, the payback period on this project is 3⅓ years, which is more than the desired payback period. Using the payback period criterion, the firm would reject this project without even considering the $9,000 cash flow in year 5.

Although the payback period is used frequently, it does have some rather obvious drawbacks that are best demonstrated through the use of an example. Consider two investment projects, A and B, which involve an initial cash outlay of $10,000 each and produce the annual cash flows shown in Table 1. Both projects have a payback period of 2 years; therefore, in terms of the payback criterion both are equally acceptable. However, if we had our choice,

TABLE 1 Payback Period Example

	PROJECTS	
	A	B
Initial cash outlay	−$10,000	−$10,000
Annual free cash inflows		
Year 1	$ 6,000	$ 5,000
2	4,000	5,000
3	3,000	0
4	2,000	0
5	1,000	0

it is clear we would select A over B, for at least two reasons. First, regardless of what happens after the payback period, project A returns more of our initial investment to us faster within the payback period ($6,000 in year 1 versus $5,000). Thus, because there is a time value of money, the cash flows occurring within the payback period should not be weighted equally, as they are. In addition, all cash flows that occur after the payback period are ignored. This violates the principle that investors desire more in the way of benefits rather than less—a principle that is difficult to deny, especially when we are talking about money. Finally, the choice of the maximum desired payback period is arbitrary. That is, there is no good reason why the firm should accept projects that have payback periods less than or equal to 3 years rather than 4 years.

Although these deficiencies limit the value of the payback period as a tool for investment evaluation, the payback period has several positive features. First, it deals with cash flows, as opposed to accounting profits, and therefore focuses on the true timing of the project's benefits and costs, even though it does not adjust the cash flows for the time value of money. Second, it is easy to visualize, quickly understood, and easy to calculate. Third, the payback period may make sense for the capital-constrained firm, that is, the firm that needs funds and is having problems raising additional money. These firms need cash flows early on to allow them to continue in business and to take advantage of future investments. Finally, although the payback period has serious deficiencies, it is often used as a rough screening device to eliminate projects whose returns do not materialize until later years. This method emphasizes the earliest returns, which in all likelihood are less uncertain, and provides for the liquidity needs of the firm. Although its advantages are certainly significant, its disadvantages severely limit its value as a discriminating capital-budgeting criterion.

Method #1

discounted payback period the number of years it takes to recapture a project's initial outlay using discounted cash flows.

$V_0 \rightarrow \$10,000$
$RR = 17\%$

Discounted Payback Period   To deal with the criticism that the payback period ignores the time value of money, some firms use the discounted payback period approach. The **discounted payback period** method is similar to the traditional payback period except that it uses discounted free cash flows rather than actual undiscounted free cash flows in calculating the payback period. The discounted payback period is defined as *the number of years needed to recover the initial cash outlay from the discounted free cash flows*. The accept-reject criterion then becomes whether the project's discounted payback period is less than or equal to the firm's maximum desired discounted payback period. Using the assumption that the required rate of return on projects A and B illustrated in Table 1 is 17 percent, the discounted cash flows from these projects are given in Table 2. On project A, after three years, only $74 of the initial outlay remains to be recaptured, whereas year 4 brings in a discounted free cash flow of $1,068. Thus, if the $1,068 comes in a constant rate over the year, it will take about 7/100s of the year ($74/$1,068) to recapture the remaining $74. The discounted payback period for project A is 3.07 years, calculated as follows:

discounted payback period$_A$ = 3.0 + $74/$1,068 = 3.07 years

[handwritten: years   remainder]

If project A's discounted payback period was less than the firm's maximum desired discounted payback period, then project A would be accepted. Project B, however, does not have a discounted payback period because it never fully recovers the project's initial cash outlay, and thus should be rejected. The major problem with the discounted payback period comes in setting the firm's maximum desired discounted payback period. This is an arbitrary decision that affects which projects are accepted and which ones are rejected. In addition, cash flows that occur after the discounted payback period are not included in the analysis. Thus, although the discounted payback period is superior to the traditional payback period, in that it accounts for the time value of money in its calculations, its use is limited by the arbitrariness of the process used to select the maximum desired payback period. Moreover, as we will soon see, the net present value criterion is theoretically superior and no more difficult to calculate.

The Net Present Value

Method #2

net present value (*NPV*) the present value of an investment's annual free cash flows less the investment's initial outlay.

The **net present value (*NPV*)** of an investment proposal is equal to the *present value of its annual free cash flows less the investment's initial outlay*. The net present value can be expressed as follows:

TABLE 2 Discounted Payback, Period Example Using a 17 Percent Required Rate of Return			
PROJECT A			
Year	Undiscounted Free Cash Flows	Discounted Free Cash Flows at 17%	Cumulative Discounted Free Cash Flows
0	−$10,000	−$10,000	−$10,000
1	6,000	5,130	−4,870
2	4,000	2,924	−1,946
3	3,000	1,872	−74
4	2,000	1,068	994
5	1,000	456	1,450
PROJECT B			
Year	Undiscounted Free Cash Flows	Discounted Free Cash Flows at 17%	Cumulative Discounted Free Cash Flows
0	−$10,000	−$10,000	−$10,000
1	5,000	4,275	−5,725
2	5,000	3,655	−2,070
3	0	0	−2,070
4	0	0	−2,070
5	0	0	−2,070

NPV = (present value of all the future annual free cash flows) − (the initial cash outlay)

$$= \frac{FCF_1}{(1 + k)^1} + \frac{FCF_2}{(1 + k)^2} + \cdots + \frac{FCF_n}{(1 + k)^n} - IO \qquad (1)$$

where FCF_t = the annual free cash flow in time period t (this can take on either positive or negative values)

k = the firm's required rate of return or cost of capital[1]

IO = the initial cash outlay

n = the project's expected life

If any of the future free cash flows (FCFs) are cash outflows rather than inflows, say for example that there is another large investment in year 2 that results in the FCF_2 being negative, then the FCF_2 would take on a negative sign when calculating the project's net present value. In effect, the NPV can be thought of as the present value of the benefits minus the present value of the costs,

$$NPV = PV_{benefits} - PV_{costs}$$

A project's NPV measures the net value of the investment proposal in terms of today's dollars. Because all cash flows are discounted back to the present, comparing the difference between the present value of the annual cash flows and the investment outlay recognizes the time value of money. The difference between the present value of the annual cash flows and the initial outlay determines the net value of the investment proposal. Whenever the project's NPV is greater than or equal to zero, we will accept the project; whenever the NPV is negative, we will reject the project. If the project's NPV is zero, then it returns the required rate of return and should be accepted. This accept/reject criterion is represented as follows:

$NPV \geq 0.0$: accept

$NPV < 0.0$: reject

> **REMEMBER YOUR PRINCIPLES**
>
> **Principle** The final three capital-budgeting criteria all incorporate **Principle 2: Money Has a Time Value** in their calculations. If we are to make rational business decisions, we must recognize that money has a time value. In examining the following three capital-budgeting techniques, you will notice that this principle is the driving force behind each of them.

[1]The required rate of return or cost of capital is the rate of return necessary to justify raising funds to finance the project or, alternatively, the rate of return necessary to maintain the firm's current market price per share.

Realize, however, that the worth of the *NPV* calculation is a function of the accuracy of the cash flow predictions.

The following example illustrates the use of *NPV* as a capital-budgeting criterion.

EXAMPLE 1

Ski-Doo is considering new machinery that would reduce manufacturing costs associated with its Mach Z snowmobile for which the free cash flows are shown in Table 3. If the firm has a 12 percent required rate of return, the present value of the free cash flow is $47,675, as calculated in Table 4. Subtracting the $40,000 initial outlay leaves an *NPV* of $7,675. Because this value is greater than zero, the *NPV* criterion indicates that the project should be accepted.

The *NPV* criterion is the capital-budgeting decision tool we find most favorable for several reasons. First of all, it deals with free cash flows rather than accounting profits. In this regard it is sensitive to the true timing of the benefits resulting from the project. Moreover, recognizing the time value of money allows the benefits and costs to be compared in a logical manner. Finally, because projects are accepted only if a positive *NPV* is associated with them, the acceptance of a project using this criterion will increase the value of the firm, which is consistent with the goal of maximizing the shareholders' wealth.

The disadvantage of the *NPV* method stems from the need for detailed, long-term forecasts of the free cash flows accruing from the project's acceptance. Despite this drawback, the *NPV* is the most theoretically correct criterion that we will examine. The following example provides an additional illustration of its application.

Handwritten notes (left margin):

$V_0 = \$40,000$

$Yr\ 1 \rightarrow \dfrac{\times 15,000}{(1+0.12)^1} = \$13,392$

$Yr\ 2 \rightarrow \dfrac{14,000}{(1+0.12)^2} = \$11,200$

$Yr\ 3 \rightarrow \dfrac{13,000}{(1+0.12)^3} = \$9,285$

$Yr\ 4 \rightarrow \dfrac{12,000}{(1+0.12)^4} = \$7,643$

$Yr\ 5 \rightarrow \dfrac{11,000}{(1+0.12)^5} = \$6,250$

$\$47,777 - \$40,000 = \$7,777$

CALCULATOR SOLUTION (USING A TEXAS INSTRUMENTS BA II PLUS):

Data and Key Input	Display
CF ; –40,000; ENTER	CF0 = –40,000.
↓ ; 15,000; ENTER	C01 = 15,000.
↓ ; 1; ENTER	F01 = 1.00
↓ ; 14,000; ENTER	C02 = 14,000.
↓ ; 1; ENTER	F02 = 1.00
↓ ; 13,000; ENTER	C03 = 13,000.
↓ ; 1; ENTER	F03 = 1.00
↓ ; 12,000; ENTER	C04 = 12,000.
↓ ; 1; ENTER	F04 = 1.00
↓ ; 11,000; ENTER	C05 = 11,000.
↓ ; 1; ENTER	F05 = 1.00
NPV	I = 0.00
12; ENTER	I = 12.00
↓ ; CPT	NPV = 7,675.

TABLE 3 Ski-Doo's Investment in New Machinery and Its Associated Free Cash Flows

	Free Cash Flow
Initial outlay	–$40,000
Inflow year 1	15,000
Inflow year 2	14,000
Inflow year 3	13,000
Inflow year 4	12,000
Inflow year 5	11,000

TABLE 4 Calculating the *NPV* of Ski-Doo's Investment in New Machinery

	PRESENT VALUE		
	Free Cash Flow ×	Factor at 12 Percent =	Present Value
Inflow year 1	$15,000 ×	$\dfrac{1}{(1 + 0.12)^1}$ =	$ 13,393
Inflow year 2	14,000 ×	$\dfrac{1}{(1 + 0.12)^2}$ =	11,161
Inflow year 3	13,000 ×	$\dfrac{1}{(1 + 0.12)^3}$ =	9,253
Inflow year 4	12,000 ×	$\dfrac{1}{(1 + 0.12)^4}$ =	7,626
Inflow year 5	11,000 ×	$\dfrac{1}{(1 + 0.12)^5}$ =	6,242
Present value of free cash flows			$ 47,675
Initial outlay			–40,000
Net present value			$ 7,675

EXAMPLE 2

A firm is considering the purchase of a new computer system, which will cost $30,000 initially, to aid in credit billing and inventory management. The free cash flows resulting from this project are provided below:

Payback Period → 3 years

	FREE CASH FLOW
Initial outlay	−$30,000
Inflow year 1	15,000
Inflow year 2	15,000
Inflow year 3	15,000

The required rate of return demanded by the firm is 10 percent. To determine the system's *NPV*, the 3-year $15,000 cash flow annuity is first discounted back to the present at 10 percent. The present value of the $15,000 annuity can be found using a calculator (as is done the margin),

$$\frac{15,000}{(1+0.10)^1} + \frac{15,000}{(1+0.10)^2} + \frac{15,000}{(1+0.10)^3} =$$

$13,636 + $12,397 + $11,279 = $37,312
$30,000 − $37,312 = $7,312

$$PV = PMT \left[\frac{1 - \frac{1}{(1+k)^n}}{k} \right].$$ Using the mathematical relationship we get:

$$PV = \$15,000 \left[\frac{1 - \frac{1}{(1+0.10)^3}}{0.10} \right] = \$15,000 \ (2.4869) = \$37,303$$

Seeing that the cash inflows have been discounted back to the present, they can now be compared with the initial outlay because both of the flows are now stated in terms of today's dollars. Subtracting the initial outlay ($30,000) from the present value of the cash inflows ($37,303), we find that the system's *NPV* is $7,303. Because the *NPV* on this project is positive, the project should be accepted.

CALCULATOR SOLUTION

STEP 1
Calculate payment value of inflows

Data Input	Function key
3	N
10	I/Y
−15,000	PMT
0	FV

Function Key	Answer
CPT	
PV	37,303

STEP 2
Subtract initial outlay from present value of inflows

$ 37,303
−30,000
$ 7,303

Using Spreadsheets to Calculate the Net Present Value

Although we can calculate the *NPV* by hand or with a financial calculator, it is more commonly done with the help of a spreadsheet. Just as with the keystroke calculations on a financial calculator, a spreadsheet can make easy work of *NPV* calculations. The only real glitch here is that in Excel, along with most other spreadsheets, the =*NPV* function only calculates the present value of only the future cash flows and ignores the initial outlay in its *NPV* calculations. Sounds strange? Well, it is. It is essentially just a carryforward of an error in one of the first spreadsheets. That means that the actual *NPV* is the Excel-calculated *NPV*, minus the initial outlay:

Actual *NPV* = Excel-calculated *NPV* − initial outlay

This can be input into a spreadsheet cell as:

=*NPV*(rate,inflow 1,inflow 2, . . . inflow 29)-initial outlay

CAN YOU DO IT?

DETERMINING THE *NPV* OF A PROJECT

Determine the *NPV* for a new project that costs $7,000, is expected to produce 10 years' worth of annual free cash flows of $1,000 per year, and has a required rate of return of 5 percent.

Looking back at the Ski-Doo example in Table 3, we can use a spreadsheet to calculate the net present value of the investment in machinery as long as we remember to subtract the initial outlay in order to get the correct number.

	A	B	C	D	E
2	Spreadsheets and NPV – the Ski-Doo Example				
3					
4	Looking at the example in Table 10-3, given a 12 percent				
5	discount rate and the following after-tax cash flows, the				
6	Net Present Value could be calculated as follows:				
7					
8			rate (k) =	12%	
9					
10			Year	Cash Flow	
11			Initial Outlay	($40.000)	
12			1	$15.000	
13			2	$14.000	
14			3	$13.000	
15			4	$12.000	
16			5	$11.000	
17					
18		NPV =	$7,674.63		
19					
20	Excel formula: =NPV(rate,inflow1,inflow2,...,inflow29)				
21					
22	Again, from the Excel NPV calculation we must then				
23	subtract out the initial outlay in order to calculate the				
24	actual NPV.				
25					
26					
27					

Entered value in cell c18:
=NPV(D8,D12:D16)−40000

Method #3

The Profitability Index (Benefit–Cost Ratio)

profitability index (PI) or benefit–cost ratio the ratio of the present value of an investment's future free cash flows to the investment's initial outlay.

The **profitability index (PI), or benefit–cost ratio,** is the *ratio of the present value of the future free cash flows to the initial outlay*. Although the *NPV* investment criterion gives a measure of the absolute dollar desirability of a project, the profitability index provides a relative measure of an investment proposal's desirability—that is, the ratio of the present value of its future net benefits to its initial cost. The profitability index can be expressed as follows:

$$PI = \frac{\text{present value of all the future annual free cash flows}}{\text{initial cash outlay}}$$

$$= \frac{\dfrac{FCF_1}{(1 + k)^1} + \dfrac{FCF_2}{(1 + k)^2} + \cdots + \dfrac{FCF_n}{(1 + k)^n}}{IO} \tag{2}$$

where FCF_t = the annual free cash flow in time period t (this can take on either positive or negative values)
k = the firm's required rate of return or cost of capital
IO = the initial cash outlay
n = the project's expected life

The decision criterion is to accept the project if the *PI* is greater than or equal to 1.00 and to reject the project if the *PI* is less than 1.00.

$PI \geq 1.0$: accept
$PI < 1.0$: reject

Looking closely at this criterion, we see that it yields the same accept/reject decision as the *NPV* criterion. Whenever the present value of the project's free cash flows is greater than the initial cash outlay, the project's *NPV* will be positive, signaling a decision to accept. When this is true, then the project's *PI* will also be greater than 1 because the present value

DID YOU GET IT?

DETERMINING THE *NPV* OF A PROJECT

You were asked to determine the *NPV* for a project with an initial outlay of $7,000 and free cash flows in years 1 through 10 of $1,000, given a 5 percent required rate of return.

NPV = (present value of all future free cash flows) − (initial outlay)

1. **Using the Mathematical Formulas.**

   STEP 1 Determine the present value of the future cash flows.

   Substituting these example values in equation (5-4), we find

   $$PV = \$1,000 \left[\frac{1 - \dfrac{1}{(1 + 0.05)^{10}}}{0.05} \right]$$

   $$= \$1,000 \, [(1 - 1/1.62889463)/0.05]$$

   $$= \$1,000 \, [(1 - 0.61391325)/0.05]$$

   $$= \$1,000 \, (7.72173493) = \$7,721.73$$

   STEP 2 Subtract the initial outlay from the present value of the free cash flows.

   $7,721.73
   − $7,000.00
   $ 721.73

2. **Using a Financial Calculator.**

   STEP 1 Determine the present value of the future cash flows.

Data Input	Function Key
10	N
5	I/Y
−1,000	PMT
0	FV

Function Key	Answer
CPT	
PV	7,721.73

STEP 2 Subtract the initial outlay from present value of the free cash flows.

$7,721.73
− $7,000.00
$ 721.73

Alternatively, you could use the CF button on your calculator (using a TI BA II Plus).

Data and Key Input	Display
CF ; 2nd ; CE/C	CF0 = 0. (this clears out any past cash flows)
−7,000; ENTER	CF0 = −7,000.
↓ ; 1,000; ENTER	C01 = 1,000.
↓ ; 10; ENTER	F01 = 10.00
NPV	I = 0.
5; ENTER	I = 5.00
↓	NPV = 0.
CPT	NPV = 721.73

of the free cash flows (the *PI*'s numerator) is greater than the initial outlay (the *PI*'s denominator). Thus, these two decision criteria will always yield the same decision, although they will not necessarily rank acceptable projects in the same order. This problem of conflicting ranking is dealt with at a later point.

Because the *NPV* and *PI* criteria are essentially the same, they have the same advantages over the other criteria examined. Both employ free cash flows, recognize the timing of the cash flows, and are consistent with the goal of maximizing shareholders' wealth. The major disadvantage of the *PI* criterion, similar to the *NPV* criterion, is that it requires long, detailed free cash flow forecasts.

EXAMPLE 3

A firm with a 10 percent required rate of return is considering investing in a new machine with an expected life of 6 years. The free cash flows resulting from this investment are given in Table 5. Discounting the project's future net free cash flows back to the present yields a present value of $53,682; dividing this value by the initial outlay of $50,000 yields a profitability index of 1.0736, as shown in Table 6. This tells us that the present value of the future benefits accruing from this project is 1.0736 times the level of the initial outlay. Because the profitability index is greater than 1.0, the project should be accepted.

TABLE 5 The Free Cash Flows Associated with an Investment in New Machinery	
	Free Cash Flow
Initial outlay	−$50,000
Inflow year 1	15,000
Inflow year 2	8,000
Inflow year 3	10,000
Inflow year 4	12,000
Inflow year 5	14,000
Inflow year 6	16,000

TABLE 6 Calculating the *PI* of an Investment in New Machinery

	Free Cash Flow	×	Present Value Factor at 10 Percent =	Present Value
Inflow year 1	15,000	×	$\dfrac{1}{(1 + .10)^1}$	= 13,636
Inflow year 2	8,000	×	$\dfrac{1}{(1 + .10)^2}$	= 6,612
Inflow year 3	10,000	×	$\dfrac{1}{(1 + .10)^3}$	= 7,513
Inflow year 4	12,000	×	$\dfrac{1}{(1 + .10)^4}$	= 8,196
Inflow year 5	14,000	×	$\dfrac{1}{(1 + .10)^5}$	= 8,693
Inflow year 6	16,000	×	$\dfrac{1}{(1 + .10)^6}$	= 9,032

$$PI = \frac{\dfrac{FCF_1}{(1 + k)^1} + \dfrac{FCF_2}{(1 + k)^2} + \cdots + \dfrac{FCF_n}{(1 + k)^n}}{IO}$$

$$= \frac{\$13,636 + \$6,612 + \$7,513 + \$8,196 + \$8,693 + \$9,032}{\$50,000}$$

$$= \frac{\$53,682}{\$50,000}$$

$$= 1.0736$$

Method #4

The Internal Rate of Return

internal rate of return (*IRR*) the rate of return that the project earns. For computational purposes, the internal rate of return is defined as the discount rate that equates the present value of the project's free cash flows with the project's initial cash outlay.

The **internal rate of return (*IRR*)** attempts to answer the question, what rate of return does this project earn? For computational purposes, the internal rate of return is defined as *the discount rate that equates the present value of the project's free cash flows with the project's initial cash outlay*. Mathematically, the internal rate of return is defined as the value *IRR* in the following equation:

IRR = the rate of return that equates the present value of the project's free cash flows with the initial outlay

$$IO = \frac{FCF_1}{(1 + IRR\%)^1} + \frac{FCF_2}{(1 + IRR\%)^2} + \cdots + \frac{FCF_n}{(1 + IRR\%)^n} \tag{3}$$

where FCF_t = the annual free cash flow in time period t (this can take on either positive or negative values)
IO = the initial cash outlay
n = the project's expected life
IRR = the project's internal rate of return

In effect, the *IRR* is analogous to the concept of the yield to maturity for bonds. In other words, a project's *IRR* is simply the rate of return that the project earns.

The decision criterion is to accept the project if the *IRR* is greater than or equal to the firm's required rate of return. We reject the project if its *IRR* is less than the required rate of return. This accept/reject criterion can be stated as

IRR ≥ firm's required rate of return or cost of capital: accept

IRR < firm's required rate of return or cost of capital: reject

If the *IRR* on a project is equal to the firm's required rate of return, then the project should be accepted because the firm is earning the rate that its shareholders are demanding. By contrast, accepting a project with an *IRR* below the investors' required rate of return will decrease the firm's stock price.

If the *NPV* is positive, then the *IRR* must be greater than the required rate of return, *k*. Thus, all the discounted cash flow criteria are consistent and will result in similar accept/reject decisions. One disadvantage of the *IRR* relative to the *NPV* deals with the implied reinvestment rate assumptions made by these two methods. The *NPV* assumes that cash flows over the life of the project are reinvested back in projects that earn the required rate of return. That is, if we have a mining project with a 10-year expected life that produces a $100,000 cash flow at the end of the second year, the *NPV* technique assumes that this $100,000 is reinvested over years 3 though 10 at the required rate of return. The use of the *IRR*, however, implies that cash flows over the life of the project can be reinvested at the *IRR*. Thus, if the mining project we just looked at has a 40 percent *IRR*, the use of the *IRR* implies that the $100,000 cash flow that is received at the end of year 2 could be reinvested at 40 percent over the remaining life of the project. In effect, *the NPV method implicitly assumes that cash flows over the life of the project can be reinvested at the project's required rate of return, whereas the use of the IRR method implies that these cash flows could be reinvested at the IRR.* The better assumption is the one made by the *NPV*—that the cash flows can be reinvested at the required rate of return because they can either be (1) returned in the form of dividends to shareholders, who demand the required rate of return on their investments, or (2) reinvested in a new investment project. If these cash flows are invested in a new project, then they are simply substituting for external funding on which the required rate of return is again demanded. Thus, the opportunity cost of these funds is the required rate of return.

The bottom line of all this is that the *NPV* method makes the best reinvestment rate assumption, and, as such, is superior to the *IRR* method. Why should we care which method is used if both methods result in similar accept/reject decisions? The answer, as we will see, is that although they may result in the same accept/reject decision, they may rank projects differently in terms of desirability.

Computing the *IRR* with a Financial Calculator   With today's calculators, determining an *IRR* is merely a matter of a few keystrokes. Earlier in the book, whenever we were solving time value of money problems for *i*, we were really solving for the *IRR*. For instance, earlier in the book when we solved for the rate at which $100 must be compounded annually for it to grow to $179.10 in 10 years, we were actually solving for that problem's *IRR*. Thus, with financial calculators we need only input the initial outlay, the cash flows, and their timing and then input the function key "I/Y" or the "IRR" button to calculate the *IRR*. On some calculators it is necessary to press the compute key, CPT, before pressing the function key to be calculated.

Computing the *IRR* with a Spreadsheet   Calculating the *IRR* using a spreadsheet is extremely simple. Once the cash flows have been entered on the spreadsheet, all you need to do is input the Excel *IRR* function into a spreadsheet cell and let the spreadsheet do the calculations for you. Of course, at least one of the cash flows must be positive and at least one must be negative. The *IRR* function to be input into a spreadsheet cell is: **=IRR(values)**, where "values" is simply the range of cells in which the cash flows including the initial outlay are stored.

	A	B	C	D	E
1					
2		**Spreadsheets and the IRR**			
3					
4	Three investment proposals being examined have the following				
5	cash flows:				
6					
7	Year	Project A	Project B	Project C	
8	Initial Outlay	($10.000)	($10.000)	($10.000)	
9	1	3.362	0	1.000	
10	2	3.362	0	3.000	
11	3	3.362	0	6.000	
12	4	3.362	13.605	7.000	
13					
14	IRR=	13.001%	8.000%	19.040%	
15					
16	Excel Formula: =IRR(values)				
17					
18	where:				
19	values = the range of cells where the cash flows are stored.				
20	Note: There must be at least one positive and one				
21	negative cash flow.				

Entered value in cell B14:=IRR(B8:B12)
Entered value in cell C14:=IRR(C8:C12)
Entered value in cell D14:=IRR(D8:D12)

Computing the *IRR* for Uneven Cash Flows with a Financial Calculator   Solving for the *IRR* when the cash flows are uneven is quite simple with a calculator: One need only key in the initial cash outlay, the cash flows, and their timing and press the "IRR" button. Let's take a look at how you might solve a problem with uneven cash flows using a financial calculator. Every calculator works a bit differently, so you'll want to be familiar with how to input data into yours, but that being said, they all work essentially the same way. As you'd expect, you will enter all the cash flows, then solve for the project's *IRR*. With a Texas Instruments BA II Plus calculator, you begin by hitting the CF button. Then, CFo indicates the initial outlay, which you'll want to give a negative value; C01 is the first free cash flow; and F01 is the number of years in which the first free cash flow appears. Thus, if the free cash flows in years 1, 2, and 3 are all $1,000, then F01 = 3. C02 then becomes the second free cash flow, and F02 is the number of years in which the second free cash flow appears. You'll notice that you move between the different cash flows using the down arrow (↓) located on the top row of your calculator. Once you have inputted the initial outlay and all the free cash flows, you then calculate the project's *IRR* by hitting the "IRR" button followed by "CPT," the compute button. Let's look at a quick example. Consider the following investment proposal:

Initial outlay	−$5,000
FCF in year 1	2,000
FCF in year 2	2,000
FCF in year 3	3,000

**CALCULATOR SOLUTION
(USING A TI BA II PLUS):**

Data and Key Input	Display
CF ;−5,000; ENTER	CFo = −5,000.00
↓ 2,000; ENTER	C01 = 2,000.00
↓ 2; ENTER	F01 = 2.00
↓ 3,000; ENTER	C02 = 3,000.00
↓ 1; ENTER	F02 = 1.00
IRR ; CPT	IRR = 17.50%

CAN YOU DO IT?

DETERMINING THE *IRR* OF A PROJECT

Determine the *IRR* for a new project that costs $5,019 and is expected to produce 10 years' worth of annual free cash flows of $1,000 per year.

EXAMPLE 4

Consider the following investment proposal:

Initial outlay	−$10,010
FCF in year 1	1,000
FCF in year 2	3,000
FCF in year 3	6,000
FCF in year 4	7,000

**CALCULATOR SOLUTION
(USING A TI BA II PLUS)**

Data and Key Input	Display
CF ; −10,010; ENTER	CF0 = −10,010.00
↓ 1,000; ENTER	C01 = 1,000.00
↓ 1; ENTER	F01 = 1.00
↓ 3,000; ENTER	C02 = 3,000.00
↓ 1; ENTER	F02 = 1.00
↓ 6,000; ENTER	C03 = 6,000.00
↓ 1; ENTER	F03 = 1.00
↓ 7,000; ENTER	C04 = 7,000.00
↓ 1; ENTER	F04 = 1.00
IRR ; CPT	IRR = 19.00%

Viewing the *NPV–IRR* Relationship: The Net Present Value Profile

Perhaps the easiest way to understand the relationship between the *IRR* and the *NPV* value is to view it graphically through the use of a **net present value profile**. A net present value profile is simply *a graph showing how a project's NPV changes as the discount rate changes.* To graph a project's net present value profile, you simply need to determine the project's *NPV*, first using a 0 percent discount rate, then slowly increasing the discount rate until a representative curve has been plotted. How does the *IRR* enter into the net present value profile? The *IRR* is the discount rate at which the *NPV* is zero.

Let's look at an example of a project that involves an after-tax initial outlay of $105,517 with free cash flows expected to be $30,000 per year over the project's 5-year life.

net present value profile a graph showing how a project's *NPV* changes as the discount rate changes.

DID YOU GET IT?

DETERMINING THE *IRR* OF A PROJECT

You were asked to determine the *IRR* for a project with an initial outlay of $5,019 and free cash flows in years 1 through 10 of $1,000.

1. **Using a Financial Calculator.** Substituting in a financial calculator, we are solving for *i*.

Data Input	Function Key
10	N
−5,019	PV
1,000	PMT
0	FV

Function Key	Answer
CPT	
I/Y	15

Alternatively, you could use the CF button on your calculator (using a TI BA II Plus):

Data and Key Input	Display
CF ; −5,019; ENTER	CF0 = −5,019.
↓; 1,000; ENTER	C01 = 1,000.
↓; 10; ENTER	F01 = 10.00
IRR; CPT	IRR = 15

2. **Using Excel.** Using Excel, the *IRR* could be calculated using the = **IRR** function.

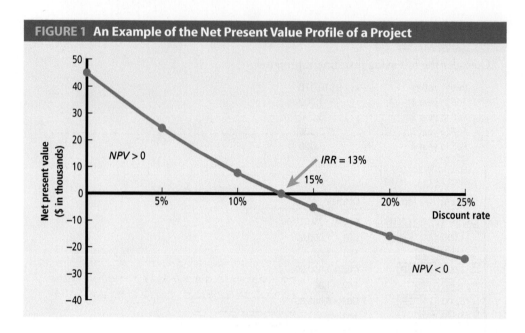

FIGURE 1 An Example of the Net Present Value Profile of a Project

Calculating the *NPV* of this project at several different discount rates results in the following:

Discount Rate	Project's *NPV*
0%	$44,483
5%	$24,367
10%	$ 8,207
13%	$ 0
15%	−$ 4,952
20%	−$15,798
25%	−$24,839

Plotting these values yields the net present value profile in Figure 1.

Where is the *IRR* in this figure? Recall that the *IRR* is the discount rate that equates the present value of the inflows with the present value of the outflows; thus, the *IRR* is the point at which the *NPV* is equal to zero—in this case, 13 percent. This is exactly the process that we use in computing the *IRR* for a series of uneven cash flows—we simply calculate the project's *NPV* using different discount rates and the discount rate that makes the *NPV* equal to zero is the project's *IRR*.

From the net present value profile you can easily see how a project's *NPV* varies inversely with the discount rate—as the discount rate is raised, the *NPV* drops. By analyzing a project's net present value profile, you can also see how sensitive the project is to your selection of the discount rate. The more sensitive the *NPV* is to the discount rate, the more important it is that you use the correct one in your calculations.

Complications with the *IRR*: Multiple Rates of Return

Although any project can have only one *NPV* and one *PI*, a single project under certain circumstances can have more than one *IRR*. The reason for this can be traced to the calculations involved in determining the *IRR*. Equation (3) states that the *IRR* is the discount rate that equates the present value of the project's future net cash flows with the project's initial outlay:

$$IO = \frac{FCF_1}{(1 + IRR)^1} + \frac{FCF_2}{(1 + IRR)^2} + \cdots + \frac{FCF_n}{(1 + IRR)^n} \tag{3}$$

However, because equation (3) is a polynomial of a degree *n*, it has *n* solutions. Now if the initial outlay (*IO*) is the only negative cash flow and all the annual free cash flows (*FCF*) are positive, then all but one of these *n* solutions is either a negative or imaginary number and there is no problem. But problems occur when there are sign reversals in the cash flow stream; in fact, there can be as many solutions as there are sign reversals. A normal, or "conventional,"

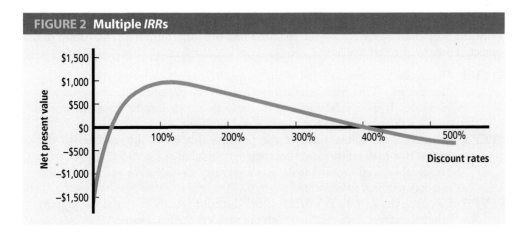

FIGURE 2 Multiple *IRRs*

pattern with a negative initial outlay and positive annual free cash flows after that (−, +, +, +, . . . , +) has only one sign reversal, hence, only one positive *IRR*. However, an "unconventional" pattern with more than one sign reversal can have more than one *IRR*.

	FREE CASH FLOW
Initial outlay	−$ 1,600
Year 1 free cash flow	+$10,000
Year 2 free cash flow	−$10,000

In this pattern of cash flows, there are two sign reversals: one from −$1,600 to +$10,000 and one from +$10,000 to −$10,000, so there can be as many as two positive *IRRs* that will make the present value of the free cash flows equal to the initial outlay. In fact, two internal rates of return solve this problem: 25 percent and 400 percent. Graphically, what we are solving for is the discount rate that makes the project's *NPV* equal to zero. As Figure 2 illustrates, this occurs twice.

Which solution is correct? The answer is that neither solution is valid. Although each fits the definition of *IRR*, neither provides any insight into the true project returns. In summary, when there is more than one sign reversal in the cash flow stream, the possibility of multiple *IRRs* exists, and the normal interpretation of the *IRR* loses its meaning. In this case, try the *NPV* criterion instead.

The Modified Internal Rate of Return (*MIRR*)[2]

Problems with multiple rates of return and the reinvestment rate assumption make the *NPV* superior to the *IRR* as a capital-budgeting technique. However, because of the ease of interpretation, the *IRR* is preferred by many practitioners. Recently, a new technique, the modified internal rate of return (*MIRR*), has gained popularity as an alternative to the *IRR* method because it avoids multiple *IRRs* and allows the decision maker to directly specify the appropriate reinvestment rate. As a result, the *MIRR* provides the decision maker with the intuitive appeal of the *IRR* coupled with an improved reinvestment rate assumption.

Is this really a problem? The answer is yes. One of the problems of the *IRR* is that it creates unrealistic expectations both for the corporation and for its shareholders. For example, the consulting firm McKinsey & Company examined one firm that approved 23 major projects over 5 years based on average *IRRs* of 77 percent.[3] However, when McKinsey adjusted the reinvestment rate on these projects to the firm's required rate of return, this return rate fell to 16 percent. The ranking of the projects also changed with the top-ranked project falling to the 10th most attractive project. Moreover, the returns on the highest-ranked projects with *IRRs* of 800, 150, and 130 percent dropped to 15, 23, and 22 percent, respectively, once the reinvestment rate was adjusted downward.

---

[2]This section is relatively complex and can be omitted without loss of continuity.
[3]John C. Kellecher and Justin J. MacCormack, "Internal Rate of Return: A Cautionary Tale," *McKinsey Quarterly*, September 24, 2004, pp. 1–4.

The driving force behind the *MIRR* is the assumption that all free cash flows over the life of the project are reinvested at the required rate of return until the termination of the project. Thus, to calculate the *MIRR*, we:

STEP 1 Determine the present value of the project's free cash *out*flows. We do this by discounting all the free cash *out*flows back to the present at the required rate of return. If the initial outlay is the only free cash *out*flow, then the initial outlay is the present value of the free cash *out*flows.

STEP 2 Determine the future value of the project's free cash *in*flows. Take all the annual free cash *in*flows and find their future value at the end of the project's life, compounded forward at the required rate of return. We will call this the project's *terminal value*, or *TV*.

STEP 3 Calculate the *MIRR*. The *MIRR* is the discount rate that equates the present value of the free cash outflows with the project's terminal value.[4]

Mathematically, the modified internal rate of return is defined as the value of *MIRR* in the following equation:

$$PV_{\text{outflows}} = \frac{TV_{\text{inflows}}}{(1 + MIRR)^n} \tag{4}$$

where PV_{outflows} = the present value of the project's free cash *out*flows

TV_{inflows} = the project's terminal value, calculated by taking all the annual free cash *in*flows and finding their future value at the end of the project's life, compounded forward at the required rate of return

n = the project's expected life

$MIRR$ = the project's modified internal rate of return

EXAMPLE 5   Calculating the *MIRR*

Let's look at an example of a project with a 3-year life and a required rate of return of 10 percent assuming the following cash flows are associated with it:

	FREE CASH FLOWS
Initial outlay	−$6,000
Year 1	2,000
Year 2	$3,000
Year 3	4,000

The calculation of the *MIRR* can be viewed as a three-step process, which is also shown graphically in Figure 3.

STEP 1 Determine the present value of the project's free cash *out*flows. In this case, the only *out*flow is the initial outlay of $6,000, which is already at the present; thus, it becomes the present value of the cash *out*flows.

STEP 2 Determine the terminal value of the project's free cash *in*flows. To do this, we merely use the project's required rate of return to calculate the future value of the project's three cash *in*flows at the termination of the project. In this case, the *terminal value* becomes $9,720.

STEP 3 Determine the discount rate that equates the present value of the *terminal value* and the present value of the project's cash *out*flows. Thus, the *MIRR* is calculated to be 17.446 percent.

---

[4]You will notice that we differentiate between annual cash inflows and annual cash outflows, compounding all the inflows to the end of the project and bringing all the outflows back to the present as part of the present value of the cost. Although there are alternative definitions of the *MIRR*, this is the most widely accepted definition.

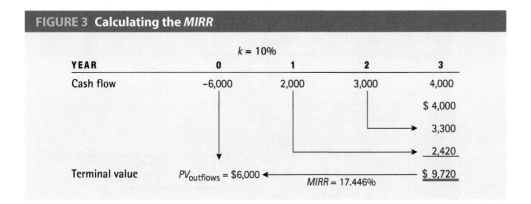

FIGURE 3 Calculating the *MIRR*

For our example, the calculations are as follows:

$$\$6,000 = \frac{TV_{inflows}}{(1 + MIRR)^n}$$

$$\$6,000 = \frac{\$2,000(1 + 0.10)^2 + \$3,000(1 + 0.10)^1 + \$4,000(1 + 0.10)^0}{(1 + MIRR)^3}$$

$$\$6,000 = \frac{\$2,420 + \$3,300 + \$4,000}{(1 + MIRR)^3}$$

$$\$6,000 = \frac{\$9,720}{(1 + MIRR)^3}$$

$$MIRR = 17.45\%$$

Thus, the *MIRR* for this project (17.45% percent) is less than its *IRR*, which comes out to 20.614 percent. In this case, it only makes sense that the *IRR* should be greater than the *MIRR*, because the *IRR* implicitly assumes intermediate cash *in*flows to grow at the *IRR* rather than the required rate of return.

In terms of decision rules, if the project's *MIRR* is greater than or equal to the project's required rate of return, then the project should be accepted; if not, it should be rejected:

MIRR ≥ required rate of return: accept
MIRR < required rate of return: reject

Because of the frequent use of the *IRR* in the real world as a decision-making tool and its limiting reinvestment rate assumption, the *MIRR* has become increasingly popular as an alternative decision-making tool.

Using Spreadsheets to Calculate the *MIRR*

As with other financial calculations using a spreadsheet, calculating the *MIRR* is extremely simple. The only difference between this calculation and that of the traditional *IRR* is that with a spreadsheet you also have the option of specifying both a *financing rate* and a *reinvestment rate*. The financing rate refers to the rate at which you borrow the money needed for the investment, whereas the reinvestment rate is the rate at which you reinvest the cash flows. Generally, it is assumed that these two values are one and the same. Thus, we enter the value of *k*, the appropriate discount rate, for both of these values. Once the cash flows have been entered on the spreadsheet, all you need to do is input the Excel *MIRR* function into a spreadsheet cell and let the spreadsheet do the calculations for you. Of course, as with the *IRR* calculation, at least one of the cash flows must be positive and at least one must be negative. The *MIRR* function to be input into a spreadsheet cell is: **=MIRR(values,finance rate,reinvestment rate)**, where values is simply the range of cells where the cash flows are stored, and *k* is entered for both the finance rate and the reinvestment rate.

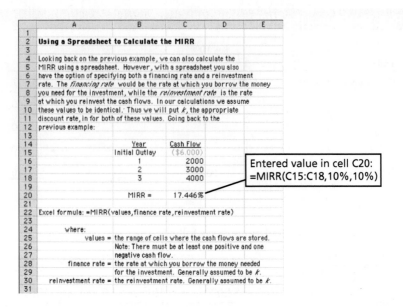

Concept Check

1. Provide an intuitive definition of an internal rate of return for a project.
2. What does a net present value profile tell you, and how is it constructed?
3. What is the difference between the *IRR* and the *MIRR*?
4. Why do the net present value and profitability index always yield the same accept or reject decision for any project?

3 Explain how the capital-budgeting decision process changes when a dollar limit is placed on the capital budget.

capital rationing placing a limit on the dollar size of the capital budget.

Capital Rationing

The use of our capital-budgeting decision rules developed in this chapter implies that the size of the capital budget is determined by the availability of acceptable investment proposals. However, a firm may *place a limit on the dollar size of the capital budget*. This situation is called **capital rationing**. As we will see, examining capital rationing not only better enables us to deal with complexities of the real world but also serves to demonstrate the superiority of the *NPV* method over the *IRR* method for capital budgeting. It is always somewhat uncomfortable to deal with problems associated with capital rationing because, under rationing, projects with positive net present values are rejected. This is a situation that violates the firm's goal of shareholder wealth maximization. However, in the real world, capital rationing does exist, and managers must deal with it. Often when firms impose capital constraints, they are recognizing that they do not have the ability to profitably handle more than a certain number of new and/or large projects.

Using the *IRR* as the firm's decision rule, a firm accepts all projects with an *IRR* greater than the firm's required rate of return. This rule is illustrated in Figure 4, where projects A through E would be chosen. However, when capital rationing is imposed, the dollar size of the total investment is limited by the budget constraint. In Figure 4, the budget constraint of $X precludes the acceptance of an attractive investment, project E. This situation obviously contradicts prior decision rules. Moreover, choosing the projects with the highest *IRR* is complicated by the fact that some projects are indivisible. For example, it may be illogical to recommend that half of project D be undertaken.

The Rationale for Capital Rationing

In general, three principal reasons are given for imposing a capital-rationing constraint. First, managers may think market conditions are temporarily adverse. In the period surrounding the downturn in the economy in the late 2000s, this reason was frequently given.

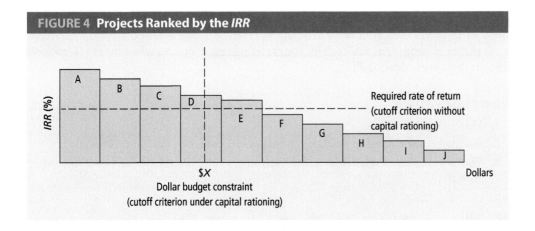

FIGURE 4 Projects Ranked by the *IRR*

At that time stock prices were depressed, which made the cost of funding projects high. Second, there may be a shortage of qualified managers to direct new projects; this can happen when projects are of a highly technical nature. Third, there may be intangible considerations. For example, managers may simply fear debt, wishing to avoid interest payments at any cost. Or perhaps the firm wants to limit the issuance of common stock to maintain a stable dividend policy.

So what is capital rationing's effect on the firm? In brief, the effect is negative. To what degree it is negative depends on the severity of the rationing. If the rationing is minor and short-lived, the firm's share price will not suffer to any great extent. In this case, capital rationing can probably be excused, although it should be noted that any capital-rationing action that rejects projects with positive *NPV*s is contrary to the firm's goal of maximization of shareholders' wealth. If the capital rationing is a result of the firm's decision to limit dramatically the number of new projects or to use only internally generated funds for projects, then this policy will eventually have a significantly negative effect on the firm's share price. For example, a lower share price will eventually result from lost competitive advantage if, because of a decision to arbitrarily limit its capital budget, a firm fails to upgrade its products and manufacturing processes.

Capital Rationing and Project Selection

If a firm decides to impose a capital constraint on its investment projects, the appropriate decision criterion is to select the set of projects with the highest *NPV* subject to the capital constraint. In effect, it should select the projects that increase shareholders' wealth the most. This guideline may preclude merely taking the highest-ranked projects in terms of the *PI* or the *IRR*. If the projects shown in Figure 4 are divisible, the last project accepted will be only partially accepted. Although partial acceptance may be possible, as we have said, in some cases, the indivisibility of most capital investments prevents it. For example, purchasing half a sales outlet or half a truck is impossible.

Consider a firm with a budget constraint of $1 million and five indivisible projects available to it, as given in Table 7. If the highest-ranked projects were taken, projects A and B would be taken first. At that point there would not be enough funds available to take on

Project	Initial Outlay	Profitability Index	Net Present Value
A	$200,000	2.4	$280,000
B	200,000	2.3	260,000
C	800,000	1.7	560,000
D	300,000	1.3	90,000
E	300,000	1.2	60,000

TABLE 7 Capital Rationing: Choosing among Five Indivisible Projects

project C; hence, projects D and E would be taken on. However, a higher total *NPV* is provided by the combination of projects A and C. Thus, projects A and C should be selected from the set of projects available. This illustrates our guideline: to select the set of projects that maximizes the firm's *NPV*.

Concept Check

1. What is capital rationing?
2. How might capital rationing conflict with the goal of maximizing shareholders' wealth?
3. What are mutually exclusive projects? How might they complicate the capital-budgeting process?

 Discuss the problems encountered in project ranking.

mutually exclusive projects projects that, if undertaken, would serve the same purpose. Thus, accepting one will necessarily mean rejecting the others.

Ranking Mutually Exclusive Projects

In the past, we have proposed that all projects with a positive *NPV*, a *PI* greater than 1.0, or an *IRR* greater than the required rate of return be accepted, assuming there is no capital rationing. However, this acceptance is not always possible. In some cases, when two projects are judged acceptable by the discounted cash flow criteria, it may be necessary to select only one of them because they are mutually exclusive. **Mutually exclusive projects** *are projects that, if undertaken, would serve the same purpose*. For example, a company considering the installation of a computer system might evaluate three or four systems, all of which have positive *NPV*s. However, the acceptance of one system automatically means rejection of the others. In general, to deal with mutually exclusive projects, we simply rank them by means of the discounted cash flow criteria and select the project with the highest ranking. On occasion, however, problems of conflicting ranking may arise. As we will see, in general, the *NPV* method is the preferred decision-making tool because it leads to the selection of the project that increases shareholder wealth the most.

When dealing with mutually exclusive projects, there are three general types of ranking problems: the size-disparity problem, the time-disparity problem, and the unequal-lives problem. Each involves the possibility of conflict in the ranks yielded by the various discounted cash flow, capital-budgeting criteria. As noted previously, when one discounted cash flow criterion gives an accept signal, they will all give an accept signal, but they will not necessarily rank all projects in the same order. In most cases this disparity is not critical; however, for mutually exclusive projects the ranking order is important.

The Size-Disparity Problem

The size-disparity problem occurs when mutually exclusive projects of unequal size are examined. This problem is most easily clarified with an example.

EXAMPLE 6

Suppose a firm is considering two mutually exclusive projects, A and B; both have required rates of return of 10 percent. Project A involves a $200 initial outlay and a cash inflow of $300 at the end of 1 year, whereas project B involves an initial outlay of $1,500 and a cash inflow of $1,900 at the end of 1 year. The net present values, profitability indexes, and internal rates of return for these projects are given in Table 8.

In this case, if the *NPV* criterion is used, project B should be accepted; whereas if the *PI* or *IRR* criterion is used, project A should be chosen. The question now becomes, which project is better? The answer depends on whether capital rationing exists. Without capital rationing, project B is better because it provides the largest increase in shareholders' wealth; that is, it has a larger *NPV*. If there is a capital constraint, the problem then focuses on what can be done with the additional $1,300 that is freed up if project A is chosen (costing $200, as opposed to $1,500). If the firm can earn more on project A plus the project financed with the additional $1,300 than it can on project B, then project A and the marginal project should be accepted. In effect, we are attempting to select the set of projects that maximize the firm's *NPV*. Thus, if the marginal project has an *NPV* greater than $154.55 ($227.28 − $72.73), selecting it plus project A with an *NPV* of $72.73 will provide an *NPV* greater than $227.28, the *NPV* for project B.

TABLE 8 The Size-Disparity Ranking Problem		
PROJECT A:		
		$k = 10\%$
YEARS	0	1
Cash Flow	−200	300
NPV = $72.73		
PI = 1.36		
IRR = 50%		
PROJECT B:		
		$k = 10\%$
YEARS	0	1
Cash Flow	−1,500	1,900
NPV = $227.28		
PI = 1.15		
IRR = 27%		

In summary, whenever the size-disparity problem results in conflicting rankings between mutually exclusive projects, the project with the largest *NPV* will be selected, provided there is no capital rationing. When capital rationing exists, the firm should select the set of projects with the largest *NPV*.

The Time-Disparity Problem

The time-disparity problem and the conflicting rankings that accompany it result from the differing reinvestment assumptions made by the net present value and internal rate of return decision criteria. The *NPV* criterion assumes that cash flows over the life of the project can be reinvested at the required rate of return or cost of capital, whereas the *IRR* criterion implicitly assumes that the cash flows over the life of the project can be reinvested at the *IRR*. One possible solution to this problem is to use the *MIRR* method introduced earlier. As you recall, this method allows you to explicitly state the rate at which cash flows over the life of the project will be reinvested. Again, this problem may be illustrated through the use of an example.

EXAMPLE 7

Suppose a firm with a required rate of return or cost of capital of 10 percent and with no capital constraint is considering the two mutually exclusive projects illustrated in Table 9. The *NPV* and *PI* indicate that project A is the better of the two, whereas the *IRR* indicates that project B is the better. Project B receives its cash flows earlier than project A, and the different assumptions made about how these flows can be reinvested result in the difference in rankings. Which criterion would be followed depends on which reinvestment assumption is used. The *NPV* criterion is preferred in this case because it makes the most acceptable assumption for the wealth-maximizing firm. It is certainly the most conservative assumption that can be made, because the required rate of return is the lowest possible reinvestment rate. Moreover, as we have already noted, the *NPV* method maximizes the value of the firm and the shareholders' wealth.

273

TABLE 9 The Time-Disparity Ranking Problem				
PROJECT A:				
		$k = 10\%$		
YEARS	**0**	**1**	**2**	**3**
Cash Flow	−1000	100	200	2000
NPV = $758.83				
PI = 1.759				
IRR = 35%				
PROJECT B:				
		$k = 10\%$		
YEARS	**0**	**1**	**2**	**3**
Cash Flow	−1000	650	650	650
NPV = $616.45				
PI = 1.616				
IRR = 43%				

The Unequal-Lives Problem

The final ranking problem to be examined asks whether it is appropriate to compare mutually exclusive projects with different life spans. The incomparability of projects with different lives arises because future, profitable investment proposals will be precluded without ever having been considered. For example, let's say you own an older hotel on some prime beachfront property on Hilton Head Island, and you're considering either remodeling the hotel, which will extend its life by 5 years, or tearing it down and building a new hotel that has an expected life of 10 years. Either way you're going to make money because beachfront property is exactly where everyone would like to stay. But clearly, you can't do both.

Is it fair to compare the *NPV*s on these two projects? No. Why not? Because if you accept the 10-year project, you will not only be rejecting the 5-year project but also the chance to do something else profitable with the property in years 5 through 10. In effect, if the project with the shorter life were taken, at its termination you could either remodel again or rebuild and receive additional benefits, whereas accepting the project with the longer life would exclude this possibility, which is not included in the analysis. The key question thus becomes: Does today's investment decision include all future profitable investment proposals in its analysis? If not, the projects are not comparable.

EXAMPLE 8

Suppose a firm with a 10 percent required rate of return must replace an aging machine and is considering two replacement machines, one with a three-year life and one with a six-year life. The relevant cash flow information for these projects is given in Figure 5.

Examining the discounted cash flow criteria, we find that the net present value and profitability index criteria indicate that project B is the better project, whereas the internal rate of return favors project A. This ranking inconsistency is caused by the different life spans of the projects being compared. In this case, the decision is a difficult one because the projects are not comparable.

There are several methods to deal with this situation. The first option is to assume that the cash inflows from the shorter-lived investment will be reinvested at the required rate of return until the termination of the longer-lived asset. Although this approach is the simplest because it merely involves calculating the net present value, it actually ignores the problem at hand—the possibility of undertaking another replacement oppor-

FIGURE 5 Unequal Lives Ranking Problem

PROJECT A:

	k = 10%			
YEARS	**0**	**1**	**2**	**3**
Cash Flows	−1,000	500	500	500

NPV = $243.43
PI = 1.243
IRR = 23.4%

PROJECT B:

	k = 10%					
YEARS	**0**	**1**	**2**	**3**	**4**	**5**	**6**
Cash Flows	−1,000	300	300	300	300	300	300

NPV = $306.58
PI = 1.307
IRR = 19.9%

tunity with a positive net present value. Thus, the proper solution involves projecting reinvestment opportunities into the future—that is, making assumptions about possible future investment opportunities. Unfortunately, whereas the first method is too simplistic to be of any value, the second is extremely difficult, requiring extensive cash flow forecasts. The final technique for confronting the problem is to assume that the firm's reinvestment opportunities in the future will be similar to its current ones. The two most common ways of doing this are by creating a replacement chain to equalize the life spans of projects or by calculating the equivalent annual annuity (*EAA* of the projects). Using a replacement chain, the present example would call for the creation of a two-chain cycle for project A; that is, we assume that project A can be replaced with a similar investment at the end of 3 years. Thus, project A would be viewed as two A projects occurring back to back, as illustrated in Figure 6. The first project begins with a $1,000 outflow in year 0, or the beginning of year 1. The second project would have an initial outlay of $1,000 at the beginning of year 4, or end of year 3, followed by $500 cash flows in years 4 through 6. As a result, in year 3 there would be a $500 inflow associated with the first project along with a $1,000 outflow associated with repeating the project, resulting in a net cash flow in year 3 of −$500. The net present value on this replacement chain is $426.32, which can be compared with project B's net present value. Therefore, project A should be accepted because the net present value of its replacement chain is greater than the net present value of project B.

One problem with replacement chains is that, depending on the life of each project, it can be quite difficult to come up with equivalent lives. For example, if the two projects

FIGURE 6 Replacement Chain Illustration: Two Project A's Back to Back

	k = 10%					
YEARS	**0**	**1**	**2**	**3**	**4**	**5**	**6**
Cash Flows	−1,000	500	500	−500	500	500	500

NPV = $426.32

equivalent annual annuity (*EAA*) an annuity cash flow that yields the same present value as the project's *NPV*.

had 7- and 13-year lives, because the lowest common denominator is $7 \times 13 = 91$, a 91-year replacement chain would be needed to establish equivalent lives. In this case, it is easier to determine the project's **equivalent annual annuity (*EAA*)**. A project's *EAA* is simply *an annuity cash flow that yields the same present value as the project's NPV*. To calculate an *EAA*, we need only calculate a project's *NPV* and then determine what annual annuity (PMT on your financial calculator) it is equal to. This can be done in two steps as follows:

STEP 1 Calculate the project's *NPV*. In Figure 5 we determined that project A had an *NPV* of $243.43, whereas project B had an *NPV* of $306.58.

STEP 2 Calculate the *EAA*. The *EAA* is determined by using the *NPV* as the project's present value (PV), the number of years in the project as (N), the required rate of return as (I/Y), entering a 0 for the future value (FV), and solving for the annual annuity (PMT). This determines the level of an annuity cash flow that would produce the same *NPV* as the project. For project A the calculations are:

CALCULATOR SOLUTION

Date Input	Function Key
3	N
10	I/Y
−243.43	PV
0	FV

Function Key	Answer
CPT	
PMT	97.89

For project B, the calculations are:

CALCULATOR SOLUTION

Data Input	Function Key
6	N
10	I/Y
−306.58	PV
0	FV

Function Key	Answer
CPT	
PMT	70.39

How do we interpret the *EAA*? For a project with an *n*-year life, it tells us what the dollar value is of an *n*-year annual annuity that would provide the same *NPV* as the project. Thus, for project A, it means that a 3-year annuity of $97.89 with a discount rate of 10 percent would produce a net present value the same as project A's net present value, which is $243.43. We can now compare the equivalent annual annuities directly to determine which project is better. We can do this because we now have found the level of annual annuity that produces an *NPV* equivalent to the project's *NPV*. Thus, because they are both annual annuities, they are comparable.

Concept Check

1. What are the three general types of ranking problems?

ETHICS IN FINANCIAL MANAGEMENT

THE FINANCIAL DOWNSIDE OF POOR ETHICAL BEHAVIOR

Ethics and trust are essential elements of the business world. Knowing the inevitable outcome—for truth does percolate—why do bright and experienced people ignore it? For even if the truth is known only within the confines of the company, it will get out. Circumstances beyond even the best manager's control take over once the chance has passed to act on the moment of truth. Consider the following cases:

Dow Corning didn't deserve its bankruptcy or the multibillion-dollar settlements for its silicone implants because the science didn't support the alleged damages. However, there was a moment of truth when those implants, placed on a blotter, left a stain. The company could have disclosed the possible leakage, researched the risk, and warned doctors and patients. Given the congressional testimony on the implants, many women would have chosen them despite the risk. Instead, they sued because they were not warned.

Beech-Nut's crisis was a chemical concoction instead of apple juice in its baby food products. Executives there ignored an in-house chemist who tried to tell them they were selling adulterated products.

Kidder-Peabody fell despite warnings from employees about a glitch in its accounting system that was reporting bond swaps as sales and income.

In 2004, Merck removed one of the world's best-selling painkillers from the market after a study showed Vioxx caused an increased risk of serious cardiovascular events, such as stroke and heart attack. Producing Vioxx wasn't Merck's problem, its problem was that, according to an editorial in the *New England Journal of Medicine*, Merck was alleged to have withheld data and information that would affect conclusions drawn in an earlier study that appeared in the *New England Journal of Medicine*

in 2000. Now, Merck faces thousands of lawsuits, and studies continue to deliver bad news about the drug. In fact, in one case, a jury awarded $51 million to a retired FBI agent who suffered a heart attack after taking the drug.

As a now-infamous memo reveals, Ford and Firestone did not feel obligated to reveal to the U.S. Transportation Department that certain tires were being recalled in overseas markets. The companies should have realized that it was not a question of whether the recall would be reported, but by whom.

These cases all have several things in common. First, their moments of truth came and went while the companies took no action. Second, employees who raised the issue were ignored or, in some cases, fired. Third, there were lawyers along for the ride, as they were with Ford and Firestone.

Never rely on a lawyer in these moments of truth. Lawyers are legal experts but are not particularly good at controlling damage. They shouldn't make business decisions; managers should. More importantly, moments of truth require managers with strong ethics who will do more than the law requires.

Do businesses ever face a moment of truth wisely? One example is Foxy brand lettuce, which in 2006, shortly after E. coli-contaminated spinach was linked to three deaths, recalled all its lettuce after they discovered irrigation water on their farms tested positive for the bacterium. Although their lettuce was not found to be carrying any bacterium, they did everything possible to protect the public and, as a result, have very loyal customers.

Source: Kevin Kingsbury, "Corporate News: Merck Settles Claims Over Vioxx Ads," *Wall Street Journal*, May 21, 2008, page B3; "Manager's Journal: Ford-Firestone Lesson: Heed the Moment of Truth," *Wall Street Journal*, September 11, 2000, page A44; "Foxy's lettuce recalled after E. coli scare," *USA Today*, October 9, 2006, page A10; and Joe Queenan, "Juice Men—Ethics and the Beech-Nut Sentences," *Barron's*, June 20, 1988, page 14.

Ethics in Capital Budgeting

5 Explain the importance of ethical considerations in capital-budgeting decisions.

Although it may not seem obvious, ethics play a role in capital budgeting. Firestone and Ford, Merck, Dow Corning, and Beech-Nut provide examples of how ethical rules have been violated in the past and what the consequences can be. The most damaging event a business can experience is a loss of the public's confidence in the business's ethical standards. In making capital-budgeting decisions, we must be aware of this and that ethical behavior is doing the right thing and is the right thing to do. The "Ethics in Financial Management" article, The Financial Downside of Poor Ethical Behavior, explains how important it is for firms to not only tell the truth but also make sure that consumers have all the facts they need.

A Glance at Actual Capital-Budgeting Practices

6 Discuss the trends in the use of different capital-budgeting criteria.

During the past 40 years, the popularity of each of the capital-budgeting methods has shifted rather dramatically. In the 1960s, the payback period method dominated capital budgeting. Through the 1970s and 1980s, the *IRR* and the *NPV* techniques slowly gained popularity and are used by the majority of major corporations today.

Interestingly, a recent survey of 392 CFOs by John Graham and Campbell Harvey of Duke University found that 74.9 percent of CFOs always or almost always use net present value and 75.7 percent always or almost always use the internal rate of return.[5] The payback period was also found to be very popular; 56.7 percent indicated that they always or almost always use the payback period. The profitability index was found to be considerably less popular; only 11.9 percent of the CFOs surveyed indicated that they always or almost always use it. Moreover, the survey found that in firms headed by older CEOs and those without an MBA, the use of the payback period was more common.

The survey also found that large firms are significantly more likely to use *NPV* to evaluate capital-budgeting projects than are small firms. On the other hand, when it comes to capital budgeting, small firms use the payback period almost as frequently as they use *NPV* and *IRR*. Apart from the survey, one of the reasons commonly given for the use of the payback period approach is that it makes sense for the capital-constrained firm. However, the survey didn't find any evidence of this being the case.

Without taking on new projects, a company simply wouldn't continue to exist. For example, Polaroid's inability to come up with a product to replace its instant camera resulted in that company going under in 2001. Finding new profitable projects and correctly evaluating them are central to a firm's continued existence—and that's what capital budgeting is all about. In fact, much of what is done within a business involves the capital-budgeting process. Many times it's referred to as strategic planning, but it generally involves capital-budgeting decisions. For example, you may be involved in market research dealing with a proposed new product or its marketing plan, or be analyzing its costs—these are all part of the capital-budgeting process. Once all this information has been gathered, it is analyzed using the techniques and tools that we have presented in this chapter. Actually, almost any business decision can be analyzed using the framework we presented here. That's because the *NPV* method "values" the project under consideration. That is, it looks at the present value of its benefits relative to the present value of its costs, and if the present value of the benefits outweighs the costs, the project is accepted. That's a pretty good decision rule, and it can be applied to any decision a business faces.

Concept Check

1. What capital-budgeting criteria seem to be used most frequently in the real world? Why do you think this is so?

Explain how foreign markets provide opportunities for finding new capital-budgeting projects.

Finance and the Multinational Firm: Capital Budgeting

Without question, the key to success in capital budgeting is to identify good projects, and for many companies these good projects are overseas. Just look at the success that Coca-Cola has had in the international markets. More than 80 percent of its beverage profits come from foreign markets, and the company earns more in Japan than in the United States. Likewise, ExxonMobil earns over half its profits from abroad and is involved in gas and oil exploration projects in West Africa, the Caspian Sea, Russia, the Gulf of Mexico, and South America.

But how do you enter these markets initially? One approach that has been used successfully is through international joint ventures or strategic alliances. Under these arrangements two or more corporations merge their skills and resources on a specific project, trading things such as technology and access to marketing channels. For example, Northwest Airlines and KLM Royal Dutch Airlines entered into a joint venture that provides Northwest

---

[5]John R. Graham and Campbell R. Harvey, "The Theory and Practice of Corporate Finance: Evidence from the Field," *Journal of Financial Economics* 60, 1–2 (May/June 2001), 187–243.

with routes to Europe where KLM has a strong presence, and provides KLM with routes in the U.S. and Asia where Northwest is well established.

Similarly, U.S. oil giant Armco formed a joint venture with Mitsubishi to sell Armco's lightweight plastics in Japan. Georgia-Pacific and Canfor Japan Corporation have a joint venture in which Georgia-Pacific gained access to Canfor's marketing expertise in Japan to sell pulp and paper products there. Likewise, H. J. Heinz Co. announced a joint venture with an Indonesian firm to gain access to its Indonesian marketing channels. Joint ventures also provide a way to get around trade barriers. For example, India and Mexico require joint ventures for entry into their markets. As a result, U.S. firms such as Apple Computer and Hewlett-Packard have been forced to enter into Mexican joint ventures in order to be allowed to ship their products into Mexico.

What is the alternative to not looking abroad for projects? It is losing out on potential revenues. Keep in mind that firms such as Xerox, Hewlett-Packard, Dow Chemical, IBM, and Gillette all earn more than 50 percent of their profits from sales abroad. International boundaries no longer apply in finance.

Concept Check

1. What methods do corporations use to enter international markets?

Summary

The process of capital budgeting involves decision making with respect to investments in fixed assets. Before a profitable project can be adopted, it must be identified or found. Unfortunately, coming up with ideas for new products, for ways to improve existing products, or for ways to make existing products more profitable is extremely difficult. In general, the best source of ideas for new, potentially profitable products is within the firm.

 Discuss the difficulty encountered in finding profitable projects in competitive markets and the importance of the search.

We examine four commonly used criteria for determining the acceptance or rejection of capital-budgeting proposals. The first method, the payback period, does not incorporate the time value of money into its calculations. However, the net present value, profitability index, and internal rate of return methods do account for the time value of money. These methods are summarized in Table 10.

 Determine whether a new project should be accepted or rejected using the payback period, the net present value, the profitability index, and the internal rate of return.

There are several complications related to the capital-budgeting process. First, we examined capital rationing and the problems it can create by imposing a limit on the dollar size of the capital budget. Although capital rationing does not, in general, maximize shareholders' wealth, it does exist. The goal of maximizing shareholders' wealth remains, but it is now subject to a budget constraint.

 Explain how the capital-budgeting decision process changes when a dollar limit is placed on the capital budget.

There are a number of problems associated with evaluating mutually exclusive projects. Mutually exclusive projects occur when different investments, if undertaken, would serve the same purpose. In general, to deal with mutually exclusive projects, we rank them by means of the discounted cash flow criteria and select the project with the highest ranking. Conflicting rankings can arise because of the projects' size disparities, time disparities, and unequal lives. The incomparability of projects with different life spans is not simply a result of the different life spans; rather, it arises because future profitable investment proposals will be rejected without being included in the initial analysis. Replacement chains and equivalent annual annuities can solve this problem.

 Discuss the problems encountered in project ranking.

Ethics and ethical decisions continuously crop up in capital budgeting. Just as with all other areas of finance, violating ethical considerations results in a loss of public confidence, which can have a significant negative effect on shareholder wealth.

 Explain the importance of ethical considerations in capital-budgeting decisions.

Over the past 40 years, the discounted capital-budgeting techniques have continued to gain in popularity and today dominate in the decision-making process.

 Discuss the trends in the use of different capital-budgeting criteria.

The international markets provide another source for finding good capital-budgeting projects. In fact, many times a new project simply involves taking an existing product and selling it in a foreign market. Joint ventures and strategic alliances have been successfully used to enter foreign markets.

 Explain how foreign markets provide opportunities for finding new capital-budgeting projects.

TABLE 10 Capital-Budgeting Methods: A Summary

1A. Payback period = number of years required to recapture the initial investment

Accept if payback period ≤ maximum acceptable payback period
Reject if payback period > maximum acceptable payback period

Advantages:	Disadvantages:
• Uses free cash flows.	• Ignores the time value of money.
• Is easy to calculate and understand.	• Ignores cash flows occurring after the payback period.
• Benefits the capital-constrained firm.	• Selection of the maximum acceptable payback period is arbitrary.
• May be used as rough screening device.	

1B. Discounted payback period = the number of years needed to recover the initial cash outlay from the *discounted net cash flows*

Accept if discounted payback ≤ maximum acceptable discounted payback period
Reject if discounted payback > maximum acceptable discounted payback period

Advantages:	Disadvantages:
• Uses cash flows.	• Ignores cash flows occurring after the payback period.
• Is easy to calculate and understand.	• Selection of the maximum acceptable discounted payback period is arbitrary.
• Considers time value of money.	

2. Net present value = present value of the annual free cash flows less the investment's initial outlay

NPV = present value of all the future annual free cash flows − the initial cash outlay

$$= \frac{FCF_1}{(1 + k)^1} + \frac{FCF_2}{(1 + k)^2} + \cdots + \frac{FCF_n}{(1 + k)^n} - IO$$

where FCF_t = the annual free cash flow in time period t (this can take on either positive or negative values)
$\quad\quad k$ = the required rate of return or the cost of capital
$\quad\quad IO$ = the initial cash outlay
$\quad\quad n$ = the project's expected life

Accept if $NPV \geq 0.0$
Reject if $NPV < 0.0$

Advantages:	Disadvantages:
• Uses free cash flows.	• Requires detailed long-term forecasts of a project's cash flows.
• Recognizes the time value of money.	
• Is consistent with the firm's goal of shareholder wealth maximization.	

3. Profitability index = the ratio of the present value of the future free cash flows to the initial outlay.

$$PI = \frac{\text{present value of all the future annual free cash flows}}{\text{initial cash outlay}}$$

$$= \frac{\frac{FCF_1}{(1 + k)^1} + \frac{FCF_2}{(1 + k)^2} + \cdots + \frac{FCF_n}{(1 + k)^n}}{IO}$$

Accept if $PI \geq 1.0$
Reject if $PI < 1.0$

Advantages:	Disadvantages:
• Uses free cash flows.	• Requires detailed long-term forecasts of a project's cash flows.
• Recognizes the time value of money.	
• Is consistent with the firm's goal of shareholder wealth maximization.	

4A. Internal rate of return = the discount rate that equates the present value of the project's future free cash flows with the project's initial outlay

IRR = the rate of return that equates the present value of the project's free cash flows with the initial outlay

$$IO = \frac{FCF_1}{(1 + IRR\%)^1} + \frac{FCF_2}{(1 + IRR\%)^2} + \cdots + \frac{FCF_n}{(1 + IRR\%)^n}$$

where IRR = the project's internal rate of return

Accept if $IRR \geq$ required rate of return
Reject if $IRR <$ required rate of return

Advantages:

- Uses free cash flows.
- Recognizes the time value of money.
- Is, in general, consistent with the firm's goal of shareholder wealth maximization.

Disadvantages:

- Requires detailed long-term forecasts of a project's cash flows.
- Possibility of multiple *IRR*s.
- Assumes cash flows over the life of the project can be reinvested at the *IRR*.

4B. Modified internal rate of return = the rate of return that equates the present value of the cash outflows with the terminal value of the cash inflows

$$PV_{outflows} = \frac{TV_{inflows}}{(1 + MIRR)^n}$$

where $PV_{outflows}$ = the present value of the project's free cash outflows

$TV_{inflows}$ = the project's terminal value, calculated by taking all the annual free cash inflows and finding their future value at the end of the project's life, compounded forward at the required rate of return

$MIRR$ = the project's modified internal rate of return

Accept if $MIRR \geq$ required rate of return
Reject if $MIRR <$ required rate of return

Advantages:

- Uses free cash flows.
- Recognizes the time value of money.
- Is consistent with the firm's goal of shareholder wealth maximization.
- Allows reinvestment rate to be directly specified.

Disadvantages:

- Requires detailed long-term cash flow forecasts.

Key Terms

Capital budgeting

Capital rationing

Discounted payback period

Equivalent annual annuity (*EAA*)

Internal rate of return (*IRR*)

Mutually exclusive projects

Net present value (*NPV*)

Net present value profile

Payback period

Profitability index (*PI*) or benefit–cost ratio

Review Questions

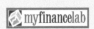

All Review Questions and Study Problems are available in MyFinanceLab.

10-1. Why is capital budgeting such an important process? Why are capital-budgeting errors so costly?

10-2. What are the disadvantages of using the payback period as a capital-budgeting technique? What are its advantages? Why is it so frequently used?

10-3. In some countries, the expropriation (seizure) of foreign investments is a common practice. If you were considering an investment in one of those countries, would the use of the payback period criterion seem more reasonable than it otherwise might? Why or why not?

10-4. Briefly compare and contrast the *NPV*, *PI*, and *IRR* criteria. What are the advantages and disadvantages of using each of these methods?

10-5. What are mutually exclusive projects? Why might the existence of mutually exclusive projects cause problems in the implementation of the discounted cash flow capital-budgeting criteria?

10-6. What are common reasons for capital rationing? Is capital rationing rational?

10-7. How should managers compare two mutually exclusive projects of unequal size? Should the approach change if capital rationing is a factor?

10-8. What causes the time-disparity ranking problem? What reinvestment rate assumptions are associated with the *NPV* and *IRR* capital-budgeting criteria?

10-9. When might two mutually exclusive projects having unequal lives be incomparable? How should managers deal with this problem?

Self-Test Problem

(The solution to this problem is provided at the end of this chapter.)

ST-1. You are considering buying a machine that will require an initial outlay of $54,200. The machine has an expected life of 5 years and will generate free cash flows to the company as a whole of $20,608 at the end of each year over its 5-year life. In addition to the $20,608 cash flow from operations during the fifth and final year, there will be an additional free cash inflow of $13,200 at the end of the fifth year associated with the salvage value of the machine, making the cash flow in year 5 equal to $33,808. Thus, the cash flows associated with this project look like this:

	CASH FLOW
Initial outlay	−$54,200
Inflow year 1	20,608
Inflow year 2	20,608
Inflow year 3	20,608
Inflow year 4	20,608
Inflow year 5	33,808

Given a required rate of return of 15 percent, calculate the following:

a. Payback period   b. *NPV*   c. *PI*   d. *IRR*

Should this project be accepted?

Study Problems

10-1. (*IRR calculation*) Determine the *IRR* on the following projects:

   a. An initial outlay of $10,000 resulting in a single free cash flow of $17,182 after 8 years
   b. An initial outlay of $10,000 resulting in a single free cash flow of $48,077 after 10 years
   c. An initial outlay of $10,000 resulting in a single free cash flow of $114,943 after 20 years
   d. An initial outlay of $10,000 resulting in a single free cash flow of $13,680 after 3 years

10-2. (*IRR calculation*) Determine the *IRR* on the following projects:

   a. An initial outlay of $10,000 resulting in a free cash flow of $1,993 at the end of each year for the next 10 years
   b. An initial outlay of $10,000 resulting in a free cash flow of $2,054 at the end of each year for the next 20 years
   c. An initial outlay of $10,000 resulting in a free cash flow of $1,193 at the end of each year for the next 12 years
   d. An initial outlay of $10,000 resulting in a free cash flow of $2,843 at the end of each year for the next 5 years

10-3. (*IRR calculation*) Determine to the nearest percent the *IRR* on the following projects:

   a. An initial outlay of $10,000 resulting in a free cash flow of $2,000 at the end of year 1, $5,000 at the end of year 2, and $8,000 at the end of year 3
   b. An initial outlay of $10,000 resulting in a free cash flow of $8,000 at the end of year 1, $5,000 at the end of year 2, and $2,000 at the end of year 3
   c. An initial outlay of $10,000 resulting in a free cash flow of $2,000 at the end of years 1 through 5 and $5,000 at the end of year 6

10-4. (*NPV, PI, and IRR calculations*) Fijisawa Inc. is considering a major expansion of its product line and has estimated the following cash flows associated with such an expansion. The initial outlay would be $1,950,000, and the project would generate incremental free cash flows of $450,000 per year for 6 years. The appropriate required rate of return is 9 percent.

   a. Calculate the *NPV*.
   b. Calculate the *PI*.
   c. Calculate the *IRR*.
   d. Should this project be accepted?

10-5. (*Payback period, NPV, PI, and IRR calculations*) You are considering a project with an initial cash outlay of $80,000 and expected free cash flows of $20,000 at the end of each year for 6 years. The required rate of return for this project is 10 percent.

   a. What is the project's payback period?

b. What is the project's *NPV*?

c. What is the project's *PI*?

d. What is the project's *IRR*?

10-6. (*NPV, PI, and IRR calculations*) You are considering two independent projects, project A and project B. The initial cash outlay associated with project A is $50,000, and the initial cash outlay associated with project B is $70,000. The required rate of return on both projects is 12 percent. The expected annual free cash inflows from each project are as follows:

	PROJECT A	PROJECT B
Initial outlay	−$50,000	−$70,000
Inflow year 1	12,000	13,000
Inflow year 2	12,000	13,000
Inflow year 3	12,000	13,000
Inflow year 4	12,000	13,000
Inflow year 5	12,000	13,000
Inflow year 6	12,000	13,000

Calculate the *NPV*, *PI*, and *IRR* for each project and indicate if the project should be accepted.

10-7. (*Payback period calculations*) You are considering three independent projects, project A, project B, and project C. Given the following cash flow information, calculate the payback period for each.

	PROJECT A	PROJECT B	PROJECT C
Initial outlay	−$1,000	−$10,000	−$5,000
Inflow year 1	600	5,000	1,000
Inflow year 2	300	3,000	1,000
Inflow year 3	200	3,000	2,000
Inflow year 4	100	3,000	2,000
Inflow year 5	500	3,000	2,000

If you require a 3-year payback before an investment can be accepted, which project(s) would be accepted?

10-8. (*NPV with varying required rates of return*) Gubanich Sportswear is considering building a new factory to produce aluminum baseball bats. This project would require an initial cash outlay of $5,000,000 and will generate annual free cash inflows of $1,000,000 per year for 8 years. Calculate the project's *NPV* given:

a. A required rate of return of 9 percent

b. A required rate of return of 11 percent

c. A required rate of return of 13 percent

d. A required rate of return of 15 percent

10-9. (*IRR calculations*) Given the following free cash flows, determine the *IRR* for the three independent projects A, B, and C.

	PROJECT A	PROJECT B	PROJECT C
Initial outlay	−$50,000	−$100,000	−$450,000
Cash inflows:			
Year 1	$10,000	$125,000	$200,000
Year 2	15,000	25,000	200,000
Year 3	20,000	25,000	200,000
Year 4	25,000	25,000	—
Year 5	30,000	25,000	—

10-10. (*NPV with varying required rates of return*) Big Steve's, a maker of swizzle sticks, is considering the purchase of a new plastic stamping machine. This investment requires an initial outlay of $100,000 and will generate free cash inflows of $18,000 per year for 10 years.

a. If the required rate of return is 10 percent, what is the project's *NPV*?

b. If the required rate of return is 15 percent, what is the project's *NPV*?

c. Would the project be accepted under part a or b?

d. What is the project's *IRR*?

10-11. (*Mutually exclusive projects*) Nanotech, Inc. currently has a production electronics facility and it is cost prohibitive to expand this production facility. Nanotech is deciding between the following four contracts:

	CONTRACT'S *NPV*	USE OF PRODUCTION FACILITY
A	$100 million	100%
B	$90 million	80%
C	$60 million	60%
D	$50 million	40%

Which project or projects should they accept?

10-12. (*IRR with uneven cash flows*) The Tiffin Barker Corporation is considering introducing a new currency verifier that has the ability to identify counterfeit dollar bills. The required rate of return on this project is 12 percent. What is the *IRR* on this project if it is expected to produce the following cash flows?

Initial outlay	−$927,917
FCF in year 1	200,000
FCF in year 2	300,000
FCF in year 3	300,000
FCF in year 4	200,000
FCF in year 5	200,000
FCF in year 6	160,000

10-13. (*NPV calculation*) Calculate the *NPV* given the following cash flows if the appropriate required rate of return is 10%.

YEAR	CASH FLOWS
0	−$60,000
1	20,000
2	20,000
3	10,000
4	10,000
5	30,000
6	30,000

Should the project be accepted?

10-14. (*NPV calculation*) Calculate the *NPV* given the following cash flows if the appropriate required rate of return is 10%.

YEAR	CASH FLOWS
0	−$70,000
1	30,000
2	30,000
3	30,000
4	−30,000
5	30,000
6	30,000

Should the project be accepted?

10-15. (*MIRR calculation*) Calculate the *MIRR* given the following cash flows if the appropriate required rate of return is 10% (use this as the reinvestment rate).

YEAR	CASH FLOWS
0	−$50,000
1	25,000
2	25,000
3	25,000
4	−25,000
5	25,000
6	25,000

Should the project be accepted?

10-16. (*PI calculation*) Calculate the *PI* given the following cash flows if the appropriate required rate of return is 10%.

YEAR	CASH FLOWS
0	−$55,000
1	10,000
2	10,000
3	10,000
4	10,000
5	10,000
6	10,000

Should the project be accepted? Without calculating the *NPV*, do you think it would be positive or negative? Why?

10-17. (*Discounted payback period*) Gio's Restaurants is considering a project with the following expected cash flows:

YEAR	PROJECT CASH FLOW
0	−$150 million
1	90 million
2	70 million
3	90 million
4	100 million

If the project's appropriate discount is 12 percent, what is the project's discounted payback?

10-18. (*Discounted payback period*) You are considering a project with the following cash flows:

YEAR	PROJECT CASH FLOW
0	−$50,000
1	20,000
2	20,000
3	20,000
4	20,000

If the appropriate discount rate is 10 percent, what is the project's discounted payback period?

10-19. (*Mutually exclusive projects and NPV*) You have been assigned the task of evaluating two mutually exclusive projects with the following projected cash flows:

YEAR	PROJECT A CASH FLOW	PROJECT B CASH FLOW
0	−$100,000	−$100,000
1	33,000	0
2	33,000	0
3	33,000	0
4	33,000	0
5	33,000	220,000

If the appropriate discount rate on these projects is 10 percent, which would be chosen and why?

10-20. (*IRR*) Jella Cosmetics is considering a project that costs $800,000, and is expected to last for 10 years and produce future cash flows of $175,000 per year. If the appropriate discount rate for this project is 12 percent, what is the project's *IRR*?

10-21. (*IRR*) Your investment advisor has offered you an investment that will provide you with one cash flow of $10,000 at the end of 20 years if you pay premiums of $200 per year at the end of each year for 20 years. Find the internal rate of return on this investment.

10-22. (*IRR, payback, and calculating a missing cash flow*) Mode Publishing is considering a new printing facility that will involve a large initial outlay and then result in a series of positive cash flows for four years. The estimated cash flows are associated with this project are:

YEAR	PROJECT CASH FLOW
0 (initial outlay)	?
1	$800 million
2	400 million
3	300 million
4	500 million

If you know that the project has a regular payback of 2.5 years, what is the project's internal rate of return?

10-23. (*Discounted payback period*) Sheinhardt Wig Company is considering a project that has the following cash flows:

YEAR	PROJECT CASH FLOW
0	−$100,000
1	20,000
2	60,000
3	70,000
4	50,000
5	40,000

If the appropriate discount rate is 10 percent, what is the project's discounted payback?

10-24. (*IRR of uneven cash flow stream*) Microwave Oven Programming, Inc. is considering the construction of a new plant. The plant will have an initial cash outlay of $7 million, and will produce cash flows of $3 million at the end of year 1, $4 million at the end of year 2, and $2 million at the end of years 3 through 5. What is the internal rate of return on this new plant?

10-25. (*MIRR*) Dunder Mifflin Paper Company is considering purchasing a new stamping machine that costs $400,000. This new machine will produce cash inflows of $150,000 each year at the end of years 1 through 5, then at the end of year 7 there will be a cash *out*flow of $200,000. The company has a weighted average cost of capital of 12 percent (use this as the reinvestment rate). What is the MIRR of the investment?

10-26. (*MIRR calculation*) Artie's Wrestling Stuff is considering building a new plant. This plant would require an initial cash outlay of $8 million and will generate annual free cash inflows of $2 million per year for 8 years. Calculate the project's MIRR given:

    a. A required rate of return of 10 percent
    b. A required rate of return of 12 percent
    c. A required rate of return of 14 percent

10-27. (*Size-disparity problem*) The D. Dorner Farms Corporation is considering purchasing one of two fertilizer-herbicides for the upcoming year. The more expensive of the two is better and will produce a higher yield. Assume these projects are mutually exclusive and that the required rate of return is 10 percent. Given the following free cash flows:

	PROJECT A	PROJECT B
Initial outlay	−$500	−$5,000
Inflow year 1	700	6,000

    a. Calculate the NPV of each project.
    b. Calculate the PI of each project.
    c. Calculate the IRR of each project.
    d. If there is no capital-rationing constraint, which project should be selected? If there is a capital-rationing constraint, how should the decision be made?

10-28. (*Time-disparity problem*) The State Spartan Corporation is considering two mutually exclusive projects. The free cash flows associated with those projects are as follows:

286

	PROJECT A	PROJECT B
Initial outlay	−$50,000	−$50,000
Inflow year 1	15,625	0
Inflow year 2	15,625	0
Inflow year 3	15,625	0
Inflow year 4	15,625	0
Inflow year 5	15,625	100,000

The required rate of return on these projects is 10 percent.

a. What is each project's payback period?
b. What is each project's *NPV*?
c. What is each project's *IRR*?
d. What has caused the ranking conflict?
e. Which project should be accepted? Why?

10-29. (*Capital rationing*) The Cowboy Hat Company of Stillwater, Oklahoma, is considering seven capital investment proposals for which the total funds available are limited to a maximum of $12 million. The projects are independent and have the following costs and profitability indexes associated with them:

PROJECT	COST	PROFITABILITY INDEX
A	$4,000,000	1.18
B	3,000,000	1.08
C	5,000,000	1.33
D	6,000,000	1.31
E	4,000,000	1.19
F	6,000,000	1.20
G	4,000,000	1.18

a. Under strict capital rationing, which projects should be selected?
b. What problems are there with capital rationing?

Mini Case

Your first assignment in your new position as assistant financial analyst at Caledonia Products is to evaluate two new capital-budgeting proposals. Because this is your first assignment, you have been asked not only to provide a recommendation but also to respond to a number of questions aimed at assessing your understanding of the capital-budgeting process. This is a standard procedure for all new financial analysts at Caledonia, and it will serve to determine whether you are moved directly into the capital-budgeting analysis department or are provided with remedial training. The memorandum you received outlining your assignment follows.

To: The New Financial Analysts
From: Mr. V. Morrison, CEO, Caledonia Products
Re: Capital-Budgeting Analysis

Provide an evaluation of two proposed projects, both with 5-year expected lives and identical initial outlays of $110,000. Both of these projects involve additions to Caledonia's highly successful Avalon product line, and as a result, the required rate of return on both projects has been established at 12 percent. The expected free cash flows from each project are as follows:

	PROJECT A	PROJECT B
Initial outlay	−$110,000	−$110,000
Inflow year 1	20,000	40,000
Inflow year 2	30,000	40,000
Inflow year 3	40,000	40,000
Inflow year 4	50,000	40,000
Inflow year 5	70,000	40,000

In evaluating these projects, please respond to the following questions:

a. Why is the capital-budgeting process so important?
b. Why is it difficult to find exceptionally profitable projects?
c. What is the payback period on each project? If Caledonia imposes a 3-year maximum acceptable payback period, which of these projects should be accepted?
d. What are the criticisms of the payback period?
e. Determine the *NPV* for each of these projects. Should they be accepted?
f. Describe the logic behind the *NPV*.
g. Determine the *PI* for each of these projects. Should they be accepted?
h. Would you expect the *NPV* and *PI* methods to give consistent accept/reject decisions? Why or why not?
i. What would happen to the *NPV* and *PI* for each project if the required rate of return increased? If the required rate of return decreased?
j. Determine the *IRR* for each project. Should they be accepted?
k. How does a change in the required rate of return affect the project's internal rate of return?
l. What reinvestment rate assumptions are implicitly made by the *NPV* and *IRR* methods? Which one is better?

You have also been asked for your views on three unrelated sets of projects. Each set of projects involves two mutually exclusive projects. These projects follow.

m. Caledonia is considering two investments with 1-year lives. The more expensive of the two is the better and will produce more savings. Assume these projects are mutually exclusive and that the required rate of return is 10 percent. Given the following free cash flows:

	PROJECT A	PROJECT B
Initial outlay	−$195,000	−$1,200,000
Inflow year 1	240,000	1,650,000

1. Calculate the *NPV* for each project.
2. Calculate the *PI* for each project.
3. Calculate the *IRR* for each project.
4. If there is no capital-rationing constraint, which project should be selected? If there is a capital-rationing constraint, how should the decision be made?

n. Caledonia is considering two additional mutually exclusive projects. The free cash flows associated with these projects are as follows:

	PROJECT A	PROJECT B
Initial outlay	−$10,000	−$100,000
Inflow year 1	32,000	0
Inflow year 2	32,000	0
Inflow year 3	32,000	0
Inflow year 4	32,000	0
Inflow year 5	32,000	200,000

The required rate of return on these projects is 11 percent.
1. What is each project's payback period?
2. What is each project's *NPV*?
3. What is each project's *IRR*?
4. What has caused the ranking conflict?
5. Which project should be accepted? Why?

Self-Test Solution

SS-1.

a. Payback period $= \dfrac{\$54,200}{\$20,608} = 2.630$ years

b. $NPV = $ present value of all the future annual free cash flows $-$ the initial cash outlay

$$= \frac{FCF_1}{(1 + k)^1} + \frac{FCF_2}{(1 + k)^2} + \cdots + \frac{FCF_n}{(1 + k)^n} - IO$$

$$= \$20,608(2.855) + \$33,808(0.497) - \$54,200$$

$$= \$58,836 + \$16,803 - \$54,200$$

$$= \$21,439$$

c. $PI = \dfrac{\text{present value of all the future annual free cash flows}}{\text{initial cash outlay}}$

$$= \frac{\dfrac{FCF_1}{(1 + k)^1} + \dfrac{FCF_2}{(1 + k)^2} + \cdots + \dfrac{FCF_n}{(1 + k)^n}}{IO}$$

$$= \frac{\$75,639}{\$54,200}$$

$$= 1.396$$

d. Using your financial calculator:

CALCULATOR SOLUTION
(USING A TI BA II PLUS):

Data and Key Input	Display
CF ; −54,200; ENTER	CF0 = −54,200.
↓ ; 20,608; ENTER	C01 = 20,608.
↓ ; 4; ENTER	F01 = 4.00
↓ ; 33,808; ENTER	C02 = 33,808.
↓ ; 1; ENTER	F02 = 1.00
NPV	I = 0.00
15;	I = 15.00
↓ ; CPT	NPV = 21,444.
IRR ; CPT	IRR = 29.5907

APPENDIX

USING A CALCULATOR

As you prepare for a career in business, the ability to use a financial calculator is essential, whether you are in the finance division or the marketing department. For most positions, it will be assumed that you can use a calculator in making computations that at one time were simply not possible without extensive time and effort. The following examples let us see what is possible, but they represent only the beginning of using the calculator in finance.

With just a little time and effort, you will be surprised at how much you can do with the calculator, such as calculating a stock's beta, or determining the value of a bond on a specific day given the exact date of maturity, or finding net present values and internal rates of return, or calculating the standard deviation. The list is almost endless.

In demonstrating how calculators may make our work easier, we must first decide which calculator to use. The options are numerous and largely depend on personal preference. We have chosen the Texas Instruments BA II Plus and the Hewlett-Packard 10bII.

We will limit our discussion to the following issues:

   I. Introductory Comments
  II. An Important Starting Point
 III. Calculating Table Values for:
     A. Appendix (Compound sum of $1)
     B. Appendix (Present value of $1)
     C. Appendix (Sum of an annuity of $1 for *n* periods)
     D. Appendix (Present value of an annuity of $1 for *n* periods)
  IV. Calculating Present Values
   V. Calculating Future Values (Compound sum)
  VI. Calculating the Number of Payments or Receipts
 VII. Calculating the Payment Amount
VIII. Calculating the Interest Rate
  IX. Bond Valuation
     A. Computing the value of a bond
     B. Calculating the yield to maturity of a bond
   X. Computing the Net Present Value and Internal Rate of Return
     A. Where future cash flows are equal amounts in each period (annuity)
     B. Where future cash flows are unequal amounts in each period

I. Introductory Comments

In the examples that follow, you are told (1) which keystrokes to use, (2) the resulting appearance of the calculator display, and (3) a supporting explanation.

The keystrokes column tells you which keys to press. The keystrokes shown in a white box tell you to use one of the calculator's dedicated or "hard" keys. For example, if +/− is shown in the keystrokes instruction column, press that key on the keyboard of the calculator. With the Texas Instruments BA II Plus, to use a function printed in a shaded box above a dedicated key, always press the shaded key 2nd first, then the function key. The HP 10bII has two shift keys, one purple (PRP) and one orange (ORG). To use the functions printed in purple (stats) on the keypad press the purple button first. To use the functions printed in orange (shift) on the keypad, press the orange button first.

II. AN IMPORTANT STARTING POINT - TEXAS INSTRUMENTS BA II PLUS

Example: You want to display four numbers to the right of the decimal.

Keystrokes	Display	Explanation
2nd		
FORMAT	DEC =	
4 ENTER	DEC = 4.0000	Sets display to show four numbers to the right of the decimal
CE/C CE/C	0.0000	Clears display

Example: You want to display two payments per year to be paid at the end of each period.

Keystrokes	Display	Explanation
2nd		
P/Y	P/Y =	
2 ENTER	P/Y = 2.0000	Sets number of payments per year at 2
2nd		
BGN	END	Sets timing of payment at the end of each period
CE/C CE/C	0.0000	Clears display

II. AN IMPORTANT STARTING POINT - HEWLETT-PACKARD 10BII

Example: You want to display four numbers to the right of the decimal. Note that ORG refers to the orange key, which is a "shifted" function used to access the functions printed in orange. There is also a purple shift key that gives you access to the statistical functions in purple.

Keystrokes	Display	Explanation
ORG, C ALL	0.00	Clears registers
ORG, Disp, 4	0.0000	Displays 4 decimal places

Example: You want to display two payments per year to be paid at the end of the period.

Keystrokes	Display	Explanation
ORG, C ALL	0.0000	Clears registers
2, ORG, P/YR	2.0000	Sets payments per year
ORG, BEG/END	2.0000	Sets END mode unless BEGIN enunciator on

III. CALCULATING TABLE VALUES - TEXAS INSTRUMENTS BA II PLUS

A. The compound sum of $1 (Appendix)

Example: What is the table value for the compound sum of $1 for 5 years at a 12 percent annual interest rate?

Keystrokes	Display	Explanation
2nd		
P/Y	P/Y =	
1 ENTER	P/Y = 1.0000	Sets number of payments per year at 1
2nd		
BGN	END	Sets timing of payment at the end of each period
CE/C CE/C	0.0000	Clears display
2nd		
CLR TVM	0.0000	Clears TVM variables
1 +/−	PV = −1.0000	Stores initial $1 as a negative present value.
PV		Otherwise the answer will appear as negative.
5 N	N = 5.0000	Stores number of periods
12 I/Y	I/Y = 12.0000	Stores interest rate
CPT FV	FV = 1.7623	Table value

B. The present value of $1 (Appendix)

Example: What is the table value for the present value of $1 for 8 years at a 10 percent annual interest rate?

Keystrokes	Display	Explanation
2nd		
P/Y	P/Y =	
1 ENTER	P/Y = 1.0000	Sets number of payments per year at 1
2nd		
BGN	END	Sets timing of payment at the end of each period
CE/C CE/C	0.0000	Clears display
2nd		
CLR TVM	0.0000	Clears TVM variables
1 +/−	FV = −1.0000	Stores future amount as negative value
FV		
8 N	N = 8.0000	Stores number of periods
10 I/Y	I/Y = 10.0000	Stores interest rate
CPT PV	PV = 0.4665	Table value

C. The sum of an annuity of $1 for _n_ periods (Appendix)

Example: What is the table value for the compound sum of an annuity of $1 for 6 years at a 14 percent annual interest rate?

Keystrokes	Display	Explanation
2nd		
P/Y	P/Y =	
1 ENTER	P/Y = 1.0000	Sets number of payments per year at 1
2nd		
BGN	END	Sets timing of payment at the end of each period
CE/C CE/C	0.0000	Clears display
2nd		
CLR TVM	0.0000	Clears TVM variables
1 +/−	PMT = −1.0000	Stores annual payment (annuity) as a negative number.
PMT		Otherwise the answer will appear as a negative.
6 N	N = 6.0000	Stores number of periods
14 I/Y	I/Y = 14.0000	Stores interest rate
CPT FV	FV = 8.5355	Table value

D. The present value of an annuity of $1 for _n_ periods (Appendix)

Example: What is the table value for the present value of an annuity of $1 for 12 years at a 9 percent annual interest rate?

Keystrokes	Display	Explanation
2nd		
P/Y	P/Y =	
1 ENTER	P/Y = 1.0000	Sets number of payments per year at 1
2nd		
BGN	END	Sets timing of payment at the end of each period
CE/C CE/C	0.0000	Clears display
2nd		
CLR TVM	0.0000	Clears TVM variables
1 +/−	PMT = −1.0000	Stores annual payment (annuity) as a negative number.
PMT		Otherwise the answer will appear as a negative.
12 N	N = 12.0000	Stores number of periods
9 I/Y	I/Y = 9.0000	Stores interest rate
CPT PV	PV = 7.1607	Table value

III. CALCULATING TABLE VALUES - HEWLETT-PACKARD 10BII

A. The compound sum of $1 (Appendix)

Example: What is the table value for the compound sum of $1 for 5 years at 12 percent annual interest rate?

Keystrokes	Display	Explanation
ORG, C ALL	0.0000	Clears registers
1, ORG, P/YR	1.0000	Sets number of payments per year at 1
ORG, BEG/END	1.0000	Sets timing of payment at the end of each period
		(If BEGIN shows then press ORG, BEG/END again)
1, +/−, PV	−1.0000	Stores initial $1 as a negative present value.
		Otherwise the answer will appear as a negative.
5, N	5.0000	Stores number of periods
12, I/YR	12.0000	Stores interest rate
FV	1.7623	Table value

B. The Present Value of $1 (Appendix)

Example: What is the table value for the present value of $1 for 8 years at a 10 percent annual interest rate?

Keystrokes	Display	Explanation
ORG, C ALL	0.0000	Clears registers
1, ORG, P/YR	1.0000	Sets number of payments per year at 1
ORG, BEG/END	1.0000	Sets timing of payment at the end of each period
		(If BEGIN shows press ORG, BEG/END again)
1, +/−, FV	−1.0000	Stores future amount as negative value
8, N	8.0000	Stores number of periods
10, I/YR	10.0000	Stores interest rate
PV	0.4665	Table value

C. The sum of an annuity of $1 for *n* periods (Appendix)

Example: What is the table value for the compound sum of an annuity of $1 for 6 years at a 14 percent annual interest rate?

Keystrokes	Display	Explanation
ORG, C ALL	0.0000	Clears registers
1, ORG, P/YR	1.0000	Sets number of payments per year at 1
ORG, BEG/END	1.0000	Sets timing of payment at the end of each period
		(If BEGIN shows press ORG, BEG/END again)
1, +/−, PMT	−1.0000	Stores the annual payment (annuity) as a negative number. Otherwise the answer will appear as a negative.
6, N	6.0000	Stores the number of periods
14, I/YR	14.0000	Stores interest rate
FV	8.5355	Table value

D. The present value of an annuity of $1 for *n* periods (Appendix)

Example: What is the table value for the present value of an annuity of $1 for 12 years at a 9 percent annual interest rate?

Keystrokes	Display	Explanation
ORG, C ALL	0.0000	Clears registers
1, ORG, P/YR	1.0000	Sets number of payments per year at 1
ORG, BEG/END	1.0000	Sets timing of payment at the end of each period
		(If BEGIN shows press ORG, BEG/END again)
1, +/−, PMT	−1.0000	Stores the annual payment (annuity) as a negative number.
		Otherwise the answer will appear as a negative.
12, N	12.0000	Stores number of periods
9, I/Y	9.0000	Stores interest rate
PV	7.1607	Table value

IV. CALCULATING PRESENT VALUES - TEXAS INSTRUMENTS BA II PLUS

Example: You are considering the purchase of a franchise of quick oil-change locations, which you believe will provide an annual cash flow of $50,000. At the end of 10 years, you believe that you will be able to sell the franchise for an estimated $900,000. Calculate the maximum amount you should pay for the franchise (present value) in order to realize at least an 18 percent annual yield.

Keystrokes	Display	Explanation
2nd		
BGN	END	Sets timing of payment at the end of each period
CE/C CE/C	0.0000	Clears display
2nd		
CLR TVM	0.0000	Clears TVM variables
10 N	N = 10.0000	Stores n, the holding period
18 I/Y	I/Y = 18.0000	Stores i, the required rate of return
50,000 PMT	PMT = 50,000.0000	Stores PMT, the annual cash flow to be received
900,000 FV	FV = 900,000.0000	Stores FV, the cash flow to be received at the end of the project
CPT PV	PV = −396,662.3350	The present value, given a required rate of return of 18 percent. (Note: The present value is displayed with a minus sign since it represents cash paid out.)

IV. CALCULATING PRESENT VALUES - HEWLETT-PACKARD 10BII

Example: You are considering the purchase of a franchise of quick oil-change locations, which you believe will provide an annual cash flow of $50,000. At the end of 10 years, you believe that you will be able to sell the franchise for an estimated $900,000. Calculate the maximum amount you should pay for the franchise (present value) in order to realize at least an 18 percent annual yield.

Keystrokes	Display	Explanation
ORG, C ALL	0.0000	Clears registers
ORG, BEG/END	0.0000	Sets timing of payment at the end of each period (If BEGIN shows press ORG, BEG/END again)
10, N	10.0000	Stores n, the holding period
18, I/Y	18.0000	Stores i, the required rate of return
50,000, PMT	50,000.0000	Stores PMT, the annual cash flow to be received
900,000, FV	900,000.0000	Stores FV, the cash flow to be received at the end of the project
PV	−396,662.3350	The present value, given a required rate of return of 18 percent. (Note: The present value is displayed with a minus sign since it represents cash paid out.)

V. CALCULATING FUTURE VALUES (COMPOUND SUM) - TEXAS INSTRUMENTS BA II PLUS

Example: If you deposit $300 a month (at the beginning of each month) into a new account that pays 6.25 percent annual interest compounded monthly, how much will you have in the account after 5 years?

Keystrokes	Display	Explanation
2nd		
BGN	END	Sets timing of payment at the end of each period
2nd		
SET	BGN	Sets timing of payments to beginning of each period
2nd		
P/Y	P/Y =	
12 ENTER	P/Y = 12.0000	Sets 12 payments per year
CE/C CE/C	0.0000	Clears display

(continues on next page)

Keystrokes	Display	Explanation
2nd		
CLR TVM	0.0000	Clears TVM variables
60 N	N = 60.0000	Stores n, the number of months for the investment
6.25 I/Y	I/Y = 6.2500	Stores i, the annual rate
300 +/− PMT	PMT = −300.0000	Stores PMT, the monthly amount invested (with a minus sign for cash paid out)
CPT FV	FV = 21,175.7613	The future value after 5 years

V. CALCULATING FUTURE VALUES (COMPOUND SUM) - HEWLETT-PACKARD 10BII

Example: If you deposit $300 a month (at the beginning of each month) into a new account that pays 6.25 percent annual interest compounded monthly, how much will you have in the account after 5 years?

Keystrokes	Display	Explanation
ORG, C ALL	0.0000	Clears registers
ORG, BEG/END	0.0000(BEGIN)	Sets timing of payments to beginning of each period
12, ORG, P/YR	12.0000	Sets 12 payments per year
60, N	60.0000	Stores n, the number of months for the investment
6.25, I/Y	6.2500	Stores I, the annual rate
300, +/−, PMT	−300.0000	Stores PMT, the monthly amount invested (with a minus sign for cash paid out)
FV	21,175.7613	The future value after 5 years

VI. CALCULATING THE NUMBER OF PAYMENTS OR RECEIPTS - TEXAS INSTRUMENTS BA II PLUS

Example: If you wish to retire with $500,000 saved, and can only afford payments of $500 at the beginning of each month, how long will you have to contribute toward your retirement if you can earn a 10 percent return on your contributions?

Keystrokes	Display	Explanation
2nd		
BGN	BGN	Verifies timing of payment at the beginning of each period
2nd		
P/Y	P/Y = 12.0000	
12 ENTER	P/Y = 12.0000	Sets 12 payments per year
CE/C CE/C	0.0000	Clears display
2nd		
CLR TVM	0.0000	Clears TVM variables
10 I/Y	I/Y = 10.0000	Stores i, the interest rate
500 +/− PMT	PMT = −500.0000	Stores PMT, the monthly amount invested (with a minus sign for cash paid out)
500,000 FV	FV = 500,000.0000	The value we want to achieve
CPT N	N = 268.2539	Number of months (since we considered monthly payments) required to achieve our goal

VI. CALCULATING THE NUMBER OF PAYMENTS OR RECEIPTS - HEWLETT-PACKARD 10BII

Example: If you wish to retire with $500,000 saved and can only afford payments of $500 at the beginning of each month, how long will you have to contribute toward your retirement if you can earn a 10 percent return on your contributions?

Keystrokes	Display	Explanation
ORG, C ALL	0.0000	Clears registers
ORG, BEG/END	0.0000(BEGIN)	Sets timing of payments to beginning of each period

12, ORG, P/YR	12.0000	Sets 12 payments per year
10, I/YR	10.0000	Stores I, the interest rate
500, +/−, PMT	500.0000	Stores PMT, the monthly amount invested (with a minus sign for cash paid out)
500,000, FV	500,000.0000	The value we want to achieve
N	268.2539	Number of months (since we considered monthly payments) required to achieve our goal

VII. CALCULATING THE PAYMENT AMOUNT - TEXAS INSTRUMENTS BA II PLUS

Example: Suppose your retirement needs were $750,000. If you are currently 25 years old and plan to retire at age 65, how much will you have to contribute at the beginning of each month for retirement if you can earn 12.5 percent on your savings?

Keystrokes	Display	Explanation
2nd		
BGN	BGN	Verifies timing of payment at the beginning of each period
2nd		
P/Y	P/Y = 12.0000	
12 ENTER	P/Y = 12.0000	Sets 12 payments per year
CE/C CE/C	0.0000	Clears display
2nd		
CLR TVM	0.0000	Clears TVM variables
12.5 I/Y	I/Y = 12.5000	Stores i, the interest rate
480 N	N = 480.0000	Stores n, the number of periods until we stop contributing (40 years × 12 months/year = 480 months)
750,000 FV	FV = 750,000.0000	The value we want to achieve
CPT PMT	PMT = −53.8347	Monthly contribution required to achieve our ultimate goal (shown as negative since it represents cash paid out)

VII. CALCULATING THE PAYMENT AMOUNT - HEWLETT-PACKARD 10BII

Example: Suppose your retirement needs are $750,000. If you are currently 25 years old and plan to retire at age 65, how much will you have to contribute at the beginning of each month for retirement if you can earn 12.5 percent on your savings?

Keystrokes	Display	Explanation
ORG, C ALL	0.0000	Clears registers
ORG, BEG/END	0.0000(BEGIN)	Sets timing of payments to the beginning of each period
12, ORG, P/YR	12.0000	Sets 12 payments per year
12.5, I/YR	12.5000	Stores I, the interest rate
480 N	N = 480.0000	Stores n, the number of periods until we stop contributing (40 years × 12 months/year = 480 months)
750,000, FV	750,000.0000	The value we want to achieve
PMT	−53.8347	Monthly contribution required to achieve our ultimate goal (shown as a negative since it represents cash paid out)

VIII. CALCULATING THE INTEREST RATE - TEXAS INSTRUMENTS BA II PLUS

Example: If you invest $300 at the end of each month for 6 years (72 months) for a promised $30,000 return at the end, what interest rate are you earning on your investment?

Keystrokes	Display	Explanation
2nd		
BGN	BGN	Sets timing of payments to beginning of each period

Keystrokes	Display	Explanation
2nd		
SET	END	Sets timing of payments to end of each period
2nd		
P/Y	P/Y = 12.0000	
12 ENTER	P/Y = 12.0000	Sets 12 payments per year
CE/C CE/C	0.0000	Clears display
2nd		
CLR TVM	0.0000	Clears TVM variables
72 N	N = 72.0000	Stores n, the number of deposits (investments)
300 +/–	PMT = −300.0000	Stores *PMT*, the monthly amount invested (with a minus sign for cash
PMT		paid out)
30,000 FV	FV = 30,000.0000	Stores the future value to be received in 6 years
CPT I/Y	I/Y = 10.5892	The annual interest rate earned on the investment

---

VIII. CALCULATING THE INTEREST RATE - HEWLETT-PACKARD 10BII

Example: If you invest $300 at the end of each month for 6 years (72 months) for a promised $30,000 return at the end, what interest rate are you earning on your investment?

Keystrokes	Display	Explanation
ORG, C ALL	0.0000	Clears registers
ORG, BEG/END	0.0000	Sets timing of payments to the end of each period
72, N	72.000	Stores n, the number of deposits (investments)
300, +/–, PMT	−300.0000	Stores PMT, the monthly amount invested (with a minus sign for cash
		paid out)
30,000, FV	30,000.0000	Stores the future value to be received in 6 years
I/YR	10.5892	The annual interest rate earned on the investment

---

IX. BOND VALUATION - TEXAS INSTRUMENTS BA II PLUS

A. Computing the value of a bond

Example: Assume the current date is January 1, 2006, and that you want to know the value of a bond that matures in 10 years and has a coupon rate of 9 percent (4.5 percent semiannually). Your required rate of return is 12 percent.

Keystrokes	Display	Explanation
2nd		
BGN	END	Verifies timing of payments to end of each period
2nd		
P/Y	P/Y = 12.0000	
2 ENTER	P/Y = 2.0000	Sets 2 payments per year; end mode (END) assumes cash flows are at
		the end of each 6-month period
CE/C CE/C	0.0000	Clears display
2nd		
CLR TVM	0.0000	Clears TVM variables
20 N	N = 20.0000	Stores the number of semiannual periods (10 years × 2)
12 I/Y	I/Y = 12.0000	Stores annual rate of return
45 PMT	PMT = 45.0000	Stores the semiannual interest payment
1,000 FV	FV = 1,000.0000	Stores the bond's maturity or par value
CPT PV	PV = −827.9512	Value of the bond, expressed as a negative number

SOLUTION Using the Bond Feature:

CE/C CE/C	0.0000	Clears display
2nd		
BOND	SDT = 1-01-1970	(This will be the last date entered)

2nd		
CLR WORK	SDT = 1-01-1970	Clears BOND variables
1.01.06 ENTER	SDT = 1-01-2006	Stores the current date (month, date, year)
↓	CPN = 0.0000	
9 ENTER	CPN = 9.0000	Stores the coupon interest rate
↓	RDT = 12-31-1990	(This will be the last date entered)
1.01.16 ENTER	RDT = 1-01-2016	Stores the maturity date in 10 years
↓	RV = 100.0000	Verifies bond maturity or par value
↓	ACT	
2nd		
SET	360	Sets calculations to be based on 360-day year
↓	2/Y	Verifies semiannual compounding rate
↓	YLD = 0.0000	
12 ENTER	YLD = 12.0000	Stores the investor's required rate of return
↓	PRI = 0.0000	
CPT	PRI = 82.7951	Value of bond as a percent of par value; i.e., value of bond is $827.95

B. Computing the yield to maturity of a bond

Example: Assume the current date is January 1, 2006, and that you want to know your yield to maturity on a bond that matures in 8 years and has a coupon rate of 12 percent (6 percent semiannually). The bond is selling for $1,100.

Keystrokes	Display	Explanation
2nd		
BGN	END	Verifies timing of payments to end of each period
2nd		
P/Y	P/Y = 12.0000	
2 ENTER	P/Y = 2.0000	Sets 2 payments per year; end mode (END) assumes cash flows are at the end of each 6-month period
CE/C CE/C	0.0000	Clears display
2nd		
CLR TVM	0.0000	Clears TVM variables
16 N	N = 16.0000	Stores the number of semiannual periods (8 years × 2)
1100 +/–	PV = –1,100.0000	Value of the bond, expressed as a negative number
PV		
60 PMT	PMT = 60.0000	Stores the semiannual interest payments
1,000 FV	FV = 1,000.0000	Stores the bond's maturity or par value
CPT I/Y	I/Y = 10.1451	The yield to maturity, expressed on an annual basis

SOLUTION Using the Bond Feature:

CE/C CE/C	0.0000	Clears display
2nd		
Bond	SDT = 1-01-1993	(This will be the last date entered)
2nd		
CLR WORK	SDT = 1-01-1993	Clears BOND variables
1.01.06 ENTER	SDT = 1-01-2006	Stores the current date (month, date, year)
↓	CPN = 0.0000	
12 ENTER	CPN = 12.0000	Stores the coupon interest rate
↓	RDT = 1-01-2003	(This will be the last date entered)
1.01.14 ENTER	RDT = 1-01-2014	Stores the maturity date in 8 years
↓	RV = 100.0000	Verifies bond's maturity or par value
↓	360	
2nd		

(continues on next page)

Keystrokes	Display	Explanation
SET	ACT	Sets calculations to be based on 360-day year
		Verifies semiannual compounding rate
↓	2/Y	
↓	YLD = 0.0000	
↓	PRI = 0.0000	
110 ENTER	PRI = 110.0000	Stores the bond value as a percentage of par value
↑	YLD = 0.0000	
CPT	YLD = 10.1451	Bond's yield to maturity

IX. BOND VALUATION - HEWLETT-PACKARD 10BII

A. Computing the value of a bond

Example: Assume the current date is January 1, 2006, and that you want to know the value of a bond that matures in 10 years and has a coupon rate of 9 percent (4.5 percent semiannually). Your required rate of return is 12 percent.

Keystrokes	Display	Explanation
ORG, C ALL	0.0000	Clears registers
2, ORG, P/YR	2.0000	Sets payments at 2 per year END mode
20, N	20.0000	Stores the number of semiannual periods
12, I/YR	12.0000	Stores annual rate of return
45, PMT	45.0000	Stores the semiannual interest payments
1000, FV	1,000.0000	Stores the bond's maturity or par value
PV	−827.9512	Value of the bond, expressed as a negative number

B. Computing the yield to maturity of a bond

Example: Assume the current date is January 1, 2006, and that you want to know your yield to maturity on a bond that matures in 8 years and has a coupon rate of 12 percent (6 percent semiannually). The bond is selling for $1,100.

Keystrokes	Display	Explanation
ORG, C ALL	0.0000	Clears registers
2, ORG, P/YR	2.0000	Sets payments at 2 per year END mode
16, N	16.0000	Stores the number of semiannual periods (8 years × 2)
1100, +/−, PV	−1,100.0000	Value of the bond expressed as a negative number
60, PMT	60.0000	Stores the semiannual interest payments
1000, FV	1,000.0000	Stores the bond's maturity or par value
I/YR	10.1451	The yield to maturity expressed on an annual basis

X. COMPUTING THE NET PRESENT VALUE AND INTERNAL RATE OF RETURN - TEXAS INSTRUMENTS BA II PLUS

A. Where future cash flows are equal amounts in each period (annuity)

Example: The firm is considering a capital project that would cost $80,000. The firm's cost of capital is 12 percent. The project life is 10 years, during which time the firm expects to receive $15,000 per year. Calculate the *NPV* and *IRR*.

Keystrokes	Display	Explanation
2nd		
BGN	END	Verifies timing of payments to end of each period
2nd		
P/Y	P/Y = 12.0000	
1 ENTER	P/Y = 1.0000	Sets 1 payment per year; end mode (END) assumes cash flows are at the end of each year
CE/C CE/C	0.0000	Clears display

2nd		
CLR TVM	0.0000	Clears TVM variables
15,000 PMT	PMT = 15.0000	Stores the annual cash flows of $15,000
10 N	N = 10.0000	Stores the life of the project
12 I/Y	I/Y = 12.0000	Stores the cost of capital
CPT PV	PV = −84,753.3454	Calculates present value
+/−	84,753.3454	Changes PV to positive
−80,000 =	4,753.3454	Calculates net present value by subtracting the cost of the project
80,000 +/−	−80,000.0000	
PV	PV = −80,000.0000	
CPT I/Y	I/Y = 13.4344	Calculates the IRR

B. Where future cash flows are unequal amounts in each period

Example: The firm is considering a capital project that would cost $110,000. The firm's cost of capital is 15 percent. The project life is 5 years, with the following expected cash flows: $−25,000, $50,000, $60,000, $60,000 and $70,000. In addition, you expect to receive $30,000 in the last year from the salvage value of the equipment. Calculate the NPV and IRR.

Keystrokes	Display	Explanation
CE/C CE/C	0.0000	Clears display
CF	CF_0 = 0.0000	
2nd		
CLR WORK	CF_0 = 0.0000	Clears cash flow variables
110,000 +/−	CF_0 = −110,000.0000	Stores CF_0, the initial investment (with a minus sign for a negative cash flow)
ENTER		
↓	C01 = 0.0000	Stores CF_1, the first year's cash flow (with a minus sign for a negative
25,000 +/−	C01 = −25,000.0000	cash flow)
ENTER		
↓	F01 = 1.0000	Stores the number of years CF_1 is repeated (in this case, 1 year only)
ENTER		
↓	C02 = 0.0000	
50,000	C02 = 50,000.0000	Stores CF_2
ENTER		
↓	F02 = 1.0000	
ENTER	F02 = 1.0000	Stores the number of years CF_2 is repeated
↓	C03 = 0.0000	
60,000	C03 = 60,000.0000	Stores CF_3
ENTER		
↓	F03 = 2.0000	Stores the number of years CF_3 is repeated
2 ENTER		(here, 2 years, so our response is 2 to the FO_3 prompt)
↓	C04 = 0.0000	
100,000	C04 = 100,000.0000	Stores CF_4, $70,000 plus expected $30,000
ENTER		
↓	F04 = 1.0000	Stores the number CF_4
ENTER		
2nd		
QUIT	0.0000	Ends storage of individual cash flows
NPV	I = 0.0000	
15 ENTER	I = 15.0000	Stores interest rate

(continues on next page)

Keystrokes	Display	Explanation
↓	NPV = 0.0000	
CPT	NPV = 29,541.8951	Calculates the project's *NPV* at the stated interest rate
IRR	IRR = 0.0000	
CPT	IRR = 22.0633	Calculates the project's *IRR*

X. COMPUTING THE NET PRESENT VALUE AND INTERNAL RATE OF RETURN - HEWLETT-PACKARD 10BII

A. Where future cash flows are equal amounts in each period (annuity)

Example: The firm is considering a capital project that would cost $80,000. The firm's cost of capital is 12 percent. The project life is 10 years, during which time the firm expects to receive $15,000 per year. Calculate the *NPV* and *IRR*.

Keystrokes	Display	Explanation
ORG, C ALL	0.0000	Clears registers
ORG, BEG/END	0.0000	Verifies timing of payments to end of each period
1, ORG, P/YR	1.0000	Sets 1 payment per year; end mode (END); assumes cash flows are at the end of each year
15,000, PMT	15,000.0000	Stores annual cash flows of $15,000
10, N	10.0000	Stores the life of the project
12, I/YR	12.0000	Stores the cost of capital
PV	−84,753.3454	Calculates present value
+/−	84,753.3454	Changes *PV* to positive
−80,000, =	4753.3454	Calculates net present value by subtracting the cost of the project
80,000, +/−	−80,000.0000	
PV	−80,000.0000	
I/YR	13.4344	Calculates the *IRR*

B. Where future cash flows are unequal amounts in each period

Example: The firm is considering a capital project that would cost $110,000. The firm's cost of capital is 15 percent. The project life is 5 years, with the following expected cash flows: −$25,000, $50,000, $60,000, $60,000, and $70,000. In addition, you expect to receive $30,000 in the last year from the salvage value of the equipment. Calculate the *NPV* and *IRR*.

Keystrokes	Display	Explanation
ORG, C ALL	0.0000	Clears registers
1, ORG, P/YR	1.0000	Sets 1 payment per year END mode
110,000, +/−, CFj	−110,000.0000	Stores CF0, the initial investment (with a minus sign for negative cash flow)
25,000, +/−, CFJ	−25,000.0000	Stores CF1, the first year's cash flow (with a minus sign for negative cash flow)
50,000, CFj	50,000.0000	Stores CF2
60,000, CFj	60,000.0000	Stores CF3
2, ORG, Nj	2.0000	Stores the number of years CF3 is repeated
100,000, CFj	100,000.0000	Stores CF4, $70,000 plus expected $30,000
15, I/YR	15.0000	Stores interest rate
ORG, NPV	29,541.8951	Calculates the project's *NPV* at the stated interest rate
ORG, IRR/YR	22.0633	Calculates the project's *IRR*

APPENDIX

COMPOUND SUM OF $1 – $FVIF_{i\%, n \text{ years}}$

n	1%	2%	3%	4%	5%	6%	7%	8%	9%	10%
1	1.010	1.020	1.030	1.040	1.050	1.060	1.070	1.080	1.090	1.100
2	1.020	1.040	1.061	1.082	1.102	1.124	1.145	1.166	1.188	1.210
3	1.030	1.061	1.093	1.125	1.158	1.191	1.225	1.260	1.295	1.331
4	1.041	1.082	1.126	1.170	1.216	1.262	1.311	1.360	1.412	1.464
5	1.051	1.104	1.159	1.217	1.276	1.338	1.403	1.469	1.539	1.611
6	1.062	1.126	1.194	1.265	1.340	1.419	1.501	1.587	1.677	1.772
7	1.072	1.149	1.230	1.316	1.407	1.504	1.606	1.714	1.828	1.949
8	1.083	1.172	1.267	1.369	1.477	1.594	1.718	1.851	1.993	2.144
9	1.094	1.195	1.305	1.423	1.551	1.689	1.838	1.999	2.172	2.358
10	1.105	1.219	1.344	1.480	1.629	1.791	1.967	2.159	2.367	2.594
11	1.116	1.243	1.384	1.539	1.710	1.898	2.105	2.332	2.580	2.853
12	1.127	1.268	1.426	1.601	1.796	2.012	2.252	2.518	2.813	3.138
13	1.138	1.294	1.469	1.665	1.886	2.133	2.410	2.720	3.066	3.452
14	1.149	1.319	1.513	1.732	1.980	2.261	2.579	2.937	3.342	3.797
15	1.161	1.346	1.558	1.801	2.079	2.397	2.759	3.172	3.642	4.177
16	1.173	1.373	1.605	1.873	2.183	2.540	2.952	3.426	3.970	4.595
17	1.184	1.400	1.653	1.948	2.292	2.693	3.159	3.700	4.328	5.054
18	1.196	1.428	1.702	2.026	2.407	2.854	3.380	3.996	4.717	5.560
19	1.208	1.457	1.753	2.107	2.527	3.026	3.616	4.316	5.142	6.116
20	1.220	1.486	1.806	2.191	2.653	3.207	3.870	4.661	5.604	6.727
21	1.232	1.516	1.860	2.279	2.786	3.399	4.140	5.034	6.109	7.400
22	1.245	1.546	1.916	2.370	2.925	3.603	4.430	5.436	6.658	8.140
23	1.257	1.577	1.974	2.465	3.071	3.820	4.740	5.871	7.258	8.954
24	1.270	1.608	2.033	2.563	3.225	4.049	5.072	6.341	7.911	9.850
25	1.282	1.641	2.094	2.666	3.386	4.292	5.427	6.848	8.623	10.834
30	1.348	1.811	2.427	3.243	4.322	5.743	7.612	10.062	13.267	17.449
40	1.489	2.208	3.262	4.801	7.040	10.285	14.974	21.724	31.408	45.258
50	1.645	2.691	4.384	7.106	11.467	18.419	29.456	46.900	74.354	117.386

n	11%	12%	13%	14%	15%	16%	17%	18%	19%	20%
1	1.110	1.120	1.130	1.140	1.150	1.160	1.170	1.180	1.190	1.200
2	1.232	1.254	1.277	1.300	1.322	1.346	1.369	1.392	1.416	1.440
3	1.368	1.405	1.443	1.482	1.521	1.561	1.602	1.643	1.685	1.728
4	1.518	1.574	1.630	1.689	1.749	1.811	1.874	1.939	2.005	2.074
5	1.685	1.762	1.842	1.925	2.011	2.100	2.192	2.288	2.386	2.488
6	1.870	1.974	2.082	2.195	2.313	2.436	2.565	2.700	2.840	2.986
7	2.076	2.211	2.353	2.502	2.660	2.826	3.001	3.185	3.379	3.583
8	2.305	2.476	2.658	2.853	3.059	3.278	3.511	3.759	4.021	4.300
9	2.558	2.773	3.004	3.252	3.518	3.803	4.108	4.435	4.785	5.160
10	2.839	3.106	3.395	3.707	4.046	4.411	4.807	5.234	5.695	6.192
11	3.152	3.479	3.836	4.226	4.652	5.117	5.624	6.176	6.777	7.430
12	3.498	3.896	4.334	4.818	5.350	5.936	6.580	7.288	8.064	8.916
13	3.883	4.363	4.898	5.492	6.153	6.886	7.699	8.599	9.596	10.699
14	4.310	4.887	5.535	6.261	7.076	7.987	9.007	10.147	11.420	12.839
15	4.785	5.474	6.254	7.138	8.137	9.265	10.539	11.974	13.589	15.407
16	5.311	6.130	7.067	8.137	9.358	10.748	12.330	14.129	16.171	18.488
17	5.895	6.866	7.986	9.276	10.761	12.468	14.426	16.672	19.244	22.186
18	6.543	7.690	9.024	10.575	12.375	14.462	16.879	19.673	22.900	26.623
19	7.263	8.613	10.197	12.055	14.232	16.776	19.748	23.214	27.251	31.948
20	8.062	9.646	11.523	13.743	16.366	19.461	23.105	27.393	32.429	38.337
21	8.949	10.804	13.021	15.667	18.821	22.574	27.033	32.323	38.591	46.005
22	9.933	12.100	14.713	17.861	21.644	26.186	31.629	38.141	45.923	55.205
23	11.026	13.552	16.626	20.361	24.891	30.376	37.005	45.007	54.648	66.247
24	12.239	15.178	18.788	23.212	28.625	35.236	43.296	53.108	65.031	79.496
25	13.585	17.000	21.230	26.461	32.918	40.874	50.656	62.667	77.387	95.395
30	22.892	29.960	39.115	50.949	66.210	85.849	111.061	143.367	184.672	237.373
40	64.999	93.049	132.776	188.876	267.856	378.715	533.846	750.353	1051.642	1469.740
50	184.559	288.996	450.711	700.197	1083.619	1670.669	2566.080	3927.189	5988.730	9100.191

Foundations of Finance: The Logic and Practice of Financial Management, Sixth Edition. Arthur J. Keown, John D. Martin, J. William Petty.

n	21%	22%	23%	24%	25%	26%	27%	28%	29%	30%
1	1.210	1.220	1.230	1.240	1.250	1.260	1.270	1.280	1.290	1.300
2	1.464	1.488	1.513	1.538	1.562	1.588	1.613	1.638	1.664	1.690
3	1.772	1.816	1.861	1.907	1.953	2.000	2.048	2.097	2.147	2.197
4	2.144	2.215	2.289	2.364	2.441	2.520	2.601	2.684	2.769	2.856
5	2.594	2.703	2.815	2.932	3.052	3.176	3.304	3.436	3.572	3.713
6	3.138	3.297	3.463	3.635	3.815	4.001	4.196	4.398	4.608	4.827
7	3.797	4.023	4.259	4.508	4.768	5.042	5.329	5.629	5.945	6.275
8	4.595	4.908	5.239	5.589	5.960	6.353	6.767	7.206	7.669	8.157
9	5.560	5.987	6.444	6.931	7.451	8.004	8.595	9.223	9.893	10.604
10	6.727	7.305	7.926	8.594	9.313	10.086	10.915	11.806	12.761	13.786
11	8.140	8.912	9.749	10.657	11.642	12.708	13.862	15.112	16.462	17.921
12	9.850	10.872	11.991	13.215	14.552	16.012	17.605	19.343	21.236	23.298
13	11.918	13.264	14.749	16.386	18.190	20.175	22.359	24.759	27.395	30.287
14	14.421	16.182	18.141	20.319	22.737	25.420	28.395	31.691	35.339	39.373
15	17.449	19.742	22.314	25.195	28.422	32.030	36.062	40.565	45.587	51.185
16	21.113	24.085	27.446	31.242	35.527	40.357	45.799	51.923	58.808	66.541
17	25.547	29.384	33.758	38.740	44.409	50.850	58.165	66.461	75.862	86.503
18	30.912	35.848	41.523	48.038	55.511	64.071	73.869	85.070	97.862	112.454
19	37.404	43.735	51.073	59.567	69.389	80.730	93.813	108.890	126.242	146.190
20	45.258	53.357	62.820	73.863	86.736	101.720	119.143	139.379	162.852	190.047
21	54.762	65.095	77.268	91.591	108.420	128.167	151.312	178.405	210.079	247.061
22	66.262	79.416	95.040	113.572	135.525	161.490	192.165	228.358	271.002	321.178
23	80.178	96.887	116.899	140.829	169.407	203.477	244.050	292.298	349.592	417.531
24	97.015	118.203	143.786	174.628	211.758	256.381	309.943	374.141	450.974	542.791
25	117.388	144.207	176.857	216.539	264.698	323.040	393.628	478.901	581.756	705.627
30	304.471	389.748	497.904	634.810	807.793	1025.904	1300.477	1645.488	2078.208	2619.936
40	2048.309	2846.941	3946.340	5455.797	7523.156	10346.879	14195.051	19426.418	26520.723	36117.754
50	13779.844	20795.680	31278.301	46889.207	70064.812	104354.562	154942.687	229345.875	338440.000	497910.125

n	31%	32%	33%	34%	35%	36%	37%	38%	39%	40%
1	1.310	1.320	1.330	1.340	1.350	1.360	1.370	1.380	1.390	1.400
2	1.716	1.742	1.769	1.796	1.822	1.850	1.877	1.904	1.932	1.960
3	2.248	2.300	2.353	2.406	2.460	2.515	2.571	2.628	2.686	2.744
4	2.945	3.036	3.129	3.224	3.321	3.421	3.523	3.627	3.733	3.842
5	3.858	4.007	4.162	4.320	4.484	4.653	4.826	5.005	5.189	5.378
6	5.054	5.290	5.535	5.789	6.053	6.328	6.612	6.907	7.213	7.530
7	6.621	6.983	7.361	7.758	8.172	8.605	9.058	9.531	10.025	10.541
8	8.673	9.217	9.791	10.395	11.032	11.703	12.410	13.153	13.935	14.758
9	11.362	12.166	13.022	13.930	14.894	15.917	17.001	18.151	19.370	20.661
10	14.884	16.060	17.319	18.666	20.106	21.646	23.292	25.049	26.924	28.925
11	19.498	21.199	23.034	25.012	27.144	29.439	31.910	34.567	37.425	40.495
12	25.542	27.982	30.635	33.516	36.644	40.037	43.716	47.703	52.020	56.694
13	33.460	36.937	40.745	44.912	49.469	54.451	59.892	65.830	72.308	79.371
14	43.832	49.756	54.190	60.181	66.784	74.053	82.051	90.845	100.509	111.190
15	57.420	64.358	72.073	80.643	90.158	100.712	112.410	125.366	139.707	155.567
16	75.220	84.953	95.857	108.061	121.713	136.968	154.002	173.005	194.192	217.793
17	98.539	112.138	127.490	144.802	164.312	186.277	210.983	238.747	269.927	304.911
18	129.086	148.022	169.561	194.035	221.822	253.337	289.046	329.471	375.198	426.875
19	169.102	195.389	225.517	260.006	299.459	344.537	395.993	454.669	521.525	597.625
20	221.523	257.913	299.937	348.408	404.270	468.571	542.511	627.443	724.919	836.674
21	290.196	340.446	398.916	466.867	545.764	637.256	743.240	865.871	1007.637	1171.343
22	380.156	449.388	530.558	625.601	736.781	865.668	1018.238	1194.900	1400.615	1639.878
23	498.004	593.192	705.642	838.305	994.653	1178.668	1394.986	1648.961	1946.854	2295.829
24	652.385	783.013	938.504	1123.328	1342.781	1602.988	1911.129	2275.564	2706.125	3214.158
25	854.623	1033.577	1248.210	1505.258	1812.754	2180.063	2618.245	3140.275	3761.511	4499.816
30	3297.081	4142.008	5194.516	6503.285	8128.426	10142.914	12636.086	15716.703	19517.969	24201.043
40	49072.621	66519.313	89962.188	121388.437	163433.875	219558.625	294317.937	393684.687	525508.312	700022.688

APPENDIX

PRESENT VALUE OF $1 – $PVIF_{i\%, n\text{ years}}$

n	1%	2%	3%	4%	5%	6%	7%	8%	9%	10%
1	.990	.980	.971	.962	.952	.943	.935	.926	.917	.909
2	.980	.961	.943	.925	.907	.890	.873	.857	.842	.826
3	.971	.942	.915	.889	.864	.840	.816	.794	.772	.751
4	.961	.924	.888	.855	.823	.792	.763	.735	.708	.683
5	.951	.906	.863	.822	.784	.747	.713	.681	.650	.621
6	.942	.888	.837	.790	.746	.705	.666	.630	.596	.564
7	.933	.871	.813	.760	.711	.665	.623	.583	.547	.513
8	.923	.853	.789	.731	.677	.627	.582	.540	.502	.467
9	.914	.837	.766	.703	.645	.592	.544	.500	.460	.424
10	.905	.820	.744	.676	.614	.558	.508	.463	.422	.386
11	.896	.804	.722	.650	.585	.527	.475	.429	.388	.350
12	.887	.789	.701	.625	.557	.497	.444	.397	.356	.319
13	.879	.773	.681	.601	.530	.469	.415	.368	.326	.290
14	.870	.758	.661	.577	.505	.442	.388	.340	.299	.263
15	.861	.743	.642	.555	.481	.417	.362	.315	.275	.239
16	.853	.728	.623	.534	.458	.394	.339	.292	.252	.218
17	.844	.714	.605	.513	.436	.371	.317	.270	.231	.198
18	.836	.700	.587	.494	.416	.350	.296	.250	.212	.180
19	.828	.686	.570	.475	.396	.331	.277	.232	.194	.164
20	.820	.673	.554	.456	.377	.312	.258	.215	.178	.149
21	.811	.660	.538	.439	.359	.294	.242	.199	.164	.135
22	.803	.647	.522	.422	.342	.278	.226	.184	.150	.123
23	.795	.634	.507	.406	.326	.262	.211	.170	.138	.112
24	.788	.622	.492	.390	.310	.247	.197	.158	.126	.102
25	.780	.610	.478	.375	.295	.233	.184	.146	.116	.092
30	.742	.552	.412	.308	.231	.174	.131	.099	.075	.057
40	.672	.453	.307	.208	.142	.097	.067	.046	.032	.022
50	.608	.372	.228	.141	.087	.054	.034	.021	.013	.009

n	11%	12%	13%	14%	15%	16%	17%	18%	19%	20%
1	.901	.893	.885	.877	.870	.862	.855	.847	.840	.833
2	.812	.797	.783	.769	.756	.743	.731	.718	.706	.694
3	.731	.712	.693	.675	.658	.641	.624	.609	.593	.579
4	.659	.636	.613	.592	.572	.552	.534	.516	.499	.482
5	.593	.567	.543	.519	.497	.476	.456	.437	.419	.402
6	.535	.507	.480	.456	.432	.410	.390	.370	.352	.335
7	.482	.452	.425	.400	.376	.354	.333	.314	.296	.279
8	.434	.404	.376	.351	.327	.305	.285	.266	.249	.233
9	.391	.361	.333	.308	.284	.263	.243	.225	.209	.194
10	.352	.322	.295	.270	.247	.227	.208	.191	.176	.162
11	.317	.287	.261	.237	.215	.195	.178	.162	.148	.135
12	.286	.257	.231	.208	.187	.168	.152	.137	.124	.112
13	.258	.229	.204	.182	.163	.145	.130	.116	.104	.093
14	.232	.205	.181	.160	.141	.125	.111	.099	.088	.078
15	.209	.183	.160	.140	.123	.108	.095	.084	.074	.065
16	.188	.163	.141	.123	.107	.093	.081	.071	.062	.054
17	.170	.146	.125	.108	.093	.080	.069	.060	.052	.045
18	.153	.130	.111	.095	.081	.069	.059	.051	.044	.038
19	.138	.116	.098	.083	.070	.060	.051	.043	.037	.031
20	.124	.104	.087	.073	.061	.051	.043	.037	.031	.026
21	.112	.093	.077	.064	.053	.044	.037	.031	.026	.022
22	.101	.083	.068	.056	.046	.038	.032	.026	.022	.018
23	.091	.074	.060	.049	.040	.033	.027	.022	.018	.015
24	.082	.066	.053	.043	.035	.028	.023	.019	.015	.013
25	.074	.059	.047	.038	.030	.024	.020	.016	.013	.010
30	.044	.033	.026	.020	.015	.012	.009	.007	.005	.004
40	.015	.011	.008	.005	.004	.003	.002	.001	.001	.001
50	.005	.003	.002	.001	.001	.001	.000	.000	.000	.000

Foundations of Finance: The Logic and Practice of Financial Management, Sixth Edition. Arthur J. Keown, John D. Martin, J. William Petty.

APPENDIX: PRESENT VALUE OF $1 — $PVIF_{i\%, n \text{ years}}$

n	21%	22%	23%	24%	25%	26%	27%	28%	29%	30%
1	.826	.820	.813	.806	.800	.794	.787	.781	.775	.769
2	.683	.672	.661	.650	.640	.630	.620	.610	.601	.592
3	.564	.551	.537	.524	.512	.500	.488	.477	.466	.455
4	.467	.451	.437	.423	.410	.397	.384	.373	.361	.350
5	.386	.370	.355	.341	.328	.315	.303	.291	.280	.269
6	.319	.303	.289	.275	.262	.250	.238	.227	.217	.207
7	.263	.249	.235	.222	.210	.198	.188	.178	.168	.159
8	.218	.204	.191	.179	.168	.157	.148	.139	.130	.123
9	.180	.167	.155	.144	.134	.125	.116	.108	.101	.094
10	.149	.137	.126	.116	.107	.099	.092	.085	.078	.073
11	.123	.112	.103	.094	.086	.079	.072	.066	.061	.056
12	.102	.092	.083	.076	.069	.062	.057	.052	.047	.043
13	.084	.075	.068	.061	.055	.050	.045	.040	.037	.033
14	.069	.062	.055	.049	.044	.039	.035	.032	.028	.025
15	.057	.051	.045	.040	.035	.031	.028	.025	.022	.020
16	.047	.042	.036	.032	.028	.025	.022	.019	.017	.015
17	.039	.034	.030	.026	.023	.020	.017	.015	.013	.012
18	.032	.028	.024	.021	.018	.016	.014	.012	.010	.009
19	.027	.023	.020	.017	.014	.012	.011	.009	.008	.007
20	.022	.019	.016	.014	.012	.010	.008	.007	.006	.005
21	.018	.015	.013	.011	.009	.008	.007	.006	.005	.004
22	.015	.013	.011	.009	.007	.006	.005	.004	.004	.003
23	.012	.010	.009	.007	.006	.005	.004	.003	.003	.002
24	.010	.008	.007	.006	.005	.004	.003	.003	.002	.002
25	.009	.007	.006	.005	.004	.003	.003	.002	.002	.001
30	.003	.003	.002	.002	.001	.001	.001	.001	.000	.000
40	.000	.000	.000	.000	.000	.000	.000	.000	.000	.000
50	.000	.000	.000	.000	.000	.000	.000	.000	.000	.000

n	31%	32%	33%	34%	35%	36%	37%	38%	39%	40%
1	.763	.758	.752	.746	.741	.735	.730	.725	.719	.714
2	.583	.574	.565	.557	.549	.541	.533	.525	.518	.510
3	.445	.435	.425	.416	.406	.398	.389	.381	.372	.364
4	.340	.329	.320	.310	.301	.292	.284	.276	.268	.260
5	.259	.250	.240	.231	.223	.215	.207	.200	.193	.186
6	.198	.189	.181	.173	.165	.158	.151	.145	.139	.133
7	.151	.143	.136	.129	.122	.116	.110	.105	.100	.095
8	.115	.108	.102	.096	.091	.085	.081	.076	.072	.068
9	.088	.082	.077	.072	.067	.063	.059	.055	.052	.048
10	.067	.062	.058	.054	.050	.046	.043	.040	.037	.035
11	.051	.047	.043	.040	.037	.034	.031	.029	.027	.025
12	.039	.036	.033	.030	.027	.025	.023	.021	.019	.018
13	.030	.027	.025	.022	.020	.018	.017	.015	.014	.013
14	.023	.021	.018	.017	.015	.014	.012	.011	.010	.009
15	.017	.016	.014	.012	.011	.010	.009	.008	.007	.006
16	.013	.012	.010	.009	.008	.007	.006	.006	.005	.005
17	.010	.009	.008	.007	.006	.005	.005	.004	.004	.003
18	.008	.007	.006	.005	.005	.004	.003	.003	.003	.002
19	.006	.005	.004	.004	.003	.003	.003	.002	.002	.002
20	.005	.004	.003	.003	.002	.002	.002	.002	.001	.001
21	.003	.003	.003	.002	.002	.002	.001	.001	.001	.001
22	.003	.002	.002	.002	.001	.001	.001	.001	.001	.001
23	.002	.002	.001	.001	.001	.001	.001	.001	.001	.000
24	.002	.001	.001	.001	.001	.001	.001	.000	.000	.000
25	.001	.001	.001	.001	.001	.000	.000	.000	.000	.000
30	.000	.000	.000	.000	.000	.000	.000	.000	.000	.000
40	.000	.000	.000	.000	.000	.000	.000	.000	.000	.000

SUM OF AN ANNUITY OF $1 FOR n PERIODS – $FVIFA_{i\%,n\ years}$

n	1%	2%	3%	4%	5%	6%	7%	8%	9%	10%
1	1.000	1.000	1.000	1.000	1.000	1.000	1.000	1.000	1.000	1.000
2	2.010	2.020	2.030	2.040	2.050	2.060	2.070	2.080	2.090	2.100
3	3.030	3.060	3.091	3.122	3.152	3.184	3.215	3.246	3.278	3.310
4	4.060	4.122	4.184	4.246	4.310	4.375	4.440	4.506	4.573	4.641
5	5.101	5.204	5.309	5.416	5.526	5.637	5.751	5.867	5.985	6.105
6	6.152	6.308	6.468	6.633	6.802	6.975	7.153	7.336	7.523	7.716
7	7.214	7.434	7.662	7.898	8.142	8.394	8.654	8.923	9.200	9.487
8	8.286	8.583	8.892	9.214	9.549	9.897	10.260	10.637	11.028	11.436
9	9.368	9.755	10.159	10.583	11.027	11.491	11.978	12.488	13.021	13.579
10	10.462	10.950	11.464	12.006	12.578	13.181	13.816	14.487	15.193	15.937
11	11.567	12.169	12.808	13.486	14.207	14.972	15.784	16.645	17.560	18.531
12	12.682	13.412	14.192	15.026	15.917	16.870	17.888	18.977	20.141	21.384
13	13.809	14.680	15.618	16.627	17.713	18.882	20.141	21.495	22.953	24.523
14	14.947	15.974	17.086	18.292	19.598	21.015	22.550	24.215	26.019	27.975
15	16.097	17.293	18.599	20.023	21.578	23.276	25.129	27.152	29.361	31.772
16	17.258	18.639	20.157	21.824	23.657	25.672	27.888	30.324	33.003	35.949
17	18.430	20.012	21.761	23.697	25.840	28.213	30.840	33.750	36.973	40.544
18	19.614	21.412	23.414	25.645	28.132	30.905	33.999	37.450	41.301	45.599
19	20.811	22.840	25.117	27.671	30.539	33.760	37.379	41.446	46.018	51.158
20	22.019	24.297	26.870	29.778	33.066	36.785	40.995	45.762	51.159	57.274
21	23.239	25.783	28.676	31.969	35.719	39.992	44.865	50.422	56.764	64.002
22	24.471	27.299	30.536	34.248	38.505	43.392	49.005	55.456	62.872	71.402
23	25.716	28.845	32.452	36.618	41.430	46.995	53.435	60.893	69.531	79.542
24	26.973	30.421	34.426	39.082	44.501	50.815	58.176	66.764	76.789	88.496
25	28.243	32.030	36.459	41.645	47.726	54.864	63.248	73.105	84.699	98.346
30	34.784	40.567	47.575	56.084	66.438	79.057	94.459	113.282	136.305	164.491
40	48.885	60.401	75.400	95.024	120.797	154.758	199.630	295.052	337.872	442.580
50	64.461	84.577	112.794	152.664	209.341	290.325	406.516	573.756	815.051	1163.865

n	11%	12%	13%	14%	15%	16%	17%	18%	19%	20%
1	1.000	1.000	1.000	1.000	1.000	1.000	1.000	1.000	1.000	1.000
2	2.110	2.120	2.130	2.140	2.150	2.160	2.170	2.180	2.190	2.200
3	3.342	3.374	3.407	3.440	3.472	3.506	3.539	3.572	3.606	3.640
4	4.710	4.779	4.850	4.921	4.993	5.066	5.141	5.215	5.291	5.368
5	6.228	6.353	6.480	6.610	6.742	6.877	7.014	7.154	7.297	7.442
6	7.913	8.115	8.323	8.535	8.754	8.977	9.207	9.442	9.683	9.930
7	9.783	10.089	10.405	10.730	11.067	11.414	11.772	12.141	12.523	12.916
8	11.859	12.300	12.757	13.233	13.727	14.240	14.773	15.327	15.902	16.499
9	14.164	14.776	15.416	16.085	16.786	17.518	18.285	19.086	19.923	20.799
10	16.722	17.549	18.420	19.337	20.304	21.321	22.393	23.521	24.709	25.959
11	19.561	20.655	21.814	23.044	24.349	25.733	27.200	28.755	30.403	32.150
12	22.713	24.133	25.650	27.271	29.001	30.850	32.824	34.931	37.180	39.580
13	26.211	28.029	29.984	32.088	34.352	36.786	39.404	42.218	45.244	48.496
14	30.095	32.392	34.882	37.581	40.504	43.672	47.102	50.818	54.841	59.196
15	34.405	37.280	40.417	43.842	47.580	51.659	56.109	60.965	66.260	72.035
16	39.190	42.753	46.671	50.980	55.717	60.925	66.648	72.938	79.850	87.442
17	44.500	48.883	53.738	59.117	65.075	71.673	78.978	87.067	96.021	105.930
18	50.396	55.749	61.724	68.393	75.836	84.140	93.404	103.739	115.265	128.116
19	56.939	64.439	70.748	78.968	88.211	98.603	110.283	123.412	138.165	154.739
20	64.202	72.052	80.946	91.024	102.443	115.379	130.031	146.626	165.417	186.687
21	72.264	81.698	92.468	104.767	118.809	134.840	153.136	174.019	197.846	225.024
22	81.213	92.502	105.489	120.434	137.630	157.414	180.169	206.342	236.436	271.028
23	91.147	104.602	120.203	138.295	159.274	183.600	211.798	244.483	282.359	326.234
24	102.173	118.154	136.829	158.656	184.166	213.976	248.803	289.490	337.007	392.480
25	114.412	133.333	155.616	181.867	212.790	249.212	292.099	342.598	402.038	471.976
30	199.018	241.330	293.192	356.778	434.738	530.306	647.423	790.932	966.698	1181.865
40	581.812	767.080	1013.667	1341.979	1779.048	2360.724	3134.412	4163.094	5529.711	7343.715
50	1668.723	2399.975	3459.344	4994.301	7217.488	10435.449	15088.805	21812.273	31514.492	45496.094

Foundations of Finance: The Logic and Practice of Financial Management, Sixth Edition. Arthur J. Keown, John D. Martin, J. William Petty. Copyright © 2008 by Pearson Education. All rights reserved.

n	21%	22%	23%	24%	25%	26%	27%	28%	29%	30%
1	1.000	1.000	1.000	1.000	1.000	1.000	1.000	1.000	1.000	1.000
2	2.210	2.220	2.230	2.240	2.250	2.260	2.270	2.280	2.290	2.300
3	3.674	3.708	3.743	3.778	3.813	3.848	3.883	3.918	3.954	3.990
4	5.446	5.524	5.604	5.684	5.766	5.848	5.931	6.016	6.101	6.187
5	7.589	7.740	7.893	8.048	8.207	8.368	8.533	8.700	8.870	9.043
6	10.183	10.442	10.708	10.980	11.259	11.544	11.837	12.136	12.442	12.756
7	13.321	13.740	14.171	14.615	15.073	15.546	16.032	16.534	17.051	17.583
8	17.119	17.762	18.430	19.123	19.842	20.588	21.361	22.163	22.995	23.858
9	21.714	22.670	23.669	24.712	25.802	26.940	28.129	29.369	30.664	32.015
10	27.274	28.657	30.113	31.643	33.253	34.945	36.723	38.592	40.556	42.619
11	34.001	35.962	38.039	40.238	42.566	45.030	47.639	50.398	53.318	56.405
12	42.141	44.873	47.787	50.895	54.208	57.738	61.501	65.510	69.780	74.326
13	51.991	55.745	59.778	64.109	68.760	73.750	79.106	84.853	91.016	97.624
14	63.909	69.009	74.528	80.496	86.949	93.925	101.465	109.611	118.411	127.912
15	78.330	85.191	92.669	100.815	109.687	119.346	129.860	141.302	153.750	167.285
16	95.779	104.933	114.983	126.010	138.109	151.375	165.922	181.867	199.337	218.470
17	116.892	129.019	142.428	157.252	173.636	191.733	211.721	233.790	258.145	285.011
18	142.439	158.403	176.187	195.993	218.045	242.583	269.885	300.250	334.006	371.514
19	173.351	194.251	217.710	244.031	273.556	306.654	343.754	385.321	431.868	483.968
20	210.755	237.986	268.783	303.598	342.945	387.384	437.568	494.210	558.110	630.157
21	256.013	291.343	331.603	377.461	429.681	489.104	556.710	633.589	720.962	820.204
22	310.775	356.438	408.871	469.052	538.101	617.270	708.022	811.993	931.040	1067.265
23	377.038	435.854	503.911	582.624	673.626	778.760	990.187	1040.351	1202.042	1388.443
24	457.215	532.741	620.810	723.453	843.032	982.237	1144.237	1332.649	1551.634	1805.975
25	554.230	650.944	764.596	898.082	1054.791	1238.617	1454.180	1706.790	2002.608	2348.765
30	1445.111	1767.044	2160.459	2640.881	3227.172	3941.953	4812.891	5873.172	7162.785	8729.805
40	9749.141	12936.141	17153.691	22728.367	30088.621	39791.957	52570.707	69376.562	91447.375	120389.375

n	31%	32%	33%	34%	35%	36%	37%	38%	39%	40%
1	1.000	1.000	1.000	1.000	1.000	1.000	1.000	1.000	1.000	1.000
2	2.310	2.320	2.330	2.340	2.350	2.360	2.370	2.380	2.390	2.400
3	4.026	4.062	4.099	4.136	4.172	4.210	4.247	4.284	4.322	4.360
4	6.274	6.362	6.452	6.542	6.633	6.725	6.818	6.912	7.008	7.104
5	9.219	9.398	9.581	9.766	9.954	10.146	10.341	10.539	10.741	10.946
6	13.077	13.406	13.742	14.086	14.438	14.799	15.167	15.544	15.930	16.324
7	18.131	18.696	19.277	19.876	20.492	21.126	21.779	22.451	23.142	23.853
8	24.752	25.678	26.638	27.633	28.664	29.732	30.837	31.982	33.167	34.395
9	33.425	34.895	36.429	38.028	39.696	41.435	43.247	45.135	47.103	49.152
10	44.786	47.062	49.451	51.958	54.590	57.351	60.248	63.287	66.473	69.813
11	59.670	63.121	66.769	70.624	74.696	78.998	83.540	88.335	93.397	98.739
12	79.167	84.320	89.803	95.636	101.840	108.437	115.450	122.903	130.822	139.234
13	104.709	112.302	120.438	129.152	138.484	148.474	159.166	170.606	182.842	195.928
14	138.169	149.239	161.183	174.063	187.953	202.925	219.058	236.435	255.151	275.299
15	182.001	197.996	215.373	234.245	254.737	276.978	301.109	327.281	355.659	386.418
16	239.421	262.354	287.446	314.888	344.895	377.690	413.520	452.647	495.366	541.985
17	314.642	347.307	383.303	422.949	466.608	514.658	567.521	625.652	689.558	759.778
18	413.180	459.445	510.792	567.751	630.920	700.935	778.504	864.399	959.485	1064.689
19	542.266	607.467	680.354	761.786	852.741	954.271	1067.551	1193.870	1334.683	1491.563
20	711.368	802.856	905.870	1021.792	1152.200	1298.809	1463.544	1648.539	1856.208	2089.188
21	932.891	1060.769	1205.807	1370.201	1556.470	1767.380	2006.055	2275.982	2581.128	2925.862
22	1223.087	1401.215	1604.724	1837.068	2102.234	2404.636	2749.294	3141.852	3588.765	4097.203
23	1603.243	1850.603	2135.282	2462.669	2839.014	3271.304	3767.532	4336.750	4989.379	5737.078
24	2101.247	2443.795	2840.924	3300.974	3833.667	4449.969	5162.516	5985.711	6936.230	8032.906
25	2753.631	3226.808	3779.428	4424.301	5176.445	6052.957	7073.645	8261.273	9642.352	11247.062
30	10632.543	12940.672	15737.945	19124.434	23221.258	28172.016	34148.906	41357.227	50043.625	60500.207

PRESENT VALUE OF AN ANNUITY OF $1 FOR *n* PERIODS – $PVIFA_{i\%,n \text{ years}}$

n	1%	2%	3%	4%	5%	6%	7%	8%	9%	10%
1	.990	.980	.971	.962	.952	.943	.935	.926	.917	.909
2	1.970	1.942	1.913	1.886	1.859	1.833	1.808	1.3783	1.759	1.736
3	2.941	2.884	2.829	2.775	2.723	2.673	2.624	2.577	2.531	2.487
4	3.902	3.808	3.717	3.630	3.546	3.465	3.387	3.312	3.240	3.170
5	4.853	4.713	4.580	4.452	4.329	4.212	4.100	3.993	3.890	3.791
6	5.795	5.601	5.417	5.242	5.076	4.917	4.767	5.623	4.486	4.355
7	6.728	6.472	6.230	6.002	5.786	5.582	5.389	5.206	5.033	4.868
8	7.652	7.326	7.020	6.733	6.463	6.210	5.971	5.747	5.535	5.335
9	8.566	8.162	7.786	7.435	7.108	6.802	6.515	6.247	5.995	5.759
10	9.471	8.983	8.530	8.111	7.722	7.360	7.024	6.710	6.418	6.145
11	10.368	9.787	9.253	8.760	8.306	7.887	7.499	7.139	6.805	6.495
12	11.255	10.575	9.954	9.385	8.863	8.384	7.943	7.536	7.161	6.814
13	12.134	11.348	10.635	9.986	9.394	8.853	8.358	7.904	7.487	7.103
14	13.004	12.106	11.296	10.563	9.899	9.295	8.746	8.244	7.786	7.367
15	13.865	12.849	11.938	11.118	10.380	9.712	9.108	8.560	8.061	7.606
16	14.718	13.578	12.561	11.652	10.838	10.106	9.447	8.851	8.313	7.824
17	15.562	14.292	13.166	12.166	11.274	10.477	9.763	9.122	8.544	8.022
18	16.398	14.992	13.754	12.659	11.690	10.828	10.059	9.372	8.756	8.201
19	17.226	15.679	14.324	13.134	12.085	11.158	10.336	9.604	8.950	8.365
20	18.046	16.352	14.878	13.590	12.462	11.470	10.594	9.818	9.129	8.514
21	18.857	17.011	15.415	14.029	12.821	11.764	10.836	10.017	9.292	8.649
22	19.661	17.658	15.937	14.451	13.163	12.042	11.061	10.201	9.442	8.772
23	20.456	18.292	16.444	14.857	13.489	12.303	11.272	10.371	9.580	8.883
24	21.244	18.914	16.936	15.247	13.799	12.550	11.469	10.529	9.707	8.985
25	22.023	19.524	17.413	15.622	14.094	12.783	11.654	10.675	9.823	9.077
30	25.808	22.397	19.601	17.292	15.373	13.765	12.409	11.258	10.274	9.427
40	32.835	27.356	23.115	19.793	17.159	15.046	13.332	11.925	10.757	9.779
50	39.197	31.424	25.730	21.482	18.256	15.762	13.801	12.234	10.962	9.915

n	11%	12%	13%	14%	15%	16%	17%	18%	19%	20%
1	.901	.893	.885	.877	.870	.862	.855	.847	.840	.833
2	1.713	1.690	1.668	1.647	1.626	1.605	1.585	1.566	1.547	1.528
3	2.444	2.402	2.361	2.322	2.283	2.246	2.210	2.174	2.140	2.106
4	3.102	3.037	2.974	2.914	2.855	2.798	2.743	2.690	2.639	2.589
5	3.696	3.605	3.517	3.433	3.352	3.274	3.199	3.127	3.058	2.991
6	4.231	4.111	3.998	3.889	3.784	3.685	3.589	3.498	3.410	3.326
7	4.712	4.564	4.423	4.288	4.160	4.039	3.922	3.812	3.706	3.605
8	5.146	4.968	4.799	4.639	4.487	4.344	4.207	4.078	3.954	3.837
9	5.537	5.328	5.132	4.946	4.772	4.607	4.451	4.303	4.163	4.031
10	5.889	5.650	5.246	5.216	5.019	4.833	4.659	4.494	4.339	4.192
11	6.207	5.938	5.687	5.453	5.234	5.029	4.836	4.656	4.487	4.327
12	6.492	6.194	5.918	5.660	5.421	5.197	4.988	4.793	4.611	4.439
13	6.750	6.424	6.122	5.842	5.583	5.342	5.118	4.910	4.715	4.533
14	6.982	6.628	6.303	6.002	5.724	5.468	5.229	5.008	4.802	4.611
15	7.191	6.811	6.462	6.142	5.847	5.575	5.324	5.092	4.876	4.675
16	7.379	6.974	6.604	6.265	5.954	5.669	5.405	5.162	4.938	4.730
17	7.549	7.120	6.729	6.373	6.047	5.749	5.475	5.222	4.990	4.775
18	7.702	7.250	6.840	6.467	6.128	5.818	5.534	5.273	5.033	4.812
19	7.839	7.366	6.938	6.550	6.198	5.877	5.585	5.316	5.070	4.843
20	7.963	7.469	7.025	6.623	6.259	5.929	5.628	5.353	5.101	4.870
21	8.075	7.562	7.102	6.687	6.312	5.973	5.665	5.384	5.127	4.891
22	8.176	7.645	7.170	6.743	6.359	6.011	5.696	5.410	5.149	4.909
23	8.266	7.718	7.230	6.792	6.399	6.044	5.723	5.432	5.167	4.925
24	8.348	7.784	7.283	6.835	6.434	6.073	5.747	5.451	5.182	4.937
25	8.422	7.843	7.330	6.873	6.464	6.097	5.766	5.467	5.195	4.948
30	8.694	8.055	7.496	7.003	6.566	6.177	5.829	5.517	5.235	4.979
40	8.951	8.244	7.634	7.105	6.642	6.233	5.871	5.548	5.258	4.997
50	9.042	8.305	7.675	7.133	6.661	6.246	5.880	5.554	5.262	4.999

n	21%	22%	23%	24%	25%	26%	27%	28%	29%	30%
1	.826	.820	.813	.806	.800	.794	.787	.781	.775	.769
2	1.509	1.492	1.474	1.457	1.440	1.424	1.407	1.392	1.376	1.361
3	2.074	2.042	2.011	1.981	1.952	1.923	1.896	1.868	1.842	1.816
4	2.540	2.494	2.448	2.404	2.362	2.320	2.280	2.241	2.203	2.166
5	2.926	2.864	2.803	2.745	2.689	2.635	2.583	2.532	2.483	2.436
6	3.245	3.167	3.092	3.020	2.951	2.885	2.821	2.759	2.700	2.643
7	3.508	3.416	3.327	3.242	3.161	3.083	3.009	2.937	2.868	2.802
8	3.726	3.619	3.518	3.421	3.329	3.241	3.156	3.076	2.999	2.925
9	3.905	3.786	3.673	3.566	3.463	3.366	3.273	3.184	3.100	3.019
10	4.054	3.923	3.799	3.682	3.570	3.465	3.364	3.269	3.178	3.092
11	4.177	4.035	3.902	3.776	3.656	3.544	3.437	3.335	3.329	3.147
12	4.278	4.127	3.985	3.851	3.725	3.606	3.493	3.387	3.286	3.190
13	4.362	4.203	4.053	3.912	3.780	3.656	3.538	3.427	3.322	3.223
14	4.432	4.265	4.108	3.962	3.824	3.695	3.573	3.459	3.351	3.249
15	4.489	4.315	4.153	4.001	3.859	3.726	3.601	3.483	3.373	3.268
16	4.536	4.357	4.189	4.003	3.887	3.751	3.623	3.503	3.390	3.283
17	4.576	4.391	4.219	4.059	3.910	3.771	3.640	3.518	3.403	3.295
18	4.608	4.419	4.243	4.080	3.928	3.786	3.654	3.529	3.413	3.304
19	4.635	4.442	4.263	4.097	3.942	3.799	3.664	3.539	3.421	3.311
20	4.657	4.460	4.279	4.110	3.954	3.808	3.673	3.546	3.427	3.316
21	4.675	4.476	4.292	4.121	3.963	3.816	3.679	3.551	3.432	3.320
22	4.690	4.488	4.302	4.130	3.970	3.822	3.684	3.556	3.436	3.323
23	4.703	4.499	4.311	4.137	3.976	3.827	3.689	3.559	3.438	3.325
24	4.713	4.507	4.318	4.143	3.981	3.831	3.692	3.562	3.441	3.327
25	4.721	4.514	4.323	4.147	3.985	3.834	3.694	3.564	3.442	3.329
30	4.746	4.534	4.339	4.160	3.995	3.842	3.701	3.569	3.447	3.332
40	4.760	4.544	4.347	4.166	3.999	3.846	3.703	3.571	3.448	3.333
50	4.762	4.545	4.348	4.167	4.000	3.846	3.704	3.571	3.448	3.333

n	31%	32%	33%	34%	35%	36%	37%	38%	39%	40%
1	.763	.758	.752	.746	.741	.735	.730	.725	.719	.714
2	1.346	1.331	1.317	1.303	1.289	1.276	1.263	1.250	1.237	1.224
3	1.791	1.766	1.742	1.719	1.696	1.673	1.652	1.630	1.609	1.589
4	2.130	2.096	2.062	2.029	1.997	1.966	1.935	1.906	1.877	1.849
5	2.390	2.345	2.302	2.260	2.220	2.181	2.143	2.106	2.070	2.035
6	2.588	2.534	2.483	2.433	2.385	2.339	2.294	2.251	2.209	2.168
7	2.739	2.677	2.619	2.562	2.508	2.455	2.404	2.355	2.308	2.263
8	2.854	2.786	2.721	2.658	2.598	2.540	2.485	2.432	2.380	2.331
9	2.942	2.868	2.798	2.730	2.665	2.603	2.544	2.487	2.432	2.379
10	3.009	2.930	2.855	2.784	2.715	2.649	2.587	2.527	2.469	2.414
11	3.060	2.978	2.899	2.824	2.752	2.683	2.618	2.555	2.496	2.438
12	3.100	3.013	2.931	2.853	2.779	2.708	2.641	2.576	2.515	2.456
13	3.129	3.040	2.956	2.876	2.799	2.727	2.658	2.592	2.529	2.469
14	3.152	3.061	2.974	2.892	2.814	2.740	2.670	2.603	2.539	2.477
15	3.170	3.076	2.988	2.905	2.825	2.750	2.679	2.611	2.546	2.484
16	3.183	3.088	2.999	2.914	2.834	2.757	2.685	2.616	2.551	2.489
17	3.193	3.097	3.007	2.921	2.840	2.763	2.690	2.621	2.555	2.492
18	3.201	3.104	3.012	2.926	2.844	2.767	2.693	2.624	2.557	2.494
19	3.207	3.109	3.017	2.930	2.848	2.770	2.696	2.626	2.559	2.496
20	3.211	3.113	3.020	2.933	2.850	2.772	2.698	2.627	2.561	2.497
21	3.215	3.116	3.023	2.935	2.852	2.773	2.699	2.629	2.562	2.498
22	3.217	3.118	3.025	2.936	2.853	2.775	2.700	2.629	2.562	2.498
23	3.219	3.120	3.026	2.938	2.854	2.775	2.701	2.630	2.563	2.499
24	3.221	3.121	3.027	2.939	2.855	2.776	2.701	2.630	2.563	2.499
25	3.222	3.122	3.028	2.939	2.856	2.776	2.702	2.631	2.563	2.499
30	3.225	3.124	3.030	2.941	2.857	2.777	2.702	2.631	2.564	2.500
40	3.226	3.125	3.030	2.941	2.857	2.778	2.703	2.632	2.564	2.500
50	3.226	3.125	3.030	2.941	2.857	2.778	2.703	2.632	2.564	2.500

GLOSSARY

accounting book value   the value of an asset as shown on a firm's balance sheet. It represents the historical cost of the asset rather than its current market value or replacement cost.

accounts payable (trade credit)   money owed to suppliers for goods or services purchased in the ordinary course of business.

accounts receivable turnover ratio   a firm's credit sales divided by its accounts receivable. This ratio expresses how often accounts receivable are "rolled over" during a year.

accounts receivable   money owed by customers who purchased goods or services from the firm on credit.

accrual basis accounting   a method of accounting whereby revenue is recorded when it is earned, whether or not the revenue has been received in cash. Likewise, expenses are recorded when they are incurred, even if the money has not actually been paid out.

accrued expenses   expenses that have been incurred but not yet paid in cash.

accumulated depreciation   the sum of all depreciation taken over the entire life of a depreciable asset.

acid-test (quick) ratio   a firm's current assets and accounts receivable divided by its current liabilities. This ratio is a more stringent measure of liquidity than the current ratio in that it excludes inventories and other current assets (those that are least liquid) from current assets.

additional paid-in capital   the amount a company receives from selling stock to investors above par value.

agency costs   the costs, such as a reduced stock price, associated with potential conflict between managers and investors when these two groups are not the same.

agency problem   problems and conflicts resulting from the separation of the management and ownership of the firm.

amortized loan   a loan that is paid off in equal periodic payments.

annual percentage yield (APY)   or **effective annual rate (EAR)**   the annual compound rate that produces the same return as the nominal, or quoted, rate when something is compounded on a nonannual basis. In effect, the APY, or EAR, provides the true rate of return.

annuity due   an annuity in which the payments occur at the beginning of each period.

annuity   a series of equal dollar payments made for a specified number of years.

anticipatory buying   buying in anticipation of a price increase to secure goods at a lower cost.

arbitrageur   an individual involved in the process of buying and selling in more than one market to make a riskless profit.

asked rate   the rate the bank or the foreign exchange trader "asks" the customer to pay in home currency for foreign currency when the bank is selling and the customer is buying. The asked rate is also known as the selling rate or the offer rate.

asset allocation   identifying and selecting the asset classes appropriate for a specific investment portfolio and determining the proportions of those assets within the portfolio.

asset efficiency   how well a firm is managing its assets.

average collection period   a firm's accounts receivable divided by the company's average daily credit sales (annual credit sales ÷ 365). This ratio expresses how rapidly the firm is collecting its credit accounts.

balance sheet   a statement that shows a firm's assets, liabilities, and shareholder equity at a given point in time. It is a snapshot of the firm's financial position on a particular date.

beta   the relationship between an investment's returns and the market's returns. This is a measure of the investment's nondiversifiable risk.

bid rate   the rate at which the bank buys the foreign currency from the customer by paying in home currency. The bid rate is also known as the buying rate.

bid-asked spread   the difference between the asked quote and the bid quote.

bird-in-the-hand dividend theory   the view that dividends are more certain than capital gains.

bond   a long-term (10-year or more) promissory note issued by the borrower, promising to pay the owner of the security a predetermined, fixed amount of interest each year.

book value   (1) the value of an asset as shown on the firm's balance sheet. It represents the historical cost of the asset rather than its current market value or replacement cost. (2) The depreciated value of a company's assets (original cost less accumulated depreciation) less outstanding liabilities.

budget   an itemized forecast of a company's expected revenues and expenses for a future period.

business risk   the relative dispersion or variability in the firm's expected earnings before interest and taxes (EBIT). The nature of the firm's operations causes its business risk. This type of risk is affected by the firm's cost structure, product demand characteristics, and intra-industry competitive position. In capital structure theory, business risk is distinguished from financial risk. Compare **Financial Risk**.

buying rate   the rate at which the bank buys the foreign currency from the customer by paying in home currency. The buying rate is also known as the bid rate.

call protection period   a prespecified time period during which a company cannot recall a bond.

call provision   a provision that entitles the corporation to repurchase its preferred stock from investors at stated prices over specified periods.

callable bond (redeemable bond)   an option available to a company issuing a bond whereby the issuer can call (redeem) the bond before it matures. This is usually done if interest rates decline below what the firm is paying on the bond.

capital asset pricing model (CAPM)   an equation stating that the expected rate of return on a project is a function of (1) the risk-free rate, (2) the investment's systematic risk, and (3) the expected risk premium for the market portfolio of all risky securities.

capital budgeting   the process of decision making with respect to investments made in fixed assets that is, should a proposed project be accepted or rejected.

capital gain (or loss) as defined by the revenue code, a gain or loss resulting from the sale or exchange of a capital asset.

capital market all institutions and procedures that facilitate transactions in long-term financial instruments.

capital rationing placing a limit on the dollar size of the capital budget.

capital structure the mix of long-term sources of funds used by the firm. This is also called the firm's capitalization. The relative total (percentage) of each type of fund is emphasized.

capital structure the mix of long-term sources of funds used by the firm. This is also called the firm's capitalization. The relative total (percentage) of each type of fund is emphasized.

cash budget a detailed plan of future cash flows. This budget is composed of four elements: cash receipts, cash disbursements, net change in cash for the period, and new financing needed.

cash cash on hand, demand deposits, and short-term marketable securities that can quickly be converted into cash.

cash currency and coins plus demand deposit accounts.

characteristic line the line of "best fit" through a series of returns for a firm's stock relative to the market's returns. The slope of the line, frequently called beta, represents the average movement of the firm's stock returns in response to a movement in the market's returns.

chattel mortgage agreement a loan agreement in which the lender can increase his or her security interest by having specific items of inventory identified in the loan agreement. The borrower retains title to the inventory but cannot sell the items without the lender's consent.

clientele effect the belief that individuals and institutions that need current income will invest in companies that have high dividend payouts. Other investors prefer to avoid taxes by holding securities that offer only small dividend income but large capital gains. Thus, we have a "clientele" of investors.

commercial paper short-term unsecured promissory notes sold by large businesses in order to raise cash. Unlike most other money-market instruments, commercial paper has no developed secondary market.

common stock shares that represent ownership in a corporation.

common stock shares that represent the ownership in a corporation.

common stockholders investors who own the firm's common stock. Common stockholders are the residual owners of the firm.

common-sized balance sheet a balance sheet in which a firm's assets and sources of debt and equity are expressed as a percentage of its total assets.

common-sized income statement an income statement in which a firm's expenses and profits are expressed as a percentage of its sales.

company-unique risk see Unsystematic risk.

compensating balance a balance of a given amount that the firm maintains in its demand deposit account. It may be required by either a formal or informal agreement with the firm's commercial bank. Such balances are usually required by the bank (1) on the unused portion of a loan commitment, (2) on the unpaid portion of an outstanding loan, or (3) in exchange for certain services provided by the bank, such as check-clearing or credit information. These balances raise the effective rate of interest paid on borrowed funds.

competitive-advantage period the number of years a firm's managers believes it can sustain a competitive advantage, given the company's present strategies.

compound annuity depositing an equal sum of money at the end of each year for a certain number of years and allowing it to grow.

compound interest the situation in which interest paid on an investment during the first period is added to the principal. During the second period, interest is earned on the original principal plus the interest earned during the first period.

constant dividend payout ratio a dividend payment policy in which the percentage of earnings paid out in dividends is held constant. The dollar amount fluctuates from year to year as profits vary.

contribution-to-firm risk the amount of risk that the project contributes to the firm as a whole; this measure considers the fact that some of the project's risk will be diversified away as the project is combined with the firm's other projects and assets, but ignores the effects of diversification of the firm's shareholders.

convertible bond a debt security that can be converted into a firm's stock at a prespecified price.

convertible preferred stock preferred shares that can be converted into a predetermined number of shares of common stock, if investors so choose.

corporation an entity that legally functions separate and apart from its owners.

cost of goods sold the cost of producing or acquiring a product or service to be sold in the ordinary course of business.

coupon interest rate the interest rate contractually owed on a bond as a percent of its par value.

covered-interest arbitrage designed to eliminate differentials across currency and interest rate markets.

credit scoring the numerical evaluation of credit applicants where the score is evaluated relative to a predetermined standard.

cross rate the computation of an exchange rate for a currency from the exchange rates of two other currencies.

cumulative feature a requirement that all past, unpaid preferred stock dividends be paid before any common stock dividends are declared.

cumulative voting voting in which each share of stock allows the shareholder a number of votes equal to the number of directors being elected. The shareholder can then cast all of his or her votes for a single candidate or split them among the various candidates.

currency swaps the exchange of principal and interest in one currency for the same in another currency for an agreed period of time.

current assets (gross working capital) current assets consist primarily of cash, marketable securities, accounts receivable, inventories, and prepaid expenses.

current debt (short-term liabilities) due to be paid within 12 months.

current ratio a firm's current assets divided by its current liabilities. This ratio indicates the firm's degree of liquidity by comparing its current assets to its current liabilities.

current yield the ratio of a bond's annual interest payment to its market price.

date of record date at which the stock transfer books are to be closed for determining the investor to receive the next dividend payment.

debenture any unsecured long-term debt.

debt capacity the maximum proportion of debt that the firm can include in its capital structure and still maintain its lowest composite cost of capital.

debt ratio a firm's total liabilities divided by its total assets. It is a ratio that measures the extent to which a firm has been financed with debt.

debt ratio a firm's total liabilities divided by its total assets. This ratio measures the extent to which a firm has been financed with debt.

debt   liabilities consisting of such sources as credit extended by suppliers or a loan from a bank.

declaration date   the date upon which a dividend is formally declared by the board of directors.

delivery-time stock   the inventory needed between the order date and the receipt of the inventory ordered.

depreciation expense   a noncash expense to allocate the cost of depreciable assets, such as plant and equipment, over the life of the asset.

depreciation   the means by which an asset's value is expensed over its useful life for federal income tax purposes.

direct costs   see **Variable Costs.**

direct quote   the exchange rate that indicates the number of units of the home currency required to buy one unit of foreign currency.

direct sale   the sale of securities by a corporation to the investing public without the services of an investment-banking firm.

discount bond   a bond that sells at a discount, or below par value.

discretionary financing   sources of financing that require an explicit decision on the part of the firm's management every time funds are raised. An example is a bank note that requires that negotiations be undertaken and an agreement signed setting forth the terms and conditions of the financing.

diversifiable risk   see Unsystematic risk.

dividend payout ratio   the amount of dividends relative to the company's net income or earnings per share.

dividend-payout ratio   dividends as a percentage of earnings.

dividends per share   the amount of dividends a firm pays for each share outstanding.

Dutch auction   a method of issuing securities (common stock) where investors place bids indicating how many shares they are willing to buy and at what price. The price the stock is then sold for becomes the lowest price at which the issuing company can sell all the available shares.

earnings before taxes (taxable income) operating income minus interest expense.

earnings per share   net income on a per share basis.

EBIT-EPS indifference point   the level of earnings before interest and taxes (EBIT) that will equate earnings per share (EPS) between two different financing plans.

economic exposure   the impact of exchange rate changes on the value of the firm including both the strategic impact of comparative relationships arising from exchange rate change and the economic impact of transaction exposure.

economic profit   differs from accounting profit in that it incorporates explicit consideration for opportunity cost of equity financing, as well as debt financing.

efficient market   a market in which the prices of securities at any instant in time fully reflect all publicly available information about the securities and their actual public values.

equity   stockholders' investment in the firm and the cumulative profits retained in the business up to the date of the balance sheet.

equivalent annual annuity (EAA)   an annuity cash flow that yields the same present value as the project's *NPV*.

eurobond   a bond issued in a country different from the one in which the currency of the bond is denominated; for example, a bond issued in Europe or Asia by an American company that pays interest and principal to the lender in U.S. dollars.

exchange rate risk   the risk that tomorrow's exchange rate will differ from today's rate.

exchange rate   the price of a foreign currency stated in terms of the domestic or home currency.

ex-dividend date   the date upon which stock brokerage companies have uniformly decided to terminate the right of ownership to the dividend, which is two days prior to the date of record.

expectations theory   the concept that, no matter what the decision area, how the market price responds to management's actions is not determined entirely by the action itself; it is also affected by investors' expectations about the ultimate decision to be made by management.

expected rate of return   (1) the discount rate that equates the present value of the future cash flows of a bond (interest and maturity value) with the current market price of the bond. It is the rate of return an investor will earn if the bond is held to maturity. (2) The rate of return the investor expects to receive on an investment by paying the market price of the security. (3) The arithmetic mean or average of all possible outcomes where those outcomes are weighted by the probability that each will occur.

expected rate of return   (1) the discount rate that equates the present value of the future cash flows (interest and maturity value) of a bond with its current market price. It is the rate of return an investor will earn if the bond is held to maturity.

(2) The rate of return the investor expects to receive on an investment by paying the existing market price of the security.

expected rate of return   (1) the discount rate that equates the present value of the future cash flows (interest and maturity value) of a bond with the current market price of the bond. It is the rate of return an investor will earn if the bond is held to maturity. (2) The rate of return investors expect to receive on an investment by paying the current market price of the security. (3) The arithmetic mean, or average, of all possible outcomes where those outcomes are weighted by the probability that each will occur.

external financing needs   that portion of a firm's requirements for financing that exceeds its sources of internal financing (i.e., the retention of earnings) plus spontaneous sources of financing (e.g., trade credit).

factor   a firm that, in acquiring the receivables of other firms, bears the risk of collection and, for a fee, services the accounts.

factoring accounts receivable   the outright sale of a firm's accounts receivable to another party (the factor) without recourse. The factor, in turn, bears the risk of collection.

fair value   the present value of an asset's expected future cash flows.

field warehouse agreement   a security agreement in which inventories pledged as collateral are physically separated from the firm's other inventories and placed under the control of a third-party field-warehousing firm.

financial leverage   the use of securities bearing a fixed (limited) rate of return to finance a portion of a firm's assets. Financial leverage can arise from the use of either debt or preferred stock financing. The use of financial leverage exposes the firm to financial risk.

financial policy   the firm's policies regarding the sources of financing it plans to use and the particular mix (proportions) in which they will be used.

financial ratios   accounting data restated in relative terms in order to help people identify some of the financial strengths and weaknesses of a company.

financial structure   the mix of all funds sources that appears on the right-hand side of the balance sheet.

financing cash flows   cash flows paid to or received from investors and lenders.

financing cost   cost incurred by a company that often includes interest expenses and preferred dividends.

finished-goods inventory goods on which the production has been completed but that are not yet sold.

fixed asset turnover a firm's sales divided by its net fixed assets. This ratio indicates how efficiently the firm is using its fixed assets.

fixed assets assets such as equipment, buildings, and land.

fixed costs costs that do not vary in total dollar amount as sales volume or quantity of output changes. Also called indirect costs.

float the length of time from when a check is written until the actual recipient can draw upon or use the "good funds."

floating lien agreement an agreement, generally associated with a loan, whereby the borrower gives the lender a lien against all its inventory.

floating-rate international currency system a system in which the exchange rates of different currencies are allowed to fluctuate with supply and demand conditions.

flotation costs the transaction cost incurred when a firm raises funds by issuing a particular type of security.

forward exchange contract a forward contract that requires delivery, at a specified future date, of one currency for a specified amount of another currency.

forward transaction an agreement today to deliver a specified number of units of a currency on a future date in return for a specified number of units of another currency.

forward-spot differential the premium or discount between forward and spot currency exchange rates.

free cash flow valuation valuing a firm as the present value of its expected future cash flows.

free cash flows the amount of cash available from operations after the firm pays for the investments it has made in operating working capital and fixed assets. This cash is available to distribute to the firm's creditors and owners.

future-value interest factor ($FVIF_{i,n}$) the value $(1 1 i)^n$ used as a multiplier to calculate an amount's future value.

future-value interest factor for an annuity ($FVIFA_{i,n}$) the value used as a multiplier to calculate the future value of an annuity.

general partnership a partnership in which all partners are fully liable for the indebtedness incurred by the partnership.

gross fixed assets the original cost of a firm's fixed assets.

gross income a firm's dollar sales from its product or services less the cost of producing or acquiring them.

gross profit margin gross profit divided by net sales. It is a ratio denoting the gross profit earned by the firm as a percentage of its net sales.

gross profit sales or revenue minus the cost of goods sold.

hedging principle (principle of self-liquidating debt) a working-capital management policy which states that the cash flow–generating characteristics of a firm's investments should be matched with the cash flow requirements of the firm's sources of financing. Very simply, short-lived assets should be financed with short-term sources of financing while long-lived assets should be financed with long-term sources of financing.

high-yield bond see Junk bond.

holding-period return the return an investor would receive from holding a security for a designated period of time. For example, a monthly holding-period return would be the return for holding a security for a month.

income statement (profit and loss statement) a basic accounting statement that measures the results of a firm's operations over a specified period, commonly 1 year. Also known as the profit and loss statement. The bottom line of the income statement shows the firm's profit or loss for the period.

incremental after-tax free cash flows the funds that the firm receives and is able to reinvest, as opposed to accounting profits, which are shown when they are earned rather than when the money is actually in hand.

incremental cash flow the cash flows that result from the acceptance of a project the firm takes on.

indenture the legal agreement between the firm issuing bonds and the bond trustee who represents the bondholders, providing the specific terms of the loan agreement.

indirect costs see Fixed Costs.

indirect quote the exchange rate that expresses the number of units of a foreign currency that can be bought for one unit of the home currency.

information asymmetry the difference in accessibility to information between managers and investors, which may result in a lower stock price than would be true in conditions of certainty.

initial outlay the immediate cash outflow necessary to purchase the asset and put it in operating order.

initial public offering, IPO the first time a company issues its stock to the public.

insolvency the inability to meet interest payments or to repay debt at maturity.

interest rate parity (IRP) theory a theory that states that (except for the effects of small transaction costs) the forward premium or discount should be equal and opposite in size to the difference in the national interest rates for securities of the same maturity.

interest rate risk (1) the variability in a bond's value (risk) caused by changing interest rates. (2) The uncertainty that envelops the expected returns from a security caused by changes in interest rates. Price changes induced by interest rate changes are greater for long-term than for short-term financial instruments.

internal growth a firm's growth rate resulting from reinvesting the company's profits rather than distributing them as dividends. The growth rate is a function of the amount retained and the return earned on the retained funds.

internal rate of return (IRR) the rate of return that the project earns. For computational purposes, the internal rate of return is defined as the discount rate that equates the present value of the project's free cash flows with the project's initial cash outlay.

intrinsic, or economic, value the present value of an asset's expected future cash flows. This value is the amount the investor considers to be fair value, given the amount, timing, and riskiness of future cash flows.

inventories raw materials, work in progress, and finished goods held by the firm for eventual sale.

inventory loans loans secured by inventories. Examples include floating or blanket lien agreements, chattel mortgage agreements, field-warehouse receipt loans, and terminal-warehouse receipt loans.

inventory management the control of assets used in the production process or produced to be sold in the normal course of the firm's operations.

inventory turnover a firm's cost of goods sold divided by its inventory. This ratio measures the number of times a firm's inventories are sold and replaced during the year, that is, the relative liquidity of the inventories.

investment banker a financial specialist who underwrites and distributes new securities and advises corporate clients about raising new funds.

junk bond any bond rated BB or below.

just-in-time inventory control system a production and management system in which inventory is cut down to a minimum through adjustments to the time and physical distance between the various production operations. Under this system the firm keeps a minimum level of inventory on hand, relying upon suppliers to furnish parts "just in time" for them to be assembled.

law of one price a proposition that in competitive markets in which there are no transportation costs or barriers to trade, the same goods sold in different countries sell for the same price if all the different prices are expressed in terms of the same currency.

limited liability company (LLC) a cross between a partnership and a corporation under which the owners retain limited liability but the company is run and is taxed like a partnership.

limited liability a protective provision whereby the investor is not liable for more than the amount he or she has invested in the firm.

limited partnership a partnership in which one or more of the partners has limited liability, restricted to the amount of capital he or she invests in the partnership.

line of credit generally an informal agreement or understanding between a borrower and a bank as to the maximum amount of credit the bank will provide the borrower at any one time. Under this type of agreement there is no "legal" commitment on the part of the bank to provide the stated credit.

liquidation value the dollar sum that could be realized if an asset were sold.

liquidity preference theory the theory that the shape of the term structure of interest rates is determined by an investor's additional required interest rate in compensation of additional risks.

liquidity premium the additional return required by investors for securities that cannot be quickly converted into cash at a reasonably predictable price.

liquidity a firm's ability to pay its bills on time. Liquidity is related to the ease and quickness with which a firm can convert its noncash assets into cash, as well as the size of the firm's investment in noncash assets relative to its short-term liabilities.

long-term debt loans from banks or other sources that lend money for longer than 12 months.

majority voting voting in which each share of stock allows the shareholder one vote, and each position on the board of directors is voted on separately. As a result, a majority of shares has the power to elect the entire board of directors.

marginal tax rate the tax rate that would be applied to the next dollar of income.

market risk see Systematic risk.

market segmentation theory the theory that the shape of the term structure of interest rates implies that the rate of interest for a particular maturity is determined solely by demand and supply for a given maturity. This rate is independent of the demand and supply for securities having different maturities.

market value added (MVA) the difference in the market value of a firm's total assets and their book value.

market value the value observed in the marketplace.

marketable securities security investments (financial assets) the firm can quickly convert to cash balances. Also known as near cash or near-cash assets.

maturity premium the additional return required by investors in longer-term securities to compensate them for the greater risk of price fluctuations on those securities caused by interest rate changes.

maturity the length of time until the bond issuer returns the par value to the bondholder and terminates the bond.

money market all institutions and procedures that facilitate transactions for short-term instruments issued by borrowers with very high credit ratings.

mortgage bond a bond secured by a lien on real property.

mortgage a loan to finance real estate where the lender has first claim on the property in the event the borrower is unable to repay the loan.

multinational corporation (MNC) a corporation with holdings and/or operations in more than one country.

mutually exclusive projects projects that, if undertaken, would serve the same purpose. Thus, accepting one will necessarily mean rejecting the others.

net fixed assets gross fixed assets minus the accumulated depreciation taken over the life of the assets.

net income (earnings available to common stockholders) a figure representing a firm's profit or loss for the period. It also represents the earnings available to the firm's common and preferred stockholders.

net operating loss carryback and carryforward a tax provision that permits the taxpayer first to apply a loss against the profits earned in the 2 prior years (carryback). If the loss has not been completely absorbed by the profits in these 2 years, it may be applied to taxable profits in each of the 20 following years (carryforward).

net present value (NPV) the present value of an investment's annual free cash flows less the investment's initial outlay.

net present value profile a graph showing how a project's *NPV* changes as the discount rate changes.

net profit margin net income divided by sales. A ratio that measures the net income of the firm as a percent of sales.

net working capital the difference between a firm's current assets and its current liabilities. When the term *working capital* is used, it is frequently intended to mean net working capital.

net working capital the difference between the firm's current assets and its current liabilities.

nominal rate of interest the interest rate paid on debt securities without an adjustment for any loss in purchasing power.

nondiversifiable risk see Systematic risk.

non-interest-bearing current liabilities (NIBCL) current liabilities that incur no interest expense, such as accounts payable and accrued expenses.

operating expense marketing and selling expenses, general and administrative expenses, and depreciation expense.

operating income (earnings before interest and taxes) sales less the cost of goods sold less operating expenses.

operating leverage the incurring of fixed operating costs in a firm's income stream.

operating profit margin a firm's operating income (earnings before interest and taxes) divided by sales. This ratio serves as an overall measure of operating effectiveness.

operating profit margin operating income divided by sales. This ratio serves as an overall measure of the company's operating effectiveness.

operating return on assets (OROA) the ratio of a firm's operating income divided by its total assets. This ratio indicates the rate of return being earned on the firm's assets.

operating working capital the firm's current assets less its *non-interest-bearing* current liabilities (rather than *all* of its current liabilities).

opportunity cost of funds the next-best rate of return available to the investor for a given level of risk.

optimal capital structure the capital structure that minimizes the firm's composite cost of capital (maximizes the common stock price) for raising a given amount of funds.

optimal range of financial leverage the range of various capital structure combinations that yield the lowest overall cost of capital for the firm.

order point problem   determining how low inventory should be depleted before it is reordered.

order quantity problem   determining the optimal order size for an inventory item given its usage, carrying costs, and ordering costs.

ordinary annuity   an annuity where the cash flows occur at the end of each period.

organized security exchanges   formal organizations that facilitate the trading of securities.

over-the-counter markets   all security markets except organized exchanges. The money market is an over-the-counter market. Most corporate bonds also are traded in this market.

par value   on the face of a bond, the stated amount that the firm is to repay upon the maturity date.

par value   on the face of a bond, the stated amount that the firm is to repay upon the maturity date.

partnership   an association of two or more individuals joining together as co-owners to operate a business for profit.

payable-through drafts (PTD)   a legal instrument that has the physical appearance of an ordinary check but is not drawn on a bank. A payable-through draft is drawn on and paid by the issuing firm. The bank serves as a collection point and passes the draft on to the firm.

payback period   The number of years it takes to recapture a project's initial outlay.

payment date   the date on which the company mails a dividend check to each investor of record.

percent of sales method   a method of financial forecasting that involves estimating the level of an expense, asset, or liability for a future period as a percent of the sales forecast.

perfect capital markets   an assumption that allows one to study the effect of dividend decisions in isolation. It assumes that (1) investors can buy and sell stocks without incurring any transaction costs, such as brokerage commissions; (2) companies can issue stocks without any cost of doing so; (3) there are no corporate or personal taxes; (4) complete information about the firm is readily available; (5) there are no conflicts of interest between management and stockholders; and (6) financial distress and bankruptcy costs are nonexistent.

permanent investments   an investment that the firm expects to hold longer than one year. The firm makes permanent investments in fixed and current assets.

perpetuity   an annuity with an infinite life.

pledging accounts receivable   a loan the firm obtains from a commercial bank or a finance company using its accounts receivable as collateral.

portfolio beta   the relationship between a portfolio's returns and the market returns. It is a measure of the portfolio's nondiversifiable risk.

preemptive right   the right entitling the common shareholder to maintain his or her proportionate share of ownership in the firm.

preferred stock   a hybrid security with characteristics of both common stock and bonds. Preferred stock is similar to common stock in that it has no fixed maturity date, the nonpayment of dividends does not bring on bankruptcy, and dividends are not deductible for tax purposes. Preferred stock is similar to bonds in that dividends are limited in amount.

preferred stockholders   stockholders who have claims on the firm's income and assets after creditors, but before common stockholders.

premium bond   a bond that is selling above its par value.

present value   the value in today's dollars of a future payment discounted back to present at the required rate of return.

present-value interest factor ($PVIF_{i,n}$)   the value $[1/(1 + i)^n]$ used as a multiplier to calculate an amount's present value.

present-value interest factor for an annuity ($PVIFA_{i,n}$)   the value used as a multiplier to calculate the present value of an annuity.

price/book ratio   the market value of a share of the firm's stock divided by the book value per share of the firm's reported equity in the balance sheet.

price/earnings ratio   the price the market places on $1 of a firm's earnings. For example, if a firm has an earnings per share of $2, and a stock price of $30 per share, its price/earnings ratio is 15 ($30 ÷ $2).

primary market   a market in which securities are offered for the first time for sale to potential investors.

private placement   a security offering limited to a small number of potential investors.

privileged subscription   the process of marketing a new security issue to a select group of investors.

profit margins   financial ratios (sometimes simply referred to as margins) that reflect the level of the firm's profits relative to its sales. Examples include the gross profit margin (gross profit divided by sales), operating profit margin (operating earnings

divided by sales), and the net profit margin (net profit divided by sales).

profitability index (PI) or benefit–cost ratio   the ratio of the present value of an investment's future free cash flows to the investment's initial outlay.

profit-retention rate   the company's percentage of profits retained.

project standing alone risk   a project's risk ignoring the fact that much of this risk will be diversified away as the project is combined with the firm's other projects and assets.

protective provisions   provisions for preferred stock that protect the investor's interest. The provisions generally allow for voting in the event of nonpayment of dividends, or they restrict the payment of common stock dividends if sinking-fund payments are not met or if the firm is in financial difficulty.

proxy fight   a battle between rival groups for proxy votes in order to control the decisions made in a stockholders' meeting.

proxy   a means of voting in which a designated party is provided with the temporary power of attorney to vote for the signee at the corporation's annual meeting.

public offering   a security offering where all investors have the opportunity to acquire a portion of the financial claims being sold.

purchasing-power parity (PPP) theory   a theory that states that, in the long run, exchange rates adjust so that the purchasing power of each currency tends to be the same. Thus, exchange rate changes tend to reflect international differences in inflation rates.

pure play method   a method for estimating a project's or division's beta that attempts to identify publicly traded firms engaged solely in the same business as the project or division.

raw-materials inventory   the basic materials purchased from other firms to be used in the firm's production operations.

real rate of interest   the nominal (quoted) rate of interest less any loss in purchasing power of the dollar during the time of the investment.

required rate of return   minimum rate of return necessary to attract an investor to purchase or hold a security.

residual dividend theory   a theory that a company's dividend payment should equal the cash left after financing all the investments that have positive net present values.

residual value   the present value of a firm's post-competitive-advantage period cash flows.

retained earnings cumulative profits retained in a business up to the date of the balance sheet.

return on equity a firm's net income divided by its common book equity. This ratio is the accounting rate of return earned on the common stockholders' investment.

revolving credit agreement an understanding between the borrower and the bank as to the amount of credit the bank will be legally obligated to provide the borrower.

right a certificate issued to common stockholders giving them an option to purchase a stated number of new shares at a specified price during a 2- to 10-week period.

risk premium the additional return expected for assuming risk.

risk potential variability in future cash flows. The likely variability associated with revenue or income streams. Risk can be measured as the standard deviation or beta.

risk-adjusted discount rate a method of risk adjustment when the risk associated with the investment is greater than the risk involved in a typical endeavor. Using this method, the discount rate is adjusted upward to compensate for this added risk.

risk-free rate of return the rate of return on risk-free investments. The interest rates on short-term U.S. government securities are commonly used to measure this rate.

safety stock inventory held to accommodate any unusually large and unexpected usage during delivery time.

scenario analysis a simulation approach for gauging a project's risk under the worst, best, and most likely outcomes. The firm's management examines the distribution of the outcomes to determine the project's level of risk and then makes the appropriate adjustment.

seasoned equity offering, SEO the sale of additional stock by a company whose shares are already publicly traded.

secondary market a market in which currently outstanding securities are traded.

secured loan sources of credit that require security in the form of pledged assets. In the event the borrower defaults in payment of principal or interest, the lender can seize the pledged assets and sell them to settle the debt.

security market line the return line that reflects the attitudes of investors regarding the minimum acceptable return for a given level of systematic risk associated with a security.

selling rate the rate the bank or the foreign exchange trader "asks" the customer to pay in home currency for foreign currency when the bank is selling and the customer is buying. The selling rate is also known as the asked rate or the offer rate.

sensitivity analysis a method for dealing with risk where the change in the distribution of possible net present values or internal rates of return for a particular project resulting from a change in one particular input variable is calculated. This is done by changing the value of one input variable while holding all other input variables constant.

short-term notes (debt) amounts borrowed from lenders, mostly financial institutions such as banks, where the loan is to be repaid within 12 months.

simple arbitrage trading to eliminate exchange rate differentials across the markets for a single currency.

simulation a method for dealing with risk where the performance of the project under evaluation is estimated by randomly selecting observations from each of the distributions that affect the outcome of the project and continuing with this process until a representative record of the project's probable outcome is assembled.

sinking-fund provision a protective provision that requires the firm periodically to set aside an amount of money for the retirement of its preferred stock. This money is then used to purchase the preferred stock in the open market or through the use of the call provision, whichever method is cheaper.

small, regular dividend plus a year-end extra a corporate policy of paying a small regular dollar dividend plus a year-end extra dividend in prosperous years to avoid the connotation of a permanent dividend.

sole proprietorship a business owned by a single individual.

spontaneous financing the trade credit and other accounts payable that arise "spontaneously" in the firm's day-to-day operations.

spot transaction a transaction made immediately in the marketplace at the market price.

stable dollar dividend per share a dividend policy that maintains a relatively stable dollar dividend per share over time.

standard deviation a statistical measure of the spread of a probability distribution calculated by squaring the difference between each outcome and its expected value, weighting each value by its probability, summing over all possible outcomes, and taking the square root of this sum.

stock dividend a distribution of shares of up to 25 percent of the number of shares currently outstanding, issued on a pro rata basis to the current stockholders.

stock repurchase (stock buyback) the repurchase of common stock by the issuing firm for any of a variety of reasons, resulting in reduction of shares outstanding. Also called **Stock Buyback**.

stock split a stock dividend exceeding 25 percent of the number of shares currently outstanding.

S-type corporation a corporation that, because of specific qualifications, is taxed as though it were a partnership.

subordinated debenture a debenture that is subordinated to other debentures in terms of its payments in case of insolvency.

syndicate a group of investment bankers who contractually assist in the buying and selling of a new security issue.

systematic risk (1) the risk related to an investment return that cannot be eliminated through diversification. Systematic risk results from factors that affect all stocks. Also called market risk or nondiversifiable risk. (2) The risk of a project from the viewpoint of a well-diversified shareholder. This measure takes into account that some of the project's risk will be diversified away as the project is combined with the firm's other projects, and, in addition, some of the remaining risk will be diversified away by shareholders as they combine this stock with other stocks in their portfolios.

systematic risk the risk of the project from the viewpoint of a well-diversified shareholder; this measure takes into account that some of a project's risk will be diversified away as the project is combined with the firm's other projects, and, in addition, some of the remaining risk will be diversified away by shareholders as they combine this stock with other stocks in their portfolios.

tax shield the element from the federal tax code that permits interest costs to be deductible when computing a firm's tax bill. The dollar difference (the shield) flows to the firm's security holders.

taxable income gross income from all sources, except for allowable exclusions, less any tax-deductible expenses.

temporary investments a firm's investments in current assets that will be liquidated and not replaced within a period of one year or less. Examples include seasonal expansions in inventories and accounts receivable.

tender offer a formal offer by the company to buy a specified number of shares at a predetermined and stated price.

The tender price is set above the current market price in order to attract sellers.

term structure of interest rates the relationship between interest rates and the term to maturity, where the risk of default is held constant.

terminal warehouse agreement a security agreement in which the inventories pledged as collateral are transported to a public warehouse that is physically removed from the borrower's premises. This is the safest (though costly) form of financing secured by inventory.

terms of sale the credit terms identifying the possible discount for early payment.

times interest earned a firm's earnings before interest and taxes (EBIT) divided by interest expense. This ratio measures a firm's ability to meet its interest payments from its annual operating earnings.

total asset turnover a firm's sales divided by its total assets. This ratio is an overall measure of asset efficiency based on the relation between a firm's sales and the total assets.

total revenue total sales dollars.

trade credit credit made available by a firm's suppliers in conjunction with the acquisition of materials. Trade credit appears in the accounts payable section of the balance sheet.

trade credit credit made available by a firm's suppliers in conjunction with the acquisition of materials. Trade credit appears on the balance sheet as accounts payable.

transaction exposure risk associated with transaction exposure, that is, risk associated with contracts on which the monetary value is fixed at a time different from when the transaction is actually completed and will be impacted by exchange rate changes.

transaction loan a loan where the proceeds are designated for a specific purpose for example, a bank loan used to finance the acquisition of a piece of equipment.

transfer price the price a subsidiary or a parent company charges other companies that are part of the MNC for its goods or services.

translation exposure risk that arises because the foreign operations of MNCs have financial statements denominated in the local currencies of the countries in which the operation are located. These denominations must be translated into the MNCs home currency at the prevailing exchange rate.

treasury stock the firm's stock that has been issued and then repurchased by the firm.

triangular arbitrage arbitrage across three markets for three currencies.

unbiased expectations theory the theory that the shape of the term structure of interest rates is determined by an investor's expectations about future interest rates.

underwriter's spread the difference between the price the corporation raising money gets and the public offering price of a security.

underwriting the purchase and subsequent resale of a new security issue. The risk of selling the new issue at a satisfactory (profitable) price is assumed (underwritten) by the investment banker.

unsecured loans all sources of credit that have as their security only the lender's faith in the borrower's ability to repay the funds when due.

unsystematic risk the risk related to an investment return that can be eliminated through diversification. Unsystematic risk is the result of factors that are unique to the particular firm. Also called company-unique risk or diversifiable risk.

variable costs costs that are fixed per unit of output but vary in total as output changes. Also called **Direct Costs**.

venture capital funds made available to start-up companies or companies in the early stages of business, as well as firms in "turn-around" situations. These are risky investments, generally in innovative enterprises and many times in high-technology areas.

volume of output a firm's level of operations expressed either in sales dollars or as units of output.

weighted average cost of capital a composite of the individual costs of financing incurred by each capital source. A firm's weighted cost of capital is a function of (1) the individual costs of capital, (2) the capital structure mix, and (3) the level of financing necessary to make the investment.

working capital a concept traditionally defined as a firm's investment in current assets. Compare Net Working Capital.

work-in-process inventory partially finished goods requiring additional work before they become finished goods.

yield to maturity (1) see Term structure of interest rates. (2) The rate of return a bondholder will receive if the bond is held to maturity. (It is equivalent to the expected rate of return.)

yield to maturity the rate of return a bondholder will receive if the bond is held to maturity.

zero and very low coupon bond a bond issued at a substantial discount from its $1,000 face value and that pays little or no interest.

zero balance accounts (ZBA) a cash management tool that permits centralized control over cash outflow while maintaining divisional disbursing authority. Objectives are (1)to achieve better control over cash payments; (2) to reduce excess cash balances held in regional banks for disbursing purposes; and (3) to increase disbursing float.

Index